CLASS 1/26/14 - AM

THE PHARISEES

The Sociological Background of Their Faith

I

Professor Morris Loeb, of
New York, the distinguished
chemist, scholar and public
worker, who died on
October 8, 1912, by his last
Will and Testament, created
a Fund under the following
terms: "I give and bequeath
to The Jewish Publication Society
of America the sum of Ten
Thousand Dollars as a permanent
fund, the income of which alone
shall, from time to time, be
utilized for and applied to
the preparation and publication
of a scholarly work devoted to
the interests of Judaism."

The present work, published in
1938, is the second issued under
this Fund. The first, *Saadia Gaon—
His Life and Works,* by Henry
Malter, was published in 1921.
The third, *The Jews in Spain—
Their Social, Political and
Cultural Life During the Middle
Ages,* by Abraham A. Neuman, was
published in 1942. The fourth,
*The Jewish Community—Its History
and Structure to the American
Revolution,* by Salo Wittmayer Baron,
was published in 1942. The fifth,
The Jews of Ancient Rome, by
Harry J. Leon, was published in 1960.

This new edition of *The Pharisees—
The Sociological Background of
Their Faith* was made possible
by the generous participation of the
Stroock Publication Fund.

THE MORRIS LOEB SERIES

THE PHARISEES

The Sociological Background of Their Faith

LOUIS FINKELSTEIN

Chancellor and Solomon Schechter Professor of Theology
at the Jewish Theological Seminary of America

VOLUME

WITH SUPPLEMENT **I** THIRD EDITION

The Jewish Publication Society of America
Philadelphia 1966–5726

TO
SOL M. STROOCK

WHO, LIKE THE ANCIENT TEACHERS, COMBINES
IN HIMSELF PROFOUND LOVE OF MAN WITH THE
SCHOLAR'S REVERENCE FOR LAW AND TRUTH.

OTHER BOOKS BY THE SAME AUTHOR

Jewish Self-Government in the Middle Ages

Kimhi's Commentary on Isaiah

A Critical Edition of the Sifre on Deuteronomy

Akiba: Scholar, Saint and Martyr

Editor: The Jews: Their History, Culture, and Religion

TABLE OF CONTENTS

VOLUME I

TABLE OF CONTENTS

VOLUME II

FOREWORD TO THE FIRST EDITION

The Pharisees constituted a religious Order of singular influence in the history of civilization. Judaism, Christianity, and Mohammedanism all derive from this ancient Palestinian Society; and through their influence in the preservation and advancement of learning, it has become the cornerstone of modern civilization. Even Buddhism and Confucianism, which alone among other religions can compare with it in depth of ethical teaching, fall far short of it in the spread of their doctrines. Fully half of the world adheres to Pharisaic faiths; only one fourth as many people follow Confucius, and less than one sixth as many are Buddhists.

What particularly distinguishes the Pharisees from all other religious groups, is the fact that they achieved this influence without sacrifice of their individuality, or compromise of their principles. Zoroastrianism, which set out to be a world religion, remained the cult of Persia; Pharisaism, which cherished no such ambitions, was adopted by people thousands of miles from Palestine. Clearly the Simeon ben Shattahs and Judah ben Tabbais of the Palestinian academies served the world in a more profound manner than they themselves imagined. They considered themselves teachers of Israel alone; they were destined to become the mentors of mankind. The ideals which Paul and his fellow Apostles carried with them out of Pharisaism into the world proved of more lasting importance in history than

the battles of any general, or the discoveries of any philosopher. Time came when the researches of Aristotle were
forgotten, and the conquests of Caesar were rendered futile;
but never in the last nineteen centuries has the influence
of Pharisaism ceased to be felt wherever in the western
world civilized people have thought and worked.

Even more astonishing than the influence of Paul and
the Apostles on the Roman world, was that of Mohammed,
the camel-driver of Mecca, whom a few neighboring Jews
and Christians transformed into the founder of one of the
world's foremost civilizations. Neither his time nor his
personality might have seemed particularly suitable for
the mission he undertook. The rabbinical schools in Palestine had reached a low ebb; and those of Babylonia had
just completed the redaction of the Talmud and were
passing through a critical transformation. Rome was at
the nadir of its influence; and Constantinople was ruled by
bigoted obscurantists who had driven the schools of learning
into distant Persia.

Yet there was sufficient energy even in these ashes of
ancient Pharisaism to kindle a fire in the heart of the Arab,
which blazing forth in a mighty flame was within a century
to illumine the whole world. Civilization, which internecine
war had destroyed in Europe, found a new home prepared
for it in its most ancient cradle, that narrow ribbon of
fertile land, lining the Tigris-Euphrates, the eastern coast
of the Mediterranean, and the Nile. In time immemorial,
this singular strip of territory, the earliest scene of recorded
human conflict and intercourse, had been allegorically tele-
scoped into a compact Garden of Eden, the home of Adam,
the ancestor of the human race. The energies which Pharisaism called out of the Arab Peninsula, brought new life to

this ancient country and made it once more the center of world thought, commerce, and even government. The Arab, last of Mediterranean races to be brought into the complex of civilized life, became its focal center. The ignorant idolater became an ardent monotheist, as well as an avid student and an indefatigable teacher. From the Pyrenees to the Indus, his disciples studied Arabic translations of ancient Greek mathematical, medical, and philosophical works, and added their own comments to them. Europeans, entirely cut off from ancient classical literature, had to rely on Latin versions of these Arabic and kindred Hebrew texts. Thomas Aquinas, Albertus Magnus, and Duns Scotus, three of the mightiest of medieval minds and the builders of Europe's intellectual renaissance, were the disciples of Avicenna, Averroes, and the Jewish philosopher, Maimonides.

The spread of Pharisaism to the ends of the Roman Empire and throughout the Arabic world was not due, as is commonly supposed, to the lack of opposing forces. Two strong philosophical movements — Stoicism and Epicureanism — each practically a religion, had tens of thousands of adherents throughout the Roman Empire. The Stoics, appealing primarily to Reason and Justice, had brilliant exponents of their doctrine in the Greek slave, Epictetus, and the Roman Emperor, Marcus Aurelius. The Epicureans, relying on the natural attractiveness of their hedonistic doctrine, had their poetical sweet-singing Lucretius. More dangerous to infant Christianity than either of these movements, was the dualistic religion of Mithras, which as late as the third century C. E., challenged the advance of the Church in almost every province of the Empire. Of Persian origin, this religion, with its concept of a cosmic battle between Good and Evil, had a subtle fascination for the Roman legions. So powerful was this attraction, that a synthesis between the dogmas of Mithraism and those of Christianity was proposed in the form of Manichaeism; and that, too, had tens of thousands of adherents. Indeed Saint Augustine himself was for a time a follower of that faith.

The Arabic world offered Pharisaism no rivals of the type of Mithraism, Stoicism, or Epicureanism. Yet the difficulties which the doctrine had to overcome among the nomads might well have seemed insuperable to the contemporary observer. The Arabs of the seventh century C.E. were involved in no such intellectual chaos as filled the Roman Empire at the beginning of the Christian Era. In spite of the conversion of scattered tribes to Judaism and Christianity, the nomads generally were loyal to the idolatry of their race. And the ignorant, self-indulgent, uxorious Mohammed, who became the apostle to the Arabs, was no Paul of Tarsus either in his intellectual or in his moral attainments. The result of these difficulties is still evident in Mohammedanism, which has no share in the Jewish-Christian doctrines of world peace or the equality of the sexes. But these deficiencies, grave as they are, do not lessen the marvel of the rapid, dramatic, though necessarily partial, victory of Pharisaism in the Arabic world. To have brought the desire for learning and the appreciation of the ethical life and of God to the nomads, was a magnificent achievement, though they were not won over to a complete acceptance of Pharisaic dogma.

The victorious energy of Pharisaism did not inhere, as is commonly supposed, merely in the doctrine of the Resurrection. This doctrine had been held by the Egyptians and the Zoroastrians, long before the rise of Pharisaism; yet neither of them was able to convert the world. And the Pharisees, themselves, drew most of their converts not from the gullible peasantry, but from the sceptical towns-folk, who might have ventured to doubt the reality of an eschatological promise.

Pharisaism won its world victory, as it won its initial victory in Palestine, not through a promise, but by a fulfil-ment. Its doctrines did not offer redemption; they brought it. They were in effect an announcement of "freedom to all the earth." The submerged were the equals of the patri-cians;* women were the equals of men; slaves were the equals of masters. All alike were children of God, created in His Image. The mere declaration of such principles aroused the latent sense of human dignity in the breast of the downtrodden, and he gratefully embraced the faith which brought him such salvation and comfort.

The urban plebeian responded to the call more readily than the rural serf, who was less conscious of enslavement. The women of the city responded more readily than the men for a subtler reason. They intuitively discovered in Pharisaism that amalgam of urban perspicacity and rural tenderness which had a natural appeal to them. A complete analysis of this aspect of Pharisaism is impossible in the limited space of this Foreword or even this book; it can only be discussed in passing, below and in some of the relevant chapters of the text.

The Arabic world which had no metropolitan plebeians, and where the women were too degraded and enslaved to share in any part of cultural life, was also attracted by the

---

*It is necessary to note that the words "plebeian" and "patrician" are used in this book as general terms, and do not imply any correlation between the classes of Jerusalem and those of Rome.

Pharisaic principle of human dignity; but, as we have seen, it placed its own interpretation on the concept. Human equality was limited to believers in Mohammed, and to males. The women were to be kept as soulless tools of their husbands, and the unbelievers were to be exterminated or enslaved.

No wonder that such a mighty force, as Pharisaism proved itself to be, had from the beginning both intense admirers and bitter opponents, but few neutral observers or objective students. The brilliant light which emanated from the East either attracted or repelled men; it never left them undisturbed. The royal family of Adiabene became converted to Pharisaism, and some of its members left their kingdom to reside in Jerusalem; Aquila, a Roman noble, became a disciple of the rabbinical academies; Shemaya, the foremost Pharisaic teacher of the age immediately before Herod, was of pagan descent. Frequently the Romans who became converted to Palestinian religion were quite unaware of the denominational differences which loomed so large in Jerusalem. Like some modern Chinese, they could not distinguish Judaism from Christianity, and considered them one faith. As a result, both Christianity and Judaism claim these converts as their own; but obviously it was the Pharisaism, common to both faiths, which won them.

So rapidly did Pharisaism spread in the palaces of Rome that the patricians became alarmed — not merely for their gods, but for themselves. The Romans were a tolerant people, but they drew the line at a religion which openly preached the equality of mankind and the futility and wickedness of war. Under the Emperor Tiberius the Jews were for a time driven from Rome; later they were made the butt of satirical ridicule; and on occasion were forbidden to practice their faith. The Christians, whose proselytizing activity was more vigorous, were treated with correspondingly greater severity, especially after they were recognized as a separate sect. It is important to remember that it was no special detail in either Christian or Jewish practice or theology which evoked these harsh measures, but the Pharisaic teachings and spiritual energy which were shared by both. The Roman writer and general saw in the Jew and the Christian who were so ready and even eager to die for their faith, precisely what the earlier opponents of Pharisaism had seen in the undivided sect — a group of narrow-minded bigots.

For Pharisaism itself, the passage of the centuries has by no means removed the ancient stigma. To this day, the word "Pharisee" remains a byword; and is still interpreted in the Oxford English Dictionary as meaning, "a self-righteous person; a formalist; a hypocrite."

The animosity reflected in this usage is not to be associated merely with the family quarrel between the early Christians and the main body of the Pharisees. It antedates the beginnings of Christianity; and indeed an early chronicler of Herod, whose words Josephus transcribes in his *Antiquities* (XVII, 2.4) records it. "For there was," he says, "a certain sect of Jews, who valued themselves highly upon the exact skill they had in the law of their fathers; and made men believe they were highly favored of God . . . These are those who are called the sect of the Pharisees." In the bitterness of conflict, it was natural for the early Christians to apply these epithets to their former comrades, who continued loyal to unaltered Pharisaism. Nevertheless, the Pharisee and the Christian remained sufficiently close to regard one another with respect. Rabbi Eliezer ben Hyrcanus, one of the most orthodox of the sages, offered high praise to an interpretation of Scripture given by an early Christian (Aboda Zara 17a); Paul, after his conversion, still declared himself a Pharisee (Acts 23.6); Gamaliel, the head of the Pharisees, was praised for his learning and tolerance in saving the Apostles from punishment (ibid. 5.34); a devout Pharisee was declared by Jesus to be "not far from the Kingdom of God" (Mk. 12.34); and Jesus himself, being asked what is the first of the commandments, replied, as might any other Pharisee, "Hear, O Israel; the Lord our God is one Lord" (ibid. 12.29).

Undoubtedly the Pharisees drew the energy which enabled them to remake world-thought, from the Prophets. The passionate call of Isaiah, the plaintive cry of Jeremiah, and the lofty exhortations of Deutero-Isaiah had at last struck a responsive chord in men's hearts. But what made the chord so responsive? While the present inquiry deals with the subject only indirectly, I believe it gives the answer to this question. Pharisaism was Prophecy in action; the difference is merely one between denunciation and renunciation. The kinship is more than ideological, however; it derives from the very nature and essence of the groups, for the Pharisees were drawn from the same social classes as the earlier prophetic following itself. The converts to prophecy among other classes might render it lip-service and even a certain measure of devotion; to the Pharisees the words of the ancient seers were like flames of fire out of their own hearts.

The true relation between Prophecy and Pharisaism is illuminated by the recurrence of the same phenomenon sixteen centuries later, in a country unknown to either

Prophets or Pharisees, the England of the sixteenth and seventeenth centuries. Once more, as in Palestine during the eighth and third centuries B.C.E., there was gathered into a growing metropolis — London — a group of traders and artisans, capable of taking a cultural stand against the dominant city patricians, ecclesiastics, and country gentry. And once more did these plebeians feel the impact of prophetic exhortation, for the English translation of the Scriptures had just been made available to the people. And just as the impact of Prophecy on the market place of Jerusalem created Pharisaism, so its impact on the market place of London created Puritanism.

The Puritans did not, of course, recognize themselves as successors to the Pharisees; nor would they have wished to identify themselves with the ancient Order. Yet such is the power of circumstance that they were compelled to be Pharisees, in spite of themselves! Thomas Huxley, who could have known only part of the evidence for the kinship between Puritanism and Pharisaism, was able to recognize it, through the generosity of his spirit and his deep penetration. "Of all the strange ironies of history," he says, "perhaps the strangest is that the word 'Pharisee' is current as a term of reproach among the theological descendants of the sect of Nazarenes who, without the martyr spirit of those primitive Puritans, would never have come into existence. They, like their historical successors our own Puritans, have shared the general fate of the poor wise men who save cities."

The researches into Pharisaism and Puritanism which have been made since Huxley's time, have confirmed this amazing intuition. In their indefatigable energy, in their devout piety, and in many aspects of their history, we are continually discovering new points of resemblance between the purists of Jerusalem at the beginning of the Christian Era and those of London in the age of Elizabeth and the early Stuarts. A strong sense of duty; an astonishing talent for self-discipline; a hunger for learning; an inner, partially unrecognized, urge for freedom; a curious mixture of idealism and realism; and, above all, profound but carefully concealed affections; hatred of the ornate and devotion to the simple: these and many other attributes of mind and character mark Pharisaism and Puritanism as twin movements, though they were born in different countries and in utterly different times.

This resurgence of Pharisaism, in a somewhat different guise, is so important for an appreciation of the original Order, that it is appropriate to review, even cursorily, some of the evidence of kinship between the two movements. The two foremost literary figures of Puritanism (using the term in its broadest sense) in the seventeenth century were, of course, John Milton and John Bunyan, both of whom had a large admixture of Pharisaism in their thought. Milton may decry the rabbinic sages, and "ask the Talmudist what ails the modesty of his marginal Keri, that Moses and all the prophets cannot persuade him to pronounce the textual Chetiv," but the very *Areopagitica* in which he makes this charge is an argument for the intellectual freedom which is the basis of Pharisaism! His paradoxical sympathy for the rebel, as personified in Satan and his cohorts, and for authority as hypostasized in God, which helps to make *Paradise Lost* so moving an epic, was characteristic of the original Pharisaism. The Pharisees loved the Temple, but opposed the priests. The Pharisees could not, like the Sect of Damascus and the Christians, withdraw from the

Jerusalem ritual; and yet they would not have hesitated to call their contemporary clerics, as Milton did those of his day, "blind mouths"—bishops who do not see, and shepherds who consume their flocks.

John Bunyan rejects the "burden of the Law," but on every page of his *Pilgrim's Progress* reveals himself as a resurrected Pharisee. Christian struggling through the Slough of Despond or writhing in the hands of the Giant, Despair, might be a personification not only of Bunyan himself, but of a host of rabbinic students, who lived a millennium before him. The advice which Pappias gave R. Akiba, or that which R. Jose ben Kisma gave R. Hanina ben Teradyon, might have come verbatim from Worldly Wiseman. "This government of Rome has been appointed from Heaven," the "prudent" counsellors said. "You can see for yourself that she has destroyed God's Temple, and burned His city, and murdered His saints, and yet she flourishes. Why then do you not obey her decree, and desist from teaching the Torah to your disciples?" (Aboda Zara 18a). And when the ancient pilgrims replied with simple faith, "God will have mercy;" what comment would Worldly Wiseman have made, other than that of R. Jose ben Kisma, "I am talking common sense to you; and you say, 'God will have mercy.'"

It is perhaps no coincidence that at one time in his life Bunyan actually fancied himself an Israelite; and John Milton immersed himself deeply not only in the Hebrew Scriptures, but in rabbinic tradition as well.

Seen in the light of these facts, the curious affection of the seventeenth century pietists, generally, for the Hebrew language and even Hebrew nomenclature, assumes a new significance. The Hephzibahs and Mehitabels, the Leahs and the Rachels, whose names we still find on old New England tombstones, prove that the inner spirit recognized the relationship with ancient Hebraism, even when the conscious mind denied it. It is even more striking that the opponents of Puritanism grasped its similarity to ancient Pharisaism. Ben Jonson does not hesitate to caricature his contemporary Puritan as "Rabbi Busy", and make him speak like a hair-splitting casuist. And the Oxford Dictionary which cites such irreverent remarks about the Pharisees, also quotes an early seventeenth century source where "Puritan" is used in the sense of "hypocritical, dissembling." As so often happens, the critical was accused of being hypercritical, and the hypercritical of being hypocritical.

The most striking resemblance between the Pharisees and the Puritans lay in their destiny. Both struggled to overcome the tendency toward luxury, licentiousness, and autocracy; both were driven by the logic of their views to extreme asceticism; both were accused of the divergent sins of profligacy and bigotry; both sought to retain the rural virtues of forthrightness and tenderness, together with the urban virtues of intellectualism and discipline; both became involved in civil wars; both discovered that force could not bring them anything but ultimate defeat; and, finally, both found their fulfilment, at least in a sense, not in the lands which gave them birth, but in distant countries, whither they were driven by the force of circumstance. The apogee of Pharisaism is the Talmud of Babylonia; that of Puritanism is the culture of New England.

The spread of a modified Pharisaism to the ends of the earth has fortunately not prevented the endurance throughout the centuries of the unchanged faith, in Rabbinic

Judaism. Pharisaism became Talmudism, Talmudism became Medieval Rabbinism, and Medieval Rabbinism became Modern Rabbinism. But throughout these changes of name, inevitable adaptation of custom, and adjustment of Law, the spirit of the ancient Pharisee survives unaltered. When the Jew reads his prayers, he is reciting formulae prepared by pre-Maccabean scholars; when he dons the cloak prescribed for the Day of Atonement and Passover Eve, he is wearing the festival garment of ancient Jerusalem; when he studies the Talmud, he is actually repeating the arguments used in the Palestinian academies.

Nor is it merely the outer accoutrements of Pharisaism which have survived in his life; the spirit of the doctrine has remained quick and vital. The story of this achievement has not yet been fully told; it lies concealed in the history of the repeated persecutions to which the later bearers of Pharisaism were subjected. When ultimately the fragmentary record is pieced together, it will be discovered as an epic, replete with heroic adventure. From Palestine to Babylonia; from Babylonia to North Africa, Italy, Spain, France, and Germany; from these to Poland, Russia, and eastern Europe generally, ancient Pharisaism has wandered. In the midst of new conditions of life, faced with new worlds of thought, the disciples of the Pharisees have sought on the one hand to preserve the old, and on the other to create the new. With the fifteenth and sixteenth centuries their energies began to wane, and an unprecedented weakness appeared in their academies. This was, however, but for the moment. The enlightenment of the eighteenth and nineteenth centuries produced spirits of diverse types, yet united in their common loyalty to the ancient teaching, in Rabbi Israel Baal Shem Tob (ca. 1700–1760) the founder of the modern Hasidic movement, Rabbi Elijah Gaon of Wilna (1720–1797) the founder of the critical school of Talmudical exegesis, and Moses Mendelssohn (1729–1786) the creator of a renewed synthesis between traditional Judaism and the learning of the West.

As recently as the latter half of the nineteenth century, there were rabbis who in their mode of life, in their courage, and in their realization that the Law was given man for his happiness, were the equals of the greatest of the Pharisaic or the Talmudic sages. I am especially mindful of the lives and activities of two of these men, because my father, to whose inspiration I am so much indebted, in his youth stood in close touch with them — Rabbi Isaac Elhanan Spektor (1817–1896), a statesman-scholar, and Rabbi Israel Salanter (ca. 1800–1883), a saintly ascetic, and founder of the Musar (ethicist) movement in Lithuanian Judaism.

A number of incidents recorded of the lives of these men indicate how nearly they approached the ancient Pharisees in their human pity and realization that the Law was given to man for his happiness and his development. It is impossible to cite these stories here, but reference may be made to the excellent biography of Rabbi Israel Salanter in Professor Louis Ginzberg's *Students, Saints and Scholars*, and to the brief statement about Rabbi Isaac Elhanan Spektor in the Jewish Encyclopedia.

The lives of these men, and numerous others like them, demonstrate the enduring importance which attaches to Pharisaism as a religious movement. Yet it would have been alien to the purpose of this book to consider the Order from this point of view. This inquiry is essentially historical and sociological, seeking to determine how the Pharisees came into existence, and what their distinctive teachings were. It is based primarily on the objective, almost scientific, approach of the Talmud, and its kindred writings. The apologetic literature which the long series of polemics against Pharisaism has evoked from its friends, has no prototype in the Talmud. With engaging candor, that ancient work informs us that there are seven types of Pharisee, only one of whom attains the ideal of "serving God out of love for Him" (Sotah 22b). It cites, with approval, the warning of the dying King, Alexander Jannaeus, to his wife: "Have no fear of the Sadducees, nor yet of the Pharisees. But beware the hypocrites who do the work of Zimri, and seek the reward of Phineas!" (ibid.). In several instances the arguments of both the Pharisees and the Sadducees relating to moot questions of law are cited, and we are enabled to see the Sadducean teaching from their point of view.

No less significant for the purpose of this study than the Talmud's judicial approach to the Pharisees, is its objective evaluation of city and rural life. If one marries a woman from the country, it rules, one cannot compel her to remove to the city, "for life in the cities is hard" (Ketubot 110b). Nor, conversely, if one marries a woman from the city can one compel her to remove to the country, "for everything is available in the city" (ibid.). Ezekiel, who described the Heavenly Chariot in detail, was "like a villager who sees the King;" Isaiah who used a few simple sentences for his theophany, was "like a townsman who sees the King" (Hagigah 13b).

While these statements are almost unique in their judicial objectivity, the recognition of rural-urban differences is by no means rare in ancient literature. The Scriptures, significantly, attribute the construction of the first city to Cain, the fratricide (Gen. 4.16); and that of the second city to

the arrogant men who built the Tower of Babel (Gen. 11.4).
Classical writers exhaust their vocabulary in descriptions
of the mendacity, cowardice, and pusillanimity of city-
folk. Aristophanes makes the simple farmer, Strepsiades,
amuse us by ascribing all of his misfortunes to marriage
with a city wife:

> "Ah! then I married — I a rustic — her
> A fine town-lady, niece of Megacles.
> A regular, proud, luxurious, Coesyra . . ."

> "Well, when at last to me and my good woman
> This hopeful son was born, our son and heir,
> Why then we took to wrangle on the name.
> She was for giving him some knightly name,
> 'Callippides,' 'Xanthippus,' or 'Charippus:'
> I wished 'Pheidonides,' his grandsire's name.
> Thus for some time we argued: till at last
> We compromised it in Pheidippides.
> This boy she took, and used to spoil him, saying,
> *Oh! when you are driving to the Acropolis, clad*
> *Like Megacles, in your purple;* whilst I said
> *Oh! when the goats you are driving from the fells,*
> *Clad like your father, in your sheepskin coat.*
> Well, he cared nought for my advice, but soon
> A galloping consumption caught my fortunes."

The tirade against the city did not, of course, end with
the ancient world; it has continued practically until our
own day. The poet Cowley, like Varro and Rabelais before
him, notes that:

> "God the first garden made, and the first city, Cain."

Our own Thomas Jefferson echoes the ancient Cato's praise of the farmer; and in the middle of the Victorian age, Betsey Trotwood vigorously asserted her conviction that a chicken bought in a London shop might be anything, but could hardly be a fowl.

In our own generation, Oswald Spengler devoted two massive volumes to the proof that urbanization means the destruction of the world, and predicted that western civilization would fall under the weight of city life.

As we glance through this literature, of which only the smallest fragment can be cited here, it becomes clear that the rural-urban conflict is one of the few constants in the recorded history of civilization. Amazing as it must seem at first glance, the ancient townsman, who lived in what we should regard as a little village, considered his neighbor, in a still smaller hamlet, a provincial, and treated him with condescension or contempt. The vineyards, granaries, and threshing floors which lay within a few miles of Jerusalem were spiritually as far from its market place, as the modern farm is from our own industrial centers. To the visitor from Ono or Anathoth, the noise of Jerusalem was as deafening, its metropolitan excitement as confusing, and its sophistication — to us so simple and transparent — as overwhelming, as those of the modern metropolis, with its millions of inhabitants and its endless traffic, are to the contemporary provincial. The reason for this is obvious: man's intellectual and emotional responses to differences of social environment are conditioned by relative, rather than by absolute, space. It is a question of time and ease of access, rather than of simple distance.

The permanence of the rural-urban conflict suggests the possibility that the formula for dealing with it may be equally permanent. It is futile to deny that despite its many advantages, urbanization involves grave perils for the human race. A predominantly urban culture tends to become prosaic, self-centered, materialistic, and cynical. And even graver than the influence of the city on its inhabitants, is that which it frequently exerts on the neighboring country-side. The peasant who comes into fleeting contact with urban life tends to absorb its weakness, without gaining its strength. He imitates its vices, but cannot attain to its vir-tues. His faith is shaken, his family loyalties are loosened, his forthrightness is perverted. But only rarely does he sub-stitute for these losses the intellectual or cultural vigor which makes city life a true civilization. Hence, long after the city trader has outgrown the habits of childish suspicion, shrewd bargaining, and foxy disingenuousness, these tendencies can still be found in the semi-urbanized peasantry. Given appropriate conditions, the city may produce the Pharisee and the Puritan; the decadent countryside can only rise to the pharisaical and the puritanical.

It is this wider spiritual decay which is reflected in three symptoms which Eduard Meyer, almost half a century ago, recognized as presaging the collapse of ancient Rome: a decreasing birthrate; a large group of economically uprooted, who had to be supported by the State; and a weakened sense of communal responsibility, particularly on the part of the intellectuals.[*]

The extent to which the spiritual disintegration character-istic of later Rome has affected our own life is a subject of de-bate; but there can be little doubt of the reappearance through-out the civilized world of all three symptoms which Eduard

---

[*] Eduard Meyer, *Kleine Schriften*, pp. 147 ff.

Meyer enumerates. Nor can there be any question of the widespread fear that political antagonisms are moving toward the destruction of our inherited civilization. Perhaps at such a time the ancient amalgam of urbanity and rusticity, the intellectual *rus in urbe*, which formulated itself successively in the profoundly spiritual movements of Prophecy and Pharisaism may be studied not only out of curiosity or historical interest, but also for guidance.

The thesis presented in this work was first proposed, in a simpler form, in an article published through the courtesy of Professors G. F. Moore and James Ropes in Harvard Theological Review, XXII (1929), pp. 185–261. Feeling that the subject required further analysis, I continued my researches, and in 1933 prepared the first draft of the present book. This was read by a number of scholars and friends, including President Cyrus Adler, Professor Julius A. Bewer, Professor Philip Leon, President Julian Morgenstern, Mr. Maurice Samuel, and Professor Charles C. Torrey. The fundamental criticisms which they offered induced me to undertake a complete revision of the work, which I present herewith.

The extent to which I relied on the basic researches made by others is indicated in the bibliography as well as in the notes, where mention is made of several oral communications which I have used for the present study. In addition to this assistance, I have received help from my wife, and a large number of friends who, I know, would prefer to remain anonymous. I must, however, express my gratitude to Professor A. D. Nock, the present editor of the Harvard Theological Review, for his permission to reproduce verbatim those parts of the article just mentioned, which are relevant to the present work; and to the librarians of the Jewish Theological Seminary of America, the Union Theological Seminary, the Dropsie College, the Hebrew Union College, the Jewish Institute of Religion, Columbia University, and the New York Public Library, for their unfailing courtesy. Part of Chapter XV was printed in *The Menorah Journal*, XXIV (January, 1936).

The transliteration used in this work is that adopted by the Jewish Publication Society for all of its books.

The English translation of the Hebrew Scriptures issued by the Jewish Publication Society of America (1917) has been used, in general, for quotations from the Bible.

The abbreviation "R." is used for Rabbinic Sages, who bore the title Rabbi or Rab, and lived in talmudic times. Those who lived after the close of the Talmud are described as "Rabbi."

When used for a book title the word *Akiba* refers to the present author's *Akiba: Scholar, Saint, and Martyr*.

FOREWORD TO THE SECOND EDITION

Pharisaism is the anomaly of religious history. Nationalist and ritualistic in origin, it became universal and philosophic in outlook. Though it admitted but thousands to formal membership, it included millions — of whom many were not Jews — among the believers in its doctrine. The Pharisees disappeared as an organized society in the third century of the Christian Era, but their influence on western spiritual thought still endures.

Two antagonisms, neither of which has any valid basis, stand in the way of a sociological study of Pharisaism. One is the antagonism between the social sciences and religion; the other is that among the religious faiths themselves.

The disregard of social science by the theologian has been due in large measure to misunderstanding. The facts, and even the theories of social science, are entirely consistent with religious teachings. The theories of the humble origin of religious ceremonial are no more disconcerting to the theologian than the theory of evolution. Even the doctrine of the material basis of the intellectual life is no denial of religion. Like other scientific observations and theories, it becomes a factor in the philosophy of religion, indicating for the religious thinker one of the ways in which human society has been impelled toward higher planes of civilization.

The hostility of some sociologists to religious thought is not inherent in the science. Humility comes to sciences, as to individuals, only with maturity. Given further development and more adequate research, the social sciences must

inevitably prove as valuable to religious thought as the
natural sciences. Indeed, social science may prove even
more valuable; for the natural sciences can be helpful only
in the development of religious philosophy, while the intro-
spective sciences can advance also the technique of religious
teaching.

The contribution which sociology can make to religion is
illustrated by a study of the Pharisees. The sect came into
being in the second century B.C.E., just before ancient civilization, having attained its complete expression in Greek
philosophy and Roman imperial administration, began to
show signs of decay. Factional in its beginnings, Pharisaism
finally became the religion of the Jewish people. From them
its major dogmas spread to the ends of the Roman empire.
When the empire fell, the Pharisaic tradition helped preserve much of classical civilization from destruction.

Told as a simple chronicle, the story assumes the proportions of an epic. Its meaning is enhanced, rather than
diminished, by sociological study which demonstrates that
the founders of the sect built far better than they knew.
Tradesmen of ancient Jerusalem, they thought they were
banding together for the protection of their ritual. Actually,
they were laying the foundations for a world civilization.

The sociological study of Pharisaism has been further im-
peded by the misunderstandings among the religious faiths.
Dogmatic theology is rightly suspicious of partial agreement.
The experience of centuries has taught religions to beware
the dangers which lurk in half-truths. "Travelers from one
religion to another," Santayana wisely remarks, "people who
have lost their spiritual nationality, may often retain a
neutral and confused residuum of belief, which they may
egregiously regard as the essence of all religion, so little

may they remember the graciousness and naturalness of that ancestral accent which a perfect religion should have." The very indebtedness of modern religions to Pharisaic doctrine has thus compelled theologians to stress the extent of their deviation from it. Nevertheless, there is so much common to all western, theistic religion — the doctrine of God and Man, the belief in the sanctity of truth, and the value of mercy — that the antipathy between the various religious traditions is tragic. Theological distinctions may be recognized and even stressed without being transformed into religious animosities. The recognition of the enduring value of the different religious traditions of the western world, both Jewish and Christian, is entirely consistent with an appreciation of their common heritage.

This thesis is not based on the assumption that the early Christians were members of the Pharisaic Order. Obviously they were not. But among the merits of Pharisaism was its ability to differentiate from the very beginning between acceptance of its dogma and adherence to the Order. The number of *haberim*, regularly enrolled Pharisees, was small; that of the co-workers of the Order was large, including the Essenes, the Therapeutae, the Sect of Damascus, and the early Christians.

Josephus was careful to draw this distinction between membership in the Order and the acceptance of its chief tenets, when he describes his own relation to Pharisaism (*Life*, 8).

The Alexandrian Jews who inquired of Hillel (the Pharisaic leader of Herod's day) about the legality of their betrothal customs (Tosefta Ketubot 4.9) were like Josephus not members of the Order, but followers of its precepts. Had these Alexandrines been Pharisees, their betrothal customs would have been identical with those of Palestine. Their deviation from Palestinian custom marks them as non-Pharisaic; their inquiry to Hillel reflects their acceptance of the Pharisaic interpretation of the Law.

The Pharisaic movement thus transcended by far the Pharisaic Order. Nothing is more vital for an understanding of Palestinian religious history than a clear appreciation of this fact. The ability of the Pharisee to impress his doctrine on others without drawing them into the Order was a direct outgrowth of the discovery of religious dogma. The Pharisee did not demand universal obedience to his discipline. He sought primarily an admission of his philosophical truth and an acceptance of his universal ethics. To admit the belief in the Resurrection or the validity of the Oral Law was perhaps not as righteous as to accept the full "yoke of the Law." But it was far better than associating oneself with the Sadducees by a denial of the Pharisaic doctrines. He who violated a Pharisaic interpretation transgressed the Law; he who rejected a major Pharisaic dogma lost his immortality.

This idea and the technique it introduced was as important in the history of religious teaching as the Macedonian phalanx in the history of military tactics. In this way the faith was spread, but was not diluted. The Pharisee of the second century of the Christian era was as firm, as devout, and as uncompromising, as his ancestor three hundred years earlier.

As Professor Frank Gavin and others have intimated, this form of organization was also adopted by the early Christian community. It, too, was a *haburah*, an association, which spread its doctrine to all, but admitted to its membership only the limited few.

But the relation of Church and Synagogue during the first century was even closer than that indicated by the similarity of doctrine and of organization. The two institutions were so intimately related, that the changes introduced in the one necessarily affected the other. Thus, the establishment of an obligatory evening service in the Synagogue was almost immediately followed by the establishment of a similar service in the early Church.*

The intolerance of the Middle Ages did not entirely destroy this close relationship between the Church and the Synagogue. There is a similarity between their music, between many of the rites introduced into their worship, and even between many of their later forms of organization. The history of the rabbinical synods of the Middle Ages bears a close resemblance to that of the Church synods; there was a close association between the Jewish, Christian and Mohammedan scholastics; and there is even a suggestion in the *Book of the Pious*** that the habits and ways of the Jews in the different communities varied as did those of their Christian neighbors.

To recognize the kinship of the faiths derived from the Prophets is not to advocate their reduction to any common denominator. The three faiths, and their subdivisions, have

*The evidence that the evening service became obligatory in the synagogue only toward the end of the first century C.E. is to be found in B. Berakot 27b. The Book of Acts which is sometimes cited as a source for three daily services in the early Christian Church (cf. W. O. E. Oesterley, *The Jewish Background of the Christian Liturgy*, p. 125) actually refers only to two services. The prayer of the ninth hour mentioned in Acts 3.1, was identical with the prayer which was recited "about the sixth hour" (Acts 10.9). It was the afternoon service, and might be recited either early or late in the afternoon. The first reference to three services in the Church occurs, therefore, in the *Didache* 8, the date of which is generally fixed at about the year 100 C.E.

**Book of the Pious*, ed. Bologna, section 1101.

come into existence to fulfill purposes of which we can be only vaguely aware. But in view of the modern attacks on all theistic religion, the future strength and development of these faiths may depend as much on their cooperation as on the preservation of their individuality. Working together with the sciences, these faiths may be able to create the synthesis of science and theology needed to guide men out of the intellectual confusion of our time. The events of the last decade have demonstrated that science and liberalism cannot survive in a world bereft of religion; and that religion cannot survive in a world bereft of liberty and science.

Out of man's present spiritual chaos may emerge an ordered, pluralistic universe of thought. It will be a universe in which the principle of federalism is applied to the realm of the spirit, as it has been to the realm of political life. Unity will be achieved with no sacrifice of liberty; cooperation without imposing uniformity.

Through the generosity of the Jewish Publication Society, some errors in the text have been corrected, and a map of Palestine during the Second Commonwealth and a chronological table have been added in this edition of *The Pharisees*. In making the corrections, I have had the assistance of valuable oral and written communications from several friends to whom I am profoundly grateful.

FOREWORD TO THE THIRD EDITION

It is customary to think of modern civilization as dynamic and developing, and of the ancient world as static and lethargic. This is largely correct, so far as the knowledge and control of the material world are concerned. A single decade of the twentieth century probably sees greater advances in therapeutic medicine, in the physical and the biological sciences, in technology and in industry than all the aeons before the Industrial Revolution. Progress in these fields has also affected, stimulated, and even revolutionized the social and psychological sciences, some types of historical research, and a few humanistic disciplines.

Yet this progress in many specific skills is distressingly associated with virtual stagnation, if not retrogression, in the area of thought where some of the ancients, at certain periods and in certain places, proved themselves so remarkably resourceful and creative—the development of wisdom. Buddha and Confucius did not invent a flying machine, but they set in motion human impulses which have made life eminently livable and significant for millions of their fellow men. Whatever be the drawbacks of the systems which grew out of these teachings and others like them, they have helped to give zest and meaning to individual and group existence and to soften the harshness of conflict between man and man.

Karl Marx's indictment of religion as the opiate of the people could be made only by one without sympathy for the real agony of mankind. To enable men to see in the perspective of the ages (as did Buddha and his peers in other traditions) the tragedies to which all flesh is heir, and to remain serene amid the confusions of life, is no small achievement.

Bertrand Russell observes that the only real contribution of religion to civilization was the determination of certain astronomical data by the ancient Egyptians. To arrive at this conclusion, he must equate civilization with the growth of natural science, and hold inconsequential the development of the saints found in all great religions together with a degree of saintliness in the level of conduct by large multitudes. It is astonishing that in a few generations antiquity produced in such widely dispersed areas as China, India, the Middle East, and Greece, men of such wisdom and enduring influence for good as Lao Tze, Confucius, Buddha, Zoroaster, the Second Isaiah, Ezra the Scribe, and Socrates. Why all these protagonists of revolutionary approaches to life and its problems appeared at approximately the same time, although in different regions, still remains a mystery. But there can be little doubt of their enduring importance in human affairs and their significance for the destiny of mankind.

The magnificent achievements of the ancient sages were both culmination of long processes of increasing wisdom and beginning of new efforts, deepening human insight and enlightening the mind of man. The present book is an effort to discern some of the socio-psychological forces which helped mould one of these efforts, namely, that of Ezra and his followers, and to perpetuate its influence.

This is—hopefully—the first in a series of monographs (one other in print—*Akiba: Scholar, Saint and Martyr*—but several in manuscript or in first drafts) showing how the disciples of Ezra, calling themselves Hasideans, and ultimately dubbed Pharisees, came into being. The series will ultimately describe the difficulties they encountered from men who had special skills but lacked the very wisdom the Pharisees sought to inculcate; how the Pharisees laid the foundation for all Western religion; how they overcame the obstacles in their way; and how they survived through wise insight. It is also necessary to understand the nature of the opposition to them and their predecessors, the prophets; and to recognize why in some generations opponents who seemed right in the immediate crisis proved wrong in the perspective of man's enduring crisis—his effort to make his brief stay on earth bearable. The Pharisees will be seen as materially disadvantaged people who found life a delightful experience, who looked forward serenely to old age and to death, who rejoiced in each of God's works, and who yet shunned the intoxicating diversions of momentary pleasure, of temporal success, and of what Rabbi Elijah Gaon of Wilna called "seeming glory." Had their counsel been taken seriously in the highest quarters of the realm, the Roman Empire might have escaped the agony of dissolution and thus spared mankind the horrors of the Dark Ages.

"The beginning of wisdom," says the author of Proverbs (1.7) "is fear of the Lord," or correctly, "awe before the Lord." For the Pharisees, all discussions regarding private and public life began with the implied question, "What is God's pleasure?" In other words, "What is right in the sight of the cosmic Creator of all mankind?" They did not ask "What is more convenient or comfortable?" or "What is more likely to lead to worldly success?" No wonder that Eduard Meyer with uncanny historical insight regarded them as "unworldly." They were unworldly, if worldliness means the sacrifice of ultimate goals to individual or national "success," which in their very nature must be ephemeral, no matter how prolonged. On the other hand, the Pharisees did not, like the Essenes (who may or may not have been identical with the sect of the Qumram Scrolls), withdraw from participation in world affairs. They never flinched from meeting problems which were difficult, and never desisted from answers which seemed demanding.

The Pharisees lived in a way other traditions might expect only from members of Holy Orders, but followed these standards in the market place, in lowly homes, in royal courts, when they walked by the way, when they lay down, and when they arose. Their material concerns became secondary to those of the spirit, and the business of God was the core of their lives.

Their distinctive way of life did not negate the possibility of others achieving similar moral discipline in other ways. They did not deny the existence of "saints of peoples of the world." On the contrary, the Pharisees held that these saints were on a level with those of their own faith. But the Pharisees were keenly aware of the peril of acculturation which, destroying the spiritual and moral values absorbed from parents and tradition, fails to provide the excellence available in other traditions and in other ways. The Pharisees assumed the Torah had been revealed to them for a Divine purpose and it would be treason to God for them to use any other way to Him, even if revealed to others, and no matter how much more convenient that path might be.

They considered it the will of God that man should live out his complete span of life. Martyrdom for the faith, or to avoid murder or infringement of a woman's chastity was permitted and commanded. Except for such extreme circumstances, prolongation of life, even one's own, was a cardinal commandment. Therefore physicians were permitted and even encouraged to practice and study their science and art. Not a goal in itself, length of life was valuable because, for the good, it offered more opportunity for righteousness; for the wicked, opportunity for repentance.

Moral and character education being the goal of life, the duty to train his child was to the Pharisee no less important than that to discipline himself.

Moderation has its uses, but these are secondary. Never did the Pharisee forget that in the wise life almost all that counts is excellence. Compromise with mediocrity in this field was not for him. While varied individual gifts might suggest different degrees of intellectual achievement, "he who gives little and he who gives much are alike, provided that their intention is alike to serve God."

The modern reader may find it difficult to associate wise insight with the arguments over ritualistic issues which occupy many of the pages of this book and a large part of the Supplement to the new edition. He may find even stranger the grave debates over such questions as whether a prayer service should open with the formula, "Blessed be the Lord," or "Blessed be the Lord, Who is blessed." Few issues could seem more remote from the development of wise outlook on life and realistic perspectives on the world.

But these gestures were part of the harmonious good life and could no more be taken lightly than notes in an opera or symphony. The Pharisees and their predecessors insisted that the whole world was a Divine Temple in which each man served as priest. Their rituals of worship at home, in the market place, and in the synagogue were as carefully thought through as similar gestures in the Temple of Jerusalem by the Aaronid priests. Naturally this doctrine seemed obnoxious to many Aaronid priests, and especially High Priests, who liked to believe that they alone were God's courtiers on earth.

The main ethical concern of the Pharisees and their predecessors was never directly challenged by their opponents. In general, no one minded their remarkable docility, their extreme gentleness, their predisposition to anonymity, their preoccupation with study, their philanthropy, their wide humanitarianism, including charity toward their opponents. Their theory of education might be deemed unsuitable for children of the rich, because it placed so great a value on the spiritual life as to discourage in some the virtues of thrift, diligence, and hard work. Their theology, making the future world of transcendent importance and reducing the present one to the level of a corridor leading to immortal life, might seem dangerous to the "practical-minded." Not subjects of debate, such disagreements rarely became part of the overt historical record.

The ethical, theological, and educational views of the opponents of the Pharisees have, in general, to be reconstructed from stray hints scattered through the Rabbinic and Jewish - Hellenistic literatures. Moreover, the Pharisaic notions in these areas could not be reduced to norms and were challenged within Pharisaism itself, when that movement came to include a large number whose emotional outlook was essentially Sadducean, even though they followed the specific Pharisaic rituals.

When Pharisaism became Talmudism it did not lose its basic character, and even in modern times its main exponents have included such saintly figures as Rabbi Israel Salanter, the Hafetz Hayyim, and the Hazon Ish. Yet the mask of pure ritualism, which ultimately covered so much of life under the Law, has frequently, for many of its lesser interpreters, tended to conceal the reality. As Professor Louis Ginzberg remarked, the Gaonic period, that is, the period in Judaism from the seventh to the tenth centuries, failed to produce a single luminary of first-rate brightness before the emergence of Rab Saadia Gaon. Ironically, those accepting the tradition of the selfless Hillel came to regard it simply as ritual, and to forget that his basic teachings were primarily a system of morals and ethics. Study itself became a ritual, instead of a means of transforming the student.

When the nature of Pharisaism was forgotten its past was re-created in the image of the lesser present. Hillel's apothegms were, indeed, remembered and repeated by rote. So were the prayers composed by earlier Pharisees and Proto-Pharisees. But their significance was lost for ever-widening circles. The efforts of Rashi, Maimonides, the French Tosafists, Nahmanides, and Rabbi Solomon ibn Aderet to get to the heart of the talmudic discussions, "to study for the sake of observing and doing," were succeeded (as persecution and harassment demanded their toll from the spirit as well as the body of the Jewish community) by the invention of complicated systems of argument and casuistry which obscured rather than illumined the thought of the ancient Talmudists. Thus the great and pregnant saying of Hillel that the "Illiterate [i.e., the observant illiterate person] is not fearful of sin [but only of its consequences], and the *'am ha-arez*" [meaning not "the ignorant" as later usage had it, but the contemporary peasant], no matter how careful of the ritual, "will not be a *hasid*" or a lover of mankind, became [despite the clear interpretation of Maimonides and Rabbenu Jonah] perverted into the doctrine that "the ignorant cannot be pious."

The clear relation of decisions in marginal cases to in-

evitable psychological and social predispositions of the
scholar, recognized in the Talmud and its great commentators as both inevitable and useful, was completely overlooked. The Palestinian Talmud was interpreted to conform
to that of Babylonia, the doctrines of Rabbi Ishmael to
those of Rabbi Akiba: placed, as it were, on a Procrustean
bed and the limbs of a great system hewn to suit the frame
derived from traditions one knew best.

Rebelling against this form of talmudic research, a group
of teachers following the example of Rabbi Elijah, the Gaon
of Wilna, initiated an effort to return to the sources of
Pharisaic inspiration, in which rabbinic studies were recognized not merely as an end in themselves, but as instruments
for the betterment of individual and group behavior and
character. Another group of scholars, following the examples
of Rapaport and Geiger, applied to these sacred works the
canons of historical research adopted from the works of
classical scholars, and sought to create a school whose main
concern in Jewish studies would be reconstruction of the past.

There remains a vital task for our generation to which the
labors of both schools are available, to combine their merits
in an intensive study of the biblical and talmudic works for
the wisdom hidden in them. This wisdom often cannot be
distilled directly from the technical debates recorded in the
talmudic books. In these debates, each scholar sought to
persuade his opponents regarding the correctness of his own
point of view in specific matters. He could not appeal to his
personal predisposition as the premise of his argument, for
this slant was usually rejected as bias by his opponents. Inevitably he resorted to a system of hermeneutics to which
his colleagues could not take exception. Thus the debates,
while invaluable for the light they shed on talmudic dialectic

and biblical exegesis, do not in general reflect the underlying logic which led to differences in the formulated or suggested norms. To understand that reasoning, one has to penetrate the lives of the individual scholars, the environment in which they moved, the tradition which helped to mould their thought. One then discovers totally different reasons, rarely articulated, for the views the individual scholar or the group upheld. It is these reasons, primarily, which indicate the wisdom underlying the opposing courses of argument and action.

The doctrine of the Immortality of the Soul became a cornerstone of Pharisaism—not because of hints in the Pentateuch or mention in the Prophets and the Hagiographa —but because in an age of increasing materialism the doctrine was an important pedagogical device for turning man to spirituality. The Talmud gives many "proofs" of man's immortality, but its pragmatic, educational usefulness is not one of them. Yet without recognition of this usefulness, the technical argument seems dry and sometimes forced.

The recovery of the inarticulate Talmud, implied in the articulate, may be one of the great services which modern scholarship can render the future as well as the past. The student of the Talmud cannot believe that his tradition is unique in this difference between what has been articulated and what led to the articulation; between the social responsibility which guided the thinker and the academic argument in which he justified his stand to those too young to comprehend his basic motivation. If the type of analysis here proposed has its analogue in other traditions, we may finally discover why a late generation, accustomed as none before it to utter candor and frankness in teachers and colleagues, finds so many discussions of ancient traditions arid.

A study of the ethics of the Pharisees would thus include analysis of their varying conceptions of holiness, the reason underlying the passion of their earlier teachers for anonymity, and the passion of later generations to preserve and glorify the names of their teachers, the nature of their liturgy, the relation of their theology to their rituals and moral insights, the paradox by which they accepted opposing opinions as equally acceptable to God.

The type of research which this book represents seems indispensable groundwork for such further studies and analyses. Neither this work, nor the ambitious ones suggested, could have been undertaken or even imagined, without the great contributions made to talmudic studies by a series of scholars who lived in the first half of this century. Among these one of the most eminent was the Hazon Ish, whose significance will become apparent only as his studies are fully mastered by disciples in the West, as well as those in Israel. Of the scholars in the West, the leading figure bringing talmudic study to new heights in the early decades of this century was certainly Professor Louis Ginzberg who was fortunate, as he often asserted, to have associated with him Professor Alexander Marx. The immense erudition of Professor Ginzberg and his clear insight into the meaning of the Talmud were complemented by the energies of his great colleague, who provided a library of unequalled wealth and critical acumen of rare quality.

One of the privileges of my life was study under both these scholars, and each page of this book attests my indebtedness to them. During the past twenty years, I have had the rare opportunity of a second education, through communion with Professor Saul Lieberman, rightly considered "the leader among those who speak in the field of Jewish knowledge" in this generation, and through the study of his great works which open a new era in talmudic studies.

It would be impossible to enumerate all the other scholars —on the Faculty of The Jewish Theological Seminary of America and elsewhere—and the laymen and women from whom I have learned and who have helped, sometimes when they least knew it, in the studies underlying these volumes. I have learned much from my rabbinic colleagues and former, as well as present, students, both when they have agreed with my views and supplemented them and when they have dissented and argued with me. Many an insight into what I believe to be the real meaning of an ancient talmudic warning came to me as I discovered in actual life the errors the Sages had in mind. Equally often I have come to understand an obscure passage in Scripture and Talmud as I heard modern teachers struggling with the identical difficulty, but perhaps with less penetration into the enduring facts of human nature. Thus while my studies have offered me continuous commentary on the present scene, the present scene has frequently turned out to be a footnote to the wisdom of the past.

No one has labored more zealously and indefatigably on this book (as on every other literary task I have undertaken at the Seminary) than Miss Jessica Feingold, without whose help this book could not have appeared at this time.

The index was capably prepared by Dr. Naomi Cohen, who is high on the list of those deserving thanks.

Parts of the research needed in connection with this study were done by Mrs. Stanley Friedman, Mrs. Theobald Reich and Mrs. Ada Turner, who all have my deep appreciation.

Heartfelt thanks are due Dr. Solomon Grayzel, Editor of The Jewish Publication Society, not only for his many suggestions in connection with this book, but particularly for his great patience.

Finally, I follow the ancient custom of the Rabbinic Sages, thanking the God of my fathers for permitting me to devote time and energy in the study of His Torah, and praying, as I enter upon old age, that He will not cast me off; and that He will not remove His holy spirit from our generation, so that we may come to serve Him in truth.

LOUIS FINKELSTEIN

Kislev 15, 5721
December 4, 1960

INTRODUCTORY NOTE TO THE THIRD EDITION

My purpose here is to describe briefly the current interpretations of Pharisaism, and to indicate how the thesis developed in this book — especially in the Supplement to the present edition — is related to them. Further, it will show how the widespread misconception of Pharisaism as an effort to mitigate what is often called "the burden of the Law" (for the Pharisees anything but a burden) arose, and how the misconception became so popular among writers on Pharisaism.

The discussion will involve analysis of the difference between the Hasidean and the Pharisaic approach to civil law on the one hand, and to the ritual on the other. Light on this subject is shed from the Book of Jubilees and from reappraisal of the passages dealing with the Pharisees in Josephus.

Finally, the general thesis of this book requires us to consider why a rustic atmosphere pervades so many of the early tannaitic works, which are, after all, of Pharisaic origin.

Thus this Introductory Note will consist of the following sections:

1. Modern Theories about Pharisaism and the Pharisees
2. The Rural Atmosphere of Some Talmudic Documents
3. The Nature and Authority of the Hasidean Judiciary
4. The Hasidean Civil Law
5. The Hasidean Criminal Law
6. The Unwritten Hasidean Ritual Law

1. Modern Theories about Pharisaism and the Pharisees

To achieve scientific objectivity regarding an historical
movement, one must paradoxically be sympathetic to it. To
understand and explain people and human movements they
must be seen from within as well as from without. Psychological identification is indispensable to intellectual appreciation. To understand the Pharisees, one must at least for a time,
and in spirit, become their disciple, as well as an observer.

Almost all modern writers about the Pharisees have been
hostile to them and their ideas, or disciples of hostile
writers. This curious fate has obscured the meaning of
Pharisaism and has led to curious misinterpretations of the
Pharisees and their ideas. Even great scholars, such as
Julius Wellhausen, Eduard Meyer, and Abraham Geiger, or
E. Schuerer and W. Bousset, have been misled.

To say this is not to minimize the contributions these
writers have made to the understanding of Jewish history,
both in the biblical and post-biblical periods. Wellhausen
was a great Bible critic, stimulating even when in error. In
his day Meyer was a foremost historian of antiquity. Geiger
added greatly to the elucidation of Scripture and Talmud.
The wide erudition of Schuerer and Bousset make their works
(especially in the later editions) vital for the modern student.

But none of these scholars could for a moment really
imagine himself a Pharisee or desire to share their ideas.

The Pharisaic view that theology, ethics, and ritual are
all ways to articulate ideas about God and the world

remained alien. Wellhausen could not see that the Prophets, despite their preoccupation with moral problems, were in the tradition of Leviticus and Deuteronomy. His dichotomy between the Law and the Prophets inevitably led also to dichotomy between the Pharisees and the Prophets. He could not understand the claim of these later Sages that their views derived from Moses and had been transmitted to them by the Prophets.

Neither Wellhausen, Meyer, Schuerer, nor Bousset could agree that truths are often more effectively articulated in conduct than in words. A theological system whose main vehicle of expression was ritual and moral behavior remained obscure. Hence, life under the Law was despised as "legalism," an invisible prison in which the Pharisee spent his life and which he sought to impose on others. How the Pharisee could identify his life with true freedom, how he found stimulus for creativity and spontaneity, how he came to regard the Law as a home rather than a dungeon, eluded these critics.

Disparagement of the talmudist and the Pharisee, extending from people to ideas, was encouraged not only by early Christian writings, but also by predilection for the Jewish apocalyptic literature where these writers were at home. Even when preserved in strange languages, such as Ethiopic, apocalyptic literature was intelligible at least in translation, whereas the intricacies of talmudic law were mysterious. The apocalyptists might be dreamers, whose reconstruction of the past was as absurd as their conception of the future. Still, they wrote a kind of history, no matter how primitive, uninstructed, partisan, and undisciplined. To that extent they could be considered fellow craftsmen, no matter how unsophisticated.

Thus for a number of critics the apocalyptists became the true "Pharisees," the men who developed the theory of another world where the injustice of the present would be righted. They seemed to have inherited the Prophetic tradition, for did not Prophecy include at least one apocalypse? And did not the Prophets — like the apocalyptists — devote time and energy to description of the ultimate bliss awaiting mankind? The emphasis on certain ceremonials in the Book of Jubilees gave pause to some of these critics, but they could dismiss that work as a curiosity in the total literature.

Some students went so far as to discern an intimate relationship between the Apocalypse and early Christianity, and therefore could understand both how Christianity arose in ancient Israel, and why many of its protagonists opposed official Pharisaism as meticulous nonsense.

Living before the discovery of the Qumram literature, these students could not know the relation of the apocalyptic writings to the *halakah* of that sect. Otherwise they would have seen that the failure of many apocalyptists to stress the *halakah* was due neither to ignorance nor disparagement. The apocalyptists simply provided the basic homiletical and theological admonitions needed for the observances they required of their followers. Heeding this phenomenon, Wellhausen and others might have inferred that silence of the Prophetic books regarding the Pentateuchal codes, rituals, and moral norms involved no ignorance or indifference. The Prophets devoted themselves largely to denunciation of idolatry and of social injustice because stress on ritual would have detracted from their urgent, immediate task of winning the people to monotheism and ethics.

On the other hand, Geiger was led into his misinterpretation of Pharisaism not by hatred, but by specious love and admiration. He respected and loved the Pharisees and some of the talmudists — such as Hillel and R. Akiba — but re-created them in his own image. In an age which was increasingly hedonistic, Geiger — obsessed by the necessity of simplifying traditional Jewish practice to accord with what he considered the needs of the modern world or at least modern Germany — sought, in the past, support for his views of the present. Probably unconscious of his own motivation, he aspired to play a role in Judaism comparable to that of Martin Luther in Christianity, and divided the ancient teachers of Judaism into two opposing groups. There were his exemplars, who continually sought to lessen the "burden of the Law." These were his heroes, the Pharisees, Hillel, and R. Akiba. Opposed were those who anticipated his opponents, the fanatically rigid Sadducees, the Shammaites, and R. Ishmael. The first group represented the "New *Halakah*," as it emerged from the progressive, evolutionary schools; the second, the "Old *Halakah*" as transmitted from primitive days.

By implication, Geiger refuted the indictment of the Pharisees and the Talmud prevalent in German scholarship of his time. The hypocritical and fanatical Jews of early Christian writings could be identified with the supporters of the Old *Halakah*, the Sadducees and the Shammaites. The main builders of the Talmud were advocates of the New *Halakah*, free from the criticisms of the early Christian writings or of contemporary scholarship. Thus Geiger maintained that the doctrine of "an eye for an eye" was taken literally by both Sadducees and Shammaites. It was part of the Old *Halakah*. The New *Halakah* interpreted the words to involve only monetary compensation. In this way Geiger became an apologete for Pharisaism and the Talmud, as well as a religious reformer.

Defending his approach vigorously, with great learning, and through the use of texts not studied in the usual rabbinic schools of his day, Geiger came to dominate Jewish historiography not only in Germany, but throughout the West.

Essentially, his underlying premise was not dissimilar to that of Wellhausen, Meyer, Schuerer, and Bousset. Like them, he considered life under the Law a burden. He disagreed with them only in holding that the Pharisees lightened this burden, whereas they appeared arch-fanatics to the other critics.

Geiger's approach to the Pharisees and their schools was followed in its fundamentals and elaborated by H. Graetz and I. H. Weiss, who made it basic to their histories of the Pharisaic and talmudic periods.

Because of the popularity of these histories, perhaps also through the teachers' efforts to carry further into practice Geiger's views on contemporary Judaism, and finally for a special reason to be discussed below, Geiger's historiography won widespread currency in Western rabbinic thought, being taken for granted in ever-widening circles.

Devastating criticism of his analyses by H. Pineles (*Darkah shel Torah*, Vienna, 1861), by Isaac Halevy in *Dorot ha-Rischonim*, and the late Professor Louis Ginzberg in his notes to the third edition of Geiger's *Kebuzat Ma'amarim*, did not reverse this trend in Jewish historiography. Pineles was known only to a limited group. Halevy's unsystematic and polemical work played but a minor role in Jewish studies. Professor Ginzberg's significant writings on the *halakah* were obscured by his magnificent contributions to other aspects of Jewish literature.

Both R. Travers Herford and G. F. Moore realized the untenability of theories on the Pharisees developed by Wellhausen, Meyer, Schuerer, and Bousset. Herford and Moore knew men who lived under the Law, and understood that for these modern disciples of the ancient Pharisees the Law was no burden but a delight. For many twentieth century Jews the thousands of talmudic norms dealing with the Sabbath and festivals were liberating (as are the rules of grammar and syntax for a writer), enabling them to articulate joy in service of their Master. Rabbinic food laws might on occasion be inconvenient, but clearly this so-called "legalism" elevated the animal process of nourishment to an act of worship. To Herford and Moore, preservation of ancient Hebrew prayers, the rituals of the *tephilin*, *zizit*, and many others revealed deep religious meaning.

Perhaps both Herford and Moore understood the joy of Pharisaism because of their acquaintance with the Puritans. The Pharisees might well appear to such writers of England and New England simply as ancient Puritans with a special slant on life.

Projecting their observations on the history, Herford and Moore startled readers familiar with the conclusions of Wellhausen, Meyer, Schuerer, and Bousset. To Herford and to Moore, who had deeper insight and wider scholarship, the Pharisees were extremely religious men who followed a different tradition. Herford and Moore could discount attacks on the Pharisees in early Christianity as a conflict among fellow-worshippers, who sought the same goals and were often in essential agreement.

However, neither Herford nor Moore could undertake to reappraise Geiger's argument. Neither had entered the portals of talmudic *halakah;* they could not evaluate Geiger's frequently complicated arguments. Therefore, following Graetz and other Jewish writers, both Herford and Moore (like the vast majority of Jewish writers on Pharisaism) accepted the description of the Pharisees as innovators, who sought to "adjust" the Mosaic law to what they considered the needs of their time.

Writing mainly for Christian readers, Herford and Moore were especially concerned with the verbal theology of the Pharisees, tangential to the main body of the faith. Their books, particularly those by Moore, have enduring importance. For the first time in the present century, outside witnesses observe Pharisaic concepts with sympathy.

Herford, Moore, and Geiger had disciples not only in England and America, but also among later German specialists. Edited by Hugo Gressmann, Bousset's third edition departed markedly from the tone of the earlier ones. And Gressmann was but one of many later German Christian scholars to learn from both Puritan-minded English and Americans and from Geiger and his followers.

In this fashion the concept of the Pharisees developed by Geiger prevailed among virtually all writers in the field. His doctrine of the Old *Halakah* and the New *Halakah* was congenial to a generation which searched everywhere for examples of evolution, and was delighted to see Jewish law as evolving from Sadducean fanaticism to Pharisaic stress on the spirit in opposition to the letter of the Law.

A special circumstance (mentioned above) helped toward their conclusions Geiger and his rabbinically-trained followers, namely, the curriculum of the rabbinical schools. There, even today, students begin study of the Talmud with the tractates on civil law — Baba Kamma, Baba Mezi'a, and Baba Batra. Next come those discussing marriage law. We shall presently see that talmudic civil law markedly deviated from that of Scripture, and the deviations also affected discussion of the marriage law.

No wonder Geiger and his school concluded that the Pharisees used exegesis to depart from the word of Scripture. Efforts of the Talmud (notably that of Babylonia) to find Scriptural support for Pharisaic deviation, at times through forced exegesis, persuaded Geiger and his followers that the ancient Sages did not hesitate to impose their views on the Bible itself.

Geiger's judgment was fortified by a further observation. In many controversies about ritual, particularly regarding the law of impurity, the Shammaitic norms were more rigorous than the Hillelite. This was natural, because the Shammaites were priests, extremely conscious of the need for ritual purity. Removed from the market place, they were able to observe severities in that regard which were almost impossible for Hillelite traders. Where the Torah is ambiguous or silent, the Shammaites tended toward rigor in the Law. To Geiger it appeared that the original Pharisaic norm had been that of the Shammaites, and that the Hillelites had mitigated its harshness — trying to preserve its spirit, but departing from its letter.

From this conclusion Geiger and his school easily inferred that among the Hillelites R. Akiba led the innovators and R. Ishmael the traditionalists. Because R. Akiba's method of Scriptural interpretation was original, because Ben Zoma had compared him to a calf which had never known the yoke (*Abot of R. Nathan*, I, ch. 23, 38b, where Ben Zoma certainly referred to R. Akiba without specific mention), because R. Akiba was daringly independent in some ritual decisions (cf. e.g. Sifra *Mezora'*, end). Because his formulation of the Law was often contrasted in talmudic writings with that of "the ancient elders" (cf. Sifra *Hobah*, *perek* 12.1, et al.), it seemed to Geiger and his group that the Talmud itself con-

sidered R. Akiba an innovator in jurisprudence, no less than
in educational method and exegetical theory.

Geiger found additional confirmation for his theory in the
Talmud's references to the Ordinances of Hillel, especially
the *prosbul* which practically abolished the cancellation of
debts during the Sabbatical years ordained in Deuteronomy
15.2. He curiously overlooked the fact that the *takkanot* of
Hillel dealt exclusively with questions of property. Through
the *prosbul* a creditor was permitted to collect a debt after
the Sabbatical year (Mishna Shebi'it 10.3). Through another
ordinance of Hillel (Mishna 'Arakin 9.4) the seller of a house
in a walled city who wished to redeem his property in
accordance with the provisions of Leviticus 25.29 ff. could
do so, even in the absence of the purchaser.

In both *takkanot* Hillel emerged as statesman-scholar, but
neither work suggested disregard for the ritual law of the
Pentateuch.

However, we will presently show (as remarked in the
Talmud by Raba, B. Gittin 36b), the Hasideans and their
disciples carefully distinguished their approach to the laws
of property from that to the ritual. The early Hasidean
judges were essentially arbitrators to whom both litigants
submitted their respective claims, and by whose decisions
they agreed to abide. When arbitrators, the Hasidean judges
were not bound by the letter of Pentateuchal law, where in
specific cases it seemed to work hardship. When under the
Maccabees the Hasidean judges were frequently members of
a legally constituted state court, they still did not abandon
their ancient right to compel a litigant to go beyond the
requirements of the Law where justice demanded, yielding
property rights with which he seemed endowed by the letter
of the Torah.

The individual possessed his property through the grace of the Torah and the community. The Torah could demand, through its interpreters, that he take no literal advantage to enforce his rights. The community, through its properly constituted courts, could end his property rights.

At a very late period, the Babylonian Talmud reported a judge who insisted that the litigant go beyond the requirements of the Law. Some carriers had, in the course of their work, negligently broken the wine jugs of Rabbah bar Hanan. Angered and wanting compensation for his loss, he seized their clothes. When the case came before Rab, he said to Rabbah bar Hanan, "Give them their garments." Rabbah bar Hanan asked Rab, "Is this the law?" To which Rab answered, "Indeed, it is; for it is written, 'That thou mayest walk in the way of good men' " (Prov. 2.20). When they had their garments the laborers said, "We are poor; we have worked all day; we are hungry; and we have nothing" (with which to get food). Rab said to Rabbah bar Hanan, "Pay them their wages." To this the amazed Rabbah bar Hanan responded, "Is this the law?" Rab replied, "Yes; for it is also written [in the same verse] 'And keep the paths of the righteous' " (B. Baba Mezi'a 83a).

Ignoring the explanation of Raba in B. Gittin 36b, and implied in Yerushalmi Shekalim 1.2, Weiss built his whole system of rabbinic historiography on the theory that the wise, far-seeing, enlightened scholars of rabbinic literature were lenient interpreters of ritual law, given to "adjustment" of law to new conditions, and opposed, Weiss believed, by a group who subordinated necessities of life to the text of Scripture.

Later scholars, including Leo Baeck, J. Z. Lauterbach, and J. N. Simhoni, also ignored the assertion of Josephus

lviii   INTRODUCTORY NOTE TO THIRD EDITION

that the Pharisees were generally considered men of superior piety and *precision* in interpretation of the Law (*War*, I, 5.2; cf. further ibid. II, 8.14). Moreover, arbitrarily these critics assumed both that the claim of the Pharisees to have received traditions from their ancestors, requiring certain observances beyond the letter of the Law (Josephus, *Antiquities*, XIII, 10.6), was (as the Sadducees had maintained) a fiction; and that this Oral Law was merely a collection of decisions by the Pharisees themselves. Yet (we show below) Josephus simply echoed the statement of the Mishna that many detailed Pharisaic norms — some regarding the Sabbath, for instance — were known only through tradition and were "mountains hanging on a hair" (Mishna Hagigah 1.8). Nowhere did Josephus suggest that the Pharisaic interpretations in any way compromised the Written Law. On the contrary, he clearly implied that these rules involved amplification and particularization of Scriptural Law, opposed by the Sadducees who inclined toward a lesser degree of piety than the Pharisees (Josephus, loc. cit.).

The historian cannot reject out of hand the Pharisaic claim that their norms were received from their ancestors. In fact this text, and particularly its Supplement, will show that this claim seems well founded (see e.g., further below, pp. 700 ff.; 718 ff.; 742 ff.).

Opposing Geiger's interpretation of the Talmud, Professor Ginzberg suggested in an historic lecture that the controversies between the Shammaite and Hillelite wings of Pharisaism originated neither in an attempt of the Hillelites to "reform" the Law, nor in liberal exegesis of the Pentateuch, nor in evolutionary development. He held that both traditions were of very ancient origin, and arose from inevitable differences in approach to the Law (especially the ritual) between the aristocracy who were Shammaite and the masses who were Hillelite in outlook. First enunciated at an early meeting of the Rabbinical Assembly, this doctrine was developed fully in his famous address on "The Role of the *Halakah* in Jewish History." In this exposition Professor Ginzberg extended to the intra-Pharisaic conflict of the Schools the distinction drawn by Josephus between the Sadducees and the Pharisees as groups (see below pp. 80 ff.), clearly accepting as basic Josephus' differentiation of the sects, and regarding the issues between them as flowing from difference in economic status.

A similar theory on the relation of the Pharisees to the Sadducees was developed by Max Weber in his significant analysis of Pharisaism (see bibliography at the end of this book). But Weber dealt mainly with the sociological and psychological aspects of the struggle within Judaism, and did not try to analyze the specific theological and religious controversies between Sadducee and Pharisee.

However, study of this book and its Supplement will indicate that most of the recorded controversies between the Sadducees and the Pharisees cannot be directly related in any way to differences in wealth. There was no reason, for example, why the rich should oppose water-libations and the poor favor them; or why aristocrats should wish the High Priest to offer incense on the Day of Atonement in one fashion and the plebeians should prefer another. Whatever the merit of Weber's interpretation of Pharisaism (and he made a valuable contribution), he failed to explain its juristic views as recorded in the Talmud and Josephus.

The problem of the controversies was approached in another way (not altogether distinct from Weber's) by S. Dubnow (see bibliography). He recognized that an

essential difference between the Pharisees and the Sadducees
of the Hasmonean age was socio-philosophical. The history
of Judea from the Maccabean revolt until the destruction of
the Second Temple suggested to Dubnow that the Pharisees
were animated (as indicated in this book, especially pp. 281
ff.) by the conviction that the Jewish people — and in particular the state of Judea — was not an end in itself but an
instrument to advance certain cultural, ethical, and spiritual
ideas. (Such an abstract statement would probably have
been meaningless for the ancient pietists, but describes as
best we can in words what they expressed in specific decisions and behavior.) In opposition during the Hasmonean
age were the Sadducees, for whom preservation and development of the Judean state was an end in itself, a goal similar
to that of other peoples.

Dubnow vainly tried to reconcile this insight with the
thesis derived from Geiger, namely, that the Sadducees were
literalists in legal exegesis, while the Pharisees were liberals.
Yet men for whom the state was an end in itself would
scarcely hesitate to adapt the Law to community requirements, and men for whom spiritual values were life-goals
would incline to disregard material needs. This contradiction
in Dubnow's theory was revealed by Ismar Elbogen (*Jewish
Studies in Memory of Israel Abrahams*, pp. 145 ff.).

So pervasive has been the influence of Geiger on modern
Jewish historiography that, although I consciously rejected
his conclusions, much of my early writing and thinking reflect
memories of them. Maturer thought brought me grave doubt
that the saintly Hillel and R. Akiba, convinced of the Divine
revelation of the Torah, could possibly have been motivated
in their judgments, even unconsciously, by hedonistic needs,
or would dare to interpret Scripture "to adjust the Law to

life." They might consider comfort or convenience, even in the interpretation of the ritual law, where the Torah was really ambiguous or silent. But how could these God-fearing men, their predecessors, and their followers possibly be accused of "changing" the ritual Law, through pseudo-interpretation and pseudo-exegesis when its meaning was clear and beyond doubt?

On a visit to the Holy Land in 1925 I first realized the actual basis for the intra-Pharisaic controversies recorded in the Talmud, and the controversies between the Pharisees and the Sadducees. Difference in wealth was secondary. Certainly neither the Hillelites nor the Pharisees as a group wished to be innovators. But in 1925 the great difference between the climate of Jerusalem and the seashore 2,400 feet below became vivid to me as never before. I then understood that environment which in my native America changed only with hundreds or thousands of miles, in tiny Judea was sharply differentiated within an hour's journey.

At once many controversies in the Talmud, seemingly derived from arbitrary exegesis, appeared reasonable and logical. They actually derived from difference of environment. Remembering that Jerusalem, the largest city of Judea, was in the highlands, we might expect some controversies to have derived also from differences between town and country. Because the priests were large landowners in the fertile oasis of Jericho and in Galilee, they might well retain traditions of the provinces, while Levites and Jerusalem's traders adhered to the traditions of the city.

Projecting on earlier times these differences among the talmudic authorities, I concluded that many controversies between Sadducee and Pharisee also reflected differences of habitat. In the recorded controversies the Sadducean position suggested prejudice arising from rural conditions, life in the plains, and priestly bias. The Pharisees of the same era were a product of the Jerusalem market place. At first I glimpsed only vaguely that in ritual law the Pharisees simply adhered to the letter of Scripture, while the rural, priestly, aristocratic Sadducees inherited a series of deviationist interpretations opposed by the Hasideans and their predecessors — the Prophets.

The present Supplement offers arguments to buttress this view, and with them the conclusion that at least some of the controversies between Sadducee and Pharisee originated before the First Exile when Jerusalem had already become a "gate of peoples," while other disagreements go back to earlier days when Judea was divided, first between the economy of the highland shepherd and the lowland rustic, and then between enlarged Jerusalem and the rest of the country. In a subsequent study I shall try to show (as my *Akiba* does in part) how many rabbinic controversies regarding ambiguous verses or problems not discussed in the Bible reflect this difference of environment.

In earlier editions of this book some passages imply that the issues between the Pharisees and the Sadducees also concerned only ambiguous biblical texts or situations where Scripture was silent. The Supplement (pp. 637 ff.) shows that this is correct only in part. Most of the debates about ritual arose from the Pharisaic loyalty to the text of Scripture and its neglect by the Proto-Sadducees, i.e., the High Priests of the Persian and Hellenistic periods or of the First Commonwealth. A few recorded controversies deal with the civil law, and in these instances also the Pharisees adopted the simple meaning of the biblical text (see pp. 633 ff.).

In most controversies concerning ritual, Sadducean deviation from the plain meaning of Scripture was due to priestly and rural predisposition or interest. In controversies between Sadducism and Pharisaism on problems concerning which Scripture was either silent or ambiguous, the Pharisees can be shown to have followed judgments and views natural to urban lay scholars. In some instances, silence or ambiguity in the Scriptural text led to further controversy within Pharisaism itself.

I therefore maintain that Sadducism was the product of the Temple hierarchy and the provincial aristocracy, whereas Pharisaism arose from conditions governing the market place in Jerusalem. The influence of these urban scholars was most distinctly felt in later times among the peasantry of the Judean highlands, while that of the priestly aristocracy dominated religious life in the Judean lowland and in distant Galilee.

2. The Rural Atmosphere of Some Talmudic Documents

However, it must be remembered that for a large part of its history, Jerusalem was little more than a village, which became a "gate of peoples" after the destruction of the Northern Kingdom of the Ten Tribes under the later kings of Judah. Laid waste under Nebuchadnezzar during the deportation to Babylonia, Jerusalem resumed life as a village during the Persian and Hellenistic periods, becoming once more a thriving center of commerce and industry under the Hasmoneans, or perhaps slightly before them.

Because Jerusalem was long a village, part of the Talmud and much of the Mishna are marked by language, examples, analogies, and general atmosphere normally associated with the countryside. This was inevitable and does not militate against our environmental thesis.

Not only was a whole Order of the Mishna dedicated to

agricultural laws, but the laws of damages usually illustrated general principles through agricultural examples such as an ox goring a cow or grazing in a neighbor's field. The Mishna, when freeing an owner from damages committed by his slave, asserted that without such a rule "a slave might set fire to a neighbor's harvest each day," bringing ruin upon his owner (Mishna Yadayim 4.7). The principle of freeing an arsonist from responsibility for hidden valuables destroyed in a fire he set, was illustrated by the example of vessels concealed in a heap of grain (Mishna Baba Kamma 6.5). Responsibility of bailees was discussed almost wholly in rural terms (Mishna Baba Mezi'a 3; 6.4 ff.; 8.1 ff.). Laws for the festival week began with permission to water a field dependent on irrigation (Mishna Mo'ed Katan 1.1). Labors prohibited on the Sabbath (Mishna Shabbat 7.2) were enumerated in fashion normal for a rustic. The treatise Shabbat opened with enumeration of four types of property, in early sources each defined in rural terms. According to interpretation of the Yerushalmi (ad loc.) and Tosefta (cf. Professor Saul Lieberman's *Tosefta Ki-Fshutah*, ad loc.) they were the private estate, the public highway, unfenced private farmland, and public paths leading to highways. Tosefta described the private estate as land elevated above the surrounding country by at least ten handbreadths or falling below it by at least ten handbreadths. The public highway was the great road leading from locality to locality. The private unfenced farmland and the public paths leading to a highway were similarly characteristic of the rural areas. While the Talmud also applied all these norms to life in the city, it is highly instructive that the four types of property were defined in terms congenial to the country.

All this is natural. Even during the last generations of the

Second Commonwealth Judea and Galilee remained rural communities, and the dominant industry of the country was agriculture. Litigation before the courts, whether of Jerusalem's market place or the Temple, was frequently typical of rustic life. Ritual observances, even among the Hasideans, were formulated in terms deriving from provincial surroundings, because the discussions arose in the pre-Maccabean period when Jerusalem itself was a village, or because they were based on biblical verses which dealt primarily with an agricultural people.

Much of the Mishna was apparently formulated during the Persian and Hellenistic ages, but the controversies between Sadducism and Pharisaism had developed far earlier, in the later generations of the First Commonwealth, or even before.

What is remarkable about the Mishna and kindred works is not their rural atmosphere, but the extent to which they reflected urban life. Unlike the public highway discussed at the beginning of Mishna Shabbat, which was the road leading from village to village, that discussed in Mishna Baba Kamma (3.1 ff.) was a city street.

Much of the treatise 'Erubin dealt with situations typical of crowded Jerusalem. The thief who was also an artisan (discussed in Baba Kamma 9.1 ff.) was presumably a townsman. Similarly, the artisan liable for damage to goods entrusted him (ibid. 3, 4) may be assumed a city dweller. Mishna Baba Mezi'a (3.4 ff.) spoke of money entrusted to a bailee, but in a rustic world bailments of produce would be a more natural example. Mishna Baba Mezi'a (ch. 4), dealing with the laws of sale and acquisition of property, opened with consideration of exchanges of silver for gold and only afterward dealt with the sale of produce, logically

primary as shown from the talmudic discussion. Mishna
Baba Mezi'a (4.6), discussing the right of a purchaser to
claim fraud, considered first the law applying in the city,
then that applying in villages. The whole of chapter 5 of
that treatise dealt primarily with situations likely to arise
in a sizable city rather than in a village. The law on the
rights of the trained urban artisan (ibid. ch. 6) preceded
that on the farm laborer (ch. 7). The law of neighbors
opened in Mishna Baba Mezi'a, chapter 10, and Baba Batra
1.1, with the example of two persons occupying the same
house or sharing a court which was likely in a city, then went
on to discussion of peasant neighbors (Mishna Baba Batra
1.2 ff., and ch. 2). The laws of sale began with the selling
of a house (ibid. ch. 4) or a court (typical of the crowded
city), and only then proceeded to the sale of a field (ibid.
4.8). A chapter dealing with the sale of a boat (ch. 5) preceded that dealing with sale of seed which failed to produce
grain (ibid. 5.1) or of large farms (ibid. 7.1. ff.).

Each of these examples may be explained by the assumption that the Pharisaic Sages dealt with city problems no
less than with rural ones, but the precedence given the
former is suggestive.

Stress on urban situations might be held to occur more
frequently in texts from Hasmonean and post-Hasmonean
times, when Jerusalem once more became a business center,
but texts with predominant emphasis on rusticity were
essentially pre-Hasmonean.

3. The Nature and Authority of the Hasidean Judiciary

The difference between the Hasideans' approach to the
civil law, which they felt free to alter, and to the ritual law,
to which they adhered to the letter no less than to the spirit
of Scripture, is illuminated by a famous *baraita* commenting

on Deuteronomy 17.8 ff. This *baraita* has been transmitted
in three different forms. As I have shown (*Hebrew Union
College Annual*, XXXII, 1961, Morgenstern Jubilee Volume,
Hebrew section, pp. 1 ff.), the pre-Maccabean text of this
baraita can readily be reconstructed from that preserved in
the Talmud of Jerusalem and in general follows the spirit
of the biblical text.

According to this Deuteronomic passage the Temple court
was supreme. When in doubt the local judge turned to it
for guidance. But this guidance was limited to the civil and
criminal law. No mention was made of ritual. The local
judge, confused regarding a case involving matters "between
blood and blood" (homicide), "between judgment and judgment" (property), or "between stroke and stroke" (physical
injury), was told to resort for instruction to the court at the
Temple. The cases mentioned were precisely of the type
which Jethro had proposed that inferior judges bring before
Moses for adjudication (Ex. 18.22), and which Moses commanded them to bring before him (Deut. 1.18 ff.). No
mention of ceremonial was made in any of these Pentateuchal
passages. Ritual problems were left to the discretion of local
leaders, to the individual if they were home or personal
ceremonies, or to the Temple authorities if they were Temple
ceremonies.

The first effort to expand the authority of the Temple
court, we are told, was made by King Jehoshaphat (II Chron.
19.8 ff.). According to the Chronicler, that king established
a court in Jerusalem "for the judgment of the Lord and for
controversies." Characteristically, this court consisted of
Levites, priests, and heads of families. "And whensoever,"
said the king to these judges, "any controversy shall come
to you from your brethren that dwell in their cities, between

blood and blood, between law and commandment, statutes and ordinances, ye shall warn them, they be not guilty towards the Lord, and so wrath come upon you and upon your brethren."

According to King Jehoshaphat then (following the record in Chronicles), the court in Jerusalem (not necessarily in the Temple itself) was to guide the people in all matters of ceremonial — warning and instructing them, so they might not transgress the Law in any respect. King Jehoshaphat continued, "And behold Amariah the chief priest is over you in all matters of the Lord" (presumably Pentateuchal law); "Zebadiah the son of Ishmael, the ruler of the house of Judah" (a layman, "in all the king's matters" (presumably in issues of civil and criminal law, not specifically discussed in the Pentateuch). Any issue involving capital punishment (perhaps only murder) was to be brought before this court. Any other issues involving the Law, commandments, statutes, and ordinances (literally, litigations) were also to be brought before the court, if the local judge wanted to escape responsibility which might bring guilt upon him and his people. The Supreme Court was to give him an authoritative decision. If the problems were covered in the Pentateuch, the Chief Priest presided; otherwise the prince of the house of Judah presided.

Described in the Book of Chronicles, the system clearly had the purpose which many religious leaders and thinkers of the Second Commonwealth (and perhaps also the First) sought to achieve — to bridge the chasm separating Proto-Sadducism from Proto-Pharisaism, which threatened to divide the Jewish people in two. The Chronicler held that the Supreme Court would be entitled to impose uniform practice on the country not only in civil and criminal law but also in ritual, provided Levites were included in its membership, as well as priests and chiefs of clans. Lacking the Levites, it was not a Supreme Court in the sense the Book of Deuteronomy had intended; and therefore had no appellate jurisdiction. Including Levites (who would be inclined toward the Hasidean doctrine) the court might transform the divisive controversies into judicial discussion and restore unity to the people. King Jehoshaphat (or the Chronicler) interpreted the words of Deuteronomy 17.9: "And thou shalt come unto the priests, the Levites, and unto the judge that shall be in those days," to mean priests *and* Levites. A court which lacked either priests or Levites could not claim the prerogatives described in Deuteronomy. Only a court including both priests and Levites could act as the Supreme Court of the land.

The implications of the passage in Chronicles are clear. The contemporary Temple Court claimed jurisdiction not only in the areas clearly defined in Deuteronomy, but in the religious life of the nation as a whole. The decisive words of Deuteronomy, the Chronicler doubtless held, were "matters of controversy" (Deut. 17.8). Any matter of controversy could and should be brought before the court for settlement. The examples mentioned in Deuteronomy were not exclusive, for the words of Deuteronomy were to be interpreted in the light of Jethro's remark to Moses (Ex. 18.20): "And thou shalt teach them the statutes and the laws, and shalt show them the way wherein they must walk, and the work that they must do." These words were taken to describe the ceremonials and rituals of Judaism, no less than its civil and criminal law.

Later history shows that the Hasideans were willing to accept the doctrine set forth in Chronicles and ascribed to

King Jehoshaphat. Later versions of the *baraita* formulated under the Maccabean regime, greatly expanded the authority of the Temple Court; for under the early Maccabees, "the Sages of Israel," i.e., the Pharisaic scholars, sat with the priests and the heads of the clans in the Supreme Court. But even in Maccabean times the Hasideans denied that the Temple Court had final jurisdiction in the interpretation of the ritual as a whole.

The Hasideans certainly denied that the Central Court could decide controversies regarding ritual during the Persian and Hellenistic periods, when it consisted exclusively of priests and the heads of the clans.

Had the Hasideans not challenged the claim of the Temple Court, their movement would have come to an early end; for the decisions of the Court during the Persian and Hellenistic periods always followed, we may be sure, the Proto-Sadducean views. Persistence of the controversies between the Sadducees and the Pharisees demonstrated Hasidean unwillingness to submit ritual and other controversial questions to the Court. The effort of the Book of Jubilees to mediate between the two groups (see below, Section 7) would have been entirely superfluous had the Temple Court been universally recognized as an authoritative interpreter of the Law.

Because the Hasideans did not recognize the Temple Court as fulfilling the requirements set down in Deuteronomy for the Supreme Tribunal, they felt free not only to flout its decisions regarding religious ritual (which they presumably considered beyond its competence in any event), but to create an independent judicial system for the solution of civil litigation among their own members.

Such an extra-legal judicial system among the Hasideans

was not only presumed in the maxim of the Men of the Great Synagogue (Mishna Abot 1.2), but its establishment was persistently ascribed in the Talmud to Ezra the Scribe (B. Baba Kamma 82a; Ketubot 3a; Yer. Megillah 4.1, 75a).

However, during the pre-Maccabean period this judicial system had no powers of coercion. Its courts could not compel anyone to appear or to submit to their decisions. Resort to them was voluntary and out of Hasidean piety. The courts had been invented so that the Hasidean, worried lest he commit injustice, could learn from them what was right regarding obligations to his fellow-man, and regarding ritual obligations. Thus these courts never had occasion to deal with willful injury to a neighbor or with such crimes as robbery or theft. Mistrusting the regularly constituted courts, which were dominated by the Temple tribunal, and doubting their learning, piety, and authority, the Hasidean was compelled by the logic of his religious views to obey only his own judges. If his own judges considered him responsible for a debt or for unintentional injury to a neighbor, he would wish to make compensation. If his own courts did not require him to offer compensation, he would not do so. Of course, if opposed by non-Hasideans, he might be hailed before the legally constituted courts which he would be forced to obey.

Litigation involving Temple property would not be brought before these Hasidean courts. What was done in such cases? Hasidean exegesis of Scripture gave a clear answer. The owner of an ox which gored that of a neighbor had to pay half of the damages for the first offense. But the Temple could not be considered a "neighbor." Hence, if a man's ox gored one belonging to the Sanctuary, no penalty was prescribed by Scripture. If, nevertheless, the Temple

Court imposed a penalty, it simply had to be paid. On the other hand, if a man's ox was hurt by an ox belonging to the Temple, he could not collect, and simply made no effort to do so, whatever the Temple judiciary might decide (Mishna Baba Kamma 4.3).

But the word "neighbor" excluded the pagan. Hence, if his ox was gored by that of a pagan, a Hasidean could accept full damages, should the legally constituted courts impose them. Yet, if the ox of a Hasidean gored that of a pagan and the regularly constituted courts acquitted the Hasidean, he was under no obligation to offer compensation (ibid.).

That the Hasidean judicial structure had for its purpose the discovery of obligations to neighbors, rather than the opportunity for a litigant to ensure his rights, seems evident from the very language of Mishna Baba Kamma 1.2, recognized by the Talmud as singular and archaic (B. Baba Kamma 6b). It reads: "Whatever I am obliged to guard [against doing injury] I must be considered as having enabled to do injury [if I failed in my duty]. If I made possible part of the injury [through such carelessness], I am obliged to make compensation for all the injury." This rule applied only to secular property, and to that belonging to children of the covenant. The form of the statement, in the first person, rather than that of a judicial norm, indicates that the early Hasidean teachers were articulating an ethical precept required of their followers, whether or not the regularly constituted tribunals enforced it.

When in doubt as to the Law, the Hasidean judge was under no obligation to follow the provision of Deuteronomy 17.8 ff. to seek advice from the Temple Court. The Hasidean judges were acting as referees to whom the litigants submitted their quarrel, and not as the duly appointed judges described in Deuteronomy 16.18. The opposing parties had come to the Hasidean scholars for *their* decision, whether or not it accorded specifically with Pentateuchal law. Thus, if Hasidean judges felt that strict application of Pentateuchal law would work injustice in a particular case, they were free to deviate from it.

Therefore the chapter in the Mishna Sanhedrin discussing civil procedure (i.e., ch. 3) dealt almost exclusively with courts of arbitration. Each litigant chose a judge, and either the two judges, or the litigants themselves chose the third.

According to R. Meir (Mishna Sanhedrin 3.1) either litigant could veto his opponent's choice. This arrangement—doubtless preserving an ancient tradition—was indispensable; for the opponent might choose a Proto-Sadducean arbiter whose persuasiveness might affect the neutral third judge. Moreover, R. Meir held that either litigant could arbitrarily refuse to admit witnesses brought by his opponent. This astonishing norm can be explained only on the assumption that the litigant under discussion wished to fulfill his obligations under Hasidean law. Convinced that the opposing witnesses were false, he could ask the judges to disregard their testimony. (Both views of R. Meir were rejected as illogical by his colleagues; and so they were, in a time when a formal judicial system with power to enforce its decisions had been instituted for all the Jews.)

To explain the passage in the Mishna logically, R. Johanan asserted that it referred only to Jewish courts in Syria. Unlike the courts of Galilee, Judea, and Babylonia in his time, these Syrian courts had no legal status, except as courts of arbitration (B. Sanhedrin 23a; but cf. Yer. ibid. 3.2, 21a).

R. Johanan could hardly have believed that the Mishna *originally* discussed only Jewish courts in Syria. Why should the Mishna be silent about the judicial procedure of the civil courts of the Holy Land, and devote a whole chapter to the discussion of those of Syria? R. Johanan undoubtedly had received a firm tradition, according to which the Mishna dealt with a voluntary judicial system, replaced in Judea and Galilee by one clothed with authority, and surviving in its original form only in Syria.

Appearing before such a court, not to enforce his rights but to learn his obligations, the pious Jew in Syria of R. Johanan's time—like the earlier Hasidean—could reject the witnesses about to testify against him, if he knew them unlikely to be credible (cf. the discussion of the different views of R. Johanan and R. Simeon b. Lakish, in both the Babylonian and Palestinian Talmudim).

Although doubtless satisfied in his own conscience that his courts of arbitration did not come under the rules of Deuteronomy 17.8 ff., and had no reason to refer to the Temple Court cases in which they needed guidance, the Hasidean, like others of his time and like judges of all times, had to prove for his opponents and some skeptics that his views conformed to the Written Word, or rather how the Written Word confirmed his judgment. Perhaps, too, he felt the need to delimit the authority of the Temple Court over the regularly constituted tribunals, even more narrowly than did the express word of Deuteronomy. Just as the Qumram Sect, opposing the High Priests who claimed descent from Zadok, resorted to a forced interpretation of Ezekiel 44.15, where the Zadokites were selected for particular and loving praise (see S. Schechter, *Documents of Jewish Sectaries*, I, p. 4), so the early Hasideans resorted to ingenious explanations of Deuteronomy 17.8 ff. in support of their right to create an independent judiciary even for civil litigation.

Playing on the words *ki yippale* (literally, "If doubt arise") the Hasidean *baraita* asserted that the whole passage dealt exclusively with the *mufla*, a legally selected judge, and not one chosen by the opposing litigants. (For a discussion of the meaning of *mufla*, cf. Professor Ginzberg's *Commentary on the Yerushalmi*, II, pp. 212 ff., and my own discussion in *Louis Ginzberg Jubilee Volume*, Hebrew Section, p. 314; it seems clear from Mishna Horayot 1.3 that the word refers to the duly appointed head of the court: see Sifre Deut. 152, p. 205; B. Sanhedrin 87a; Yer. ibid. 11.4, 30a.) But even such a judge in a quandary need not refer a difficult case to the Temple Court. According to the pre-Maccabean version of the *baraita* under discussion (see article in Morgenstern volume already mentioned), he need appeal to the Temple Court only when confused as to interpretation of the facts before him or the logic of his legal analysis. He need not be guided by the tradition of the Temple Court.

The Temple Court also had a role in defining areas of jurisdiction. A local court, according to Hasidean theory, could not decide cases involving capital punishment. If litigation arose which was on the surface only a claim for monetary compensation, but might possibly involve the capital penalty, the local judge would rightly refer it to the Temple marriage court. One such case was that of the newly married bride whose husband claimed he had not found her a virgin (discussed in Deut. 22.13 ff.).

By the charge the husband might be demanding only the right to divorce his wife without repayment of her dower—a claim to be adjudicated in civil courts. He might accuse her of licentiousness before the *erusim* (literally, betrothal).

On the other hand, the presentation of his case might lead to her being charged with adultery while an *arusah*, a crime punishable by death. Because of this possibility, the local court would properly refer the case to the Temple authorities for adjudication. Such a case, according to the Hasidean *baraita* in its earliest form (see Yer. Sanhedrin 11.4, 30a) was meant by the phrase "between blood and blood."

The words, "between judgment and judgment," meant— according to Hasidean exegesis—a decision whether any other case before the local judge possibly involved capital punishment.

Finally, the words, "between blow and blow" could not be interpreted by the Hasideans as referring to physical injury. As shown below (p. 721 ff.) they held that such injuries were subject only to monetary payment. In later times most talmudic authorities in Babylonia held that while such injuries were subject only to compensation, they could not be tried in their courts (see B. Baba Kamma 27b, 84b), but the Talmud encountered great difficulty in its effort to explain the difference between such cases and civil suits for the repayment of loans. Rab Nahman called payments for physical injuries "fines." *Tosafot*, Baba Kamma 27b (catchword, *Kenasa*), explained that this remark was not to be taken literally; for general talmudic theory held payment for physical injury was not a fine at all, but compensation. It would appear that at an early time, when the Babylonian authorities set up their autonomous judicial system, they limited its authority to the collection of debts, because they agreed with the Shammaitic principle (see below, pp. 721 ff.) that physical injury should be punished with the *talio*, but that the defendant could *redeem* his limbs through appropriate payment. This theory seems to have been accepted by the Hasmoneans, and from them to have spread to Babylonia: the reason that the Babylonian judges, who had no authority to enforce the *talio*, did not exact payment for physical injury. There was no reconciliation between this practice and the early Hasidean theory, preserved among the Hillelites and stressed by R. Akiba in particular, that compensation for physical injury was under no circumstances other than monetary damages. Hence Rab Hisda—the disciple of Rab Huna, himself the disciple of Rab, who followed the views of Rabbi Judah the Patriarch and R. Akiba—considered it proper to collect damages for physical injury through Babylonian Jewish courts.

The word for "blow" (*nega'*) was interpreted by the Hasidean scholars to mean the plague of leprosy. A local judge faced with a case of suspected leprosy would be wise to refer it for judgment to the Temple Court, whose priestly members were skilled in these problems. (The discussion of the *baraita* here amplifies that in the *Hebrew Union College Annual* mentioned and differs from it slightly. The article in the *Annual* should be corrected accordingly.)

This exegesis enabled the Hasideans to interpret the verse suggesting that the priests had authority in all issues of physical struggle and in controversy (Deut. 21.5) in such a way as to limit the authority of the priestly court. Once more the word "stroke" (*nega'*) was explained to mean "leprosy," and the word "controversy" was held to refer to rituals specifically assigned to the priesthood, such as the ordeal of the suspected wife (Num. 5.11 ff.), the expiation of an unexplained murder (Deut. loc. cit.), and the ceremony of the red heifer.

4. THE HASIDEAN CIVIL LAW

As already observed, because the Hasidean courts of pre-Maccabean times were technically courts of arbitration to which litigants submitted voluntarily, the civil law of the group did not have to conform to the written text of Scripture. Seeking both peace and justice among the litigants, the courts could deviate from the word of the Pentateuch whenever they held that literal application of the Law would work hardship or injustice. Hence, precedents established by Hasidean courts often differed greatly from civil law prescribed in the Pentateuch.

We do not know what the Sadducean civil law was or how the pre-Maccabean Temple Courts functioned. However, there are hints in the Book of Jubilees and the Testaments of the Twelve Patriarchs (see below, p. 268) that one issue between the Hasideans and the Proto-Sadducees concerned interpretation of the word *na'arah* (maiden) in the Bible. According to the Hasideans, in this instance followed by the Book of Jubilees and the Testaments of the Twelve Patriarchs, the term referred only to a pubescent girl, i.e., one above the age of twelve but not yet twelve and a half (B. Niddah 65a; cf. Mishna ibid. 5.8). The Pharisees held such a girl to be a grown woman, only partly under the authority of her father. After she became twelve and a half her father's rights over her ceased completely. Thus fines paid for rape (Deut. 22.29) or seduction (Ex. 22.16) or slander (Deut. 21.19) of his daughter belonged to a father only until she was twelve and a half years old. Only before that age could he choose her husband (ibid. 22.13). If the father sold her into concubinage (an institution probably already archaic and considered only for theoretical exegesis of the biblical passages) before she was twelve, she could leave her "husband" on reaching that age, whether he agreed or not (Ex. 21.7, and Mekilta, Mishpatim, ch. 3, p. 257). If she remained with him she would not be considered a concubine or maid servant, but his wife (Ex. 21.10 and Mekilta, Mishpatim, ch. 3, p. 258).

The Hasideans further abolished slavery for debt, of the debtor himself or of his children, although such slavery was envisaged in II Kings 4.1, and was implied even in Nehemiah 5.5, as perhaps also in Exodus 21.1 ff., and Leviticus 25.29.

Under Hasidean law, a Judaite could become a slave only by selling himself into bondage (see Mekilta on Ex. 21.1) or by being sold by the Court in repayment for theft for which he could not make restitution.

The biblical law which said that a Hebrew slave preferring bondage at the expiration of his six-year term (the maximum permitted) could be kept "forever," was interpreted to mean that he remained enslaved only until the Jubilee year (see Mekilta on Ex. 21.6).

A series of norms regarding property rights was developed by the Hasideans to supplement that of Scripture. Hasidean law defined the duties of neighbors toward each other and the boundaries of their land. They were forbidden to dig near the borders lest that injure the neighbor's property. Various regulations were formulated governing purchase and sale, and obligations on finding a lost article.

Hasidean courts held that a man admitting part of a claim against him had to support his assertion by an oath; whereas one denying a claim outright was under no such obligation (Mishna Shebuot 6.1). Later sages encountered much difficulty in search for biblical foundation to this seemingly paradoxical rule (cf. B. Baba Kamma 107a,

Sanhedrin 3b). However, it seems rooted in an early Hasidean observation that outright denial of a claim was far more difficult for many than partial admission; and that litigants might resort to half-truths, unless required to substantiate their statements under oath. (This observation is mentioned in the Talmud, B. Baba Mezi'a 3a.)

Certain complications in the laws on theft unprovided for in Scripture were handled by Hasidean judges. A man who had stolen wool and dyed it, could not restore what he had stolen: what payment was to be made? The Bible offered no answer; but Hasidean law did (Mishna Baba Kamma 9.1 ff.).

Biblical labor laws were greatly expanded by the Hasideans. It was not enough that an employer desiring to deal justly with his employee should pay wages on time as provided in Deuteronomy 24.15. A worker was permitted to leave his job whenever he chose. If he ruined the material on which he was working, his liability was limited.

As already indicated, the norm limiting the meaning of the word na'arah, as used in Scripture, to girls approximately over twelve but under twelve and a half involved complications in the marriage law. Should a father, in violation of the Hasidean interpretation of Scripture, give his daughter in marriage when she was older than twelve and a half, would the marriage be valid? Hasidean courts held that a father's rights over a daughter were those of property, and therefore his action was void. Whether in pre-Maccabean times the Temple Courts accepted these decisions, is unknown. Presumably, they did not. That is probably why the Hasidean norm in this regard was the subject of specific reference in the Pseudepigraphic literature. We already observed that both the Book of Jubilees and the Testaments of the Twelve

Patriarchs seemed to agree that a girl given in marriage by her father, after she had reached maturity, was free to marry anyone else, for her father's action had no validity.

Hasidean law also defined the rights of each partner as well as the duties and rights of fellow-townsmen in relation to each other and to the community. It fixed the rights of the leaders of a community over communal property. It determined the precise moment when a sale was consummated, transferring the rights and obligations of the vendor to the purchaser. It prohibited certain types of competition, and enjoined business arrangements intended to evade the biblical law against usury.

Hasidean law admitted circumstantial evidence in civil litigation; and held that the testimony of one witness, in itself not sufficient for a decision, had to be offset by an affirmation of the opposing litigant, supported by an oath.

We have already observed that the attitude of the Temple authorities to these Mishnaic norms cannot be fully determined. But there is some evidence, in addition to that already cited, that it was disapproving. Thus their extreme sense of individual responsibility led the Pharisees to place the whole blame for wrong-doing by an agent upon him, rather than on the principal. Even a man sent to commit arson, provided he was a normally intelligent human being, had to bear sole responsibility for damage done by him (Mishna Baba Kamma 6.4). The principal was guilty, according to Hillelite law, as reported by R. Joshua, only in the eyes of Heaven, but could not be convicted by courts of mortal human beings (B. Baba Kamma 55b). Holding the owner of a slave responsible for damages done by him— even against the will of the owner (see below, pp. 285 ff.)— it seems evident that the Sadducean tradition would require compensation from a principal who deliberately caused injury to a neighbor. Therefore the Mishnaic norm must be of Hasidean origin and opposed to that of the Temple judges and priests.

One issue of civil law which apparently divided the Proto-Sadducees and the Hasideans in an unrecorded controversy concerned the law of the Jubilee year. The question was whether the law applied during the Second Commonwealth, and if so, to what extent.

The rule set down in Leviticus 25.8 ff. assumes division of the Land of Israel among the tribes, clans and families. According to Joshua 15.1 ff., this was made by lot. Sifra *Behar*, beginning, holds that, in view of this original division of the land among the whole population, the law of the Jubilee could apply only when the whole people of Israel dwelt in the Holy Land, and every person could identify the ground he possessed as that given his ancestors at the time of the allocation by Joshua. This was by no means the case during the Second Commonwealth, so the law of the Jubilee did not apply, at least to farmland.

However, the question could be raised whether the law of the Jubilee dealing with houses in walled cities, and explained in Leviticus 25.29 ff., applied during the Second Commonwealth. Under that law, houses in a walled city, when sold, could be redeemed within a year. If not so redeemed, they remained the permanent possession of the purchaser. The reason for this rule seemed to be that, unlike the rest of the country, the houses in walled cities had not been distributed by lot among tribes, clans and families. Therefore, the owner of such a house could not claim that his ancestors had been given it through the general division at the time of Joshua. Ownership was based merely on claims deriving from ordinary commercial transactions. The Torah gave the owner a year within which to redeem the house, if circumstances compelled him to sell it. But if he were unable to redeem it, the house was forfeit to the purchaser.

The right reserved to the seller to repurchase the house at the original price was of great importance in ancient Judaite society. The story of Naboth (I Kings 21.1 ff.) suggested that separation from ancestral possessions was extremely painful. Indeed, we can see from the Book of Ruth that pride in family ownership of land extended to that actually owned by somewhat distant relatives. (Similar attachment to ancestral soil and property is reflected in modern times in the literature emanating from England and the Continent, and is possibly even stronger in other regions of the world.) While the seller of a house in a walled city might not be able to prove ancestral ownership up to the time of Joshua—and even with such proof the house was not considered a family possession in the sense that farmland was —he parted with it only under dire financial necessity and at the first opportunity would seek to "redeem" it. If the purchaser could demand a larger price than he had paid, the law against usury (Lev. 25.35 ff.) could easily be circumvented. The lender could purchase the house, then resell it to the original owner at a price including a substantial profit. The Hasideans held that this had to be prevented.

Mishna 'Arakin 9.4 assumed that this law applied during the Second Commonwealth, as during the First. And indeed it is difficult to suggest why it should not. The norm was not connected (like those relating to farm territory) with the original division of the land at the time of Joshua, but simply provided that a seller had a year in which to redeem the house he had sold, though it might never have belonged to his ancestors.

Maintaining, like the other Hasideans, that the law of the Jubilee applied to houses in walled cities even in his time, Hillel resorted to an ordinance to protect the seller against injustice. As the year drew to an end, it became customary for a purchaser to hide in order to prevent the seller from returning the purchase money and re-establishing himself in the house. Hillel ordained that the seller need not hand the money to the purchaser directly, but could leave it for him in a specifically appointed place and that this would redeem the house. The regular courts did not enforce the law of the Jubilee, even in a walled city. Had they done so, Hillel's ordinance would have required their assent before becoming effective. Hillel was not dealing with juridical rights, but with Hasidean piety.

In Mishna 'Arakin, loc. cit., Jerusalem was specifically mentioned as one of the walled cities to which the law of the Jubilee applied. However, a document survives (in *Abot of R. Nathan*, I, ch. 35, 52b) indicating that the buyer of a house in Jerusalem had to return it whenever the seller wished to redeem the house, even after a year. This norm is part of a code of ten sections, all dealing with laws applying to Jerusalem. I have elsewhere shown that this code originated during the Great Rebellion against Rome (see *Alexander Marx Jubilee Volume*, Hebrew section, pp. 358 f.). It contains various hygienic provisions, which indicate concern that overcrowding might lead to disease, and other provisions which suggest fear that the Romans might plant spies in the capital city.

However, the norm in this document dealing with houses in Jerusalem contradicts that of Mishna 'Arakin (loc. cit).

The context of the norm in *Abot of R. Nathan* shows that the authors of the document accepted the theory that Jerusalem had never belonged to any of the tribes, but to the whole nation. Further, the owners of houses in Jerusalem, the document claimed, did not own the land on which they were built. Yet, it is not clear from the text why, granted this theory, houses could be redeemed in perpetuity, or be redeemable at all. Logically such houses might be classed with chattels or other unlanded property which, once sold, belonged to the buyer forever.

The answer seems to be that an old Hasidean norm granted the seller the right to redeem a house in a walled city. The compilers of the document in *Abot of R. Nathan* did not feel free to challenge this rule. On the other hand, they felt the norm inadequate and in need of extension to permit redemption in perpetuity.

Although the document, originating (as suggested above) among the leaders of the Rebellion against Rome, was presumably Shammaitic (for the Rebellion was led by Shammaites and was opposed by the Hillelites), its authors accepted the view that the sale of houses in Jerusalem had to be subject to redemption at the original price. Without such provision (we already indicated) the sale of property might simply be used to evade the laws against usury.

This innovation may have resulted, like other norms, from local conditions when the struggle with Rome began. Many country folk sought the comparative safety of Jerusalem when the Roman legions were expected or were near. Many inhabitants of Jerusalem wanted to flee. Their need to exchange all property for gold and silver and the provincials' desire for quarters in Jerusalem would have raised the prices of the houses, facilitating the flight of its inhabitants.

The seller's perpetual option to repurchase a sold house greatly reduced its value, precisely what the leaders of the Revolution desired.

From what has been said, it may be inferred that the Hasideans always held the law of the Jubilee applied to walled cities, at least during the Second Commonwealth; and that this claim was denied by the Sadducees. The Book of Jubilees was an effort to extend to the entire country the rule accepted by the Hasideans; and to demand that the law of the Jubilee be observed throughout the land, though not all the Jews dwelt in it and therefore the owners of particular tracts could not prove ancestral rights to them.

Here, as with other controversies, the author of the Book of Jubilees tried to avoid partiality through a new theory which made the difference between Sadducee and Pharisee irrelevant because it went far beyond the claims of either group.

5. THE HASIDEAN CRIMINAL LAW

Modes of punishment in the Mishna for violation of the criminal law—like its civil law—differ significantly from the letter of Scripture. Hasidean teachers seemingly considered the Torah permissive in this regard rather than mandatory.

Indicated in the Supplement (pp. 708 ff.), the spirit of biblical law itself suggested that while it is the province of the Legislator to threaten severe punishment for infringement of the Divine word, it was the duty of the judge to temper justice with mercy. The whole mishnaic and talmudic system of judicial procedure in criminal cases illustrated this point.

The Supplement (pp. 720 ff.) states that the Hasideans

denied that the punishment of burning, imposed by the Pentateuch in a few instances, meant burning at the stake. Similarly they held that death by stoning really meant by throwing from a great height. They refused to convict a criminal on his own confession, holding that the verses requiring evidence of two witnesses in capital cases (Deut. 17.6, 19.15) admitted of no exception whatsoever. They would not convict a defendant found guilty by a majority of one, although such a majority was sufficient for acquittal. Once acquitted, a criminal could not (they said) be retried, even if new evidence were discovered against him (Mishna Sanhedrin, ch. 4). In general, they considered it far better that many guilty go unpunished, than that anyone possibly innocent should be convicted.

Being courts of arbitration, the pre-Maccabean Hasidean tribunals did not claim authority to inflict punishment. But even in theory, looking forward to the time when their opinions would be authoritative, the Hasideans regarded punishment as at best a necessary evil, to be avoided whenever possible. They opposed the summary judgments of the Court of Priests which, as shown in the Supplement (pp. 720 ff.) disregarded the procedures insisted upon by Hasidean law to protect those accused of crime. We are assured by Josephus (*Antiquities*, XIII, 10.6) that later Pharisaism, at times in power under the Hasmoneans, adhered to the Hasidean doctrine of leniency in punishment. Josephus' testimony in this regard is the more significant because he generally records the Shammaite rather than the Hillelite interpretation of Hasideanism, and the Shammaite interpretation often tended to be influenced by the views of the priests who dominated that school.

Yet as indicated below (pp. 720 ff.), the talmudic record

apparently recognized the Court of Priests as *de facto* authoritative in the Temple. There is even a suggestion that this Court of Priests (to be distinguished from the tribunal known to the Pharisees as that of the Chamber of Hewn Stones, in which they claimed the right to be included) exercised authority of this type in the case of certain transgressions, even when committed outside the Temple precincts. Thus Midrash Tannaim 13.9 (p. 65) preserves a norm through which a man seeking to entice others to idolworship incurred just such summary punishment. The Mishna did not include this norm, so we must assume that Midrash Tannaim transmitted merely a claim of the Temple priesthood, rejected by authoritative Pharisaism but preserved traditionally in one of its schools.

While as shown below (pp. 720 ff.), the Hasideans and in later generations within the ranks of Pharisaism the Hillelites resisted the doctrine of the *talio*, the concept of "measure for measure" as Heavenly punishment and a law of Nature, survived in the Talmud. The concept seems to have originated with the admonition of the Temple priests to the woman brought before them by her husband on suspicion of adultery, to undergo the ordeal of the bitter waters (Num. 5.1 ff.). To obtain a confession from the woman and thus spare her the ordeal, she would, according to both Mishna (Sotah 1.4) and Tosefta (ibid. 1.6, p. 293), be addressed with moving words. Apparently these stirring admonitions included historical examples suggested by Scripture, indicating the certainty of Divine punishment "measure for measure." Samson had transgressed with his eyes (being lured by them to pursue illicit love) and ultimately was blinded. Absalom, having taken undue pride in his hair, was in the end destroyed through its abundance

(Mishna ibid. 1.8). R. Meir draws the inference from all these examples that "all the measures of God are measure for measure" (Tosefta Sotah 3.1, p. 295). And indeed probably R. Meir was in this instance, as often on other occasions, simply transmitting priestly traditions. Presumably these fragments of ancient homilies were preserved in the Mishna and Tosefta of Sotah (the treatise dealing with the ordeal of the suspected woman) because they were part of the admonition to a woman about to undergo the prescribed ordeal. This seems implied in Sifre Numbers (12, p. 18).

The priestly tradition of measure for measure seems to underlie a famous maxim of Hillel, who with the other members of his school rejected the *talio* so far as human courts were concerned. Like other maxims of Hillel, this one seems addressed especially to the priesthood. He had urged them to be disciples of Aaron, no less than his physical descendants; maintaining that Aaron was characterized by love of peace and the pursuit of peace, love of people and the desire to bring them to the Torah (Mishna Abot 1.12). Certainly the Shammaitic priests of Hillel's day could not be considered lovers of peace, for they counselled and even urged rebellion against Rome. Nor could they be described as seeking to bring the general population near the Torah, for they held that the Torah should be taught only to the wealthy and the aristocrats (*Abot of R. Nathan*, I, ch. 3, beg.).

Hillel argued that while Heavenly punishment might be marked by "measure for measure," it was apportioned not only to transgressors, but also to those who summarily (and therefore illegally) punished transgressors. From the Hasidean and Hillelite point of view, already observed, judges themselves had to be careful lest in their desire to punish the sinful they themselves fall into transgression. Hillel used the example of a skull floating on a river to admonish: "Because thou didst drown others, thou hast been drowned; but in the end, those who drowned thee, *will themselves suffer a similar fate*" (Mishna Abot 2.4). Although the man who had perished might have deserved his fate, those responsible for his death would not be held guiltless. Thus Hillel used the very doctrine of "measure for measure," exhorting the priestly judiciary to shun what he considered its extra-legal and illegal judgments.

6.   THE UNWRITTEN HASIDEAN RITUAL LAW

So far as the ritual was concerned, not only did the Hasideans adhere faithfully to the letter and spirit of the Pentateuchal text, but we have already noted that they observed many norms not found in Scripture. Hasideans claimed to have received from their forebears norms which amplified and made specific the general statements of Scripture (Josephus, *Antiquities*, XIII, 10.6).

These traditions, rejected by the Sadducees, Josephus clearly implied, dealt not with the civil or criminal law, but with ritual. Because of the restrictions which the norms involved, the Sadducees resisted them. (This statement of Josephus would alone be sufficient to refute the widespread notion that Sadducism originated in pious adherence to the Law with which the Pharisees dealt cavalierly.) These traditions received by the Pharisees from their fathers included not only many detailed rules regarding observances on the Sabbath (cf. Mishna Hagigah 1.8; Mishna Shabbat, ch. 7), but many other extrapolations of biblical law.

Thus the term "vow" as used in the Pentateuch regularly

denoted the vow of a sacrifice or other gift to the Sanctuary
(cf. Lev. 21.20; 23; Deut. 13.6; 17; 26; 24.22; cf. further
Judg. 11.30; Ps. 114.16; Eccl. 5.4). Numbers (30.3 ff.),
however, suggested that a vow might also be secular, simply
a pledge to do or not to do something otherwise permitted.
This was an extension of the law dealing with vows to the
Temple. A vow to the Temple had to be kept, as the verses
from Deuteronomy and Ecclesiastes demonstrated. When
a man declared an animal *korban*, "a sacrifice," it became
holy, so that he could use it for no purpose other than a
Temple offering.

But what if he declared part of his property "like a *korban*"; that is to say, bestowed on it the status of a sacrifice,
meaning it could not be used by him or anyone else, but yet
was not to be devoted to the Temple? Hasidean law declared such a vow valid. If he had declared the property
"like a *korban*" only so far as he was concerned, it was forbidden to him; if to anyone else, it was forbidden to that
person.

Given readily to vows, perhaps in attempts to establish
the veracity of their assertions, particularly in trade, the
ancient Judaites would resort to circumlocutions through
use of words which sounded like *korban*, but were different
(precisely as many moderns, to avoid oaths, use arbitrary
terms reminiscent of them yet different from them). All
such expressions were declared by the Hasideans to have
the effect of the word *korban* itself. The object was forbidden
either to the owner, if he said the material was *korban* to
him, or to another if the owner made the material *korban*
to that person. One could also declare another's property
to be "like a *korban*" to oneself. One could go further.
One could declare abstract or intangible benefits to be like

a *korban*. Thus, a husband could declare himself "like a *korban*" so far as his wife was concerned, or declare her "like a *korban*" so far as he was concerned. In either case normal marital association between them became prohibited (cf. Mishna Nedarim 1.1; 3; 4; 2.1; 3.1 et al.). However, resort to a scholar was open to a person who had uttered such a vow and wished to indicate his regret at having made it. The scholar would then seek "an opening" in the terms of the vow to find it inapplicable. Human speech being what it is, it was almost impossible not to find a particular situation excluded from the vow. The Hasidean scholars frequently exercised great ingenuity in discovering such "openings." Thus R. Eliezer held that a scholar might ask the person under the vow whether he had considered the honor due his parents, who might be ashamed of a son given to vows made in anger (Mishna Nedarim 9.1). R. Eliezer further held that a vow might be annulled if the person under it admitted that he had not foreseen developments which actually occurred. Thus if a person vowed that nothing belonging to him should be used or enjoyed by someone who had particularly angered him, who then achieved unexpected prominence which made the vow especially embarrassing, admission that foresight regarding this development would have prevented the vow was sufficient, according to R. Eliezer, to obtain release from it (ibid.). R. Meir held that one might ask a person under a vow whether he had realized he was violating various biblical norms, such as "Thou shalt not take vengeance" (Lev. 19.18): if the swearer admitted that he had not realized the violation the oath was deemed nullified (ibid. 9.2).

The colleagues of R. Eliezer and R. Meir considered their view too lenient, but agreed that if a man vowed no longer to associate with his wife, he might be reminded of his obligations to pay her her dower in case of divorce. If he had forgotten, and asserted that had he remembered he would not have taken the vow, he could be released from it (ibid. 9.4). All agreed that one might appeal to the sense of dignity of the person taking the vow. If reminded that it was undignified for him or a disgrace to his children to divorce his wife (on the basis of a vow), and he admitted he had not considered that, the vow was nullified (ibid. 9.5). On one occasion a man vowed not to marry his niece and then regretted it. The case came before R. Ishmael, who noticed that being underfed she seemed uncomely. R. Ishmael took her into his house, looked after her and adorned her, then introducing her to her uncle asked whether he had vowed not to marry this woman. When the man agreed that he had only made a vow against the niece in her previous condition, R. Ishmael "released" the vow (Mishna Nedarim, loc. cit.).

The Mishna admitted there was no biblical basis for scholars to offer release from vows (Mishna Hagigah 1.6). "The release of vows floats in the air, and has no verse on which to depend," the Mishna stated. But in effect so did the principle that vows were effective when not associated with a sacrifice or other gift to the Temple.

In brief, the Hasideans or their predecessors, having extrapolated the concept of the vow, also limited its binding force. We may be sure that the Proto-Sadducees recognized neither the right of the scholars to release vows nor the concept that a vow was binding in secular life.

It seems probable that Sadducean marriage law differed from that of the Hasideans in an important detail. Among Hasideans a woman became "betrothed" in the sense of

Deuteronomy 22.23, if she received as token of marriage either a gift or a writ of marriage, or if she and her prospective fiancé cohabited (Mishna Kiddushin 1.1). It seems clear that among the Proto-Sadducees betrothal consisted rather in the document by which the father of the bride transferred his rights to the prospective husband (cf. Tobit 7.13).

Cohabitation as a form of betrothal seemed inconceivable for the aristocratic Proto-Sadducees and Sadduceans in Jerusalem. It probably was limited to the lower classes in Judea (Mishna Ketubot 1.4), and as a custom originated in the primitive institution of the matriarchate. Similarly, the *mohar* paid by a husband for his wife (cf. Ex. 22.15), from which arose the symbolic presentation of a valuable gift to the woman in token of "betrothal," seems to have been characteristic of the lower classes. And so was the drafting of a document by the husband which in its original form presumably was an acceptance of a claim to pay the *mohar* on demand. This form of betrothal doubtless was instituted to help the impecunious suitor who cou'd not provide the necessary cash (cf. B. Ketubot 82b).

In any event, so great an authority as Maimonides, following a tradition going back to the Geonim, holds that betrothal through a gift is of Sopheric origin (Maim., *Yad*, *Ishut*, 1.2; cf. commentaries, ad loc.).

This may explain the assertion in the Psalms of Solomon 8.13 (12) accusing the Sadducean High Priests of living with women wedded to others. The Sadducees simply did not recognize the Pharisaic law of marriage in this regard.

In the narrower area of ritual, biblical law specifically prohibited only seething a kid in its mother's milk (Ex. 23.19, 34.26; Deut. 14.21). But this book shows (pp. 58 ff.)

that in Hasidean law this prohibition extended to all mixtures of meat and milk, and to the use of such mixtures for food. These extrapolations were entirely within the spirit of the biblical commandment, as shown in the discussion in this book (loc. cit.). But the Sadducees may have challenged them.

Surprisingly, Proto-Sadducees apparently contended that the injunction against eating the blood of animals did not apply to some sacrificial animals. The prohibition in several passages in the Pentateuch recurs in the peace-offering (cf. Lev. 3.17; 7.26; 17.10 ff.; cf. however Deut. 12.23). It was particularly noteworthy that the punishment of being "rooted out from among the people" for this transgression is mentioned only in the passage dealing with the peace-offering (Lev. 7.27; 17.10 ff.).

Perhaps, following the injunction given in Deuteronomy 12.23, the Sadducees agreed that the blood of animals slaughtered for secular use could not be eaten. But Sadducees apparently held that the blood of sacrifices, such as the sin-offering, could be eaten by priests. Indeed it was probably deemed part of the ritual for the priest to consume this blood, because through the process a transgressor obtained atonement. Regarding sacrificial meat, Sifra asserted that "the priests eat [the prescribed portions] and the persons offering the sacrifices are forgiven" (Sifra *Shemini, perek* 2.4, 47b). Similarly the Proto-Sadducean priests apparently held that the blood of the sin-offering eaten by the priests (after some had been sprinkled on the altar) helped obtain forgiveness for a transgressor.

It seems, too, that the Proto-Sadducees permitted the eating of fats which the Hasideans considered forbidden. These fats were those Leviticus 3.3 and similar passages required to be sacrificed on the altar. According to Hasidean law, the Bible forbade eating such fats from domestic animals, even if they were not sacrifices. However, the Pentateuchal injunction against eating these fats always occurred in the context of the laws of the peace-offerings, and this fact suggested to the Sadducees that only fats of specified offerings (Lev. 3.17; 7.22 ff.) were prohibited.

The law which limited the time for consumption of sacrificial meat whether by priests or laity (when permitted them at all) also occurred in the Pentateuch only in association with the peace-offering (Lev. 6.17; 19.6). According to this rule, the meat of the peace-offering might be eaten on the day of the sacrifice and on the morrow, but not later. The meat of the sacrifice of thanks, which was a variant of the peace-offering, might be eaten only on the day of the sacrifice (Lev. 6.9).

In Hasidean law the latter norm applied however to all sacrificial meat which could be eaten (Sifra *Zav*, *perek* 12.1, 35c). These included the sin-offering and the guilt-offering. According to Mishna Zebahim 6.2, it applied also to the meal-offering.

Apparently the Sadducees and their predecessors rejected such extrapolation of the Written Word. It appears that they permitted in secular food use of the type of fat which in the peace-offering was sacrificed on the altar; that they did not consider applicable the norm prohibiting meat left beyond a time limit, except where explicitly stated; and that they did not even forbid drinking the blood of some sacrifices, perhaps not even of domestic animals slaughtered for secular use. That is why Tosefta Horayot 1.17, p. 474, asserts that if the Supreme Court (that of the Chamber of Hewn Stones in the Temple) gave permission to eat such food considered prohibited by the Pharisees, it would have to bring a sacrifice of atonement, such as described in Leviticus 4.18 ff.

Emphasis on these norms in the Book of Jubilees also confirms the suggestion that they were subjects of controversy. The book repeatedly stressed the injunction against eating any blood. Pointedly, this prohibition is addressed in one passage to Levi, apparently because the priests required a special admonition on the subject (see Jub. 6.9 ff.; 7.28 ff.; 21.6, 18).

On the other hand, the Book of Jubilees mentioned only that the fat of the peace-offering was to be sacrified on the altar (21.9), and demanded only that the meat of that sacrifice be consumed within the specified time (ibid. v. 10). Presumably the author agreed with the Hasideans regarding the prohibition of blood, but with the Proto-Sadducean priests regarding the fats and the law on eating sacrificial meat after the specified time.

These controversies regarding forbidden food are replaced —in similar context—in Mishna Horayot 1.3 by three others apparently likewise subjects of differences between Proto-Sadducees and Hasideans. The Mishna mentioned first the prohibition against carrying burdens on the Sabbath which the Sadducees rejected, at least so far as it concerned carrying from house into court or from one house into another (see below, Section 7). The Mishna further hinted that while the Proto-Sadducees of course forbade idol worship, they did not consider genuflection in the presence of idols to be idolatry, if they were not accepted as Divine (cf. Yer. ad loc.). Finally, the Proto-Sadducees seem to have rejected Hasidean interpretation of the rules dealing with menstrual impurity.

This controversy requires explanation. It originated in exegesis of the passage beginning, "And if a woman have an issue of blood many days not in the time of her impurity" (Lev. 15.25). Naturally a question arose about the meaning of the phrase "many days." And precisely what was meant by "not in the time of her impurity"?

To Hasidean physiology the beginning of one menstrual period was separated from the next by at least eighteen days. Therefore if blood appeared more than eighteen days after the beginning of the preceding menstruation it was normal menstrual fluid. Moreover, once menstruation had begun, any blood appearing within seven days was menstrual. The time under consideration in the biblical passage just quoted was therefore eleven days after the end of the menstrual period.

"Many days" (the Hasideans held) could not be fewer than three. Thus a woman suffering "an issue of blood" for three successive days within the eleven day period mentioned became *zabah*, i.e., "a woman with a flow." When cured, she waited seven days (during which she was considered defiled) to make sure of her health. If she remained normal, she bathed. On the following day she brought prescribed sacrifices of purification.

However, even if "the issue" continued only for two days, the Hasideans considered the woman diseased. They declared her defiled, and required her to watch for further symptoms for seven days. If the symptoms did not recur within the week, she bathed, and was pure. She did not offer the sacrifices of purification, because sacrifices prescribed for special occasions could not be brought as voluntary offerings (Sifra *Zabim, perek* 8.4, 79a).

The Hasideans went further. Even if the "issue of blood"

appeared only once, the woman was impure for the following day, during which she had to watch for repetition of the symptom. If none occurred, she bathed, and was declared pure (Sifra, loc. cit.; cf. Mishna Niddah 10, end).

The Mishna implied that the Proto-Sadducees challenged this norm. They apparently denied that in such instances a woman became impure at all, for the biblical text specifically spoke of "many days." Hence the Document of the Sect of Damascus (following Hasidean *halakah* in this case) accused the high-priestly groups of "lying with her who sees blood of her issue" (see S. Schechter, *Documents of Jewish Sectaries*, I, p. 5; R. H. Charles, *Apochrypha and Pseudepigrapha*, II, p. 810; and cf. Professor Ginzberg's *Eine unbekannte jued. Sekte*, p. 30).

The author of the Psalms of Solomon 8.13 (12) may have referred to this controversy in his charge that the Sadducees defiled the sacrifices "with menstrual blood" (see R. H. Charles, op. cit., p. 640).

While some of these controversies dealt with sacrifices, this was only incidentally. The prohibition against eating animal blood applied generally. The Hasideans merely objected to the Proto-Saducean priests' declaration that they were exempt from part of the ban. The prohibition against eating the sacrificial meat after the prescribed time applied to the laity given part of the thank-offering, the tithed animals, and similar sacrifices.

We have already observed regarding the criminal law that early Hasideans did not generally consider themselves authorized to decide questions of Temple practice. Hence, the talmudic assertion that norms under the classification of *shebut* had no application to the Sanctuary. Such norms forbade on the Sabbath labor inconsistent with its spirit, though not included among the types of work specifically prohibited. Apparently because the priests refused to recognize the principle of *shebut*, the norms deriving from it had never been adopted by the Temple authorities. The Hasideans admitted the priests' right to reject the norms, so far as the Temple worship was concerned (Mishna 'Erubin, ch. 10; and cf. Babli, ibid. 102a).

The Temple authorities also permitted on the Sabbath labor ancillary to the sacrificial ritual, though it might have been performed before the Sabbath. The Hillelites forbade this and presumably their view retained that of the early Hasideans. Drawn largely from the priesthood, the Shammaitic Pharisees held that the Temple practice was consistent with the Law (see Mishna Pesahim 6.1, in the name of R. Eliezer). No one questioned the priests' decisions regarding the New Moon or the intercalary year.

Also accepted was the priestly view that a woman who had suffered a miscarriage should under certain circumstances bring the sacrifice required for a normal birth, but that the sacrifice should be burned rather than offered on the altar (Mishna Temurah 7.6). Although it is very difficult to find Scriptural support for their position, the priests' insistence that a proselyte or a captive could not marry into the priestly group has persisted in all rabbinic codes down to our day (cf. Maimonides, *Yad, Issure Biah*, 18.3, and commentaries, ad loc.; ibid. 18.17; and B. Kiddushin 78a; ibid. Yebamot 60b). The priests' refusal to allow a proselyte (including in the term descendants of proselytes) to act as judge was followed, so far as the Court of the Chamber of Hewn Stones (which the priests controlled) was concerned (B. Yebamot 101b).

On the other hand, the text of this book shows that (pp.

102 ff.; 115 ff.; 118 ff.; 121 ff.) and in the Supplement (pp. 641 ff.; 654 ff.; 661 ff.; 700 ff.), the Hasideans resisted priestly decisions on four issues which at first glance appear to deal with sacrifices or the Temple ritual. The Hasideans insisted that the High Priest perform according to the letter of the Law the ritual of offering the incense on the Day of Atonement. They demanded that the priest sacrificing the red heifer be a *tebul yom*, rather than entirely purified. They insisted that the heave offering (*Omer*) be sacrificed according to their tradition, rather than according to the priestly one. They offered water-libations during Sukkot, and observed the ceremonies connected with it.

In each of these cases, the Hasideans considered themselves no less involved than the priests, and therefore held that the issues were under Hasidean jurisdiction. The High Priest offered atonement for all Israel on the Day of Atonement and was the agent of the people (see below p. 659). If he violated the Law, he might imperil the whole nation and each individual within it. The ashes of the red heifer were essential to purify those defiled through contact with the dead, whether inside or outside the Temple. Therefore the ashes had to be prepared as the Hasideans demanded. Moreover, a large part of the ceremony took place on the Mount of Olives, outside Temple precincts. The days between Passover and Shabuot had to be counted by each Jew (Sifra *Emor, perek* 12.1, 100d), because each had to observe the festival of Shabuot on the appointed day. Besides, no one was permitted to eat new grain until the *Omer* had been sacrificed. The ceremony of the water-libations on Sukkot, associated with the rainfall, was of concern to the whole community, especially because it was the only Temple ritual in which the whole community could partici-

pate directly. The Hasideans seemed to believe that the
general Jewish concern for these ceremonies led to Hasidean
jurisdiction over the Temple and priestly practice regarding
them. These examples were not, therefore, really exceptions
to the principle that the early Hasideans permitted the
Temple Court to guide its ritual.

7. Light on Pharisaism and Sadducism from the Book of Jubilees

The controversies of the Proto-Pharisees and Proto-
Sadducees are illumined through one of the major attempts
during the Second Commonwealth to restore the unity of
Jewish law, the publication of the Book of Jubilees. At the
same time, the priests' tendency to deviate from the ritual
enables us to understand the daring innovations proposed
by this author. The book was almost certainly composed
in pre-Hasmonean times (see below, p. 641). Apparently, it
was the work of a patriotic, dedicated priest of the lower
classes who saw peril to the nation in the increasing bitterness between the Temple High Priests and the Sages of
Israel. (The Pharisaic scholars were regularly called by that
name in the Talmud, cf. B. Kiddushin 66a, et al., not to
distinguish them from Gentile scholars, but from the priestly
judges who were mainly Sadducees, see below, pp. 727 ff.
for the significance of the similar term, "Court of Israel.")
The author undertook to dispose of all the controversies,
through compromises and suggestions which made them
irrelevant. He seemingly held that the restoration of peace
within Israel was so vital an achievement as to justify even
departure from the text of the Pentateuch. To obtain acceptance of his work, he asserted that it had been secretly

given to Moses on Mt. Sinai and, rediscovered in the time of the Second Commonwealth, was to replace the Oral Law of the Proto-Pharisees.

a. The Date of Shabuot

The controversy concerning the time and meaning of the Shabuot festival was to be resolved through substitution of a solar for the lunar calendar. This solar calendar was so conceived that every festival day would occur on a Sunday. This would meet the economic problem of the priests whose term ended on the Sabbath before a festival and who had to look after their needs without help of the Temple authorities when several days intervened between the Sabbath day and the festival day (see below, pp. 643 ff.). On the other hand, the invention of the proposed solar calendar enabled the author to admit that Shabuot, always occurring on the same day of the month, commemorated the giving of the Law and the covenant between God and Noah. The Jubilaic author proposed that the forty-nine days between Passover and Shabuot be counted from the last day of Passover, rather than from the first as the Hasideans demanded, or from the Sabbath of the festival week as the Proto-Sadducees demanded.

The author doubtless hoped that the Hasidean scholars would accept his proposed solar calendar, for according to it the word *Shabbat*, Leviticus, chapter 23, meant festival, in agreement with their view, rather than Sabbath, as the Proto-Sadducees held. On the other hand, he believed he had satisfied the Proto-Sadducees, because they would benefit practically from the proximity of each festival to the Sabbath day.

That adoption of the solar calendar was proposed to resolve the ancient controversy regarding the date of Shabuot is evident from the fact that the author inserts the discussion of the calendar into the context of the laws pertaining to that festival.

Lest any reader suppose that the sacrifices prescribed for Shabuot might be brought as voluntary offerings at the time prescribed by his own group, the author stresses the norm requiring all the offerings mentioned in Scripture in connection with this festival to be made on the day he had set for it (Jub. 6.22). Thus it would not be possible for a conscientious Proto-Sadducee or Hasidean to bring the offering of the two loaves at some time other than that set in the Book of Jubilees, in order to satisfy the demands of his own tradition.

b. Carrying on the Sabbath Day

The author accepted the Hasidean prohibition against carrying burdens on the Sabbath day, not only from home to the public highway or from there home, but even from a house into another house or into the courtyard or *vice versa* (Jub. 2.30; 50.8). He went further. He declared it forbidden to lift a burden with *intent* to carry it out of a house. But he did not mention the law of the *'erub*, which in obvious agreement with the Proto-Sadducees he rejected (cf. above, Section 6).

c. The Sukkot Ceremonies

The author did not abolish the ceremony of the water-libations. However, he hoped once again to placate the Proto-Sadducees by removing the ritual from the Sukkot festival to the Passover (Jub. 49.22). Because the association of Sukkot with rain was rejected in the Book of Jubilees (to suit the feelings of the Proto-Sadducees), the various rituals developed in connection with willow branches were also abolished. The procession with the willows about the altar was not mentioned. On the contrary, on *each* of the Sukkot days there was to be a procession about the altar, seven times with palm branch and citron (and presumably also with willow and myrtle). This provision of Jubilees 16.31 opposed Mishna Sukkah 4.4, 5, according to which the members of the procession carried willow branches going about the altar only once on the first six days of Sukkot and seven times on the seventh.

On the other hand, the mandate of the Book of Jubilees was in conflict with another norm of the Mishna. According to the Mishna (Sukkah 4.1) the *lulab* was to be taken on the Sabbath, only if it coincided with the *first* day of Sukkot. If any of the other six days of the festival occurred on the Sabbath, the *lulab* was not to be touched. The Book of Jubilees makes no such distinction, holding that there was to be a procession carrying the citrons and palm branches on each of the seven days, although obviously one would be a Sabbath.

The author did not even provide that, in order to participate in the procession on the Sabbath, the palm branches and the fruit should be brought to the Temple on Friday, as Mishna Sukkah 4.2 required if the first day occurred on a Sabbath (when according to it, the *lulab* was to be taken in the normal manner). Probably the priestly author of the Book of Jubilees held that, whenever a Temple ceremonial was permitted on the Sabbath, all preparations for it were also permitted, even though they might have been arranged on Friday. This was exactly the position taken by R. Eliezer and the Shammaites generally, and opposed by the

Hillelites whose views were transmitted by R. Joshua (see Mishna Pesahim 6.1).

Thus the question raised by the Proto-Sadducees whether it was permitted to beat the willows on the ground on the Sabbath day was circumvented (see below, p. 703).

During each of the seven days of Sukkot the Book of Jubilees required that the Hallel be recited with joy, commemorating Abraham's celebration of the festival, in which "he praised and gave thanks to his God for all things with joy" (Jub., loc. cit.).

(It is significant that according to a *baraita*, both recorded in Tosefta Sukkah 3.1, p. 195, ed. Lieberman, p. 266, and in Babli Sukkah 43b, the Boethusians, and apparently also the Sadducees and the Proto-Sadducees, denied that the ritual of "beating the willows" could be performed on the Sabbath. Of course Professor Lieberman points out in *Tosefta Ki-Fshutah*, Sukkah, p. 870, the sectarians rejected all the ceremonies associated solely with the willows, including the procession. One would therefore expect the *baraita* to have said that they did not agree that "the willow [ceremony] sets aside the Sabbath." However, the sectarians did not recognize any violation of the Sabbath law in connection with the willow ceremonies, aside from beating the willows on the ground. This was because the sectarians already remarked in Section 6, did not regard carrying a burden from place to place on the Sabbath a violation of the Law. The Hasideans and the Pharisees did; and therefore when the seventh day of Sukkot occurred on the Sabbath, they brought their willows to the Temple on Friday.)

From the Book of Jubilees it is manifest that not only priests but all Israelites participated in these processions, following the example of Abraham. This seems to be also the meaning of the Mishna (Sukkah 4.5). It is further implied in the *baraita* already mentioned, and transmitted in Tosefta Sukkah 3.1, p. 195, ed. Lieberman, p. 266, where we are told that the *'am ha-arez*, finding the willows covered with rocks by the Boethusians, dragged the branches out, presumably to participate in the procession. The text of this *baraita* (re B. Sukkah 43b) suggested that only the "priests," and not the laity, approached the altar. Therefore Babli holds that in the famous incident, after the *'am ha-arez* had drawn the willows out from under the rocks, the priests set the branches up on the sides of the altar. Rashi (ad loc.) properly concludes that according to Babli Israelites could not march about the altar, because only qualified priests (without a blemish, and who had washed their hands and feet) could enter the area separating the altar from the Porch of the Temple building. In this Rashi was followed by all the commentators on the Mishna.

However, the question whether a priest who had failed to wash his hands and feet might enter the particularly sacred space was itself a controversial subject. Simeon the Pious told R. Eliezer that he himself had done so (Tosefta Kelim I, 1.6, p. 569). R. Eliezer retorted that Simeon had escaped alive after this transgression only because it was not detected (see ibid.; and cf. below, p. 732).

Tosefta Sukkah 4.23 (p. 200, ed. Lieberman, p. 277) reported that the shewbread was divided among the officiating priests in this very area. But the portion of the bread given the priests "with a blemish" was removed "without" (i.e., to the general space of the Court of Priests; see Professor Lieberman, *Tosefta Ki-Fshutah*, ad loc.), "because they could not enter the space between the altar and the 'porch.'"

The view that a priest "with a blemish" or who had not washed his hands and feet might not enter this sacred space was confirmed by Mishna Kelim 1.9, which added that priests with hair long uncut (that is, whose hair had been uncut for thirty days), also could not enter that space. The Mishna does not specify the rule for priests who had not washed their hands and feet. Presumably, this is because the Mishna followed the view of R. Meir, according to whom such priests might come into the sacred space (Tosefta Kelim, loc. cit.). But this lenient view was rejected by R. Meir's colleagues (ibid.). Sifre Zutta 5.2, p. 228, maintained that priests "with a blemish, or uncut hair, or who had drunk wine" could not enter that part of the Court of Priests. (However, the text of Sifre Zutta seems to have been emended in transmission, and to have dealt originally only with priests with uncut hair or who had drunk wine.)

The issue had—it appears—never really been clarified. Presumably it was the subject of an early difference of opinion. We may be able to discover this by asking, on what occasion did Simeon the Pious enter the holy place, without washing his hands and feet from the laver placed there (cf. Ex. 30.20). Obviously, he did not walk behind the altar and in front of the Sanctuary itself merely from curiosity. If he went there to receive his portion of the shewbread, he would have washed his hands and feet before taking the food, for eating the holy food was itself an act of worship. Moreover, under such circumstances, how could R. Eliezer claim that Simeon the Pious had escaped death for the transgression only because no one noticed his violation of the law? If all the priests about to receive their portion of the shewbread washed their hands and feet as they came into the holy area, and Simeon did not, his failure to do so would have been noticed very quickly.

Perhaps, we are justified in assuming that the event occurred during the Sukkot processions. Israelites participating in this ceremony did not wash their hands and feet, but priests did because they always washed their hands and feet on approaching the space between the altar and the "Porch." Simeon the Pious failed to do so, because he did not believe it necessary on that occasion. R. Eliezer maintained that if Simeon had been caught violating the law in this respect, he would have met his death. If this interpretation is correct, we may further assume that R. Eliezer was in this instance (as so frequently) transmitting traditions of the Shammaitic priesthood. Simeon the Pious followed the views of the Proto-Hillelites and the earlier Hasideans who considered the omission of washing permitted.

R. Meir, who allowed priests whose hands and feet had not been washed (Tosefta Kelim I, 1.6, p. 569) to enter this area of the Court of Priests, likewise was transmitting a Proto-Hillelite tradition, which we know from the Tosefta Sukkah 4.23 was not followed in Temple practice. (Cf. Mishna Zebahim 2.1 declaring unfit for worship a priest not clothed as prescribed, or who had drunk wine, or had not washed his hands and feet; and considering a ritual performed by one of them invalid. Cf., however, B. Sanhedrin 83a, according to which a priest who performed acts of worship while his hair had been uncut for thirty days was punishable by death, so that presumably any act of worship by him also was void. The same view was expressed by Tosefta Zebahim 12.17, p. 498.) From these sources we may conclude that no priest in those categories could enter the sacred area between the altar and the "Porch." (Cf. *Sidre Toharot*, *Kelim*, Yosepof, 1873, 68a, for a broad and profound discussion of the whole subject and the various texts bearing on it.)

Thus the question, whether a priest unfit for worship on the altar might under any conditions go into the area discussed, was debated in early times. The priests held that he might not; the Proto-Hillelites held that he might. While later authorities, like R. Eliezer, might draw a fine distinction between unqualified priests and Israelites regarding entry into the special part of the Court of Priests, in earlier times those who banished from it disqualified priests (who had not washed their hands and feet, or who had a blemish) would certainly refuse to admit non-priests.

It follows that those who allowed the non-priests to march about the altar with their willows were Proto-Hillelites and early Hasideans. The priests objected to the practice, but were unable to prevent it, as they were unable to suppress the ceremonies connected with the water-libations. Thus the tradition permitting the laity to march about the altar followed that of the Hillelites and early Hasideans. That preserved in Babli followed the practice of the Temple priests which came into Pharisaism through the Shammaite tradition.

The Book of Jubilees sided with the Hasideans in this instance, and suggested therefore that the procession could include non-priests.

The Proto-Sadducees, who objected to the ritual of water-libations and beating the willows on the Temple ground on the seventh day of Sukkot, objected also to these processions. In their eyes the processions violated the holiness of the Temple court, because even a priest with a blemish, or who had not washed his hands and feet, or whose hair had not been cut, was banned from going into this particularly sacred spot. Surely then an Israelite or Levite was not permitted to enter the area.

The Book of Jubilees, rejecting the concept that Sukkot was a period of "judgment for rain" (Mishna Rosh ha-Shanah 1.2), also rejected the theory that it was a season of sacrifice on behalf of "the peoples of the world." Scripture required seventy bullocks to be sacrificed during the seven Sukkot days, with thirteen on the first, one less each succeeding day, and ending with seven on the seventh day (Num. 29.13 ff.). These seventy bullocks were interpreted as atonement for the seventy nations of the world (B. Sukkah 55b). The fierce nationalism of the Book of Jubilees could not support this concept. Indeed, the author held that Sukkot was not a period of judgment for rain—a necessity for all mankind—and therefore the main reason for the sacrifices was lacking. So with remarkable intrepidity the Jubilaic author changed the number of sacrifices to be offered on the Sukkot days (Jub. 16.22 and 32.4).

In further vent to his anti-Gentilism, the author prohibited any but Israelites from dwelling in the Sukkot booths (Jub. 16.25; 29), a prohibition unknown to either Scripture or Talmud.

Recognizing the psychological necessity of a festival marked by libations of water, and yet desiring to please the Proto-Sadducees through abolition of these rituals on Sukkot, the author (as already noted) prescribed them for Passover (Jub. 49.22). Perhaps he felt this change was essential. The early Hasideans had called Sukkot "the season of our joy," insisting that its most significant rite was that of the popular celebrations. The author agreed with

his fellow-priests of higher rank that on Sukkot these celebrations could well detract from the importance and popularity of the rituals associated with the Day of Atonement.

On the other hand, the author seems to approve the
Proto-Hillelite and Hillelite view that private whole-burnt
offerings might be sacrificed on the festival days (Jub.
16.22; cf. Mishna Hagigah 2.3).

d. The Day of Atonement

The Book of Jubilees—conscious of the pagan rites of the
peasants—declared the Day of Atonement one of sorrow
(Jub. 34.19), opposing the Hasidean concept of the occasion
as one of solemn joy, when despite the fast (see below, pp.
54 ff. and 704 ff.) vineyard dances by the young men and
women were not only condoned but encouraged. Like some
Rabbinic Sages, the author considered the goat offered on
the Day of Atonement a sacrifice of propitiation for the
sale of Joseph into slavery. (His brothers had dipped his
garment in the blood of a goat, and brought it to Jacob, as
evidence that Joseph had met a violent death [Jub. 34.18;
cf. Sifra, *Miluim, Shemini,* beg.].)

The Talmud hinted that at one time (as remarked on
pp. 704 ff.) the Hasideans were gravely concerned because,
intended in a measure to replace the popular pagan festivities usual on the tenth of Tishri, the Sukkot celebrations
were accompanied by sexual frivolities. (Perhaps, indeed,
this was one of the reasons for Proto-Sadducean condemnation of these ceremonies.) "Originally," records a *baraita*
(Tosefta Sukkah 4.1, p. 198, ed. Lieberman, II, p. 272; cf.
Tosefta Ki-Fshutah, ad. loc.), "when witnessing the celebrations of the water-libations, the men would be within, and
the women without." That is to say, after the Court of

Israelites had been filled to capacity, crowds still gathered in the Court of Women, which would therefore be filled by men and women—the men nearer the Court of Israel, the women behind them. "When the Court noticed that this arrangement led to improprieties, it built three porches about the Court of Women, one on each of the three sides of the Court [but none on the fourth side, which led to the Court of Israelites]. In this way, the women could watch the ritual of the libations [from these porches, to which alone they were admitted during the ceremonies] and the sexes were not mingled."

The curious relation of the Sukkot festivities required by the Hasideans and used in their liturgy to describe the holiday, to those popular among the peasantry on the tenth of Tishri, the retention of the festivities in the Book of Jubilees although the author rejected the concept of Sukkot as a time of judgment for rain, the remarkable talmudic suggestion (just quoted) that these festivities sometimes led to undesirable incidents in the Temple, all indicate that the ceremony of the water-libations, the celebrations with the burning faggots, and the procession with the willows did not originate in the concept that Sukkot was a period of judgment for rain: on the contrary, the concept was developed to add an air of solemnity to the festivities. The rites were apparently of very primitive origin, so primitive that they survived although not mentioned in the Pentateuch—and this despite the opposition of the priesthood, both during the First and Second Commonwealths.

Far from inventing these rites the Hasideans simply accepted them as useful in giving the community at large opportunity for direct participation in a Temple ritual—an aspect of the ceremonies especially distasteful to the priests. To prevent the celebrations from getting out of hand, the Hasideans associated them with the solemn consideration that during the festival period the world was being judged with regard to rain. This book indicates (p. 704) that it is unlikely this association first developed during the Second Commonwealth. Instead the Talmud suggested it was made by the Prophets themselves.

e. The Jubilaic Author's Attitude to the Temple

It is not clear whether the author approved the existence of a Temple structure like that reared by Solomon. In many passages (cf. Jub. 49.18) he spoke of the Temple as a "tabernacle," but that may be an archaism, based on the word of Scripture. On the other hand, this peasant priest may well have deplored substitution for the simple wilderness tabernacle of the imposing structures built by Solomon, later by the returning Exiles, and finally made most impressive under Herod.

f. The Tithes

According to the Jubilaic author (13.26; 13.9), tithes were to be given the priests (and not the Levites), a view shared by the priestly tradition handed down in the Talmud and opposed by the Hillelites (cf. *Akiba*, p. 83). The Second Tithe (an expression found in the Talmud but already known to the Jubilaic author) could not therefore be intended for the priests in accordance with Numbers 18.26 ff. The Book of Jubilees prescribed that the Second Tithe was, like sacrificial meat, to be eaten in the Tabernacle precincts (Jub. 32.10). The Book added that the tithes of each year had to be consumed before its close, lest they be polluted as were sacrificial meats kept beyond their prescribed time (Jub. 32.11, and cf. Lev. 7.16 and 19.8).

g. The Jubilaic Author's Concept of Man's Immortality

The author undertook to end the ancient theological controversy regarding the Resurrection of the Dead, through the assertion that there would be a resurrection of the spirits but not of the bodies (Jub. 23.31). Lest this doctrine prove offensive to the Proto-Sadducees because it suggested the doctrine of Immortality of the Soul, the author insisted that the spirits would be revivified at the end of days (loc. cit.). However, according to the Book of Jubilees, it would seem that this Resurrection of the spirits was limited to those of Jews. The author opposed the Hasidean view that the pious of all peoples would achieve immortality. (This Hasidean view is preserved in Mishna Sanhedrin 10.2, where Balaam is denied participation in the future life, suggesting that other righteous Gentiles would share in it. The tradition survived among the Hillelites and was expressed by R. Joshua, but opposed by R. Eliezer. Cf. B. Sanhedrin 104a, and my discussion of the subject in *Mabo le-massektot Abot ve-Abot d'Rabbi Natan*, p. 223.)

h. The Jubilaic Author's Concept of the *Talio*

Opposing the Hasidean tendency toward leniency in punishment, and especially its refusal to inflict the *talio*, the author maintained that punishment should be measure for measure (Jub. 4.32).

i. The Law of the Jubilee Year

Perhaps the most instructive doctrine of the book was

that from which derived its usual name. The author (already observed above, Section 4) maintained that the law of the Jubilee applied in the Second Commonwealth, holding with the Hasideans it had applied also in the First. Failure to observe the law had brought calamity on the nation, and would do so again.

Under Jubilaic law no priest could own land, but during the Second Commonwealth priests were among the chief landowners. Presumably, therefore, unlike the high-priestly families, the priest who composed this work was himself landless and appealed to the landless.

No wonder that this book was deemed sacred by certain segments of the population who, obeying and expanding its commands, developed the sect of the Essenes and those of the Qumram group (perhaps identical with the Essenes). To them the need for a Messiah, sprung both from the seed of Aaron and from the seed of David, was urgent. They could not believe that a scion of the reigning High Priest would ever accede to their own revolutionary ideas. Only the miraculous intervention of God in human affairs, and more especially in those of Israel, could effect fulfillment of the Torah in their time.

But the Torah to be established in Messianic days and to be approached in this world differed from the Pentateuch. What the Hasideans and the Pharisees had done to the civil and criminal law of the Torah, and the High Priests to ritual, these socially depressed priests and laymen did to other sections of the Pentateuch. It is inconceivable that Jews like the Essenes or those of the Qumram Sect or the writer of the Book of Jubilees would dare flout the very word of Scripture, had they not consciously imitated recognized Temple authorities in their approach to matters of ritual, and in a sense the approach of Pharisaic judges to the civil and criminal law.

For the priestly deviationists who altered the ritual, the Written Law was merely a series of recommendations, to be "adjusted" to social need. The author of the Book of Jubilees could find support for his views in the fact that the Hasideans, themselves loyal to the word of Scripture, generally did not undertake to impose their tradition on the Temple ritual, where the High Priest reigned supreme.

The author of the Book of Jubilees and the sect based on his teachings by the unknown "Teacher of Righteousness" concluded from the observation of both Sadducean practice and Pharisaic acquiescence in it (so far as the Temple was concerned) that "the needs of the hour" could supersede the commandments themselves.

Because (as already noted above) no one owning land could consider himself obedient to the Jubilaic law as understood in the Book of Jubilees; because the solar calendar deprived the Temple high-priesthood of a most cherished prerogative, namely, the determination of the calendar; because the author considered all priests equal, as descendants of the first priest, Levi; because the author nowhere mentioned the High Priest to be clothed with special authority or privilege, we may rightly assume that the Jubilaic writer belonged, or at least sympathized with, the landless priests; and that the Sect founded upon his teachings drew its support from the landless masses.

Essentially provincials (but unlike the Proto-Sadducees, poor and landless), they were fiercely nationalistic, contemptuous of the Gentile world, inclined toward severity in punishment, convinced that success depended not on effort but on predestined fate, and detesting of the constant violation of the Law by the high-priesthood of their time (the later Hellenistic period). Unable to persuade the rest of Jewry that the law of the Jubilee still applied to the farm country, many in the sects withdrew from the general community, preferring to live in their own communes, usually in the wilderness near Jericho, and conducting their lives as they saw fit. Others, Josephus recorded, lived in the cities of Judea, but apparently everywhere as landless workers and artisans.

These sects opposed Hasideanism partly because they could not admit the authority of the lay scholar *vis à vis* the Temple and rejected some of the Hasidean tradition, but mostly because Hasidean stress on intellectual achievement alienated them. What this group needed was a short cut to Salvation. The high value placed by the Hasideans on constant study, the Hasidean belief that the Temple High Priests had full authority over Temple ritual, Hasidean unwillingness to demand reapportionment of the land on the principles implied in Leviticus 25.1 ff., Hasidean insistence that observance of the faith was compatible with life among a people who were largely unobservant, drove the sects to seek their salvation elsewhere. Fortunately for them (they thought) there were, going back to Moses himself but unknown to either Hasideans or Proto-Sadducees, documents such as the Book of Jubilees which set down rules precisely fitted to the needs of these sects. They looked forward to bliss in another world, a world in which the Jewish people would be dominant and which would be essentially spiritual rather than physical.

Adoption of the solar calendar forced the author of the Book of Jubilees also to accept the doctrine of personal angels. The festivals had to be cosmic, to negate prerogative of earthly authorities to determine the proper dates. For the festivals to be cosmic, the whole Law had to share that characteristic, and from this concept followed the idea of good and rebellious angels or those who obeyed the Law and those who violated it.

The future Resurrection being limited to spirits (Jub. 22.30), the sinful were condemned to eternal torment just as the spirits of the righteous were to enjoy eternal bliss. Mere denial of a share in the future world (which the Hillelites and originally all Hasideans, conceived to be the portion of everyone) could scarcely be a penalty for those who believed in neither immortality nor the Resurrection, but enjoyed mundane prosperity.

As Professor Lieberman was the first to point out, the Talmud refers to the Qumram Sect four times. (See *Proceedings of the American Academy for Jewish Research*, XX, pp. 395 ff.) Each time their ritual was declared "a deviationist way." They were not considered apostates, because in early Hasideanism even Sadducism was not equated with apostasy. Both Sadducism and Essenism were deviationist, in that their followers disregarded the Torah, as studied, taught, and understood by Hasideanism and Pharisaism. (For further discussions of the issues raised in this section, see my article on the *halakah* of the Book of Jubilees in *Harvard Theological Review*, 1923; and Ch. Albeck, *Das Buch d. Jubiläen und die Halacha.*)

8. The Description of the Pharisees by Josephus

The discussion in this Note, in the text and in the Supplement, demonstrates the accuracy of Josephus' description of the Pharisees and the Sadducees. No matter how inaccurate otherwise or how frequently he may have sacrificed precision to apologetics, his picture of the dominant groups in contemporary Judaism corresponds to fact. He knew all three groups—the Sadducees, the Pharisees, and the Essenes —intimately and had no difficulty in explaining them.

In *War*, I, 5.2, speaking of Queen Salome, Josephus asserted that "Beside Alexandra, and growing as she grew, arose the Pharisees, a body of Jews with the reputation of excelling the rest of the nation in the observances of religion, and as exact exponents of the laws."

This description of the Pharisees as the most pious of all the groups and as precise interpreters of the laws, should itself suffice to refute the current theory that they changed the Law whether through legislation or nterpretation. Josephus' account corresponds rather to that given in the Supplement to this book, in which analysis of the Pharisaic-Sadducean controversies shows that the Pharisaic ritual loyally adhered to the text of Scripture, but the Sadducean views originated among deviationists. Josephus further demonstrated the truth of the talmudic assertion (see pp. 637 ff.) that even many Sadducees of later times, and certainly the *'am ha-arez*, no matter what their practices, took for granted the Pharisees' superior learning and understanding of the Law.

Elaborating on his theme, Josephus asserted (*War*, II, 8.14) that the Pharisees

"are considered the most accurate interpreters of the laws, and hold the position of the leading sect, attribute everything to fate and to God; they hold that to act rightly or otherwise rests, indeed, for the most part with men, but that in each action, Fate co-operates. Every soul, they maintain, is imperishable, but the soul of the good alone passes into another body, while the souls of the wicked suffer eternal punishment."

The Supplement (pp. 768 f.) shows that the Pharisees with their eye on the future world disregarded success and comforts on earth, and in these respects differed from the Sadducees. The word "fate" in this passage is used with precision and (as is indicated, e.g., in B. Ta'anit 25a) means that material fortune in this world often depends on circumstances unrelated to effort or piety. However, Josephus did not forget the Pharisaic teaching that there is also Divine reward for good deeds in this world and he therefore added the words "and to God."

While the Pharisees agreed that moral decisions are in general made by man, they prayed that God might turn him to righteousness and repentance. Thus they recognized that virtuous habits, once established, facilitate the pursuit of virtue. "He who seeks to purify himself will be assisted in his efforts to do so" (B. Shabbat 104a). They also held that such accidental factors as good neighbors, good environment, and good parentage may affect the ability to achieve and act on moral judgment (Mishna Abot 2.9).

Josephus, himself a priest, usually adopted the Shammaitic interpretation of the Law (cf., e.g., his views on the talio, Antiquities, IV, 8.35). He also followed Shammaitic theology. According to the Shammaites, man's soul was indestructible. After death, its condition was that of the shades—rephaim—mentioned in Scripture.

In the Day of Judgment, there would be three groups, the Shammaites held (according to Abot of R. Nathan, I, ch. 41, 67a). The righteous would be resurrected to eternal bliss. The wicked would be condemned to eternal torment. The intermediate group would descend into Gehenna, to be scorched by its fires and, thus purified, join the righteous (The School of Hillel disagreed with these views. They considered the soul destructible [cf. Sifre Num. 112, p. 120] and held that many of the wicked would neither be resurrected nor judged [see Tosefta Sanhedrin 13.7 ff., p. 435; *Abot of R. Nathan*, I, ch. 36, 53b ff.]; and that the intermediate groups comprising the vast majority of men would be forgiven. Hence, the Hillelites foresaw no eternal torment or punishment for anyone in the future world. R. Akiba offered a compromise. He held that punishment of the wicked in Gehenna would last for twelve months. Other sages suggest shorter periods [Mishna 'Eduyyot 2.10].)

The reference to the "other body" in Josephus was unrelated to the doctrine of transmigration. Josephus explained that the resurrection was one of the spirit, which would live a physical life in the eschatological future, in a second body. The body inhabited in the present world would have decayed, or burned, or otherwise been destroyed.

Josephus continued:

"The Sadducees, the second of the orders, do away with Fate altogether, and remove God beyond, not merely the commission but the very sight of, evil. They maintain that man has the free choice of good or evil, and that it rests with each man's will whether he follows the one or the other. As for the persistence of the soul after death, penalties in the underworld, and rewards, they will have none of them."

Thus the Sadducees maintained that man's fate is entirely in his own hands; they denied that in moral decisions God ever leads a man into transgression, even through habit; and of course they denied the eschatological future.

The discussion in the Supplement (p. 748) shows how indispensable to the Sadducean theory of education were these beliefs, and how they corresponded to the record of the differences between the groups, in *Abot of R. Nathan*, I, chapter 5, 13b.

"The Pharisees," Josephus added, "are affectionate to each other, and cultivate harmonious relations with the community. The Sadducees, on the contrary, are even among themselves rather boorish in their behavior, and in their intercourse with their peers are as rude as to aliens." The precision of these remarks is demonstrated below (pp. 82 ff.).

However, Josephus may have been referring to another aspect of Pharisaism—the mutual respect of its opposing schools, discussed on pp. 631 ff. We must remember that the various talmudic stories which told about the brusqueness of such teachers as Shammai and R. Eliezer all emanated from their opponents. After all, Shammai did warn his disciples to receive all men graciously; while R. Eliezer's favorite maxim included an admonition to regard the honor due one's colleague as one's own. The Shammaites considered school discipline to require severity toward pupils (*Abot of R. Nathan*, I, ch. 6, 14a); but that view did not interfere with the concept shared with other Pharisees that in human intercourse gentleness and courtesy were enjoined in the Torah itself. Perhaps in the contrast Josephus drew between Pharisaic courtesy and Sadducean brusqueness, he had in mind another consideration. The relation of the Sadducees to the Boethusians (who shared their theology and practice) was one of bitter hostility, worlds apart from the friendship marking the relations of Shammaites and Hillelites.

In *Antiquities*, XIII, 5.9, Josephus, in addition, explained that the Pharisees

> "say that certain events are the work of Fate, but not all; as to other events, it depends on ourselves, whether they shall take place or not. . . . But the Sadducees do away with Fate, holding that there is no such thing and that human actions are not achieved in accordance with her decree, but that all things lie within our power, so that we ourselves are responsible for our well-being, while we suffer misfortune through our thoughtlessness."

These attitudes correspond to those quoted above from the *War*. Here Josephus merely added that the actions, for which men are responsible and which are associated with moral decisions, sometimes affect men's condition in this world, through the will of God.

The description in *Antiquities*, XIII, 10.5, of the Pharisaic influence on the community, enabling them effectively to criticize king or high priest, corresponds to the implications of Mishna Yoma 1.5. Josephus' assertion in the same context, XIII, 10.6, that the Pharisees tended toward leniency in punishment is also confirmed by other evidence (see below, pp. 720 ff.).

Proceeding further, Josephus noted that

> "the Pharisees had passed on to the people certain regulations handed down by former generations and not re-

corded in the Law of Moses, for which reason they are rejected by the Sadducean group, who hold that only those regulations should be considered valid which were written down [i.e., in Scripture] and that those handed down by the fathers need not be observed. And concerning these matters, the two parties came to have controversies and serious differences, the Sadducees having the confidence of the wealthy alone but no following among the populace, while the Pharisees have the support of the masses."

We have already suggested that this remark indicates clearly that the "regulations handed down by former generations," i.e., the Oral Law, consisted not of a series of lenient interpretations but of specifications and amplifications of the general statements of the Bible, as well as extrapolations of the commandments to situations not covered by the written word. All these the Sadducees rejected, and indeed their forebears had rejected parts of the Written Law itself.

It is generally agreed that the references to the Pharisees in *Antiquities*, XVII, 2.4 were taken by Josephus or his secretaries from a hostile source. At least their tone is inconsistent with Josephus' general attitude toward Pharisaism. Nevertheless, the specific assertions in this passage confirm the evidence already presented regarding the nature of Pharisaism. Josephus writes:

"For there was a certain sect of men that were Jews, who valued themselves highly upon the exact skill they had in the law of their fathers, and made men believe they were much favored by God. . . . These were they that are called the sect of the Pharisees, who were in a capacity of greatly opposing kings. A cunning sect they were, and soon elevated to a pitch of open fighting and doing mischief. Accordingly when all the people of the Jews gave assurance of their good-will to Caesar, and to the king's [i.e., Herod's] government, these very men did not swear, being above six thousand; and when the king [Herod] imposed a fine upon them, Pheroras' wife paid the fine for them. In order to requite which kindness of hers, since they were believed to have the foreknowledge of things to come by Divine inspiration, they foretold how God had decreed that Herod's government should cease, and his posterity be deprived of it; but that the kingdom should come to her and Pheroras, and to their children. These predictions were not concealed from Salome [the sister of Herod] but were told the king, as also how they perverted some persons about the palace itself. So the king slew such of the Pharisees as were principally accused. . . . He slew also all those of his own family who had consented to what the Pharisees foretold."

Once more, Josephus stressed the accuracy of the Pharisaic interpretation of the Law (in this passage, described as merely a claim on their part). Once more, too, we are told of their widespread influence, enabling Pharisees to defy a king. Apparently the writer held that they could be goaded into open fighting when resisted, but generally sought to attain their objectives through indirection.

The Pharisees could not recognize the kingship of Herod. He was one of the Idumeans, permitted to remain in their native land after subjugation by Hyrkan on condition they adopt Judaism as their faith. From the viewpoint of Pharisaic law, such forced conversion was no conversion, because it did not include the indispensable element of voluntary acceptance of "the commandments" (B. Yebamot 47a f.). Therefore, Herod was not really an Israelite, and could not under the provision of Deuteronomy 17.15 become king. Not surprisingly, the Pharisees were unwilling to swear allegiance to him.

The number of Pharisees doubtless was far greater than six thousand. The historian merely remarked that six thousand risked their lives in resistance to the oath of allegiance. Whether refusal to acknowledge the king justified martyrdom, may have been considered a debatable question among the contemporary Pharisees. At first Herod let them off with a fine paid for them by his sister-in-law, but in the end he slaughtered their leaders. In its essentials this story of Josephus was confirmed by the talmudic tradition (B. Baba Batra 3b).

Josephus' suggestion that the Pharisees had, or claimed to have, supernatural sight into the future, seems to come from a misunderstanding of their position. The Pharisees were certain that, violating the express command of the Torah, Herod's kingship would not endure, and that no child of his would inherit the throne. Such an assertion required no gift of prophecy. On the other hand, they may have assured Pheroras' wife that, because she was voluntarily an observant Jewess, her children might be eligible to the throne.

Finally, Josephus in *Antiquities*, XVIII, 1.2, returned to further analysis of Pharisaism and Sadducism:

"Now, as for the Pharisees, they live meanly, and despise delicacies in life; and they follow the conduct of reason; and what that prescribes to them as good for them, they do; and they think they ought earnestly to strive to observe reason's dictates for practice. They also pay respect to such as are in years; nor are they so bold as to contradict them in anything, which they have introduced; and while they hold that all things are done by fate, they do not take away the freedom from men of acting as they think fit; since their notion is, that it has pleased God to make a temperament whereby what He wills is done, but so that the will of men can act virtuously or viciously. They also believe that the souls have an immortal vigor in them, and that under the earth there will be rewards or punishments, according as they have lived virtuously or viciously in this life; and the latter are to be detained in an everlasting prison, but that the former shall have the power to revive and live again; on account of which doctrines, they are able greatly to persuade the body of the people; and whatsoever they do about Divine worship, prayers, and sacrifices, they perform them according to their direction; insomuch that the cities gave great attestation to them on account of their entire virtuous conduct, both in the actions of their lives, and their discourses also.

"But the doctrine of the Sadducees is thus; That souls die with the bodies; nor do they regard the observance of anything besides what the [Written] Law enjoins; for they think it a virtue to dispute with those teachers of philosophy whom they frequent; but this doctrine is received but by a few, yet by those of the greatest dignity; but they are able to do almost nothing of themselves; for when they become magistrates, as they are unwillingly and by force sometimes obliged to do, they addict themselves to the notions of the Pharisees, because the multitude would not otherwise bear them."

Once more a study of Pharisaic law and theology demonstrates that Josephus was not adapting the facts to the understanding of his Greek readers, but recording his observations. The preference of the Pharisees for "mean" living, that is, their contempt for luxury, was confirmed in *Abot of R. Nathan*, I (ch. 5, 13b) in a taunt quoted from the Sadducees. The assertion that the Pharisees "follow the conduct of reason," trying to discover its dictates, referred to their insistent study of the Torah. The Talmud was in essence an effort to apply "reason" to life, both in the interpretation of Scripture and where Scripture was silent on application of its basic principles. Granted the view that the Scriptures are the revealed word of God, and that man's life derives meaning from his service to God, the Pharisee's way of life was a Life of Reason.

The first of the petitions in his daily prayers was for "wisdom" and perception. However, the wisdom and perception were not to be artfulness or craft in search for the false goods of mundane life; but means to achieve the real, everlasting good of the eternal life with God.

The assertion that the Pharisees did not contradict their elders, applied even more emphatically to the Shammaites (whom we have already remarked Josephus regularly followed) than to the Hillelites. This seems obvious from *Abot of R. Nathan*, I (ch. 6, 14a) where the proper relation of disciple to teacher was explained in detail, and was ascribed to Jose b. Joezer, the first of the Proto-Shammaites.

The doctrine that man has a certain freedom of action, but that this does not interfere with Divine development of the world process is (as often remarked) identical with the positions articulated by R. Akiba (Mishna Abot 3.15).

We have seen that Josephus ascribed to all the Pharisees

doctrines he knew only from his earlier Shammaitic connections, and this was the case with his explanation that the sinful are subjected to everlasting torment in the future world, whereas the Resurrection is limited to the righteous.

Control of all Jewish religion by the Pharisees in the final generations of the Second Commonwealth was attested by the talmudic record (cf. Mishna Yoma 1.5, et al.). However, we have noted that the Temple ritual was conducted by Shammaitic rather than Hillelite principles, and that the Shammaitic principles themselves in some instances derived from priestly traditions to which the Sadducees had taken no exception and which indeed had been promulgated by Proto-Sadducees (see below, pp. 736 ff.).

The declaration that the "virtuous conduct" of the Pharisees was recognized by almost the whole community can only mean that in addition to their punctilious observance of the ritual the Pharisees translated the principles of the Torah into ethical norms and principles which won widespread approbation.

The description of the Sadducees in this passage by Josephus contained, beyond that found elsewhere in his works, only the reference to their disputations with the teachers of philosophy. By this phrase, Josephus seemingly meant the frequent arguments between contemporary Sadducees and the Pharisaic teachers in the final days of the Second Commonwealth. Some of these discussions have been preserved in the stories of their encounters with Rabban Johanan b. Zakkai (cf., e.g., Tosefta Parah 3(2).8, p. 631).

Having restated with some elaboration his concept of the opposing groups, Josephus suddenly added a fourth "sect" of Jewish "philosophers," namely, the Zealots and their predecessors in the later days of Herod. According to Josephus, this fourth sect faithfully followed the Pharisaic norms and rules of life. But unlike the Pharisees, this group had "an inviolable attachment to liberty; and say that God is to be their only Ruler and Lord. They also do not value dying any kinds of death, nor indeed do they heed the deaths of their relations and friends, nor can any such fear make them call any man, lord."

Josephus, pointedly identifying this "fourth philosophy" with the leaders of the final Rebellion of 66-70, sought to dissociate their movement from Pharisaism. The historian, aware in Rome of the edicts against the practice of Judaism, was impelled to distinguish from the rebels the main body of observant Jews. Perhaps he added the paragraph in question on request by the Jewish Commission, consisting of Rabban Gamaliel II, R. Joshua, R. Akiba, and R. Eleazar b. Azariah (see *Akiba*, p. 136). These scholars visited Rome and wished to impress on the Imperial government the distinction between Pharisaic practice of their faith and the warlike nationalism which had led to the rebellion against Rome. Loyalty to the Kingdom of God proclaimed each morning and night in the *Shema* and on occasion in other practices; inability to join in the deification of the Emperors; the rite of circumcision; the observance of the Passover; the carrying of *lulab* on Sukkot all could be interpreted as anti-Roman, but were not so in fact. They were merely expressions of the Jews' loyalty to the religion of their fathers which—above all—directed the use of reason in relations with fellow men.

Josephus may well have believed that it would help this important cause, vital for the survival of Judaism, to describe the Zealots and their predecessors under Herod as a "fourth sect," different from the Pharisees although, to be sure, agreeing with them in religious practice and beliefs.

The importance of this distinction became only too obvious as the Roman pressure on the Jews to abandon their faith increased, and ultimately led to the Rebellion of Bar Kokeba.

The description of the Pharisees in Josephus thus agreed fully with the implications of the talmudic writings. From both works the Pharisees emerge as a group which, accepting the Torah as the word of God and considering existence meaningful only so far as it provided opportunity for service to Him, adhered loyally to the rituals enjoined in Scripture. The Pharisees followed a series of norms in which the word of Scripture was elaborated. They studied the word of the Torah and indulged in continuous contemplation of the right, in an insistent search for the ethical life. They possessed a wide reputation for piety, tolerance, wisdom. This reputation clothed the Pharisees with enormous power used with remarkable self-restraint. They were loathe to impose punishment for crime, and when compelled by evidence to do so inclined toward leniency. They treated one another with great affection, and were generally mild and temperate to opponents. They despised present luxury, and sought instead to deserve future bliss. They realistically appraised the paradox of man's consciousness of freedom and of circumstances beyond his control, such as heredity and education, weighting his decisions. For generation after generation, this remarkable group—disciples of the Prophets—labored, studied, and taught in Jerusalem, to such effect that even Josephus (who had deserted their way of life) was stirred by profound admiration for the Pharisees and their achievements.

The material in the Introductory Note is essential, yet its inclusion meant considerable delay in publication. Nevertheless the new edition does not begin to discuss many issues which may be considered pertinent. So far as I can see these do not bear on the main theses of the book although they would be of interest. The additions might include analysis of the Hasidean liturgy and its development, showing the light it sheds on the theology and origin of Hasideanism, the relation of town and country in ancient Judea at various stages in its history, and the reconstruction of the judicial system of the Second Commonwealth before and after the Maccabean Rebellion.

In citing classical works, I have wherever possible, used standard translations, instead of replacing them with the originals which might be open to question. Thus for the Hebrew Scriptures I have used the Jewish Publication Society version. When available in the Loeb Classics Series I have in general used its translations. For the writings of Josephus not yet in the Loeb series I have used Whiston's translation where that did not seem manifestly impossible.

My discussion of the material from the Qumram literature is limited to that indispensable to the present argument, but scarcely attempts to exhaust all the implications for the history of Pharisaism.

Finally, while this book was in press there appeared Professor Saul Lieberman's historic contribution to talmudic studies: his *Tosefta Ki-Fshutah* on *Mo'ed*, of which many passages deal with issues raised in *The Pharisees*. I have taken note of some through corrections in proof. But through restrictions of time and space I was unable to do so with others. Thus the chapter on "The Customs of the Men of Jericho" is profoundly affected by his discussion of the sources in his commentary on Tosefta Pisha, chapter 3.19, ed. Lieberman, pp. 156 ff., and should be rewritten. In the course of proofreading itself literally hundreds of talmudic passages, hitherto enigmas to me seemed to become clear, and I would have liked to share these new insights with the reader. But to this process there is no end.

Rediscovery of the underlying principles of Hasideanism and its motivations is a difficult task and will require the labors of many scholars and students. I part from this book with the hope that it may prove a step in the right direction, bringing light to contemporary problems, and stimulating the pursuit of knowledge and wisdom in the unique treasury of Hasidean and Rabbinic thought.

Fifteenth of Ab, 5762
August 15, 1962

CHRONOLOGICAL TABLE

(of chief persons and events discussed in the book)

Date	Kings	Prophets	Events
		PRE-EXILIC PERIOD	
ca. 995–985	Saul		
ca. 985–955	David		
ca. 955–930	Solomon		
931–914	Rehoboam		
931–911	*Jeroboam		
912–872	Asa		
886–875	*Omri		
875–852	*Ahab	Elijah	
843–821	*Jehu	Elisha	
843–804	Jehoash		
805–790	*Jehoash		
804–776	Amaziah		
790–749	*Jeroboam II	Hosea, Amos	
734–734	Jotham		Syro-Ephraimitic War
733–722	*Hoshea		
734–715	Ahaz	Isaiah	Fall of Samaria, and end of Northern Kingdom
715–697	Hezekiah		Invasion of Sennacherib
697–643	Manasseh		
640–610	Josiah	Nahum	
		Zepahaniah	Restoration of the Law
		Jeremiah	Invasion of Necho
609	Jehoahaz		
609–598	Jehoiakim		First Babylonian Deportation
598	Jehoiachin		
598–587	Zedekiah	Ezekiel	

*Asterisk indicates Kings of Israel only . . . For the dates for the pre-Exilic period, I have adopted all those given by Mowinckel in *Die Chronologie der Israelitischen und juedischen Koenigen* (*Acta Orientalia*, X (1932), p. 271). For the later period I follow the chronology used in Margolis, M. L. and Marx, A., *History of the Jewish People*, Philadelphia, 1927.

Date	Kings	Prophets	Events
		EXILIC AND POST-EXILIC PERIODS	
562			Death of Nebuchadnezzar and accession of Evil Merodach
539			Conquest of Babylonia by Cyrus
538			First Restoration under Sheshbazzar
520		Haggai Zechariah	Zerubabel
515			Completion of the Second Temple
458			Return under Ezra
457			Mixed Marriages dissolved
445			Appointment of Nehemiah as Governor of Judea
433			Recall of Nehemiah to Persia
411			Destruction of Jewish colony at Elephantine, Egypt
334			Alexander the Great crosses the Hellespont
331			Alexander passes through Palestine
323			Alexander dies
ca. 250			Simeon II, the Righteous, High Priest
198			Victory of Antiochus III over Ptolemy at Raphia; Palestine passes into the power of the Seleucids
175			Antiochus IV succeeds to Seleucid Throne

Date	Events
168	Antiochus IV reduces Jerusalem; forbids practice of Judaism. Revolt of the Maccabees.
165	Rededication of the Temple
152	Jonathan, High Priest
142	Jonathan slain, Simeon becomes High Priest
135	Johanan Hyrcanus succeeds Simeon
103	Alexander Jannaeus becomes High Priest
76	Salome Alexandra, Queen of Judea.
63	Pompey enters Jerusalem
49	Break between Caesar and Pompey
39	Herod made King of Judea
ca. 30	Hillel and Shammai

AFTER THE CHRISTIAN ERA

Date	Events
37	Caligula, Emperor of Rome
41	Claudius, Emperor of Rome
	Agrippa I, King of Judea
50	Agrippa II
54	Nero, Emperor of Rome
66	Rebellion against Rome
69	Vespasian, Emperor of Rome
70	Destruction of Jerusalem, and burning of the Temple

JERUSALEM

New City or Bezetha
Castle of Antonia
The Temple
Herod's Palace
Asmonean Palace
Zion
Upper City
Akra or Lower City
Brook Kedron

0   500   1000 yards

PALESTINE
in Roman Times

Scale of miles
0   5 10   20   30

GREAT SEA
DEAD SEA

PHOENICIA
Coele Syria (Litani)
R. Leontes
R. Litani
Valley of Mizpah
Mt. Hermon
ITUREA
SYRIA
DAMASCENE

Gebal
R. Lycus
R. Magorus
Chalcis
Zidon
Zarephath
Zor
Hammon
Ramah
Caesarea Philippi (Panias)
Kedesh Naphtali
Waters of Merom
Merom
Akko
Gisch-halab
Seleucia
BASHAN
Giscala
Ramah
Gabara
Chorazin
Capernaum
Bethsaida
Haifa
Jodephatho
Rimmon
Sepphoris
Hazor
Magdala
Sea of Chinnereth
Gischala
Ashtaroth-Karnaim
Golan
Aphek
Gamala
GALILEE
Shihin
Nazareth
Mt. Tabor
Tarichaea
Dium
Magdiel
Endor
Dor
Megiddo
Plain of Shunem
Jezreel
Esdraelon
Yarmuk
Amatha
Gadara
Arbela
Caesarea
Hadad-Rimmon
Taanach
Mt. Gilboa
Gilboa
GILEAD
Pella
Jabesh-Gilead
Mahanaim
R. Cana
Dothan
Ramoth
Gibeah Asher
Succoth
Thebez
Gerasa
Apollonia
Samaria
Mt. Ebal
Tirzah
Ramoth-Gilead
Joppa
Schechem
Mt. Gerizim
R. Jabbok
Kaphar Saba
Rabbath
Lebonah
Alexandrium
Shiloh
Abel-Keramim
Ramathaim
Thimnathah
Phasaelis
Hadid
Jeshanah
Ophrah
Rabbah
Modein
Bethel
Rimmon
Beth-Aven
Lod
Beth-Horons
Beroth
Jericho
Ekron
Gezer
Gibethon
Michmash
Jamnia
Emmaus
Ramah
Anathoth
Gederoth
Kirjath-jearim
Mizpah
Jerusalem
Gilgal
Beth-haran
Ashdod
Hazor
Gath
Bethany
Timnah
Shemesh
Bethlehem
En-Eglaim
Ascalon
Mizpah
Socoh
Etam
Herodium
Mt. Nebo
Medeba
Eglon
Betogabri (Bet Jibrin)
Keilah
Bethzur
Hebron
Ataroth
Kiriathaim
Dibon
Gaza
Lachish
Tekoa
Machaerus
Ziph
Engeddi
Anab
Socoh
Carmel
R. Arnon
Raphia
En Rimmon
Jeshua
Rabbath Moab
Beersheba
IDUMAEA
Arad
Masada
Kir of Moab
MOAB
SAMARIA
JUDAEA
Wilderness of Judah
Plain of Sharon
Plain of Philistia
PERAEA
Mts. of Abarim
Pisgah
Zoar
R. Sared
GEBAL
Akrabbim
EDOM

THE PHARISEES

The Sociological Background of Their Faith

I. INTRODUCTION

This book is an attempt to present a comprehensive survey of the economic, social, and political factors which helped to determine the course of Jewish thought in the biblical and post-biblical periods. The method used is a commonplace of modern historical scholarship; it is only its special application which may seem to give it novelty or daring. Indeed, the groundwork for this study has already been laid in the brilliant investigations of a dozen eminent scholars.[1] Magnificent, however, as their contributions are, they remain inadequate, because it is impossible to understand any segment of Palestinian history thoroughly without reference to the whole. The underlying conditions of the country remained so nearly the same from generation to generation that the conflicts of the pre-Hebraic inhabitants are illumined by a correct understanding of Bible and Talmud; while, on the other hand, whole chapters of the Mishna can be interpreted properly only in the light of archaeological records fifteen centuries older than they.

Only when it is examined in the light of this reconstruction, does the prophetic and rabbinic literature become fully significant and intelligible. Follower of YHWH and worshiper of Baal, true prophet and false prophet, Hasid and Hellenist, Pharisee and Sadducee, Hillelite and Shammaite,[2] disciple of R. Joshua ben Hananya and of R. Eliezer ben Hyrcanus, of R. Akiba and R. Ishmael, of R. Judah ben Ilai and R. Simeon ben Yohai, of R. Jose and R. Meir —an apparent welter of names, of futile arguments, of obscure and occasionally even trivial hostilities—becomes

1

an interpreted and ordered struggle, prolonged through forty generations. The Talmud is no longer a chronicle of passionate futilities, but the record of intensely practical discussions; and even the scriptural text, viewed more closely, attains a new beauty and magnificence. The reader is able to correlate what was once an apparently arbitrary confusion of argument, which could interest only the erudite and the curious, with the problems which occupy the minds of thoughtful men today, and will continue to do so for centuries to come. The history which is revealed to us is as instructive for our social-minded generation as any other record of the past; and, by virtue of the strange rôle which these ancient groups have played in the development of human thought, even more fascinating.

The main thesis emerging out of this analysis is that the prophetic, Pharisaic and rabbinic traditions were the products of a persistent cultural battle, carried on in Palestine for fifteen centuries, between the submerged, unlanded groups, and their oppressors, the great landowners. Beginning in the primitive opposition of the semi-nomadic shepherd and the settled farmer, the struggle developed into a new alignment of the small peasant of the highland against the more prosperous farmer of the valleys and the plains. From the province the conflict was transferred to the cities, where it expressed itself in the resistance of traders and artisans to the nobles and courtiers. Finally, it appeared in the sanctuary itself in the bitter rivalry between Levite and priest.

The clash between the opposing groups of the Second Commonwealth and of the first centuries of the Christian Era was as significant, morally and spiritually, as was that between the prophets and their opponents, centuries earlier.

The formal issues changed; the fundamental differences remained the same. The social forces which had made the patrician landowner of the eleventh century B.C.E. desert the YHWH of his nomadic ancestors and worship the *baalim* of the earlier Canaanite agriculturists, and had driven his successors of the sixth century B.C.E. to imitate Assyrian and Egyptian manners, dress and worship, produced the Hellenist in the third century B.C.E., as well as the Sadducee and the Herodian of a later generation. Conversely, the follower of the prophet gave way to the Hasid, and the latter was succeeded by the Pharisee. When Pharisaism became practically synonymous with Judaism, the divisive forces made themselves felt within it, and there arose the two factions of Shammaites and Hillelites to struggle for the control of the party.

The division of these classes in life was, of course, far less sharply defined than can be indicated in the following pages. The student must use this discussion as he would a Mercator's map of the globe, making constant mental adjustment for the need of reducing the infinitely complicated facts of reality to the simplicity of words and paper. Throughout the analysis the response of the mass is recorded; that of the exceptional individual must, generally, be ignored, except where, as in the case of some of the most distinguished prophets, it affected the whole course of the normal social development. It is not that the individual, with his special idiosyncracies, is forgotten; it is rather that we have finally realized that he cannot be understood until the normal mass reaction of which he is part is fully analyzed.

Because of the fundamental polarity of ancient Palestinian economy and politics, the various social conflicts were usually lost in a single dichotomy, separating the nation into plebeians and patricians. Sometimes, however, the complications of the opposed and contrasted interests led to the growth of three, or four, or even more parties. Indeed the cross section of the sociological strata of Jewish Palestine during the last decade of the Second Commonwealth, presents the following complicated aspect:

I. JERUSALEM

Upper Classes	Lay Nobility	Generally Herodian[3] or Romanophile; sometimes Sadducean; perhaps a few Shammaitic
	Temple Nobility	Generally Sadducean; a few Shammaite
	Emancipated Women of these classes	Views unknown, probably generally assimilationist
Middle Classes	Lower Lay Patricians	Shammaitic, in the main
	Lower Aaronids	
	Emancipated Women of these classes	
Lower Classes	Levites (including Singers and Gate-Keepers of the Temple)	Hillelites
	Traders	
	Artisans	
	Women of these Classes	
Submerged Groups	Unemancipated Women	Culturally ineffective
	Paupers	
	Slaves	

II. JUDEA

Upper Classes	Landowners of Jericho	Apparently generally assimilationist or Romanophile
	Landowners of Coastal Plain and *Shefelah*	*'Am Ha-Arez*; sometimes Shammaite
	Provincial Priests	*'Am Ha-Arez*, sometimes Shammaite
Lower Classes	Farmers of Highland	Shammaite, Hillelite, Essene, Sectarian; *'Am Ha-Arez*
	Shepherds	Hillelite, Essene, Sectarian, *'Am Ha-Arez*
Submerged Classes	Women / Hired men on the farms / Slaves	Culturally Ineffective

III. GALILEE

Upper Classes	Large Landowners / Emancipated Women	*'Am Ha-Arez*, sometimes Shammaite; frequently Zealot
Middle Classes	Small Landowners / City Artisans and Traders	Usually Zealot, sometimes Sectarian
Submerged Groups	Unemancipated Women / Hired Farm-Workers / Slaves	Culturally ineffective

The division of classes in earlier times was doubtless simpler; and yet followed the same general pattern. How these various groups came to interact as they did, and the manner in which their activity led to the development of prophetic and rabbinic Judaism, are the problems which must concern us in the following chapters.

II. PALESTINE AND ITS DIVISIONS

The Mishna tells us of Palestine, that it was divided into three provinces, Judea, Galilee, and Transjordan (the Peraea of the Gospels).[1] Samaria, a beautiful and fruitful hill country, lying between Judea and Galilee, was never occupied by Jews and played no part in the development of their thought. Its people, descended in part from the Ten Tribes and in part from immigrants transplanted into Palestine by the Assyrian kings (ca. 700 B.C.E.), served the God of Israel and even accepted the Law of Moses. Yet they were bitterly hostile to the Judeans and at no time became united with them. Transjordan, too, important in early biblical days, the birthplace of Jephthah the judge and Elijah the prophet,[2] had sunk into cultural insignificance during the Second Commonwealth. However, it still was accounted part of Jewish Palestine; while Galilee and Judea, together with their capital, Jerusalem, which spiritually loomed larger than either and dominated both, constituted for the Maccabean a diversified and almost self-sustaining world.

Separated from this world by the distance of five thousand miles and the passage of twenty centuries, the modern student may regard it as a small, undifferentiated unit, an atom hardly capable of further division. To the contemporary Palestinian Jew, however, who compared his country not with the continents which are now familiar to us, not even with remote Babylonia and Persia, but with neighboring Edom and Tyre, it comprised within its ten

7

thousand square miles a "broad and goodly country" of varied climates, races, occupations and interests.

In the middle of the second century B.C.E., this tiny Jewish Commonwealth had, almost by a miracle, torn itself free from the huge Syrian Empire. Yet, within seventy years, it was destined to lie once more sick and bleeding, rent by internal conflict, a temptation to the next conqueror, Rome. The unity of the people, evoked by persecution and strengthened by the enthusiasm of unexpected victory, maintained itself only for a brief interval against the divisive forces inherent in the social structure and given freer play by the removal of external pressure. By a curious and inevitable paradox, the vehemence which had overcome internal division in the face of foreign armies was transferred to the social and religious struggles within the Commonwealth; so that the very force which alone had been able to bring victory was also fated to bring ruin. Like the virtuous maiden in the Arabian tale, Judea was herself destroyed by the magical fires which she had drawn from her inner being to conquer the evil genie. The astonishing result of the unequal struggle against Antiochus and his armies had transformed the belief in the truth and divinity of the Law not merely into a principle, but into a rigid system of Divine discipline which elevated the smallest minutiae of observance into passionate issues calling for the sacrifice of life and limb. Insignificant variations of rite and custom, born of irrelevant differences of life and environment, were given an exaggerated importance comparable to that of court etiquette and legal formality. The nation became partitioned into small groups each of which was firmly persuaded of its monopoly of universal truth, and was certain that the coming of the Messiah depended on the general acceptance of its beliefs. Fads became fetishes, congregations hardened into sects. This fanatical atmosphere gave rise to the ascetic Essenes, the anti-ecclesiastic New Covenanters, the Morning Bathers, the Water Drinkers, the Worshipers at Sunrise,[3] and, it is said, no less than a score of other tiny but determined sects and societies.[4]

Curiously, the only group among all of these which retained its poise and equanimity, which continued to be tolerant of opposition without and division within, was that of the Pharisees. Never has a religious sect been more open-minded.[5] They continued to worship at the sanctuary though a High Priest of the opposing group stood at its head. They permitted differences of opinion among their members and encouraged the preservation of variant rituals. Except during brief intervals of inflamed passion, neither of their factions attempted to foist its views on the other. "Both traditions are the words of the living God," was one of their fundamental norms.[6] "Although one group permitted what the other prohibited and one declared pure what the other declared impure, they did not refuse to prepare their food together or to intermarry with one another, fulfilling the verse, 'Love ye truth and peace.' "[7]

An unwritten law required both factions, the Shammaites and the Hillelites, to be represented in the government of the party and forbade the selection of the leader of the sect and his associate from the same group.[8] Indeed, the Pharisees attached such importance to this rule that when they achieved national power, they introduced it into the government of the Commonwealth and made bi-partisan control a cornerstone of their unwritten constitution.[9]

This tolerance is the more remarkable because it was combined with a deep passion for the Law. There have

been many periods in the world when people were broad-
minded regarding questions to which they were indifferent;
the Pharisees were almost unique in developing a liberal
attitude toward a problem which was the primary concern
of their life—the study and observance of the Torah. To
be wholeheartedly devoted to the truth as one sees it, and
yet to permit deviation from it in teaching and practice is
an attitude worthy of a modern scientist. Its occurrence
among the ancient Pharisees, and particularly among their
Hillelite faction, is doubtless to be associated with the
intellectual curiosity which was characteristic of their leadership. Whether their liberalism was the cause or the effect
of their intellectualism, or both were the results of some
more recondite force, cannot be definitely ascertained.

It was this paradoxical combination of religious passion
and intellectual objectivity which differentiated Pharisaic
tolerance from that affected by some of the Sadducees.
According to both Josephus and the Talmud, there were
many Sadducees who in their daily life observed the rules
of the Pharisees.[10] But this denial of their own principles
by the Sadducees cannot be considered true tolerance; it
was rather a result of their utter worldliness and lack of
interest in the issues which were of such deep concern to
the pious. The faithful Sadducee tended to be as narrow
and fanatical in his views as the members of any minor
sect.

The liberalism of the Pharisees and the indifference of
the Sadducees could not, however, bring about a union of
the two sects. The deep social clefts between the two parties
permitted no real meeting of minds. Natural topography
combined with man-made institutions to create differences

and stir up hatreds in the tiny Commonwealth. To appreciate the significance of these factors making for division, we must analyze the social structure of the various components of Jewish Palestine.

A. JERUSALEM

From the southern tip of a long plateau, ancient Jerusalem looked down on three sides into deep gorges, which made it quite inaccessible. Only from the North, across the range leading to Shechem and Samaria, can traders or armies approach the mountain fastness which David chose as his impregnable capital. The "sweet singer" and excellent warrior did not foresee the difficulties which his successors would have to overcome before they could contrive to transform the Jebusite village which he had elevated to the first place in Israel into a "gate of my people."[11] From a rural town, with threshing floors on its outskirts, Jerusalem became a busy market place in Josiah's day and, by the time of the Psalmist, was "As a city that is compact together" (Ps. 122.3). The temple-site which David bought from Arauna, the Jebusite, for fifty shekels of silver[12] (receiving as a gratuity the oxen that worked it) appeared to the Chronicler to be a bargain at six hundred shekels of gold.[13] Making allowance for the rapid decline in the value of silver, the enormous difference still gives eloquent and unimpeachable evidence of Jerusalem's growth from the days of its first king to those of the Levitical historian.

In this metropolis lived, at a conservative estimate, some 75,000 persons,[14] including the royal and high-priestly families, the great merchants, and the wealthy land-owning

nobility, who preferred the atmosphere and profits of court
and office to life on their own large rural estates, the Temple
priests, the lower Temple servants (i. e. the Levites), officials, traders, artisans, beggars, and slaves. Together they
constituted about one tenth of the country's population.[15]
But the influence of the city was entirely disproportionate
to the numbers of its inhabitants. Ever since the days of
David, the city had literally and figuratively towered over
its entire hinterland and had drawn to itself the most significant elements in the population. The men of wealth who
could live from the rent of their estates, the skilled artisans
who sought work, the clever traders who were ambitious
for gain, the poets, the writers, the singers, and the prophets
all drifted toward the Court, the Temple, and the metropolis. Micah, finding no response in his native Mareshah,
Jeremiah, wearied with the obstinacy of the men of Anathoth, both turned hopefully to Jerusalem. It was not only
the first of Judean cities; it had no real second. As in post-
war Austria, the entire urban population of the country
was practically concentrated in a single locality, a huge
head set with fascinating deformity upon a meager body.

In the period under discussion, the patrician and fash-
ionable quarter of Jerusalem was its higher, western mount,
which is separated from the lower, eastern knolls, by a deep
cleft, still clearly discernible, although centuries of sediment
have moderated its ancient declivity. In this cool and
breezy "Upper City," free from the odors and crowds of the
valley and the older eastern quarter, dwelt the rich of the
land, in their proud mansions, surrounded by their numerous slaves and enjoying the fear and respect of the multitude, no less than the luxuries of power and opulence. They
used gold bindings for the palm branches which they carried

in the festive Temple ceremonies of the Sukkot week;[16] and gold containers for the first fruits which they brought on Pentecost.[17] A special regulation was needed to prohibit them from covering their phylacteries with gold.[18] Such was their standard of living that when a widow of their class was given an allowance of two seahs (about eight gallons) of wine for the use of her household per day, she cursed the Court, saying, "May you make similar allowance for your own children." "And," reports one of the judges, "we answered 'Amen' to her wish."[19] It is said that this same lady paid Agrippa II three kabs (about three quarts) of gold dinars to obtain the High Priesthood for her husband.[20] Desiring to see him perform his most imposing service, that of the Day of Atonement, when it is forbidden to wear shoes, she had silk coverings spread over the streets from her house to the Temple Mount, so that she did not have to expose her bare feet to the soil.[21] The expense of maintaining a patrician household can be estimated from the fact that another widow was granted four hundred silver dinars (ca. $100) a day for her personal expenses.[22] There is good authority for the statement that when Vespasian was about to besiege Jerusalem, three of the city's nobles had stored away sufficient food to take care of the whole city for three years.[23] To this day the section of the city in which these aristocrats dwelt—approximately that now occupied by the Armenian and Christian quarters— has retained something of its ancient glory and shows marks of superior wealth and taste. In Maccabean times, it was a new part of the city, to which the patricians fled from the suffocating neighborhood of their humbler brethren. It was adorned by the Herodians with their great palaces, and during the last war against Rome (66–70 C.E.) was the haven of the aristocrats who, opposing the mutiny, fortified themselves within it and made occasional sallies against the lower city to force the submission of the rebels to recognized, pagan authority.[24]

The income of these patricians, the largest landowners in the Commonwealth, was derived in the main from their vast estates, which were worked by slaves and hired men or let to tenants.[25] "Who is a man of wealth?" remarked R. Tarfon, "he who possesses a hundred vineyards and a hundred fields and a hundred slaves to work them."[26] The ecclesiastics among this aristocracy received large perquisites, which in spite of their affluence they readily accepted and even eagerly sought.[27] Many of them, as well as the lay patricians, also engaged in "great commerce," i. e., import and export.[28] The difference between them and the plebeian traders corresponded exactly to that between the *emporoi* and *kapeloi* of the Egyptian papyri.[29]

The great valley which runs below these hills, cutting across the city from north to south, took its name (the Tyropoean) from the cheese-makers who were apparently its principal inhabitants. But it also provided room for other merchants and shop-keepers, for its southern end was apparently the center of the weaving trade.[30] It is recorded that as early as the seventh century B.C.E., Jeremiah, needing a potter, descended into this historic valley (Jer. 18.3). To the northeast of it arose the noble Temple Mount, while to the southeast lay the "Lower City" which, except for a few great palaces, was almost exclusively inhabited by Jerusalem's plebeians. The Hasmonean High Priests, desiring to be near the Temple, and perhaps also wishing to show their democracy, had built their homes there, and their example was followed by the famous Queen Helene, the Arabian proselyte who left her kingdom to live in Jerusalem. But aside from such exceptional structures, the section was given over, like the Tyropoean valley itself, to the slums of Jerusalem.

Here, in lanes so narrow that a camel laden with flax was in danger of having it ignited by the merchant's candle (litigation ensuing from such an occurrence is, in fact, discussed in the Talmud),[31] and in "houses" sometimes no more than twelve feet long and eight feet wide,[32] slept and labored the families of the artisans and traders. The available space was at most doubled by the common courtyard into which these tiny cells opened.[33] Frequently, however, the courtyard was so crowded that the pious householder had to be relieved from the duty of building a complete booth for the Autumn Festival and was permitted to assuage his conscience with a bower large enough to hold his head and his back.[34] Placing it at his door so that his table, his hands and his feet protruded into the house, he fulfilled the barest letter of the biblical commandment: "In booths shall ye dwell seven days."[35]

Except for the artisans of the Temple, who were well paid, some of the specialists among them receiving, it is said, as much as twelve minas (about three hundred dollars) per day,[36] the average wages of workers in Jerusalem were small. Usually they amounted to about one dinar (about twenty-five cents) per day, in addition to their food.[37] This was equivalent, in purchasing power, to about three-eighths of a bushel of wheat.[38] Some, however, did not receive even that much. It is recorded, for instance, that Hillel, who was later to become the foremost scholar in Israel, earned only half a *zuz* per day when he came to Jerusalem as an immigrant from Babylonia.[39] Under such circumstances, life could be maintained only at the lowest possible level. Bread and some cabbage, garlic or turnip, morning and night, meat once a week on the Sabbath day (for the more affluent)—was the usual fare.[40] A linen sheet thrown over the body served as covering at night; by many it was also used as clothing by day.[41]

While rich and poor lived in close proximity, they belonged culturally and socially to separate worlds from which neither made any effort to escape. Like the great landowners of the Middle Ages, the patricians of Jerusalem considered themselves particularly "noble"[42] and above mingling with the masses of the people. "This was the custom of the esthetically minded 'men of Jerusalem,'" we are informed, "they would not act as witnesses to a document unless they knew who the other witnesses were, nor would they sit in judgment unless they knew who the other judges were, nor would they accept an invitation to dinner, unless they knew who the other guests were."[43] Perhaps it was this snobbishness which made it necessary for them to adopt the Egyptian custom of repeating every dinner invitation on the day of the appointment.[44] In the carefully kept genealogical records of the Temple, the families of these patricians were especially noted as those into which priests might marry.[45] In their fear of plebeian contamination, the patricians generally preferred, however, to marry within their own clans.[46] So prevalent did the marriage of near relatives become among them that some of the plebeian sects, in their resentment, declared marriages between uncles and nieces nothing less than incestuous.[47]

It was entirely natural that these "men of Jerusalem" should be high-handed in their treatment of their employees and the traders who supplied their needs. When they appointed a chef to prepare a meal, a reliable authority informs us, they held him responsible for any contretemps which occurred and made him pay damages in accordance "with their social position and that of their guests."[48] A number of maxims current among them have been preserved, and are especially significant for their attitude of mind. "Do not resort to roofs," they said, "lest you fall into the sin of David; if your daughter has grown up and is still unmarried, free your slave and marry her to him; and be careful of the affection of your wife for her first son-in-law."[49]

Peculiarly enough, their consciousness of caste did not prevent them from engaging in activities of true philanthropy and humanitarianism. Even the most helpless was the recipient of some of their benefactions. When a dinner was served in one of their houses, a napkin was hung over the door to indicate that the poor were welcome to come in.[50] Both men and women organized themselves into charitable associations. The women devoted themselves more particularly to those activities which required a special degree of piety and humanitarianism. They provided for the needs of the boys who were raised with special care for their Levitical purity so that they might take part in the ceremony of the Red Heifer; and they provided the narcotic which rendered the criminal condemned to death less sensitive to pain.[51]

The poor artisan or trader bore no resentment against his wealthier neighbor, being resigned to his poverty and convinced that so wide a gulf of worldly circumstance could never be bridged. Since marriage customs, funeral rites, and festival observances could not be the same for him as for the owners of the spacious homes on the hills, his human self-respect compelled him to find a particular virtue in his own way of living. He was proud of his traditions and customs and determined to cling to them.

This pride was strengthened by the conviction of intellectual superiority. Contact with traders from all parts of Palestine and foreign countries had sharpened his wits and developed his powers of conversation. He had, indeed, social graces quite unknown among the gentry, whose life was spent in the unstimulating companionship of subjected wives,[52] intimidated children and brutalized slaves. If, like the barons of medieval Europe, the ancient Judean aristocrats affected to despise such humble arts as reading and writing, the artisan could, from the safe retreat of his narrow cell, return contempt for contempt. There were manual laborers who achieved a mastery of religious tradition and law, raising themselves, at least in the opinion of the majority class, far above the wealthiest of their neighbors. The absence of learning as a profession, subject to the temptations of an alliance with wealth, left the scholars or scribes of Palestine in the plebeian ranks from which they had sprung.

The contrast between the upper and lower classes in ancient Jerusalem had been noticed as early as the seventh century B.C.E. by Jeremiah, when he came into the capital city fresh from the simple, rural economy of Anathoth. When he found to his dismay that the traders and artisans among whom he had expected piety and devotion were expert business men intent on their own material advancement, he decided to turn to the rich for inspiration. "And I said: 'Surely these are poor, they are foolish, for they know not the way of the Lord, nor the ordinance of their

God; I will get me unto the great men, and will speak unto them; for they know the way of the Lord, and the ordinance of their God.' " Alas, he discovered that if the poor workers and merchants were wily traffickers, their "betters" "had altogether broken the yoke, and burst the bands" of religious faith and devotion (5.4 ff.).

The masses of Jerusalem thus presented a certain solidarity of opposition to the spiritual mastery of the nobility. Instead of accepting the manners of the patricians as the "respectable" standard, they actually sought—and in part successfully—to impose their own forms on the community. In earlier Jewish history, the plebeians had lacked both opportunity and desire for such self-assertion. Either they had lived in small communities, dominated spiritually as well as politically and economically by their "betters," or they had been scattered shepherds, inarticulate and few in number. Elijah the Tishbite, Amos of Tekoa, and a few anonymous writers had indeed impressed their personalities on wider circles than their immediate followers; but there was little hope for the dominance of plebeian culture until the rise of the urban center. The massing of the impoverished not by hundreds but by thousands gave them a community feeling and an ability to establish their own standards of worth which, in the end, affected also the higher strata of the population.[53] But, even more important, the struggle to maintain their cultural standards in the face of economic adversity developed in them that peculiar idealism and that purity of motive which transformed them into the spiritual mentors of the western world. While the prophets and sages were drawn, as we shall see, from all classes, the support which their teaching received in the slums of Jerusalem was the ultimate force which made for

the preservation and spread of their ideals. The market
place of Judea's capital became a dynamo of religious and
intellectual activity, producing light and energy for distant
nations and generations yet unborn.

The shift of power in Jerusalem itself was nevertheless
slow and uncertain because the receptivity of the patrician
landowners was naturally low. They were mostly wealthy,
ignorant and satisfied. Their social relations were mainly
with other large farmers, and prestige was reckoned in
acres and not in memorized texts. Some of them were
intimates of the governing officials—the Persians in their
day, and, after them, the Seleucids and the Hasmonean
High Priests. Such intercourse, however, implied neither
polish nor erudition.

The Temple hierarchy was perfectly at home in this
brutish society, for the priesthood was generally as unlettered as the rest of the nobility.[54] In the last Temple days,
when learning had achieved some standing, there were
High Priests who could not read the Bible. To make a sign,
instead of writing one's name, was so common among the
aristocracy that, like the use of the seal for the same reason,
it became a symbol of nobility. These priests cannot accu-
rately be described as the tools of the wealthy, for well-
authenticated records show that they themselves were
among the wealthiest of the people. "Most priests are
affluent,"[55] runs a rabbinic proverb of the Second Jewish
Commonwealth. The Legislator had indeed foreseen the
possibility of this development and had in vain prohibited
priests from holding land.[56] Ingenious interpreters had
found an escape from the injunction, restricting its application to the tribe as distinguished from the individual
members. In this way, it became inapplicable to their

own day when only two of the twelve tribes made up the Jewish Commonwealth. The obvious and farsighted intention of the prophetic teacher to prevent an alliance between the Temple hierarchy and the secular power was ignored. The priests seized the land and themselves became the wealthiest people in the country. Unfortunately for them, even the simplest and most credulous souls could not regard their wealth as the reward of their piety for, whatever their devotion to the ritual, they were grossly and shamelessly materialistic. Hence, it was said—and quite without irony —that their success came to them because of the Mosaic prayer, "Bless, O Lord, his possessions,"[57] in which the prophet was supposed to be speaking of the priests, the traditional "sons of Aaron."

While the priests were, in general, both economically and culturally, members of the patrician class, they had special interests of their own which divided them from the whole laity. They usually married within their own tribe[58] and tried to make it an absolute rule for the High Priest to do so.[59] When anyone offered to marry their daughters they demanded twice the usual marriage settlement.[60] According to Josephus, they refused to permit any of their number to marry a woman "who gained her livelihood through hawking or innkeeping."[61] Alone of all the Israelites, they would not countenance marriage to proselyte women or women who had had sex-relations with anyone who was "unfit for marriage into the priesthood."[62] Whether the "defilement" had occurred through marriage or otherwise made no difference. Indeed, if the wife of one of them was outraged, her husband might either divorce her or keep her; he could never again live with her. Even the slightest possibility of pollution was sufficient for them to insist on this rule. Zechariah ben ha-Kazzab, one of the foremost priests of Jerusalem, reports that when the city was taken by the armies of Titus, he remained with his wife throughout the period of murder, violence and rapine which followed. "I swear by the Temple," he cried, "that her hand did not move from mine from the time the pagans entered Jerusalem until they left it." But his colleagues refused to permit him to live with her. "No one can testify in a case in which he has a special interest," they replied.[63]

This pride of caste did not, however, prevent division from arising in their midst. A few of the wealthiest clans asserted a right to have the High Priest chosen from among their members. There was some historical basis for such a claim until the second century B.C.E. in the fact that the "high-priestly family"—there was only one in those days— was actually descended from Zadok, the first priest of Solomon's Temple. When the Hasmoneans ousted this early family because its members had become Hellenists, they or their clients invented a genealogy which made them Zadokides.[64] When, however, Herod came to power, he decided, in his eagerness to destroy the high-priesthood as a rival dynasty, to sell the office to the highest bidder and in fact gave preference to priests who could not possibly claim any ancestral privileges.[65] Yet in the course of time these new arrivals at the high-priestly dignity covered themselves, too, with the cloak of Zadok. They refused to mingle on terms of equality with the other members of their tribe; gave the highest offices in the Temple to their sons and their sons-in-law; and on occasion quarreled with the less affluent ecclesiastics about some of their perquisites.[66] There is some evidence that the most extreme among them, also, considered marriage outside their own families improper; and they certainly forbade their members to marry daughters of the laity.

Through these methods they reduced some of the other priests to poverty, so that in the last decades of the Temple we discover a small but significant priestly proletariat.[67] Even those, however, who escaped this complete impoverishment were conscious of the social ostracism which they suffered; it is probably this which drove many of them from the Sadducism which was natural to their tribe into the ranks of the Pharisees.

The true plebeians of the Temple were, of course, the propertyless Levites. They made common cause with the plebeians of the city and of the province and led the opposition against the patricians both in the Sanctuary and outside it. So powerful, however, was the caste system of the Temple, that these Levites themselves were divided into two classes: the "singers" and the "gate-keepers." The different offices descended by inheritance from father to son; and so sharp was the cleavage between them that when once a "singer" approached a "gate-keeper" and offered to help him at his work, the latter cried out, "Go back; you are a singer; and a singer who closes the gates commits a capital offense!"[68]

In spite of this apparent acceptance of aristocratic standards, the Levites were, undoubtedly, an effective force in spreading the ideal of human equality and liberty of thought among the people. If Jerusalem became the Holy City of the world, that was due not to the Temple and the priests, but to the Levites and the scribes.

B. The Provincials*

However much the inhabitants of Jerusalem disagreed among themselves, they were at one in the natural contempt of townspeople for the provincial.[69] The division between the inhabitants of Jerusalem and the rest of the country became evident as early as the ninth century B.C.E. The historian of the period says significantly that, after the revolt against the usurping queen Athaliah (ca. 835 B.C.E.), "all the people of the land rejoiced and *the city was quiet*" (II Kings 11.20). The words imply—what is also indicated in the story of what preceded the coup—that the restoration of the rightful heir was received joyously in the country but rather resignedly in the city.[70] A hundred years later Isaiah speaks regularly of "the inhabitants of Jerusalem and the men of Judah,"[71] as though the two different groups were, in his eyes at least, of equal importance. Jeremiah, whose special interest in the tribe of Benjamin might have led him to distinguish it from the rest of Judah, also accepts the earlier division of the Commonwealth into metropolis and province (7.34). A native of the country, he consistently mentions Judah before Jerusalem while Isaiah, the city-bred prophet, always gives priority to the capital.

The increased importance which came to Jerusalem in the Second Commonwealth sharpened the opposition between it and the country. The patricians of the city, proud of their urban sophistication, their governmental or hierarchal connections, and the superior wealth which enabled them to retire from active farm-life, regarded their former neighbors, who still followed the team and the plough, with pitying condescension.[72] The plebeian craftsmen and merchants of Jerusalem, though poor and landless, shared

* Cf. Supplement, pp. 754-761.

this feeling entirely. With singular opprobrium, both classes applied to the provincial the term '*am ha-arez*, meaning literally "people of the soil."[73] In pre-exilic times, this term had, strangely, been one of honor and distinction. The country squires, for whom it had been coined, had been a powerful class in the community. They formed the backbone of the militia and paid the bulk of the taxes. From the ninth century B.C.E. on, they seem to have formed a definite corporate body with recognized rights, privileges, and powers, enjoying the respect as well as the fear of the larger community. The princes and the nobles who lived in the capital frequently managed to lead them, but always had to reckon with them. Their loyalty to the Davidic dynasty was one of the main bulwarks of its strength, and their fanatical nationalism led to the repeated revolts against Assyria and Babylonia which terminated in the destruction of Jerusalem. In the fourth and third centuries B.C.E., however, when the Jewish Commonwealth was merely an unimportant dependency of the great Persian or Seleucid Empires, military service brought no glory and payment of taxes gave few privileges. The '*am ha-arez* were no longer honored as a powerful body but rather despised as brutish individuals. As the standards of patrician wealth and plebeian learning rose, the gentry, whose possessions were limited and whose learning was nil, sank progressively in the esteem of the townsmen. The expression '*am ha-arez* became, like the English word "villain," first a term of disparagement, then of opprobrium, though, to be sure, in another sense. Similarly, the English word "boor" and the Yiddish corruption "*poyer*" (meaning, simply, "dunce") are associated with the term *Bauer*, which in German has retained its honorific implications;

and the expressions *pagan* (derived from the Latin *paganus*, meaning "villager") and *heathen* (from the root "heath") are reminders that long after Christianity had made its way in the towns, the countryside remained unconverted. The expression *'am ha-arez*, passing through a similar development, had by the beginning of the Common Era come to mean nothing more than "ignorant." It is in this sense that, for instance, Hillel (ca. 30 B.C.E.–20 C.E.) uses it, when he says, "The brutish cannot be God-fearing nor can the *'am ha-arez* (the ignorant) be saintly."[74]

In addition to the ordinary contempt which any metropolitan might feel for an unsophisticated farmer, the men of Jerusalem found an impassable religious barrier set up between the provincials and themselves in the Levitical laws of purity. These laws were established in Scripture for the whole community but, in practice, came to be observed only in Jerusalem and its environs. Consequently, the whole nation, except those living in or near Jerusalem, was Levitically impure. Since an impure person contaminates any vessel or food which he touches, natural social relations between the two groups were impossible.

Yet the inhabitants of Jerusalem themselves must have realized that these laws could not be observed outside of the capital. The Law declares a person defiled by the simplest and most natural acts and occurrences. The proximity of a dead body, a cemetery, contact with the carcass of an animal, seminal issue, sexual congress, sitting on a mat previously used by a menstruous woman—these, and many other similar "accidents," defiled one. Some of these defilements were removed by the comparatively easy ceremony of ritual bathing, but others required nothing less than a visit to the Temple and the elaborate ceremonies of sacrifice or the sprinkling of the ashes of the "red heifer."[75] Since even a pious peasant could hardly be expected to undertake the difficult and arduous donkey-ride to Jerusalem whenever he had visited his ancestors' graves or attended a funeral, most of the country population was continually impure.

However, in Jerusalem, where the laws were easily observed, they were held in the highest regard. There must have been some feeling among the people that they had a hygienic as well as a religious value; and, indeed, there is a strong resemblance between the precautions against impurity prescribed in the Talmud and those against infection prescribed by modern science.[76] In a semi-tropical country a human corpse is one of the foremost sources of disease and those touching it are rightly separated from the community for a time. There is similar danger in persons suffering from various sexual diseases. The person "with a flow" was a potential focus of infection, and the Legislator wisely cut him off from the community until he was healed.[77] Significantly, he was required to bathe in "living" rather than in still waters. Such precautions might be superfluous in sparsely populated villages, but they were essential to the welfare of Jerusalem's many thousands. They were particularly important at the Temple, where people gathered in such numbers that on festival days its courts were filled to utmost capacity. Indeed, on the Passover eve, the courts would be crowded and emptied three times before the crowd of pilgrims had been accommodated.[78] Under such conditions, the Levitical laws were no longer mere ceremonial rites; they were rules of health which prevented each festival from leading to an epidemic. By one of those strange primitive intuitions which continually surprise us in the study of ancient manners and habits, the men of Jerusalem knew that the Levitical laws were means not only of serving God but of protecting man. Whatever excuse might be offered for him, the *'am ha-arez*, who neglected these laws, came inevitably to be regarded not only as intellectually debased but religiously impure.

The *'am ha-arez* was also "suspected" of violating another commandment of Scripture. The biblical law, as interpreted in the Second Commonwealth, placed two taxes of ten percent each on all agricultural products of the country. The first tithe was for the support of the Levites, the second belonged to its owner but had to be consumed in Jerusalem.[79] Like all other people, the peasants of Palestine disliked taxes, whatever their purpose, and most of them declined to give the first tithe to the Levite or take the second to Jerusalem. Just how they reconciled their inaction with the explicit commands of Scripture, as laid down in Numbers (18.21 ff.) and Deuteronomy (14.22 ff.), need not concern us. To the men of Jerusalem the failure to give the tithes seemed a patent denial of the authority of the Torah; it was simply heresy.

No less objectionable from the sophisticated urban point of view was the continued adherence of the provincial to his ancestral superstitions. It is significant that long after the Baal worship had apparently disappeared from Israel, the field which was watered by rain was still called *Bet ha-Baal*, the territory of Baal, to distinguish it from the *Bet ha-Shelahim*, the field which was watered by irrigation. In later times, the use of this name was entirely innocent, of course, like our use of the names of pagan deities to designate the days of the week. Yet there can be no doubt that in both instances the evidence of language proves the survival of primitive thought in the minds of the people, long after they had officially been converted to the dominant religion.[80] The expression *Bet ha-Baal* was especially incongruous in talmudic Judaism, because the Hasidim and their followers, the Pharisees and the rabbinic sages, considered it forbidden to mention the Baal, and frequently replaced it with the word *Boshet* (shame) even in the text of Scripture!

But more important than this archaic reference to the Baal as the source of rain and fertility was the preservation of various "Amoritic" superstitions among the provincials. Among these were such practices as the carrying of bones of the dead as amulets, pouring out wine and oil on festive occasions, and especially at the reception of honored guests, and the recognition of certain days as being ill-omened.[81]

Finally, the peasant neglected all ceremonies in which writing was involved. The biblical commandment, "And thou shalt bind them for a sign about thy hand, and they shall be for frontlets between thine eyes"[82] was taken literally in Jerusalem, where pieces of parchment containing four special chapters of the Torah were inserted into phylacteries (*tefillin*) and worn about the arm and forehead, especially during prayer. Similar scrolls were inserted into little receptacles and attached to the door-posts in accordance with the prescription of Deuteronomy 6.9 and 11.20. But the peasant could neither read the scrolls nor write them. As a result, he knew nothing of phylacteries or door-post inscriptions (*mezuzot*).[83]

The absolute enforcement of the laws of purity would not only have cut Jerusalem off from the rest of the country,

but would have ruined its commerce and probably precipi-
tated civil war. A compromise was of necessity arranged
and, since the country folk near Jerusalem were regarded
as generally observant, they were declared pure. An imagi-
nary line was drawn about Jerusalem at a distance of about
fifteen miles, through the village of Modin. Beyond that
point, the peasants were considered suspect in regard to
purity; within it, they were trusted. This led to a peculiar
but necessary paradox in the law. The Mishna states it
with the utmost frankness: "On the hither side of Modin
the peasants are trusted regarding the purity of their earthenware; beyond it they are not trusted. Thus it happens
that when a potter selling his pots passes Modin on the
way to Jerusalem, though he and the pots are the same as
before, they are now considered pure; if they return past
the line of Modin, he is no longer to be believed in regard
to their purity."[84]

Greater liberality was shown in connection with the
produce of the field. Most peasants, wishing to retain as
large a market for their crops as possible, would garner
them "in a state of purity." At least, this was true in
Judea. Hence, throughout the province of Judea, though
not in Galilee, the farmers were trusted regarding the purity
of their wines and oils.

These compromise regulations prevented the differences in practice between Jerusalem and the provinces
from developing into a major schism. The fact remained,
however, that except within a short distance from the capital or at special times such as the vintage or harvest, the
ritual prescriptions which deeply affected life in Jerusalem
were absolutely ignored. Esoteric as the whole system of
Levitical purity seems to us, a large part of the religious

life and thought of the observant Jew was occupied by it. No less than one-sixth of the Mishna[85] is devoted to a discussion of its minutiae. Such was the respect which these regulations enjoyed among the inhabitants of Jerusalem that, even after the destruction of the city, they continued to adhere to them. For those families who moved in groups to smaller villages, this entailed perhaps no extraordinary hardship. But most of the former inhabitants of the city were scattered after the year 70 C.E. in towns and hamlets where they formed a small minority. Observance of the rules of ritual purity meant separation from next-door neighbors, refusal to mingle freely with fellow-villagers, the loneliness of pedantry and snobbishness—all added to the pains of poverty in a strange environment. Yet, many preferred these sufferings to abandoning their ancestral customs and to the adoption of the less vigorous Levitical customs of the country.

One of these devoted ritualists had the presence of mind to save the ashes of the last "red heifer" when the city of Jerusalem was taken by the Romans and its Temple burned. No new heifer could be sacrificed after the fall of the Temple, but the ashes of the last one were preserved for no less than 200 years. As late as the third century C.E. the scholars still "performed the purification ceremony" in Galilee.[86] When we recall that during those centuries the Jews passed through the aftermath of the war against Vespasian, the rebellion of Bar Kokeba and the persecutions of Hadrian; that they lost not only their Temple and their capital but also the whole of the Judean province; we can readily appreciate the devotion necessary to preserve these "ashes of the red heifer." There is something intensely pathetic in the thought of these poor people, driven from their ancient city, struggling to adjust themselves to a new life and, withal, insisting almost with their last breath upon saving a peculiar ritual from the grinding jaws of devouring Time.

After the fall of Jerusalem the *'am ha-arez* could no longer be distinguished from the cultured by his habitat. The destruction of Jerusalem had made peasants or, at least, small townsmen and villagers of all its people. A new touchstone was needed to mark off those who could be trusted in matters of ritual purity from those who were suspect. The first thought that suggested itself to the scholars of the day was that the observance of the minutiae of Jewish law, which had become usual in Jerusalem and was disregarded outside, might serve as a test. "Who is an *'am ha-arez*? R. Eliezer says, 'He who does not read the *Shema'* morning and night.' R. Joshua says, 'He who does not wear the phylacteries.' Ben Azzai says, 'He who does not wear fringes (*zizit*) on his garment.' "[87]

Such signs could, however, merely distinguish, but not separate the pure from the suspect. In the painful proximity which their common defeat had brought to both classes, the bitterness, which had been only partly expressed before, broke out into open and intense hostility. Signs of violent hatred for the city man on the part of the *'am ha-arez* are not lacking even before the year 70 C.E. Indeed, Christianity owed its origin in part to the unpopularity of the city people among the peasants who confused the social grace of the trader with dissembling and hypocrisy.[88] But the vehement excoriations of Jesus against the Scribes were mildness itself compared with the almost savage ferocity which the *'am ha-arez* of the following century felt for the cultured group. Toward the end of the first century, R. Eliezer remarked, "If the *'am ha-arez* did not

need us for the purposes of trade, they would slaughter
us."[89] Another teacher maintained that "the hatred which
the 'am ha-arez bears towards the scholar is greater than
that which the pagan bears towards the Jew." R. Akiba,
whose first forty years were spent as an ignorant shepherd,
but who ultimately became one of Israel's greatest scholars,
said, "When I was an 'am ha-arez, I used to say that if I
had a scholar I would bite him like an ass."[90]

This animosity between country and city, between
ignorance and letters, can be duplicated in many ages and
lands.[91] In ancient Palestine, there was added to natural
fear and dislike of one another the passion engendered by
the cruel opposition of their common enemy, Rome, as well
as by differences of religious observances and degrees of
patriotic emotion. The country gentry had been in the van
of Jewish nationalism and had suffered most in the recurrent
repressions under the Herodians and the Romans. Their
lands had been confiscated and divided among the flunkies
and flatterers of the conquerors. Their families had been
impoverished. Their children had been sold into slavery
or driven into exile. Their leaders had been tortured, cruci-
fied and thrown to the lions. From a lofty station many
of them had been reduced to the lowest rungs of the social
ladder. In their suffering they had not even the mitigating
solace of their countrymen's respect. The Romans hated
them for their nationalism and the scholars despised them
for their ignorance.

The bitterness of their lot was aggravated by the venom
of envy. They begrudged the scholar not only his superior
pretensions and his joy in study but the respect which he
received from the Romans. R. Johanan ben Zakkai had
convinced the Romans of the pacifism of his colleagues and

disciples. He had been able to save not only those who had actively striven for peace and mediation but even such bitter nationalists as R. Eliezer ben Hyrcanus and R. Gamaliel, the son of a leader of the rebellion.[92] Many a country squire who had been robbed of his land must have wondered what virtue there was in learning to save its possessor not only from a cruel death but even from the general seizure of property.

Hate evoked hate. The scholar, who had merely despised the peasant when he was at a distance, found him unbearable in close proximity. His boorish ways, his uncouth manners, his narrow chauvinism, his lack of ideas, and his small-talk made his company galling to the more sensitive. In addition, the scholar was painfully aware of the malice which the peasant felt towards him. "Six rules are laid down in regard to the 'am ha-arez," according to one authority. "They are not to be asked to act as witnesses; they are not to be permitted to testify; secrets are not to be entrusted to them; they may not be appointed as trustees for the estates of orphans; they may not be appointed as trustees of charity funds; they may not be permitted to escort one on one's way."[93] Another authority maintains that an 'am ha-arez should be forbidden to eat meat.[94] One great teacher, R. Meir (ca. 150 C.E.), says, "Whoever marries his daughter to an 'am ha-arez might as well bind her before a lion. Just as a lion tears his victim to pieces and then consumes him, so the 'am ha-arez beats his wife and then takes her into his embrace."[95] Another authority remarks with vigor, "A man should sell all he has and marry the daughter of a scholar. If he cannot find the daughter of a scholar, let him marry the daughter of a leader of the people. If he cannot find one, let him marry the daughter of a head of the synagogue. If that too be impossible, let him marry the daughter of a distributor of charity-funds or of a teacher of children. But let him, under no circumstances, marry the daughter of an *'am ha-arez*, for the *'am ha-arez* is despicable, and his wife is like vermin, and to his daughters may be applied the verse, 'Cursed be he that lieth with any manner of beast'!" (Deut. 27.21).[96]

During a period of famine, R. Judah the Prince (ca. 200 C.E.) opened up his granaries and announced: "Let the students of Scripture or of Mishna or of Tradition or of codified norms or of ethical sayings enter and eat: but let not any *'am ha-arez* come in!" One of the disciples of the academy, feeling that the distinction was unjust, forced his way into the presence of the prince and said, "Master, feed me." R. Judah said to him, "Hast thou read Scripture?" "No," replied the student. "How then can I feed thee?" cried the Master. "Feed me like a dog or a raven." After he had fed him, R. Judah, on whom the lesson had been completely lost, was heard to moan, "Alas, that I have given of my bread to the *'am ha-arez.*"[97]

A contemporary scholar, R. Yannai, one day found a stranger in the synagogue and, noticing his scholarly appearance, immediately invited him to his home. After the meal, he requested his guest to say grace. Unfortunately, the stranger's scholarship was limited to his mien and bearing, but did not extend to a knowledge of the Law or ritual. "I am unable to say grace," he said humbly. "Say it after me," continued the haughty and indignant R. Yannai, and then he pronounced the words: "A dog has eaten the bread of Yannai." Bitterly hurt, the poor peasant said, "I have never had the opportunity of studying.

But once an itinerant preacher passed through our town and from him I heard a verse which I remember well. The Scriptures say, 'The Torah was commanded us by Moses, the inheritance of the community of Jacob' (Deut. 33.4). It does not say 'the inheritance of the community of Yannai,' but 'of Jacob.' Your learning is not yours at all but mine!"[98]

Could it have been to prevent the 'am ha-arez from seizing such useful crumbs of knowledge that scholars discouraged study in their presence? One of them remarks, "To study before the ignorant is like violating a man's betrothed in his presence."[99]

The hostility which developed between the 'am ha-arez and the scholar after the destruction of Jerusalem, and particularly in the third century, throws light on the tendencies already at work during the earlier period in which we are now primarily interested. During the second century B.C.E., when the Second Commonwealth was approaching the heyday of its glory, the vicious feelings of hatred lay, however, in the unborn future. The fundamental social division in the country was not of learned and unlearned, but of rich and poor. In Jerusalem which, like most cities, contained extremes of both wealth and poverty, this distinction necessarily obscured all others. Only when the people had lost all their property and become equally destitute, did the minor distinction of scholarship emerge into notice. Before that, men were far more ready to be dazzled by gold than by wise sayings. The 'am ha-arez still looked to the patricians of the metropolis for guidance in both spiritual and cultural affairs. He knew their contempt for his simplicity and unsophistication, but he accepted it, desiring deep in his heart to emulate them. His great hope was that one day he or his son or his grandson would join the

ranks of the courtiers in Jerusalem. The English squire
of the eighteenth century could not have felt greater awe
for "his lordship" and "her ladyship" than did the Palestinian farmer for the high-priestly nobles of his metropolis.

C. JUDEA

The *'am ha-arez* was not a uniform class. Wide differences of wealth and culture separated the dwellers of the
highland country from those of the lowland, and the inhabitants of Judea from those of Galilee. Left to themselves,
however, these country people would never have developed
any social conflict analogous to that which rent the citizenry of Jerusalem into mutually hostile halves. For while
the extremes of their rural society were far enough apart,
there was no particular point at which the social structure
was especially weak and liable to break. There was a
smooth, imperceptible gradation from the wealthiest farmer, with his many acres and herds, to the poorest peasant
whose stony ground barely provided the meanest necessities
of life.

It was only the dominion of Jerusalem over the spiritual life of Judea, similar to that of Athens over Attica,
which transferred into the peaceful, static villages the
bitter conflict which had arisen in the city. While the large
landowners looked to the patrician priests of Jerusalem
for religious guidance, the plebeian farmer, hardly distin-
guishable from the serf, depended upon the humble Levite
and the lay artisan-teacher. Simple, naïve and unsophisticated, these peasants, men of the soil, were ready to receive the imprint of the first teacher who ministered to
them. They were beneath the attention of a priesthood

more concerned with Temple ceremonial than with service
to the people. Happy indeed was the farmer if the aristocratic priest accepted his offering; to ask for religious guidance and consolation in return would have been presump-
tuous. It thus came about that, throughout this period,
the small, plebeian farmers followed the rites current among
the merchants and artisans of Jerusalem's slums, while
the aristocracy of the capital clung to the rural habits
which they had inherited from their ancestors.

This result, inevitable in any event, was intensified by
the peculiar development of Palestinian land-ownership.
From the earliest recorded period onward, it appears that
plebeian farmers occupied the stony, comparatively unpro-
ductive hill-country while the lowlands were held by the
patrician clans.[100] This had been true in the days of the
Judges when the plebeian Israelites who remained loyal
to the traditions of the wilderness, handed down from their
ancestors, inhabited the mountains and plateaus while the
richer farmers of the valleys became assimilated with the
Canaanites.[101] It was no less true during the Second Commonwealth. The lowlands of Jericho and En-gedi, famous
throughout the ancient world for their balsam, their date
palms, their semi-tropical climate, and their general fertility,[102] as well as the almost equally productive plain of
Ludd, were controlled by the foremost patricians of the
Commonwealth.[103] It was in Jericho that a number of
small farmers—probably the last survivors of impoverished families—were compelled to transfer the title of their
estates to the Temple, in order to escape expropriation
by wealthier neighbors.[104] From Ludd came such rich men
as R. Eliezer ben Hyrcanus and R. Tarfon.[105] The highlands
were inhabited by a poorer and hardier folk. Even to

this day, the inhabitants of the Judean hills are among the poorest of the country's peasants. While the farmers of the fertile valleys produce enough from the soil to keep them during the winter and the whole year, the "highland-ers" are frequently compelled to enter the service of others during the winter months.[106]

So complete was the difference between the two groups that they considered themselves derived from different tribes. The "highlanders" claimed descent from Judah, the lowlanders from Benjamin.[107] The wealth of these Benjaminite lowlanders explains the prominence of their tribe during the Second Commonwealth. The writer of the Book of Esther, for instance, wishing to describe Mordecai as an aristocrat, traces his descent to Benjamin.[108] The author of Psalm 68 declares that "young Benjamin there rules them"; and only afterward mentions "the princes of Judah" (v. 28). At the beginning of the Christian Era, Paul, the Apostle to the Gentiles, announces himself as a Benjaminite.[109] A hundred years later, R. Simeon and R. Meir, the representatives of patricianship in the School of R. Akiba, [110] espouse the cause of the Benjaminites, and claim that the Temple as well as the grave of Rachel were within the boundaries of that tribe.[111] And finally, about the year 200 C.E., we find R. Judah the Prince, foremost in his generation both in wealth and learning, boasting of his descent from that ancient tribe.[112] It is hardly credible that this tribal separation could have been preserved had not descent from the tribe of Benjamin implied social distinction.

It is noteworthy that R. Judah, the representative of the plebeians in the School of R. Akiba, denies that the Temple was situated on Benjaminite territory. Loyal to his tribe of Judah, he claims that its eponym, Judah the son of Jacob, was, alone among the ancestors of the twelve tribes, buried in the cave of Machpelah.[113] This was, of course, strenuously denied by R. Meir, who declined to grant Judah any preëminence not specifically accorded him in Scripture. It is equally illuminating to find R. Meir, the warm defender of the rights and prestige of the tribe of Benjamin, also lenient with regard to the festival observances on the farms. While R. Judah forbids a lowland farmer to water his *Bet ha-Baal* during the festival week, since it presumably can thrive on rain water, R. Meir, representing doubtless the traditions under which he was raised, holds that it is permitted.[114]

The accumulated evidence thus points to a social as well as a cultural conflict between the Judean hill country and the lowlands. This explains the sustained resistance of the lowland farmers to the plebeian influence, even after it had become dominant in the highland.

D. GALILEE

As we move northward from Jerusalem across the country of the Samaritans, we come to the luxuriant plain of Jezreel, and rising out of that into the beautiful mountains of lower and upper Galilee. This fertile land, stretching back from the plain of Tyre toward the east, bordering on Phoenicia and Syria, had always remained half pagan. Isaiah (8.23) had called it the "Galilee of the Gentiles" and as late as the time of the Maccabees[115] its Jewish population was a small minority. The early Maccabees conquered it and peopled it with men from Judea. We may take it that, as in other conquests, its lands were divided among the powerful warrior aristocrats of Jerusalem and their affiliated squires of the country, the 'am ha-arez. It thus became quite common for patricians to own two or more estates in the various provinces; and, indeed, the talmudic records refer, without special comment, to men who had properties in Judea and Galilee, with a wife and a household in each locality.[116] After the conquest of Titus, it was possible for some of the "men of Jerusalem" to leave the southern province and settle permanently in Galilee, where their holdings lay waiting to receive them.[117]

The culture of Galilee was, thus, from the beginning dominated by the patricians of Jerusalem, whose manners in turn derived largely from those of their ancestors—the provincials of Judea. But whereas the patricians who resided in Jerusalem were in the course of generations somewhat affected by its metropolitan influence, the Galileans remained from the beginning to the end bucolic. The 204 Galilean cities which Josephus mentions[118] were not towns in our sense of the word. They were mere hamlets and villages, like the "cities" which the Talmud describes as belonging to individual owners.[119] There were, however, in his time a few larger communities, like Sepphoris and Tiberias.[120] In these towns there were markets, tradesmen, artisans, craftsmen, who took care of the technical and commercial needs of the province. There were also wealthy men who had moved from their farms to these larger settlements to enjoy the social life of the city. These urban settlements thus became miniature Jerusalems with their own provincial patricians and plebeians. Yet, being far away from the metropolis, the inhabitants of these towns naturally followed the customs, rites and institutions of their province. Thus the social conflict which shook the capital and passed from it into Judea did not reach Galilee for a long time. And when it did arrive, it had lost its original form. It was no longer primarily a struggle of the plebeian against a patrician group of customs. The issues had become doctrinal and political. The plebeians of the north were unwilling to accept the social habits of Jerusalem, but they became the devoted followers and ultimately the most indefatigable missionaries of the plebeian faith and pacifism.

III. SOME TYPICAL VARIATIONS OF CUSTOM

At the beginning of the Christian Era, Judea and Galilee were divided from each other by a number of customs, most of which were astonishingly unrelated to the geographic or economic characteristics of the two provinces. It will be simple to show how all of these started as conflicts between the rich and poor in Jerusalem and were transferred from there to the hinterland. The Galilean forms are invariably what we might expect from metropolitan patricians of the day whereas the Judean countercustoms could have arisen only among urban plebeians. The Talmud does state that the "men of Jerusalem" generally agreed with the Galileans but we must not infer from this statement that *all* the inhabitants of Jerusalem followed the customs attributed to Galilee. Such a condition would be altogether inexplicable in view of the social configuration of the country. The record becomes intelligible only when we consider the fact that ancient texts, like modern writers on fashion, speak of a city as though it contained nothing but elevated classes and that by the "men of Jerusalem" our sources actually mean the patricians and "society" of the day![1]

A. MARRIAGE CUSTOMS

In a country which recognized plural marriage and where a man was expected to purchase his wife from her father, bachelorhood and celibacy were not infrequently the enforced lot of those who were kept out of the market

43

by poverty. Even when there was, so to speak, no com-
petitive bidding and the woman was as anxious as the man
for marriage, the folk-demand for appropriate payment
stood as an impassable wall between them. Just so today,
under totally different conditions, the iron conventions of
the proper home to be set up and the insistence on other
standards of social caste stand in the way of apparently
feasible and sensible marriages. So grievous and widespread was this evil that the saintly writer of the *Testaments of the Twelve Patriarchs* (ca. 100 B.C.E.) takes cognizance of it and seeks to reconcile the penniless artisan
to celibacy by depicting an ideal prototype for him in Issachar, the patient, laboring husbandman, "the strong ass,
crouching between two burdens" (Gen. 49.14) of Jacob's
blessing. Issachar is made to say, "Therefore when I was
thirty-five years old, I took to myself a wife, for my labor
wore away my strength and I never thought upon pleasure
with women; but, owing to my toil, sleep overcame me."[2]

Simeon ben Shattah (ca. 70 B.C.E.) did endeavor to
remedy the evil in part by substituting for the customary
purchase price a nominal marriage token with a note of
indebtedness for the rest, payable at the dissolution of the
marriage through death or divorce. Such a note could be
executed by the poorest, provided the wife accepted it.
Slight as this change seems, it required the consent of the
Sanhedrin, for it involved a complete revolution in Jewish
marriage forms. Hitherto, the bride's father had executed
the marriage deed, which was in effect a bill of sale, transferring to the chosen husband the full rights over his daughter. The change meant that the marriage contract was to
be drawn up by the suitor who, on becoming the husband,
assumed definite legal obligations toward his wife.[3]

While this ordinance removed an important bar to marriage, it did not meet all the difficulties. The artisan, who no longer had to pay cash for his wife, still had to find means to support her and, when there were no prospects, could as little think of marriage as before. In the talmudic annals, we meet men like R. Akiba and Ben Azzai who attained mature age before their economic condition permitted them to marry. Even in maturity, neither of these could have taken unto himself a wife, had not the bride promised to support him.

Yet there were many fathers anxious to give their daughters in suitable though impecunious marriage and many women who, living under the paternal roof, would have preferred the pains of poverty to the solitude of celibacy. The urge of life was too strong for the inherited custom and the new fashion developed of taking the husband into the bride's house instead of requiring him to set up a house for himself.[4] This change doubtless arose first in the poorer sections of the city and only then spread to the neighboring farmlands and Judea's highland. This expedient seems simple enough to us. But that is only because for us marriage has become merely a symbolic ceremony. What we regard as ritual and ceremony was living reality to the ancients. The man seeking a wife had first to propose to her father, pay the now nominal purchase money, and draw up the marriage contract.[5] This, however, constituted merely the "betrothal" (*erusim* in Hebrew), an option, as it were, preventing the maid from being married to anyone else. She still remained with her father's family till her husband was ready to receive her. The usual length of a "betrothal" was a year.[6] During this time, she was considered married to her new lord and infidelity was punishable as adultery. She could not be freed without a formal writ of divorcement and, if the husband died, she automatically became the betrothed of his oldest brother. However, she might not live with her husband till he had taken (*nasa* or *lakah*) her to his house, thus completing the marriage. Her removal from her father's to her husband's house was the occasion of a nuptial celebration, quite different in spirit from the purely commercial act of the original betrothal. Much hardihood must have been required for the early Judeans to substitute for the traditional taking of the wife to the husband's house the inverse tradition of accepting the husband into the wife's family. We may be sure that it was not done in the "best" families. Where it was done, the woman was considered still not properly married; she remained "betrothed" (*arusah*) until the husband could take her to a home of his own. The law, however, taking cognizance of the customary facts, says, "He who eats at his father-in-law's house *in Judea* cannot after marriage charge his wife with loss of virginity, for they are frequently together in private."[7]

The spread of this habit necessarily made even the most traditional and respectable relax in their rigor. Hence, in Judea the betrothed were permitted to remain together "for a time before they were brought into the nuptial chamber in order that his heart may be attracted to her." This was particularly reasonable because both the husband and the bride were of mature age. In Galilee, however, such pre-marital privacy was considered unseemly.[8]

In rich homes and in rural districts the husband's father was expected to build a "marriage home" for his son in which the young couple could live.[9] For the poor inhabitants of Jerusalem's crowded slums this was, however, out of the question, and the newly married couple had to spend their first nuptial night in the same room with the other members of the family. Even when a special room was available for them, they were expected to find place for the two groomsmen, one chosen from the bride's family and the other from the husband's. In Galilee, this custom did not prevail and the bridal pair were allowed full privacy on their wedding night.[10] The exhibition of delicacy on the part of the Galileans is especially remarkable because in general they were far less modest and refined than the Judeans.[11]

B. The Widow's Rights

It was impossible for a woman of ancient Palestine to maintain an independent livelihood, except in urban communities. In the country, people could exist only in some relation to the farm; they were either owners, the children of owners, slaves, tenants or hired workers. A propertyless man might indeed wander about the country, seeking to win his bread, without legal relation to the means of production. In biblical times, such persons, half-paupers, half-itinerant workers, were apparently common. They were classified as *Ger* (literally—*stranger*)[12] and corresponded roughly to the English vagrant or rather to the American hobo. In the later times, of which we are speaking, the growing city life of Jerusalem had absorbed most of these homeless rovers. Still, neither in biblical times nor afterward would a woman have been permitted to enjoy even this wretched form of independence. She had to be wife, daughter, or slave; she could not cut herself loose from some relation to a man and a family. When, therefore, in the rural districts, or among the aristocrats who followed the

peasant custom, a man died, his wife (or wives) continued
to live in his home and be supported as before. Hence the
marriage contract of the aristocratic land-owning families
read: "You shall remain in my house and be supported
from my properties as long as you remain a widow in my
house."

This is recorded in the Mishna as the custom of the "men
of Jerusalem" and the "men of Galilee."[13] The Judean
formula provided for the widow's support only until the
heirs might choose to pay her the dower, which was fixed
in the marriage contract. This rule was obviously based
on the usage of plebeian Jerusalem, where a woman could
find work and with the two hundred *zuz*, which constituted
the normal dower of a virgin, even set herself up in some
small business.

C. PRAISE AND PANEGYRIC

To the countryman it seems that the homes and daily
intercourse of the artisans and traders are infected with
the disingenuousness brought from the market place.[14]
This contempt of the farmer for the townsman is not altogether undeserved. Urban charm and social grace too
readily degenerate into obsequiousness and duplicity;
what passes for good manners and urbanity sometimes
turns out to be nothing more than the technique of deception. From the polite to the politic is an easy and almost
imperceptible descent. Both habits have their roots in
the city and in the nature of its merchant life.

The ingenuousness which characterized the farmer class
of ancient Palestine is reflected even in the cautious eulogies

which were part of the funeral rites. It would have been considered almost as unseemly to exaggerate the virtues of a dead friend as to expose his faults. Among the city nobility, as on the farm, words were accepted at something like their literal worth; to degrade them was as wicked as to falsify other standards and measurements. Hence we find stated in the name of R. Judah, "in Jerusalem, only the merits attained by the deceased were recited at his bier; but, in Judea [following as usual the custom of the plebeians] both those virtues which he had and those he lacked might be attributed to him."[15]

Convincing evidence that the custom attributed to Judea in our records really had its origin in the market place of Jerusalem, may be found in the similar disagreement regarding the praise to be bestowed on a bride at her wedding. The Shammaites, who were admittedly the richer group of the Pharisees, say, "every bride according to her virtues," but the Hillelites, as free from the bonds of literalness at weddings as at funerals, say, "every bride may be described as comely and charming."[16]

The Galilean custom with regard to extravagant eulogies is not recorded; but we may be certain it was that of Jerusalem's aristocracy. This conjecture is rendered the more plausible because in other respects the Galileans adopted the funeral rites of Jerusalem rather than those of the Judean countryside. In both Galilee and Jerusalem it was customary, for instance, to recite eulogies *before* the funeral at the house of the deceased; in the Judean villages that was done *after* the funeral, at the grave. Hence, people of Jerusalem and Galilee would say, "Attain merit *before* thy bier," while those of Judea said, "Attain merit *after* thy bier."[17]

The fact that the Galileans accepted this particular custom of Jerusalem shows how thoroughly they were dominated by the culture of Jerusalem's nobility. Their own needs in this instance definitely coincided with those of the Judean villages, where cemeteries were located within easy approach and the funeral services were most naturally conducted at the grave. It was otherwise in Jerusalem, where the size of the city and the fear of defilement forced people to set aside cemeteries at a considerable distance. Since most friends of a deceased person could not follow his body to the burial ground, it naturally became customary to recite the eulogies at the home before the funeral procession. This reason did not at all apply to the Galilean villages; and yet they accepted the habit of Jerusalem.[18]

The social charm of the plebeians, evident at critical occasions in life, such as marriages and funerals, was further exhibited in their observance of the usual amenities of greeting and discourse even in times of bereavement. The farmer, unused to conversation in general, could hardly be expected to rally his wits sufficiently to be conversational under the stress of overwhelming grief. Hence, the Judean mourners would readily greet those who came to comfort them as the guests entered and departed; whereas the Galileans considered even this modicum of social intercourse a mark of disrespect to the dead.[19]

D. The Paschal Festival

The Passover festival begins on the fifteenth day of the first Hebrew month (Nisan) and extends until the twenty-first day. The paschal lamb, which is eaten on the eve of

the first festival day, must be slaughtered during the afternoon of the fourteenth day of the month. In commemora-
tion of the ancient custom of the wilderness, this day was
generally observed as an additional holiday by abstention
from work.

Jerusalem, however, while acknowledging the sanctity
of the day, could not give it the status of a complete festival.
The influx of pilgrims more than doubled the population
of the city[20] and the needs of the visitors forced artisans
and tradesmen to remain at work.

Thus necessity gave birth to custom and the population
of Jerusalem worked until noon on the fourteenth day. As
usual, the custom spread from Jerusalem's market to the
whole Judean province so that "in Judea they would
work until noon but in Galilee they would do no work
at all."

Here, too, we discover that the patrician Shammaites who
had neither shops nor trades agreed with the Galileans,
while the Hillelites of rural Judea showed themselves much
more sympathetic to their fellow plebeians of the city.
The Mishna tells us that "during the night the Shammaites
prohibit all work while the Hillelites permit it—even in
places where it is prohibited during the day—till the rise
of the sun."[21] These two traditions leave no doubt that
the Hillelites, accepting the inevitable, were willing to permit
work in all places on the night preceding the sacrificial day;
while for Jerusalem's markets, the indulgence was extended
until the next noon. The patrician Shammaites and the
Galileans, leaning on the full law of festivals, forbade labor
not only during the day but also during the preceding
night.

E. The Purity of Olives

The olive, which grows readily almost anywhere in Palestine, was especially cultivated in Galilee.[22] In crowded Judea, with its smaller allotments, the soil could not easily be spared for this extensive form of cultivation. But on the hill slopes and in the valleys of spacious Galilee, there was room enough for the wide-spreading roots of the olive tree. "It is easier," says a rabbi of the second century, "to raise a legion of olives in Galilee than a single child in Judea!"[23] The olive trees of Gischcala were famed throughout the land and exaggerated tales of their productivity are told. The biblical verse, "As for Asher, his bread is fat and he yields royal dainties"[24] was applied to them. The olive came to be for Galilee what the vine was for Judea and the date for Arabia.

So great was the patrician partiality towards Galilee that this favorite fruit received special consideration in the Shammaitic legal decisions. The rigorous laws of Levitical purity on which the Shammaites laid so much stress at other times were relaxed; as, indeed, they had to be if any Galilean oil was to be recognized as pure. The Galileans, living in a land at best semi-Judaized, and so far from the Sanctuary, had never submitted fully to the biblical laws concerning Levitical defilement. According to the letter of the Law, they were all, like the Jews of the diaspora and like all Jews living today, permanently impure, and whatever they touched was defiled. Fortunately, the Law did not require them to be pure. It merely forbade them to enter the Temple or partake of holy food in the period of their impurity. Being in Galilee, they could in any event do neither, but whenever any one of them planned to undertake a pilgrimage, he had to prepare himself for purification.

The impurity of the Galilean became, however, a problem in its social aspect; whatever food he touched shared his defilement and could neither be eaten by the pure nor used for sacrifice.

Wise legislation had mitigated the impracticability of the law by providing that no fruit could receive defilement unless it had been moistened since the time of plucking (Lev. 11.38). The farmer's problem was then merely to keep liquid away from his olives or grapes or grain which could then remain uncontaminated for a long time. But, whereas he could save his products from water and other extraneous moisture, how was he to keep their own juices from breaking through the thin epidermis and exposing them to impurity? The Galileans solved this problem very conveniently: they held that the juice of an olive did not render the fruit liable to pollution.

This arbitrary but economically essential interpretation of the law was held by the Shammaites to apply to olives but they declined to extend it to other fruits, like grapes. When Hillel asked Shammai to explain this contradiction, the reply he received was equally illogical and human: "If you anger me, I shall declare the olives also impure."[25] The commentators of the Talmud, worried by this admitted inconsistency, have endeavored in vain to discover an acceptable legal reason for the Shammaitic position. None, however, can be found, for the ruling was based on necessity, not on reason. The Shammaites merely sanctioned the necessary habits of Galilee, where it was impossible to procure Levitically pure workers to garner the olives. They saw no need for extending the principle to wine, the product of Judea, for in the southern province, within easy reach of Jerusalem and the Temple, Levitically pure workers could be found for the vintage. Yet even in Judea the restriction added to the trouble and cost of the vintage. It need not surprise us therefore to find that the Hillelites, as sympathetic towards the Judean grape-growers as the patrician Shammaites were to the Galilean olive producers, should have maintained that "he who gathers grapes for the wine-press does not expose them to defile-ment through their own juice."[26]

F. The Day of Atonement

The tenth of Tishri ended the period of the New Year celebration not only among the Jews, but among many other Syrian peoples. But whereas for other nations it served as an occasion for wild merry-making, with general wine drinking, and obscene sex-ceremonies, it was for the Jews a Day of Atonement, of grave and serene contempla-tion, of mutual forgiveness and reconciliation, of abstinence from food and drink, from the wearing of sandals, from the use of ointment, and from marital congress. It was not a season of grief or sorrow. On the contrary it was a festival, during which mourning was forbidden. But it was a festival celebrated "after the manner of the angels," its joy was purely spiritual, with nothing sensuous or earthly contam-inating it.

The lofty aspirations of the Lawgiver and the sages in fixing the form of this festival could hardly, however, pre-vent the intrusion of some influence from the surrounding world. Both in patrician Jerusalem and in provincial Galilee we find vestiges of the widespread pagan agricultural vintage festival,[27] which marked the day for the neighboring peoples. Behind the Temple solemnities of ritual and sacrifice, of self-denial and prayer, R. Simeon ben Gamaliel II (ca. 170 C.E.)[28] reveals to us a chaste, attractive and wholesome picture of vineyard celebrations and country dances with maidens breaking through their coyness and calling on the youths to join them. "There were no days in Israel more festive than the fifteenth of Ab or the tenth of Tishri; for then the daughters of Jerusalem, garbed in white borrowed garments (so as not to embarrass the poor) would dance in the vineyards. What did they say? 'Young man, lift up thine eyes and see what thou choosest.' " The charm of the invitation seems to have been held in careful check, for the text continues: "Pay no regard to comeliness; think rather of the family."

The scene and its setting are rural. The participants are the aristocrats of Jerusalem, for pride of family intrudes incontinently into the picture.[29] The celebration, placed in vineyards rather than elsewhere, is unmistakably associated with the vintage, marking its beginning about the middle of Ab and its end early in Tishri.

Such was the social significance of these festivities that each vineyard was expected to have a large vacant space set aside for that express purpose. It was called the *mahol* or the dancing-place. Grave scholars disagreed regarding the necessary size of the *mahol*, with the patrician Shammaites allowing a plot 24 cubits (48 feet square) while the plebeian Hillelites were satisfied with about one-half that area.[30]

Perhaps the graver festivity arranged by the High Priest for his friends after completing the service at the Temple on the Day of Atonement had some kinship with these jollities. The Talmud supposes that the High Priest rejoiced merely in "having come forth from the sanctuary in peace."[31] Yet the solemnity of the day would seem to make actual festivities out of place. We can only assume that in the patrician minds and hearts of the High Priest and his friends there lurked vague memories of earlier rural times when the religious fast was combined with agricultural festivity.

To the patricians of Jerusalem, the momentary reversion to rural type and the release from daily conventions were attractive enough, even without food or drink, which were forbidden because of the public fast. In Galilee, however, the combination of fasting and festivity was inconceivable. "There is no joy except in meat," a sage who was akin to the provincials remarked.[32] Since banqueting on the Day of Atonement was impossible, the Galileans took pleasure and penance in turn. They feasted on the ninth of Tishri and fasted on the tenth.

The custom spread from Galilee to Babylonia, where huge banquets were arranged for the ninth of Tishri.[33] Even in our own time, observant Jews mark the day with a special holiday dinner. The origin of the custom has long been forgotten; and it is generally explained that the additional food is intended as a preparation for the next day's fast. But this interpretation is utterly unacceptable. Had the dinners on the ninth of Tishri been merely prophylactic, they would have been as customary in Judea as in Galilee. Yet the Mishna explicitly states that the custom was known only in Galilee.[34] Furthermore, the sages, in several generations, had to warn the people to stop their feasting well before dark, lest they violate the Day of Atonement.[35] Indeed the Torah itself, as if cognizant of the possible infraction of the Fast, stresses the fact that the Day of Atonement begins at nightfall. "In the ninth day of the month at even, from even unto even, shall ye keep your Sabbath" (Lev. 23.32). Since all Jewish festivals begin at dusk, this unique reminder must have some special purpose: apparently it is intended to offset the temptation to engage in agricultural frivolity into the night of the ninth of Tishri.

It is quite inconceivable that such heavy banquets would be nothing more than a preparation for the fast day. It would be far more natural for the day preceding the great Fast of Atonement to reflect something of the morrow's solemnity and spiritual concentration. An additional course or two at the final meal might be forgiven; but the origin of the general feasting must be sought in the celebration from which arose also the primitive vineyard pageantry of patrician Jerusalem.

The superlative genius of the talmudic sages as religious guides and teachers enabled them to transform the ninth of Tishri from a day of mere frivolity into one of charity to the poor, confession before God, and mutual forgiveness and reconciliation among men.[36] The custom of banqueting was retained; and yet the day was covered with a solemnity hardly inferior to that of the Day of Atonement. Before entering on the meal, the Jew was required to recite the confession of his sins, in the afternoon prayer; and the gravity of this service carried over to the feast itself. "The confession," reads an ancient record, "should properly take place at dusk (immediately before the beginning of the Day of Atonement), but the sages commanded that one should confess before one eats, lest the meal confuse one's mind."[37] No child could fail to be deeply moved when, the meal over, he heard his father, still under the influence of the solemn afternoon prayer with its confession, reciting, in a low voice.

the Grace after Meat. The words, "Blessed art Thou, O
Lord, our God, who dost feed the whole world with goodness, with graciousness, with lovingkindness and with
mercy," repeated so frequently throughout the year, assumed a new meaning on the eve of the Day of Atonement.
Few eyes remained dry as these words were spoken; few
hearts could escape the sense of complete dependence on
God and of the common hope and fate of all mankind, and
indeed all creation, which the simple phrases conveyed.
It became literally true that "he who ate and drank on the
ninth of Tishri received as much spiritual elevation as if
he had fasted on both the ninth and tenth days."[38]

G. Eating the Meat of Fowl with Milk

Biblical Law, as is well known, prohibits the seething
of a kid in its mother's milk.[39] Maimonides was the first
to suggest that the reason for this prohibition was the
desire of the Scriptures to suppress a Canaanite custom
which made the seething of the animal in its mother's milk
a religious ceremony, based, doubtless, on the superstition
that this improved the fertility or milk-producing powers
of the mother.[40] Maimonides' hypothesis, which twenty-
five years ago was rejected as preposterous by so eminent
an authority as Sir James Frazer,[41] has recently been most
remarkably vindicated by the discovery of the Ras es-
Shamra inscriptions, which for the first time actually record
the Canaanite practice of seething a kid in its mother's
milk as part of the worship of the pre-Israelite inhabitants
of Syria.[42] So abhorrent was this particular custom to
the teachers of Judaism, that they supplemented the prohibition of the practice by declaring meat of a kid seethed in

its mother's milk forbidden to eat. Yet the practice, like other superstitions, persisted among large sections of the provincials. Fearful of giving offense either to the God of Israel by seething a kid in its mother's milk, or to the gods of the Canaanites by not doing so, the simple provincial sought escape in a compromise. He seethed the kid in milk, but not in that which came from its mother. If he was particularly careful, he would substitute a calf for the kid, and cow's milk for that of the goat. But these devices helped him very little. The interpreters of the Law, alert to the danger of syncretism, and determined to wipe out the last vestiges of superstition, would accept no compromise. They extended the prohibition to include milk of other goats than the mother of the kid, and finally also to include the meat and milk of all cattle, and indeed of all mammals.[43]

This rule did not, however, end the controversy, for the provincials resorted to the scheme of cooking the meat of fowl with milk. The sages of Jerusalem thereupon declared that the law against seething a kid in its mother's milk applies also to winged fowl, though these produced no milk.

The interpretation was accepted in Judea; but half-pagan Galilee resisted it. Its provincials could not be induced to yield the last retreat into which they had been driven, and without which the superstition could not survive at all. Hence we find that as late as the second century C.E., the Galilean sage, R. Jose,[44] permits the use of fowl with milk, although all his colleagues forbid it.[45]

It is noteworthy that in this instance, too, the Shammaites gave evidence of some sympathy with the Galileans. Although the Shammaites did not actually permit the use of the milk with the meat of fowl, they considered it permissible to serve cheese on the same table with fowl, provided the same person did not eat both. But the Hillelites held that "they could neither be eaten nor served together."[46] The pertinacity of the sages in tolerating no compromise with regard to the Canaanite custom suggests that their objection to it had deeper foundations than opposition to superstition and paganism as such. It is altogether probable, as Philo suggests,[47] that they saw something particularly repulsive, cruel and barbarous in seething the offspring of an animal in the milk of its mother. They recoiled from the thought of permitting such a custom to survive in any form. So completely has this interpretation of the Law been accepted among the Jews, and so great was the influence it has exerted on the Jewish mind that to this day the prohibition against eating meat with milk is considered binding by all observant members of the faith; indeed, there are millions who, having eaten meat at one meal, will not drink milk or eat butter or cheese until the next meal, at least six hours later.[48]

Any single example of a sympathetic bond between the aristocracy of Jerusalem and the peasantry of Galilee might be attributed to chance.[49] The accumulation of these indications establishes, I believe, a logical relationship. Similarly an organic rapport is revealed between the artisans and traders of the city and the poorer farmers and peasants of the Judean table-land; a division which is highly significant for the development of Pharisaic and rabbinic thought, as well as for early Christianity.

IV. THE CUSTOMS OF JERICHO

The culture of Jericho like that of Galilee was completely dominated by the patricians. But whereas the patrician masters of Galilee were upper-class Pharisees or Shammaites, those of Jericho were of the still higher assimilationist nobility. Hence it came about that on a number of issues the "men of Jericho" rejected the Pharisaic teaching. Six of these issues are recorded in the Mishna.[1]

A. THE FOURTEENTH DAY OF NISAN

As we have seen, the fourteenth day of Nisan was observed as a full festival in Galilee and among the Shammaites of Jerusalem; and even the artisans of Jerusalem refrained from work on it after midday. But the assimilationists saw no reason for observing the day at all. They had to submit to outward recognition of those festivals on which the Scriptures commanded them to rest; but they declined to abstain from their usual business on a day which was sanctified by nothing more binding than ancestral custom. Hence the Mishna records that the men of Jericho "continued to graft their palm trees throughout the day."

B. THE OMISSION OF THE RESPONSE TO THE SHEMA'

The second custom peculiar to the "men of Jericho" was the omission of the response to the *Shema'*. How this textual variation in the service originated, and why it was considered sufficiently important for the permanent record of our Mishna, are questions which can be answered only by reference to earlier history of Jewish worship.

The introduction of the *Shemaʿ* into the Temple service may be described without extravagance as one of the most significant events in Jewish ecclesiastical history. It marked the most important victory within the walls of the Sanctuary of the adherents of "simple" worship over the lovers of the costly and the ornate. The battle between these groups, originating with Israel's entrance into Canaan, had been carried on for more than a millennium. During all that time the prophets had inveighed against a system of worship which permitted the rich to approach God more closely than the humble. The teachers of religion[2] had tried to substitute prayer for sacrifice, and as early as the Book of Samuel had declared that "to obey is better than to make offerings."[3] Some of them had even denounced the sacrificial system, declaring it unworthy of Israel's God.[4] But whatever might be their success with the people, they were without authority in the Temple itself. Supported by the combined influence of tradition and foreign example, the priests had resisted any change in the inherited forms. Such, moreover, was their vested interest in the sacrificial system, that it seemed impossible that they should ever be converted to an even partial acceptance of the plebeian view. Yet the scribe succeeded where the prophet had failed; and a High Priest was to lead the movement to supplement the sacrificial ceremonies with a call to study and the love of God.

The changed attitude of the hierarchy was due entirely to the influence of Simeon the Righteous (ca. 230 B.C.E.), the ablest of all the High Priests who presided over the Second Temple. In him, for the first time in its history, the

Temple had a governor who believed in the primacy of the intellect.[5] "Judaism," he used to say, "has three bases, study, ritual, and philanthropy."[6] Holding this principle, and aided by a Great Assembly of priests, patrician leaders, and plebeian scholars, which he convoked,[7] he compelled the other ecclesiastics to make the reading of the Scriptures a preliminary to their daily worship.[8]

The ceremony was conducted each morning in the Chamber of Hewn Stones, where later in the day the Sanhedrin met to discuss questions of Jewish law and leadership.[9] As was altogether appropriate, the service opened with a benediction of thanks to God as Creator of Light. This was followed by the recitation of the Ten Commandments. It was then that the *Shema'*, Deuteronomy 6.4–9, was read. Its touching and mellifluous cadences effectually summarized the Jewish "duties of the heart." "Hear, O Israel: the Lord our God, the Lord is One. And thou shalt love the Lord thy God, with all thy heart, and with all thy soul, and with all thy might. And these words, which I command thee this day shall be upon thy heart; and thou shalt teach them diligently unto thy children, and thou shalt talk of them when thou sittest in thy house, and when thou walkest by the way, and when thou liest down, and when thou risest up. And thou shalt bind them for a sign upon thy hand, and they shall be for frontlets between thine eyes. And thou shalt write them upon the door-posts of thy house, and upon thy gates."

The selection of the passage betrays the hand of the master thinker, and must probably be attributed to Simeon himself. The first verse was admirably suited to become, what Simeon may have intended it to be from the beginning, a confession of faith in the God of Israel. Nowhere else in Scripture are the elements of universalism and particularism in the Jewish conception of God expressed so completely or so forcefully.[10] God is declared to be One, the Ruler of all mankind, but He is also "our God," the God of Israel. No wonder that it became customary to respond to this verse with the cry, "Blessed be His glorious Name forever and aye," as though it were a formal benediction. The remainder of the passage was equally powerful and effective. It called on the hearer to "love" God, making religious observances a matter not merely of habit, but of devotion and loyalty. And finally, it emphasized in words of unique force and strength the abiding duty of study and teaching. Thus the priest was to be reminded daily of the wider significance of his routine duties, and of his permanent obligation to be a student and a guide, within the Temple and outside of it.

Once established, this ceremony was inevitably adopted also by the synagogues. The duty of knowing God and loving Him, of studying the Torah and teaching it, was too near the hearts of the synagogue leaders for them to forgo such an opportunity for stressing it. And especially since they considered their prayer ritual analogous to the sacrificial system of the Temple, it seemed quite appropriate that they should begin their service with the readings used by the priests. Ultimately the *Shema'* became so popular that every Jew recited it immediately on rising and before going to sleep. And when Jesus was asked to name the first of the commandments he quoted its first verse.[11]

In the course of time two other passages were added to the *Shema'*: Deuteronomy 11.13–21, and Numbers 15.37–41. The first passage mentions the phylacteries and the *mezuzot*; the second describes the fringes to be worn on four-cornered garments, and declares that their purpose is to remind the Jew of the commandments. Since, by this time, the wearing of phylacteries and fringed garments during prayer had become a general custom, the two paragraphs seemed appropriate supplements to the original service.

It was about the middle of the first century C.E. that there occurred the first important abbreviation of the service, the curious excision of the Decalogue. The reason for this change was the rise of a sect, perhaps that of the Christians, who maintained that only the Decalogue was revealed by God to Moses. The synagogue leaders, fearing that the importance given to the Ten Commandments in the daily ritual might be cited as evidence for this claim, decided to omit them. In the Temple, however, the old ritual was continued unchanged.

Other, purely political, events had had an even deeper effect on the significance of the service. In the year 63 B.C.E. Pompey subdued Jerusalem, and forced his way through the Temple, and into the Holy of Holies. The sight of the Roman general, fresh from his military victories and lascivious pollution stepping into the Sacred Chamber, which even the High Priest durst enter only on the Day of Atonement and after suitable purification, was a fearful shock to the Jews; his emergence, entirely unharmed, was incredible. Inevitably the event shook the faith of the people. Yet the mental conflict which ensued led to renewed and firmer faith. Mordant doubt and misgivings were silenced by sheer power of will. True, the pagan had entered the Temple; but what else had Israel deserved? They were a defiled people, and their sanctuary had suffered the punishment for their sins. But a day would come when God would arise to punish His enemies for their arrogance, when He would reveal Himself in all the glory He had promised to the prophets, and He would establish His kingdom forever.

The hope for the Kingdom of God thus ceased to be a mere eschatological fancy, and became part of the everyday thought of the pietists. There was all-conquering Rome, powerful, proud, and apparently irresistible; but behind the scenes, moving all men like marionettes, was the Mighty One of Israel.

For the pietists, who developed this new faith, the *Shema'*, and especially its first verse, assumed an altogether novel meaning. Its emphatic assertion offered them peace of mind, in the midst of intellectual struggle and sectarian controversy. "The Lord is our God, the Lord is One," was more than an avowal of the transcendence of Israel's God; it was a recognition of His sole power. Rome might conquer; it could only be for the moment. Ultimately the Lord would prove Himself unique in strength.

The recitation of the *Shema'* thus came to be "a confession of the Kingdom of Heaven." This new meaning was emphasized further by a slight change in the response, which was now made to read, "Blessed be the Name of His glorious *Kingdom* forever and aye."[12]

The new interpretation of the *Shema'*, and the changed response, were entirely satisfactory to the Pharisees, including the lower ranks of the hierarchy, who were seeking some way of giving vent to their protest against Rome's desecration of the Temple and subjugation of Israel. But it was repugnant to the highest nobility, the Herodians and their satellites, as well as to the foremost of the Sadducees, who willingly accepted the new regime. True successors to the Hellenists of pre-Maccabean days, and the assimilationists of even earlier times, they recoiled from any thought of resistance to Rome. They readily accepted subservience to the Italian pagans, which Israel shared with all other peoples. They opposed the nationalist movement, no matter what form it took, whether political, cultural, or theological, lest it irritate the governing power.

Hence it came about that the "men of Jericho" who beyond all others were under the influence of these patrician ideals, "compressed the *Shema'*," omitting the response which had become customary everywhere else.

C. Cutting the Barley before the Omer.

Jericho, lying thirteen hundred feet below the level of the Sea, is the warmest part of Palestine, and naturally produces its crops long before the rest of the country. Biblical Law, however, forbade the use of the new barley, which appeared in the spring, before the sixteenth day of Nisan,[13] when the first part of the produce was harvested as a sacrifice to God. We may imagine how the men of Jericho, watching their barley ripen, must have been irked by the rule which prohibited them from eating it. Public opinion, however, compelled them to submit. But when the scholars who hailed from the table-land demanded that they should not even harvest their grain before the sixteenth day of the month, they refused to yield. "They would cut and heap up the grain before the *Omer* (the sacrifice of the first barley on the sixteenth day)."

D. Their Use of Temple Property

It was probably during one of the periods of turmoil in the Second Commonwealth—either during the Maccabean Wars, or the Wars of the Hasmonean Succession, or the efforts of Herod to win the throne—that the great landowners of the plain of Jericho undertook to oust their poorer neighbors from their small holdings. These naturally did not consist of palm groves, such as the patricians themselves possessed; but of the less valuable sycamore trees,[14] lying in the less fruitful country, beyond the tropical, palm tree zone. Like the robber barons of the early Middle Ages, the mighty patricians would seize the property they coveted, compelling the owner to become their tenant, or lose all rights to his estate. He could appeal to no national authority, for, in the days of discord, the nominal king or High Priest would not dare to offend the powerful landowners, lest he drive them to the side of his opponents.

Anticipating the victims of the mediaeval barons who gave their property to the Church, the small landowners of Jericho averted ruin by dedicating their property to the Temple in Jerusalem.

In a sense this surrender of title was merely a form of insurance against robbery. The former owner remained on his ancestral soil. He merely lost the official designation of owner, and had to pay a suitable rent. But these were easy terms, considering the utter destitution which faced him if he neglected the arrangement.

In the course of time, the conditions which had led to the acquisition of these large properties in Jericho by the Temple were forgotten; and many of the tenant farmers, recalling their ancestral rights to the soil, resented the Temple's demand for rent. Nothing, however, could be done to release the estates; they belonged to the Temple in perpetuity. Yet one freedom the tenants allowed themselves; they would cut sprigs of their sycamore trees for replanting, without reference to the Temple ownership. This was bitterly resented by the authorities in Jerusalem.

E. Eating Fallen Fruits on the Sabbath

The necessity of standardizing the Law had led the Hasidean and Pharisaic scholars to include even plucking fruit under the prohibition against reaping on the Sabbath. This interpretation was hardly intelligible to the farmer who drew a clear distinction between the work of reaping grain or gathering fruit and the pleasure of picking a fig or a date for his immediate enjoyment. So much was the norm resented in certain sections of the country that the disciples of Jesus refused to obey it and when "he went through the cornfields on the Sabbath day, his disciples began, as they went, to pluck the ears of corn."[15]

The "men of Jericho" did not dare to violate the Pharisaic law quite so publicly; but they could not refrain from eating the fruits which fell from the tree on the Sabbath. Yet according to the Pharisaic conception of the Law this, too, was prohibited. Only that could be eaten on the Sabbath which was prepared for use when the holy day set in. Since the fruit was still attached to the tree on Sabbath eve, it remained prohibited for the entire day, no matter what happened to it.

F. The Portions Due the Poor from Vegetables

The two most important agricultural gifts commanded in Scripture are (a) the corners of the field, which must be left for the poor (Lev. 23.22), and (b) the tithe of the produce which must be given to the Levite (Num. 18.24). There was no doubt that every farmer was required to set aside both types of gift from grainfields and fruit trees. But throughout the Pharisaic and rabbinic periods there was a difference of opinion regarding the obligation of the owner of a vegetable patch. The provincials, who resented the law of tithes generally, vigorously opposed its extension to the vegetables which are not specifically included under it in Scripture. Long and intricate arguments were adduced to show that "herbs" must be tithed; and yet the provincials remained unconvinced.[16] Indeed, the sages were in the end forced to admit that "the tithe of herbs" is only a rabbinical, and not a biblical, commandment.[17] But, the provincials asked, when and by what right had the rabbinical decree been issued? "Woe unto you, Pharisees," cries Jesus, "for ye tithe mint, and rue, and all manner of herbs, and pass over judgment and the love of God."[18] The full bitterness of his irony can be appreciated only when we recall the discussions on the subject in the Talmud. "You do what is not commanded," he seems to say, "and you fail to perform what is the foundation of all Law."

On the other hand, the leaders of the Pharisees denied that there was any obligation to leave the corners of a green vegetable garden for the poor. The sociological basis of this interpretation is obvious. Even a small grain field is big enough to allow some portion to be set aside for the poor. But the corners of the tiny vegetable gardens which many of the artisans and traders possessed would hardly have been sufficient to keep even the poorest.

Furthermore, to allow the poor to come to a small garden for such herbs as they might choose to gather would involve disproportionate hardships for the owner. It would be quite impossible to limit their gleaning to the narrow strip set aside for them; and the owner would be compelled to watch the tiny field continuously lest it be destroyed altogether. We might have expected the Pharisees to face the situation frankly, and to declare large vegetable fields, but not small ones, subject to the law of "corners." Such a differentiation between rich and poor, in the observance of the Law, was, however, repugnant to the whole spirit of Pharisaism. Thus it came about that the Pharisees who insisted that herbs be tithed for the Levite, freed them from the law of "corners."

These objections did not, of course, apply to the law of tithes. Every Jew was expected to give one-tenth of his produce to the Levite; and no matter how small the crop of his field or garden might be, it was reasonable for him to set aside the due share for the ecclesiastic.

But the Pharisees were not satisfied with declaring the gardens of vegetables free from the obligation of "corners"; they maintained that those who separated the "corners" transgressed the Law. For, they said, the poor, not being required to give the Levitical tithes from their rightful gleanings, withheld them in error from those which they obtained from these "corners."

One of the wealthy followers of the sages, by the name of Boion, was once put to considerable expense because of this controversy regarding the tithes and "corners" of vegetable fields. He was visiting his charitable but unlettered son, and as he approached the garden, found a group of poor people loading their carts from the produce of the "corners." "My children," cried the pious Boion, "put down the vegetables; and I will give you twice as much of others, which are properly tithed. It is not that I begrudge these herbs, but the sages said, 'The corners must not be separated from vegetable gardens.' "[19]

The "men of Jericho," however, declined to be bound by this rabbinic ruling. Their large vegetable fields supplied them with far more than their needs; the produce could not be kept in barns, but had to be disposed of immediately; there was no market sufficiently near for them to sell the "herbs." It seemed to them far preferable to give the "herbs" to the poor than to waste them; and so they separated the "corners" from their vegetable gardens. As for the tithes which so worried the rabbis, the men of Jericho agreed with the Galileans, that they could not be collected from herbs.

The customs of Jericho, interesting in themselves, become especially significant when we realize that they were an expression of the mentality of the highest aristocracy in Judah. They reveal the extent of the provincials' and patricians' revolt against plebeian interpretation of the Law, and incidentally provide a clue to the cultural relationship of the Judaite lowland and the province of Galilee.

V. THE ORIGIN OF THE PHARISEES*

The vagaries of the Galileans and the men of Jericho, described in the last two chapters, could not lead to permanent schisms in Judaism. The scholar of Jerusalem noted, and perhaps resented, some of the differences; but he could not outlaw them. After all, the issues were of minor and purely local significance. How could the plebeians undertake to foist on others their funeral ceremonies, or their forms of marriage contract? They could not deny that their only authority for their views was the tradition of their ancestors and teachers; and it was easy to see that the Galileans and the men of Jericho were entitled to follow the traditions they had received from *their* forbears.

But there were other issues between the various groups of the population which concerned *national* policy, belief and practice. Such, for instance, were the dates of the major festivals, the manner in which the High Priest was to perform his functions at the Temple, the laws of inheritance, and the relations of the Jews to other nations. Differences regarding these and similar questions had been developing throughout the fifth, fourth and third centuries B.C.E. The plebeians, who had constructed a whole philosophical system regarding these issues, had never made any effort to compel the adoption of their views. They had patiently awaited the coming of the Messiah, who, they did not for a moment doubt, would agree with them and offer supernatural sanction for their arguments.

* Cf. Supplement, pp. 629 ff.

They might have continued indeterminately to follow this policy of eschatological hope and momentary inaction, had not their whole picture of the future been radically altered through the Maccabean Wars. The successful battles of Judah the Maccabee against outnumbering Syrian armies had transformed the Messianic Age from a distant theological dream into an imminent, practical possibility. It was obvious that definite decisions concerning the moot questions of national policy could no longer be delayed. If a Jewish State was to be created, its foundation would have to be the plebeian interpretation of the Torah.

It was characteristic of the plebeian scholars, the so-called Scribes, that they did not at once proceed to create a political party for the advancement of their views. Instead, they organized themselves and their followers[1] into a Society for the stricter and more thorough observance of that part of the Law which was being most widely ignored and flouted among the provincials—the rules of Levitical purity.

Universal obedience to these regulations seemed to the plebeians a necessary prerequisite to recognition of Israel as "a kingdom of priests and a holy nation."[2] They correctly understood that it was this the Lawgiver had in mind when he associated the laws of purity with approach to the Temple. It was clear perversion of his intent, and nothing more than a quibble, to maintain, as the provincials did, that only those who visited the Temple were required to be pure.

The choice of this issue as a basis for the plebeian organization was certainly dictated by no other motives than those of piety. Yet from a practical point of view, too, no better selection could have been made. The law of purity was one which could only be observed on a social and coöperative basis. The plebeian's concern regarding his neighbor's obedience to this law was thus not purely altruistic. Try as he might he could not be "pure" in his own home, if those with whom he dealt neglected the law. Of what use was it for him to guard his grain zealously against defilement under his roof, if it had probably become contaminated at the source, while it lay in the farmer's bin? Was it not vain and absurd for him to spend care and energy in preserving the purity of his earthenware, if the potter who made it had corrupted it beyond redemption?

There were, however, forces even more natural, impelling the pious *trader* to seek new adherents to these laws. The social bars which his observance set up between him and a large part of the population interfered with his business unless he could bring the masses to accept his view. Like the primitive Christian, a century or two later, he had to make propaganda for his faith in sheer self-defense, to escape being marooned on an island of truth in a sea of error. To recognize this human impulse is not to derogate from the sincerity of these early teachers, any more than it is hypocritical to profess love because it is part of an external, impersonal and universal hunger. Trade might grow with the spread of faith, yet from a materialistic view, renunciation would have been even more profitable. The pietist observed because he believed; but accepting his belief, he tried to win others to it.

The new society bore definite resemblances to others which had been organized, in earlier times, for various social and philanthropic purposes.[3] But two characteristics made it unique. It was probably the first organization to admit plebeians and patricians on an equal footing; and it was from the first definitely propagandist. Its emphasis on "purity" necessarily made it a primitive "Consumer's League," for its members were prevented, by their adherence to its platform, from making purchases at the shops of those suspected of transgressing the Law.[4]

The members of the Society called one another *haber*, comrade. The expression "members of the Synagogue" (*bene ha-keneset*)[5] was sometimes used to distinguish the masses of the Order from their leaders, the scholars or Scribes (*soferim*). But the wall between them and the other Jews gained them, most commonly, the name of "Separatists" (Hebrew, *Perushim*; Aramaic, *Perishaia*; Grecized into *Pharisaioi*, whence the English, Pharisees). This was not intended in any derogatory sense; it implied merely separation from impurity and defilement.

The course of Maccabean history made it inevitable that this pietist Order should in the end be transformed into a partisan opposition, whose goal was no longer the education of the simple, but the defeat of the mighty. Just as the peaceful puritans of James I's day became, with the passing of time, the Independent Army of Cromwell, so the pietist Pharisees of 150 B.C.E. gave birth to the bitterly warlike partisans of King Jannai's day. But even after Pharisaism had become a political slogan, it still did not entirely forget its original aim. As late as the Mishna, compiled three and a half centuries after the organization of the society, the term "Pharisee" was still used as the antonym of *'am ha-arez*. "The clothes of the *'am ha-arez*," we are told, "are impure for the Pharisee; the clothes of the Pharisee are impure for those who eat the heave-offering."[6] The Pharisees who declined to trust the provincial, were themselves suspected by the Temple priests, who, in their arrogance, would not rely on the purity of any layman, no matter how pious.

Another rule declares that "the Pharisee, even in his impurity, may not eat with the *'am ha-arez*,"[7] lest they grow accustomed to eat together ordinarily.

The original, pietistic character of Pharisaism appeared most clearly in its rules governing admission and expulsion, which closely resembled those recorded by Josephus for the Essenes.[8] The applicant for admission had to appear before three members of the Order and to accept as binding on him the following regulations: (a) not to give his heave-offerings or tithes to an *'am ha-arez*; (b) not to prepare his food together with an *'am ha-arez*; and (c) to eat his food in Levitical purity.[9] The admission of the head of a family qualified all the other members, including the slaves, provided he had their assurance to abide by the rules of the order.[10] Even men of learning, to whom the term *'am ha-arez*, in its derivative sense, could not possibly be applied, were subject to this form of initiation.[11] Only a person who was appointed to the High Court was exempt from it.[12] After admission, the candidate was on trial for a year, during which time he was, presumably, watched with especial care.[13] Thereafter he was considered a trusted member of the Order.

One who failed to maintain the standards required was declared "suspect." If his guilt was definitely proven, he might be expelled from the Order by a vote of the Conclave of Scholars, presumably those who were members of the Sanhedrin.[14] He was then declared *menuddeh* ("defiled")[15] and his status was that of an ordinary *'am ha-arez*. His former comrades indicated their distrust of him by withdrawing from his company, lest he defile them. He was not denominated traitor, renegade, reactionary, or Sadducee; the Order simply declined to vouch for his "purity." The social wall raised between him and the loyal members was not a punishment, it was an inevitable division between the observant and the non-observant.

Three cases of expulsion from the Order are recorded in the Talmud; in all of them the defendants were noted scholars; and in spite of special circumstances which doubtless played their part in the decisions reached, the formal charge in every case was Levitical "impurity."

The earliest recorded case of expulsion from the Order was that of Akabiah ben Mahalalel, about the middle of the first century.[16] He held a number of heretical views in theology, but these were not cited against him. He was ousted because he refused to accept the opinion of the majority in regard to the Levitical Law.[17] The same punishment was visited on another scholar, Eliezer ben Enoch, "because he made light of the hand-washing before meals." The third and greatest teacher to suffer expulsion was R. Eliezer ben Hyrcanus, a man of singular learning and intellect, as well as of great wealth and high position. His sin, like that of Akabiah, consisted in his stubborn insistence on his views, although he was outvoted. The occasion of the rupture was his declaration that a certain type of stove was "pure," although the other sages declared it impure. The Talmud gives us a vivid and touching portrayal of the scene of his punishment. His favorite pupil, R. Akiba, undertook the painful task of bringing him the verdict of the court, lest another messenger hurt the aged scholar's feeling more than necessary. Dressed in black, he approached his master and sat down at a distance of four cubits from him. "What is the trouble, Akiba?" R. Eliezer asked, when he noticed R. Akiba's clothes of mourning and his unusual reserve. "I believe that your colleagues are withdrawing from you," R. Akiba said. "Whereupon," the narrative continues, "R. Eliezer tore his garments and took off his shoes, and sat down on the ground, while his eyes overflowed with tears."[18]

As late as 170 C.E., the ancient tradition, according to which expulsion could only follow suspicion of impurity, was successfully used by R. Meir to save himself from the wrath of his colleagues. He was unpopular among them for a number of reasons. Like Akabiah and R. Eliezer, he had purely personal opinions and traditions to which he attached great importance. He was a patrician, while most of the scholars of his day were plebeians. He retained the friendship of the notorious informer, Elisha ben Abuyah, whom all the scholars hated for his merciless denunciation of the Jews to the Romans. And above all, he had led an insurrection against the quiet and meek head of the academy, R. Simeon ben Gamaliel. As a result of these circumstances a movement was initiated to expel him. But when the matter came up for trial, R. Meir simply said to his colleagues: "I decline to hear your complaint until you tell me who can be expelled and for what reasons a man can be expelled."[19] Obviously when the rules were recited, the case against R. Meir collapsed, for he was rigorously observant of the Pharisaic rules of purity.

Out of this institution of *Niddui*, there arose in later times the elaborate system of excommunication which proved so powerful a weapon in the hands of both the Synagogue and the Church. Days came when Pharisaism was no longer a part of the Jewish people, but the whole of it; and when expulsion from its midst meant absolute social ostracism. The laws of purity had long become obsolete and their practice forgotten, but the method of

expulsion from the community was for that reason all the
more effective; for now, the expelled member was tabu
not only to a small specially observant group, but to all
others as well. Men withdrew from the neighborhood of
the excommunicate as the Pharisees had withdrawn from
the company of the defiled *menuddeh*, although they were
no longer in any danger of ritual contamination from him
and would have laughed at the suggestion that he was
Levitically impure. But, as frequently, the old ritual had
become the basis for a new custom which had a powerful
influence on the course of events.

When the Pharisees became a political force, the adherents of the ruling Hasmonean dynasty, too, organized to
defend their rights against the protesting plebeians who
were undermining their regime. Since the high-priestly
family claimed descent from Zadok, the first priest of the
Solomonic Temple, their party came to be known as *Zad-
dukim* (Gr. *Saddoukaioi*; Eng. Sadducees). After the reign
of Herod, however, their opponents, deriding the fictitious
claim of the High Priests to Zadokite descent, called the
party "Boethusians." This was as much as to say, "You
are defenders not of the ancient House of Zadok, but of
the House of Simeon ben Boethus"—the ignorant priest
whom Herod had imported from Egypt as the most promising purchaser of the high-priesthood.[20]

The sources permit no doubt that the Sadducees derived
from the wealthiest strata of Jerusalem. As late as the
time of Josephus, after the Pharisees had been in full control of Jewish life for more than a century, it was still true
that the richest families adhered to their ancestral Sadducism.[21] The Pharisees had been able to win over to formal
allegiance most of the upper middle class and some of the

patricians; but the highest aristocracy resisted them to the last.

That each party had its center and focus in the metropolis is evident from even a superficial study of the history of the times. The Saducean influence radiated from the Temple, the Pharisaic from the market place. Whatever following the opposing groups might win among the peasantry, their formulated philosophy could have arisen only in the sophisticated environment of the city.

While their urban, aristocratic life inevitably gave the Sadducees special views, not shared by the farmers on the land, such is the natural conservatism of religious custom that they retained, for the most part, the ceremonies and ritual which had developed among them and their ancestors before they had been drawn into the city. What is more, the traditions of the province which continued among the Saducean aristocracy were not limited to ceremonial; they included personal habits, manner of speech, and general contempt for book-learning. The crudity, vulgarity, and boorishness of the primitive farm were shed almost as slowly as particular forms of worship. These aspects of the controversy between Pharisee and Sadducee have been astonishingly overlooked, and must be treated in a special chapter.

VI. THE URBANITY OF THE PHARISEES

While the Pharisees, according to Josephus, were "affectionate to one another and cultivated harmonious relations with the community," the Sadducees "were rather boorish in their behavior even among themselves, and in their intercourse with their comrades were as rude as to aliens."[1] In his *Antiquities*, Josephus softens this indictment, saying that the Sadducees "think it an instance of virtue to dispute with those teachers of philosophy whom they frequent." The Pharisees, on the other hand, "pay respect to such as are advanced in years nor are they so bold as to contradict them in anything which they have introduced."[2]

We need not suppose that Josephus pays these compliments to the Pharisees because he is one of them, and maligns the Sadducees because he is opposed to them. Though officially a Pharisee, Josephus was no fervent partisan. At the time he wrote his books, he had broken as much with Pharisaism as with Sadducism and led the life of a hated and despised apostate in Rome. Yet he retained sufficient affection for his people to wish to paint them all in fair colors. His description of the Sadducees cannot therefore be a mere hostile fiction; and even malice itself derives its force from a coloring of truth. The curious difference in manner which Josephus notes, is but another instance of the distinction existing since time immemorial between urbanity and rusticity. Frequent contact with strangers trained the city-dweller to soft speech and polished manners, virtues which the isolated peasant could not emulate easily.

A cheerful countenance brought custom to the door of the trader or craftsman but might destroy the authority of the landowner among his subordinates—his wives, children, slaves and employees. To the one, social grace was a notable achievement; to the other, it was sheer hypocrisy.

Following the example of earlier plebeians the Pharisees carried their tenderness not only into their home-life but into the courts of justice and were noted for leniency of their penalties while the Sadducees were distinguished by their severity.[3]

The violence and crudity of the aristocratic Sadducees were clearly an inheritance from earlier provincial surroundings. The picture of the contemporary 'am ha-arez, taken from rabbinic literature, may be somewhat overdrawn but it leaves no doubt that he, like the peasant of all time, lacked refinement and culture.[4] This fact is confirmed by the stories which the sages tell of their own colleagues who had begun life as provincials. The School of Shammai, mouthpiece of the wealthy Pharisees, was as noted for ill manners as the Sadducees themselves. "A man should always be as meek as Hillel and not as quick-tempered as Shammai," is one of the pedagogic maxims of the Talmud.[5] Hillel himself, having in mind the Shammaitic tendency to cruel punishments in school, said: "He who is quick-tempered cannot be a teacher."[6]

We learn something about the treatment accorded even grown-up, mature pupils under Shammaitically-minded instructors, from the casual statement of R. Johanan ben Nuri, an overseer in the academy conducted by the patrician R. Gamaliel II, that "Akiba ben Joseph was flogged more than five times at my instance because I made complaint against him."[7] When we bear in mind that the victim of

this humiliating correction, reserved in the Law for arch-
sinners, was none other than the great saint who as a mature,
married man sacrificed everything for the sake of learning
and in a short time rose to the foremost place in the school,
we can readily imagine the firmer discipline that was exercised over lesser pupils. The copyists of later days would
not credit the tradition and in some versions altered the
text of R. Johanan ben Nuri's remark.[8] Still, sufficient
sources record the exact words to leave the facts beyond the
possibility of doubt.

On several occasions, the easily excited Shammaites actually came to blows in the academy and at meetings of the
Sanhedrin. Hillel, bringing a sacrifice to the Temple on a
festival day in a manner of which they disapproved, barely
escaped violence at their hands.[9] Several members of their
school grossly insulted a poor colleague, R. Johanan the
Hauranite, because on a visit during the Sukkot festival
they found him in a meager hut which had space only for
his body and not for his table. Without thinking of his
penury and the suffering he underwent to comply with the
Law, they greeted him with the words, "If this is what you
have been doing all your life, you have never fulfilled the
commandment concerning booths!"[10]

R. Eliezer ben Hyrcanus, one of the most erudite among
the sages but a descendant of provincials, was noted for
his ill-breeding. He was wont to utter the most lurid curses
against those who disagreed with him. When, for instance,
R. Akiba, his favorite pupil, once refuted him in argument,
he shouted in anger: "From the laws of *shehitah* (slaughter)
have you refuted me, by *shehitah* may you find death."[11]
The fearful words haunted his amazed disciples, who doubtless saw in the cruel death which R. Akiba suffered many

years later, during the Hadrianic persecutions, the grim realization of his master's curse.

In a discussion of Temple customs, Simeon the Pious remarked that on one occasion he had come near the altar without washing his hands. R. Eliezer leaped at him with fury. "Who is greater, you or the High Priest?" he thundered. Abashed, poor Simeon held his peace, but R. Eliezer, once his ire was aroused, was not to be put off. "Are you ashamed to admit that the High Priest's dog is better than you? I swear that even if the High Priest were to come near the altar with his hands unwashed, his head would be split with a log!"[12]

This temper did not forsake him even on his death-bed. As he lay in his last illness, his son, Hyrcanus, entered to relieve him of his phylacteries in honor of the approaching Sabbath. R. Eliezer scolded him violently. Hyrcanus, astonished, remarked to those who stood by, "I fear my father is delirious." "You and your mother are delirious," the enraged dying man called back from his bed.[13]

Less uncouth than R. Eliezer but still insensitive to the pain of others was another patrician colleague, R. Eleazar ben Azariah. R. Akiba once remarked to him and Ben Azzai, a poor scholar who had abstained from marital responsibilities because of his desire to study, that "whoever spills human blood diminishes, as it were, the Image of God." To this Ben Azzai, forgetting his own celibacy, replied: "Whoever refrains from procreation may likewise be considered as diminishing the Image of God." Turning on him at once, R. Eleazar said: "Good precepts are valuable in the mouths of those who practice them. There are some who preach well and do well. Ben Azzai preaches well but does not do well." Ben Azzai, humbled and pained, simply remarked, "What shall I do? I desire to study the Torah. The world must be maintained through others."[14]

R. Tarfon, another wealthy Hillelite with Shammaitic leanings, never outgrew the rural habit of invoking the most baleful imprecations upon his children. "May I bury my children if this is not a perverted tradition!" he would cry.[15] So greatly did he shock his colleagues with these words that many years later when R. Judah the Prince visited R. Tarfon's city, he asked whether there were "any descendants left of that saint who used to curse his children."[16]

The half-Shammaite, R. Gamaliel II, a descendant of Hillel, had like the other patricians caught the contagion of speaking his mind without regard to the pain he gave. Visiting R. Joshua ben Hananya, who lived in a poor hovel, where he worked at the laborious trade of needle-making, R. Gamaliel said as he noted the walls black with soot: "From the walls of your house, one can easily guess your vocation."[17]

R. Ishmael, a leader of the patrician school of the second century C.E., actually raised unsocial behavior to a philosophy. Whereas R. Akiba, spokesman of the plebeians, taught that one should do "what is upright in the eyes of God and what is good in the eyes of man," R. Ishmael said it was "sufficient to do what is right in the eyes of God; there is no other good."[18] To this R. Akiba replied, "With whomsoever men are pleased, God is also pleased; those in whom men find no delight cannot give delight to God."[19]

Even patrician women had sharp tongues. Beruriah, the famous wife of R. Meir and daughter of the wealthy R. Hanina ben Teradyon, once called a fellow-provincial, R. Jose, who was old enough to be her father, "Galilean Fool."[20] Meeting a student who was repeating his lessons without the usual oriental swaying of the body, she kicked him and said: "If you study with all your two hundred and forty-eight limbs, you will learn; otherwise, you will always remain an ignoramus!"[21]

This bluntness of expression was not at all incompatible with a fine tenderness which frequently lay concealed beneath it. The fierce R. Eliezer had a niece who grew up in his house, and who came to love him so that she would not marry any other man. R. Eliezer's mother, who, with her womanly intuition, saw how matters stood, urged him to marry the girl, but recognizing their wide differences in age, R. Eliezer hesitated and continued to propose other matches for her. Finally, the child, despairing of her uncle's ever making any advances, said to him, "I am thy hand-maid, to wash the feet of thy slaves," whereupon he took her to wife.[22]

R. Gamaliel II, the haughty president of the academy, who did not flinch from the most severe disciplinary measures when he thought them necessary, was observed one day to be red-eyed with crying. His disciples, making inquiry about the matter, discovered that a neighboring woman whose child had died awoke at midnight to weep for her bereavement, and R. Gamaliel, hearing her voice, could not restrain his tears of sympathy.[23]

His servants, Tabbai and Tabita, who were husband and wife, received from him the utmost affection. The children were taught to call them Father Tabbai and Mother Tabita;[24] they were taught the law;[25] Tabbai was permitted to wear the phylacteries during prayer[26] and to sleep in a booth during the Sukkot week,[27] like a freeman. When the old slave died, R. Gamaliel observed the rites of mourning for him, as for a member of his household. His patrician colleagues, feeling that in this he went too far, remonstrated with him, saying, "You have taught us, our master, that one does not observe mourning for slaves." "That is so," R. Gamaliel replied; "but Tabbai was different. He was a pious slave."[28]

Indeed it was the harsh R. Gamaliel who coined the most humane and universalist maxim in the whole of rabbinic literature—one that might deservedly be accepted as basic to all religion: "He who has mercy on God's creatures will obtain mercy from Heaven."[29]

R. Tarfon, who used to curse his children, was yet so fond of them that he laughingly remarked to his colleagues, "Be careful of me, because of my daughter-in-law."[30] Once while he was delivering a public lecture in the open, according to Palestinian custom, he was interrupted by the passing of a bridal procession. Noticing that the bride was poor and that she was not properly prepared, he asked his mother and his wife to take her into the house, "and wash her, and anoint her, and adorn her, and arrange the customary dances before her until the time comes for her to go to her husband's house." Although he had many slaves and servants, he tried to please his mother by attending to her wants himself, and in her old age, would bend down so that she could use him as a step to ascend to her bed and to descend from it.[31]

R. Ishmael, a patrician, who expressed contempt for social grace, was nevertheless capable of utmost gentleness, charity and understanding. During the unrest which occurred in Palestine toward the end of Trajan's reign (ca. 115–116), he is said to have supported a number of families out of his private means.[32] Perhaps the most touching incident related of him, however, concerned his work as a judge. A young man, who had been betrothed for some time, came before him with his fiancée, saying that he no longer loved her and could not marry her. Indeed, he had taken a vow to have nothing to do with her. R. Ishmael looked at her and noticed that she still bore traces of beauty which had faded because of poverty. Instead of rendering a decision, he invited her to his house, where she was properly fed, protected, and cared for. After a time, he called her fiancé to meet her again. "Is this the woman you have vowed not to marry?" R. Ishmael asked, when he introduced them to one another. No wonder that when the sage died, the mourners took as their text, "Daughters of Israel, cry for Ishmael."[33]

These actions of love and tenderness were the expressions of the inner nature of the scholars. They were, however, as unused to repress their anger or pain as their tenderness and affection. To use R. Gamaliel's phrase, "They were from without as from within."[34]

In sharp contrast with the manners of patricians and provincials were those of the polished city plebeians, who formed the dominant faction of the Pharisees. A man once wagered four hundred *zuz* (about one hundred dollars) that he would provoke Hillel, the typical Pharisee, to anger. He waited until the Sabbath eve and, when he thought Hillel would be most occupied with his preparations for the holy day, began to walk up and down before his house, shouting, "Is there anyone here by the name of Hillel?" Hearing him, Hillel came out and said, "What is it, my son?" "I have an important question to ask," said the man. "Ask it, my son, ask it." "Why are the Babylonians long-headed?" "That is indeed an important question," Hillel replied, and then, with much more training in human nature than in anthropology, continued: "Because their midwives are unskilled." The question was intended to irritate Hillel not only by its insignificance to a Jewish legalist, but also by its personal allusion, for Hillel was a native of Babylonia. Frustrated in his first attempt, the man returned, twice going back and forth each time with his loud call: "Does anyone live here by the name of Hillel?" His second and third questions were as inconsequential as his first: "Why are the eyes of the Palmyreans red? Why are the feet of the Africans broad?" Each time Hillel replied patiently with some apparently satisfactory explanation. Exasperated at last, the man said to Hillel, "Are you the Hillel whom they call a prince in Israel? May there be few such among our people!" "Why, my son?" the scholar asked. "Because you cost me four hundred *zuz*!"[35]

The same humility was characteristic of the other great teachers of the school, R. Johanan ben Zakkai, R. Joshua ben Hananya, and R. Akiba. R. Joshua ben Hananya, for instance, used to tell how thrice in his life he had been outwitted, by a woman, a boy and a girl.

Staying at an inn for several days, he had twice neglected to observe the custom of leaving a little food in his dish for the hostess. Perhaps his plebeian spirit rebelled against this unhygienic and humiliating form of "tipping." On the third day, however, the resentful hostess filled the food with salt. He tasted a bit and pushed the plate away. "Why do you not eat?" she asked with mock innocence. "I ate earlier in the day," he prevaricated. "Perhaps, Sir, you meant to provide additional leavings to make up for the two previous days," the bold hostess ventured.

"Walking in an unknown district," R. Joshua further relates, "I came to a fork in the road where a child sat playing. 'My son, which road shall I take to the city?'

'The road to the right,' he replied 'is long and short; that to the left is short and long.' I took the one he called short and long, but after a few hundred paces discovered it was an unused road and ended in hedges of vineyards and fields. When I came back to the fork in the road, I said to the boy, 'Why did you deceive me?' 'I did not,' he insisted. 'It is indeed shorter in distance but longer in time.' "

Once R. Joshua came to a well near which a girl was sitting, and asked her for a drink. She gave him a drink and offered him one for his ass also. "You are like Rebekah," he gallantly remarked. She, apparently well-read in Scripture, replied instantly, "But you are not at all like Eliezer!"[36] Eliezer, it must be remembered, had given Rebekah costly gifts and a husband, with none of which Joshua had come provided.

R. Akiba had perhaps the most polished manners of all the plebeians for, though he had been brought up as a shepherd boy in uncultured surroundings, he had broken with his past when he entered the academy. Some traits of his noble mind have already been indicated. It is noteworthy that in an age of contempt for women he unhesitatingly proclaimed his indebtedness to his wife for all his scholarly achievement.[37]

No less significant, however, than the urbanity of the Pharisees was their respect for learning and the pleasure they derived from it. Talmudic records demonstrate the truth of Josephus' praise that the Pharisees were "the most accurate interpreters of the Law"[38] in their day. To appreciate the full meaning of this, we must bear in mind, of course, that among the Pharisees Law included far more than it does among us. It covered every aspect of human behavior: religious ceremonial, the protection of health, the interpretation of literature, the regulation of the calendar, the relation of Israel to its neighboring peoples, as well as ethics, manners and beliefs, and civil and criminal jurisprudence. The Law determined such questions as whether or not one might greet a bereaved person, praise a bride extravagantly, or arrange banquets on the ninth of Tishri and Purim. It regulated one's diet, one's dressing habits, and one's relations with one's wife. Scholars debated questions of theology as well as phases of Law. The doctrines of the Resurrection and the existence of angels, the wisdom of seeking proselytes to Judaism, and the policy to be pursued with relation to the Romans were subjects of discussion in the Academies of Law.[39]

The Law forbade the Jew to use the superstitions[40] of the Canaanites, to believe in "lucky" days, to carry bones as charms, or to imitate Roman tonsure. He was discouraged from substituting Greek for Jewish studies; and he was considered derelict in his duty if he failed to teach his child the elements of Hebrew language and literature.

Some of the ceremonial observances connected with the faith, like those regulating Levitical purity, particularly of women, involved a considerable knowledge of anatomy; the laws fixing the status of clean and unclean animals, and forbidding the use of sick animals for food, took the student into the fields of zoölogy and animal physiology; the establishment of the calendar and some aspects of the Sabbath and festival laws involved a considerable knowledge of mathematics and astronomy.

This information garnered by the trained "scribes" had to be handed down, generation by generation, to students who could spare only part of their time for study. The necessity for the preservation of the tradition involved the development of pedagogics, as well as skill in elegance and brevity of expression. The fine, easy flowing, yet marvelously compact style of the Mishna (finally compiled about 200 C.E.) was, like other such literary developments, not the creation of a single generation. It grew up very slowly and gradually, through generations of patient effort.

It is thus obvious that what the ancient Jew called the "Law" really included, in its broadest and truest sense, everything which his contemporary Greek would have considered *Sophia*, or Wisdom: ethics, physics, metaphysics, history, biology, physiology, medicine, mathematics, astronomy, as well as the rudiments of psychology, pedagogics, logic, and literary form, not to speak of ordinary jurisprudence, and the primitive economics and sociology connected with it. The only difference between Athenian and Jew was the fact that the Greek generally approached all these sciences with the question, "What is the real?" whereas the Jew asked himself, "What is the right?"

Hence Josephus could rightly say of the Pharisees, who devoted themselves to the study of the Law, that "they follow the conduct of Reason," and "observe what it prescribes as good for them," and "think they ought earnestly to strive to observe Reason's dictates in their practice."[41] An apologist as well as an historian, he is purposely using Reason instead of Law, so that the Greeks will be able to follow him; nevertheless the term is not altogether unjustified. Jewish Law, as the Pharisees interpreted it, was Reason.

It is obvious, however, that not all the Pharisees could have been Masters of the Law. The scribes, who guided the Order, were few. Yet the tendency to revere the Law and to give some time to its study was almost universal.

Certainly in this, the Pharisees, like their descendants and followers in the Jewish ghettos of medieval and modern Europe, were almost a unique phenomenon in history. It was not merely that so many of them gave their leisure to study; it was the fact that their intellectual pursuits gave them such delight, which must impress us. As a predecessor of the Pharisees, doubtless a plebeian Hasid, perhaps of the fourth or third centuries B.C.E., puts it:

"This is my comfort in my affliction,
   That Thy word hath quickened me" (Ps. 119.50).
"It is good for me that I have been afflicted [he says],
   In order that I might learn Thy statutes." (Ps. 119.71).
"Unless Thy Law had been my delight,
   I should then have perished in my affliction" (Ps. 119.92).

Suppressed by patricians, persecuted by ecclesiastics and government officials, without hope of rising out of his poverty and class degradation, denied all mundane pleasures, confined to a tiny hovel which opened into an equally narrow court or alley, with little fresh air or sunshine, and hardly any contact with field, grass or tree, a typical dweller of an ancient slum, the plebeian worker freed himself from his heavy chains by rising into the warm, life-giving atmosphere of the Study of the Torah. No wonder that to him God came to be revered primarily as the Author of the Torah. It was with no attempt at hyperbole, that he said:

"Oh, how love I Thy Law!
   It is my meditation all the day" (Ps. 119.97).

The child of such a tradition, reading the beautiful poem in praise of Nature, preserved in Psalm 19, was naturally moved to add to it another psalm, in praise of that which seemed to him greater than Nature—the Law.

"The precepts of the Lord are right [he says],
Rejoicing the heart . . .
More to be desired are they than gold, yea than much
fine gold;
Sweeter also than honey and the honeycomb" (19.9 ff.).

In their insistence on the primacy of learning the Pharisees were simply advocating a policy which had been upheld for centuries in the market place of Jerusalem. The contempt of the provincial, and the aristocrat who was descended from him, for book learning[42] has already been noted. The Deuteronomic ideal of the "wise and understanding people" (4.6) found few adherents among them. It was not they who were concerned with the obedience and study of the Law because that "was the wisdom and understanding" of Israel in the face of all the other nations. It was not they who put the words of the Torah on their hearts and "meditated therein day and night" (Josh. 1.8). Even those teachers of the Law who arose among the patricians, drew their following from the plebeian market place. This was doubtless true in the First Commonwealth when the prophet proposed to "bind up the testimony, seal the instruction" among his disciples (Isa. 8.16). But it was even more obviously true in the Second Commonwealth.

Those patricians who outgrew the provincial contempt for learning tended to train their children in a system of Wisdom, which represented prudence rather than ethics, piety or tradition.[43] It was only rare geniuses among the patricians, like Simeon the Righteous, Antigonus of Socho, and Jeshua ben Sira, who brought into their class some understanding of the value of Study.

After Pharisaism had become the dominant organization of the Commonwealth, its own patrician wing displayed an antagonism to book learning and especially its democratization, which is deeply reminiscent of the earlier aristocrats and the Sadducees. They would have limited instruction to the children of the wealthy;[44] and even for this class they established the principle that "not study is important, but practice."[45] "Speak little and do much,"[46] was one of the fundamental principles of Shammai, one of their foremost leaders. It is certainly significant that while Hillel, R. Johanan ben Zakkai and R. Akiba, the three greatest plebeians among the talmudic sages, had huge numbers of pupils and disciples, their patrician opponents, Shammai, R. Simeon ben Gamaliel and R. Ishmael, had few or no students learning under them.

The issue reached a tragic climax during the Hadrianic persecution when the government forbade the practice of the Law. The question then arose whether the study of the Torah was not of sufficient importance to justify violation of its ceremonial precepts. R. Akiba, loyal to his faction's principles, maintained that it was; R. Jose the Galilean and R. Tarfon, the representatives of the patrician group, held that Practice was more important.

The debate occurred more than half a century after the destruction of Jerusalem; yet such was the influence which the metropolis exerted on the plebeians that they still adhered to the tradition of Learning, or as Josephus would have put it, Reason, as the *summum bonum*, worthy of the sacrifice not only of life, but of the ceremonies of the Law themselves. And they carried the day. "The whole Assembly finally cried out, 'Study is great, for Study alone can lead to appropriate Practice.'"[47]

This devotion to intellectual pursuits is essentially urban, as we still indicate by the use of such expressions as "urbane" and "civilized." No wonder that because of it the Pharisees became known as the party of the scribes. Not that all the Pharisees were scholars; or that the Sadducees were entirely without men of learning. But the dominant characteristic of Pharisaism was study; that of Saducism was contempt for scholarship.

In view of the provincial character of the inhabitants of Galilee it was quite natural that they should have misinterpreted both the urbanity and the love of learning which they rightly associated with Pharisaism. To the blunt and ingenuous villager, Pharisaic amenity and politeness seemed mere dissembling and chicanery; and their love of book-learning nothing more than pedantry.[48] He could not realize that the ease of manner and conversation which was characteristic of the townsmen, as well as their polish and self-control, was so much a part of them as to be almost instinctive. He was as insensitive to the Pharisee's delight in abstruse discussions of the Law, as the modern uninitiate is to the mathematician's joy in non-Euclidean geometry and universes of multiple dimensions. The ancient Galilean was amazed when he discovered the Pharisee spending hours in a discussion of whether mint and rue ought to be tithed. Still less could he understand the fervor which would make such a scribe travel over land and sea to win a single convert to his teaching.

The accusation of hypocrisy and punctiliousness was not one against which the Pharisees could defend themselves. If by hypocrisy was meant their self-control, and by punctiliousness their insistence on the mastery and observance of detail in the Law, they were indeed guilty of both. They were, however, quite innocent of the charges of insincerity, fanaticism, and false motives which were ascribed to them, as to the Puritans of a later age. Nevertheless, so frequently were these calumnies repeated that they affected the minds of the Pharisees themselves. As their factions parted from one another, each accused the other of the vices which the outer world charged against both.

Gamaliel II, one of the leaders of the Shammaites[49] in his generation, trying to keep the Hillelites out of his academy, set up a rule that "no one who is different within from what he appears without may enter the school."[50] Somewhat earlier a Hillelite writer had spoken of his Shammaitic opponents in the following terms: "Treacherous men, self-pleasers, dissemblers in all their own affairs and lovers of banquets at every hour of the day, gluttons, gourmands . . . devourers of the goods [of the poor], saying that they do so on the ground of justice, but in reality to destroy them; complaining, deceitful, concealing themselves lest they should be recognized, impious, filled with lawlessness and iniquity from sunrise to sunset: saying, 'We shall have feastings and luxury, eating and drinking, and we shall esteem ourselves as princes.' And though their hands and their minds touch unclean things, yet their mouth speaks great things, and they say furthermore, 'Do not touch me lest thou shouldst pollute me, in the place where I stand.' "[51]

Certainly none of the excoriations which Jesus uttered against the whole Order could have exceeded this factional denunciation in bitterness. Yet there can be little doubt that the passage was written by an observant, loyal Pharisee of the gentler group. Even his gentleness gave way, however, before the ferocity of the *odium theologicum*.[52]

As we look back over the centuries which have passed since Palestine rang with the sounds of these factional and sectarian conflicts, we can appreciate the significance of Pharisaism to the world far better than could either its defenders or its opponents. We see in it a manifestation of the human spirit, which in part has its parallels in other peoples and other regions of the globe. And yet it has been unique in this: it became the foundation for the foremost intellectual and spiritual structure the world has yet seen, Western Civilization. We can now realize what the contemporary opponent failed to appreciate, that Pharisaism represented an effort to assert the supremacy of the spiritual tradition which had its roots in Prophecy, over the decadent, syncretistic Hellenism, which combined in itself the worst elements in Greek and Persian civilization. To avoid being lost in Canaanitic superstition, Persian insobriety, Egyptian licentiousness, and Roman ferocity, which had conquered Greece itself, the Pharisee determined to hold on with almost superhuman strength to the traditions of his ancestors. He succeeded long enough to bring about the partial conversion of the whole Roman world to his views, and thus to lay the basis for the rise of both Christendom and Mohammedanism, the two great moral and intellectual energies of the later world. From the perspective of these achievements, the conflicts which raged about Pharisaism can be assayed with cool impartiality.

Viewed in this light, the struggle between the Pharisees and their opponents, as well as that among the factions in their own midst, was essential to these achievements. The accusations of the sects, parties, and smaller groups against one another were, as usual in polemics, replete with exaggerations and perversions of fact. The Galileans were not mere gluttons; the Pharisees were no sanctimonious hypocrites; the Shammaites were more than quick-tempered peasants; and the Hillelites more than subtle thinkers and teachers. The quarrels between them, however, led to critical self-examination and purification, which were essential to the usefulness of the whole system to the world. The descendants of those who accused the Pharisees of being so energetic in their efforts at conversion became themselves the world's foremost religious missionaries; the subtleties of the rabbinical academies became the logic of medieval scholasticism; and the doctrines of purity, simplicity, human brotherhood and Divine Fatherhood, which were inherent in Pharisaism, have become an integral part of all civilized human thought.

VII. THE SOCIAL BACKGROUND OF THE PHARISAIC LEGISLATION

To their contemporaries, the difference in manner between the Pharisees and the Sadducees was less important than their legal controversies. Probably most of these have been forgotten; and of those which have been recorded, not all are entirely understood.[1] Yet the material which has been preserved is quite sufficient for a sociological analysis of the two systems. Both are revealed to us as vital, powerful forces, created to defend opposing interests. Neither sect determined its views by such artificial and spurious principles as "literal" and "liberal" interpretation of Scripture. They both were ready to adhere to the letter of the Law or to depart from it as best suited the needs of their following. Indeed, they would have considered themselves false to the needs of their groups had they acted otherwise. It happened, indeed, that the plebeians seeking new rights had more frequent occasion to adopt novel interpretations of the inherited law than their opponents who were merely trying to preserve what they had. But even in these instances, their liberal interpretation was a result of their view, not its cause. And, it must be added, that with respect to the recorded controversies, the literal meaning of the Bible supports the Pharisaic views more frequently than those of the Sadducees. This does not, of course, mean that the Sadducees adopted new and revolutionary opinions. It merely indicates that many of the controversies antedate by centuries the origin of the two sects; and that the plebeian predecessors of the Pharisees frequently intruded their views into Scripture itself. This did not, however, prevent the Sadducees from continuing in their ancestral ways, for, like the Pharisees, there were those among them who were not so much interested in agreeing with Scripture as in having Scripture agree with them.

A. The Sukkot Festival*

Both Josephus and the Talmud record the heated controversy between Pharisees and Sadducees in regard to the Sukkot (feast of tabernacles) ritual. The Pharisees marked this festival with several ceremonies admittedly not found in the Bible but which they held essential. Chief among these was the water-libation poured on the altar on each of the seven festival days. They also formed a procession about the altar each day carrying in their hands the citron and a cluster of palm, myrtle and willow branches. On the seventh day, they marched around the altar seven times, willow branch in hand, crying "Hosanna." After the procession, the willow branches were beaten against the floor of the Temple until their leaves fell off. Each night the Temple courts were the scene of almost riotous celebration. "Saints and pious men danced before them, carrying burning torches in their hands and chanting songs and psalms while the Levites played the harp, the flute, the cymbals, the trumpets and other instruments without number." So many torches were lit that "there was not a court in Jerusalem which remained without illumination from the light of the water-drawing celebration."[2]

To such an extent were ordinary conventions thrown over, that on one occasion R. Simeon ben Gamaliel I, the head

* Cf. Supplement, pp. 700-708.

of the Pharisees, danced around before the crowd in the Temple throwing eight torches into the air one after another and catching them before any could fall to the ground. R. Joshua ben Hananya, who was a young man in the last days of the Temple, told how he had practically no sleep during the festival week, for the wild celebrations lasted throughout the night until it was time to prepare for the morning sacrifice.[3]

All of these customs were opposed by the Sadducees who were, however, unable to suppress them. Their sect showed its opposition by forbidding them whenever it could find a reasonable pretext for doing so. Thus it objected to these ceremonies being conducted on the Sabbath.

As early a sage as R. Akiba associated these rites with the doctrine that Sukkot is a period of judgment for rain.[4] But how did the ritual become an occasion for a sectarian controversy? The answer to this question is to be sought in the biblical origins of the Sukkot festival.

The most popular as well as the most celebrated of all ancient Jewish festivals was that of the ingathering. Both in Scripture and in Talmud, it is called the Pilgrimage, *par excellence*.[5] The spring festival, Passover, was indeed a notable occasion, as was also the celebration of the wheat harvest (Pentecost). Neither of these, however, yielded so much joy as the autumn holiday which marked the end of the vintage as well as the gathering of the grain into storehouses. The joy of life, which had been accumulating throughout the summer, suddenly burst forth in unrestrained hilarity. The huts and bowers, erected during the busy season of vintage and ingathering as protection against the hot sun by day and the chill air by night, remained for the wild merriment of the ensuing festival. Such were the sweet and fragrant memories attached to it that the aged farmer, although long retired from field work, would join with the younger people in draining the final drops of this autumnal happiness. Even after he settled in the city, the landowner did not at this time of the year reconcile himself to the artificiality of civilization, and his heart turned continually to the booths of the ingathering. The formal visit to the Temple and the heavy meat of the sacrifice were no substitutes for the happy freedom of the fragrant booth. Many a city patrician doubtless spent the festival on his farm, reaping in joy although he had not sown in tears. Others, as greedy for pleasure but more averse to toil, retained the celebration, even if not at the scene of the ingathering. They erected rustic booths in their urban gardens where they could enjoy the memories of the vintage while they left its pains and labors to brawnier hands.

The Bible does not describe this development but implies it in the parallel regulations for the festival. The Book of the Covenant calls it "the feast of ingathering, at the end of the year, when thou gatherest in thy labours out of the field" (Ex. 23.16). A kindred passage speaks even more simply of "the feast of ingathering at the turn of the year" (ibid. 34.22). In both verses, obviously addressed to peasants and farmers, the Legislator takes the booths for granted and says nothing about them. But Deuteronomy, the code which primarily concerns itself with Jerusalem and its interests,[6] ordains that "thou shalt keep the feast of tabernacles seven days, after thou hast gathered in from thy threshing-floor and from thy winepress" (16.13). The passage not only commands the erection of the booths; it makes them the central feature of the festival observance, for in urban life the booths were not taken for granted as part of the harvest. On the contrary, they seemed bizarre and out-of-place—a religious symbol, which attracted attention to the holiday for which they were built.

An historical reason for the festival is supplied in the Book of Leviticus. We are there told that the booths commemorate the divine protection under which Israel wandered in the wilderness. "All that are home-born in Israel shall dwell in booths; that your generations may know that I made the children of Israel to dwell in booths, when I brought them out of the land of Egypt" (Lev. 23.42).

Neither the urban patrician nor the rural farmer needed this historical motive for the festival. For them the feast of ingathering was its own justification. But the allusion to booths in the wilderness took the lead in the minds of the artisans and traders of Jerusalem's markets and shops who were remote from the ingathering itself.

Yet the historical reason does not explain why the festival should have opened on the fifteenth day of the seventh month, or, for that matter, on any other date. No dramatic incident was associated with the particular date of the festival. The child who asked, "Why is today Passover?" was given his reply in Exodus. If he wanted to know, "Why do we celebrate Shabuot today?" the Pharisees had their answer. But if, living in the city and seeing nothing of the process of ingathering, he wanted to know, "Why is today Sukkot?" there was no point in the answer, "God provided booths for us when we were wandering in the wilderness," for the booths were presumably used every day of the year.

The Pharisees, with characteristic ingenuity, found an answer. Sukkot occurs at the season of the ingathering and about two or three weeks before the beginning of the rainy season. While the men of Jerusalem did not share the immediate thrill of the ingathering, they eagerly looked forward to the first rainfall, which was an even more immediate blessing to them than to the farmers. A drought could affect the peasant only after six or eight months, when the harvest time came; it brought misery to the poor artisan of Jerusalem at once. As the autumn equinox approached, he was watching the skies daily for signs of approaching rain, which would fill his cisterns, run almost dry through the long, hot, summer months. If the heavens failed him, there was indeed no hope. The few springs which bubbled about the city could hardly begin to meet the needs of its population.[7] Its governors had struggled for centuries to improve the water supply; but none had succeeded in making it adequate. Two thousand years were to pass before there was the possibility of bringing water by rail from the more fortunate coastal plain and *shefelah*, or to establish a western system of artificial pumps, aqueducts and reservoirs. In the third century B.C.E., the most imaginative did not dream of such inventions.

The patricians were, of course, in far less danger. Their larger and better built cisterns and pools contained enough water to meet their needs even in difficult times. If, by chance, their own supply fell short, they could turn to their neighbors, they could purchase whatever was brought into the city from outside, or, if all these expedients failed, they could retire to their lowland estates until the city's situation improved. But we may imagine with what trembling anxiety the plebeian groups of the metropolis greeted the autumn festival, which in good years heralded the first rainfall. Inevitably Sukkot became the occasion of both hope and fear: hope for the best, and fear of the worst.

The mixture of feelings became characteristic of the Pharisees' mode of celebrating the festival.

They adopted the ceremonies of fire and water which were universally used in the ancient world to stimulate the rain. They did not think of them as magical rites, but rather as methods of evoking God's pity and favor; and they rejoiced in the certainty that their prayers would be answered.

But it was not the joy of the ingathering of fruits which filled their hearts; it was the happiness that soon water would be plentiful. The men of the Sharon and Jezreel might rejoice in the crops of the past year; the men of Jerusalem were thinking of the rainfall of the morrow.

We can now see why the Sadducees could find no warrant for either of these customs in Scripture and opposed them as foreign innovations. True, they needed water for their crops, too, but the dominant emotion was at the moment the joy of the ingathering. Perhaps the high-priestly families, who were largely Sadducean, objected to the celebration lest it rival the ceremonial of the Day of Atonement. But more important than such personal considerations was the feeling that the traditional festival should not be insidiously transformed into an untraditional day of judgment.

Yet the issue was even broader than this. The water-libation was favored by the plebeian because it was essentially a plebeian offering. The semi-nomadic shepherd wandering over parched deserts considers water one of God's greatest gifts and believes it worthy of being offered in sacrifice to Him. Indeed an inscription discovered at Palmyra is dedicated "to the good and merciful God who drinks no wine."[8] When Samuel was about to pray for

Israel in Mizpah, they "drew water, and poured it out before
the Lord, and fasted on that day, and said there: 'We have
sinned against the Lord'" (I Sam. 7.6). When three friends
of David, taking his jest seriously, broke through the camp
of the Philistines and brought him water from the well of
Bethlehem, he could not drink it but "poured it out unto
the Lord" (II Sam. 23.16). Gideon, wishing to make a sacrifice to God, prepared a "kid, and unleavened cakes of an
ephah of meal; the flesh he put in a basket, and he put the
broth into a pot, and brought it out unto him under the tere-
binth, and presented it. And the angel of God said unto him,
'Take the flesh and the unleavened cakes, and lay them
upon this rock, and pour out the broth.' And he did so"
(Judg. 6.19). We cannot suppose that the angel ordered
the broth poured out in contempt. On the contrary, it was
a libation which God accepted as He did the flesh and
cakes which were burned by the fire from the rock.[9]

Even the four pitchers of water which Elijah poured over
the sacrifice and the wood on Mount Carmel (I Kings
18.34) may not have been intended, as is generally supposed,
to enhance the miracle of the divine fire. After all, it is
as much of a marvel that a small fire should come from
Heaven as a mighty conflagration. But Elijah was will-
fully pursuing his desert ritual, offering to his God a libation
of water and dramatically demonstrating to the assembled
multitude that God preferred it to the wine of the rural
grape-growers.[10]

The issue between water and wine which continued
throughout the First and Second Commonwealths was not
limited to the question of sacrifice. The plebeian water-
drinker considered it a symptom of moral deterioration for
Noah to plant a vineyard and, becoming drunk, to expose

himself to shame (Gen. 9.20). Jeremiah (35.6) deemed the Rechabites above praise because they rejected wine and clung to water. Long before him, Amos (2.12) had complained of the Israelites who gave the "Nazirites wine to drink." From the beginning of Jewish history to the end, the holy man desisted from wine. The plebeian Israelites did not, indeed, like the Nabataeans whom Diodorus describes, make the drinking of wine a capital crime;[11] but they considered abstinence characteristic of the holy man. During the Second Commonwealth, the Water Drinkers formed a significant sect,[12] and the poor, saintly R. Judah tells us that the four cups which, in accordance with custom, he drank on Passover night gave him a headache which lasted until the autumn.[13] On the other hand, the patrician High Priest, Simeon the Righteous, regarded withdrawal from wine a sin and therefore declined to partake of the sacrifice brought by a Nazirite.[14] Much later, R. Simeon ben Johai and R. Eleazar ha-Kappar, both patrician teachers of the second century, held that those who abstain from wine commit a sin and would have to answer for the dereliction on the day of judgment.[15]

These varied and conflicting opinions merely demonstrate the truism that the rural and patrician teachers, like their less educated followers, loved wine and respected its use, while the plebeian moralists tended to make a virtue out of necessity, and living in a community which could not afford intoxicants, held them to be evil.

The objection to water-libations was thus not merely theoretical; it had intense practical significance for the aristocrats and the Sadducees. To pour water to God was like giving Him a blemished animal. It was nothing short of an affront for which the direst vengeance might be exacted. The plebeian with his opposing traditions considered the libation satisfactory and acceptable, and especially appropriate when he was praying for rain.

With these facts in mind, we can understand the chagrin of the men of Jerusalem when Alexander Jannaeus, deriding their custom of water-pouring, spilt the water not on the altar but on his feet. No wonder the populace, parched with summer's thirst, anxious for the winter rains, were angered beyond measure and, forgetting the respect due to their priest and king, forgetting their debt to the house of the Hasmoneans, pelted him with the citrons which they had brought in celebration of the festival.[16] A mere deviation from ritual and even an offensive gesture directed at their prejudices could hardly have justified what was tantamount to a rebellion. The incident is most easily understood when we realize what the rain, and because of it the water-pouring, meant to the Jews of Jerusalem. To conform to a prejudice of his sect, the King was apparently prepared to sacrifice their most urgent need—water. Small wonder that their resentment almost broke all bounds. The later rabbis, whose sense of loyalty to the monarchy was strong and who lived in other parts of Palestine, could hardly believe that Jews would treat their King with indignity. They therefore tell the story, but change the central figure to an anonymous Sadducean High Priest. It is Josephus who has kept a record of the identity of the High Priest, King Alexander Jannaeus.

This explanation of the controversy between the Pharisees and the Sadducees helps to elucidate a number of other facts the meaning of which would otherwise be obscure. The Pharisees inserted in the second benediction of the *Shemoneh 'Esreh* a confession of faith in the resurrection.[17]

As part of it, they recited in the winter months or, more precisely, from the day after Sukkot till the first day of Passover, the praise of God as of "Him who causeth the wind to blow and the rain to descend." They did not mention this attribute in the summer.[18]

The variation between the summer formula and that of the winter is most striking. Note that it is not a prayer for rain that is omitted. That we might understand. Rain in the summer might conceivably be harmful. It is the praise of God as the giver of rain that is omitted; yet God is the giver of rain at all times, both summer and winter.

No less strange is it that the praise of God as rain-giver should have been inserted in the second benediction. Why was it not added to the first benediction which contains the other praises of God? The second was a controversial benediction, praising God as the one who would quicken the dead; the first contained the praises to which all sects agreed: "Blessed art thou, O Lord, our God and God of our fathers, God of Abraham, God of Isaac, and God of Jacob, the most high God, possessor of heaven and earth." It was there if anywhere that one would expect the additional glorification of God, "He who causeth the wind to blow and maketh the rain to descend." The second benediction reads merely: "Thou art mighty, feedest the living, quickenest the dead; blessed art thou, O Lord, who quickenest the dead." What is the relation of rain-giving to the resurrection? Did the Sadducees who denied the resurrection also deny that God was the rain-giver?

These difficulties disappear in view of what has been said. The Sadducees admitted that God caused the rain to descend. That is well attested in Scripture. They objected to the Pharisaic association of rain-giving with Sukkot.

The Pharisees, in order to stress their view, inserted in the second benediction, which they had established, a statement that God gave rain, but they recited it only from the day after Sukkot till Passover. This was an implied declaration that on Sukkot God decides whether He will give rain or not. To this doctrine the Sadducees made vigorous objection. The addition of the attribute, "who causeth the wind to blow and the rain to descend," occurred to the Pharisees only as part of their controversy with the Sadducees. It could not well be added to the first benediction, which had long been established, but was inserted in the second, the controversial paragraph.

It is important to note that in the closing chapters of Zechariah, which were probably composed in Jerusalem about half a century before the rise of the Pharisaic group as a definite sect, Sukkot is already intimately connected with the rain. "And it shall come to pass," we are told, "that every one that is left of all the nations that came against Jerusalem shall go up from year to year to worship the King, the Lord of hosts, and to keep the feast of tabernacles. And it shall be, that whoso of the families of the earth goeth not up unto Jerusalem to worship the King, the Lord of hosts, upon them there shall be no rain . . . This shall be the punishment of Egypt, and the punishment of all nations that go not up to keep the feast of tabernacles" (Zech. 14.16–19). The association of Sukkot with rain is thus less a Pharisaic than a Jerusalemite doctrine and its acceptance by the Pharisees points to their origin as a Jerusalem party.

There is a trace of this controversy in the Book of Chronicles, a century before Deutero-Zechariah. The Chronicler retells the story of David who poured out the water brought to him by friends, and changes the verb slightly so as to make it signify "poured it out unto the Lord" as a libation (I Chron. 11.18). This modification can have only one purpose: to stress the antiquity of water-libations and thus to justify the plebeian contention in this regard. Since Sukkot was the only festival about whose offerings there ever arose a controversy of this nature, the Chronicler is obviously here giving his support to the predecessors of Pharisaism. It is characteristic of his day that this agreement should be expressed by innuendo rather than directly, and implied in a story rather than commanded.

The transformation of Sukkot from a festival of in-gathering into a period of judgment influenced the Pharisaic interpretation of the other festivals, Pesah (Passover) and Shabuot (Feast of Weeks). In the course of time, Pharisaic theology developed the theory that there are "four seasons when the world is judged: on Passover with regard to the crops; on Shabuot with regard to the fruit of the trees; on Rosh ha-Shanah all creatures pass before God as in a regiment; and on Sukkot they are judged regarding rainfall."[19] This doctrine of four periods of judgment in the year is not an invention of the *tannaim*; it is of early Pharisaic origin. It can be traced back to the Book of Jubilees. The writer of that work, in his anxiety to please both Sadducees and Pharisees, offers a compromise between the views of the two schools and suggests that there are four days of judgment. According to him, these are not the great festivals but rather the first days of the first, fourth, seventh and tenth months.[20] Obviously, this is intended to satisfy the Pharisees by granting them four days of judgment and the Sadducees by making the four days not the festivals, as the Pharisees taught, but the first days of each quarter of the year.

The Pharisaic influence is clear in the suggestion that the four days be called "days of remembrance." The expression "days of remembrance" does not occur in Scripture but is regularly used in the liturgy for Rosh ha-Shanah. What was more likely to suggest to the reader that the four days are to take the place of the four "periods of judgment" than to call them "days of remembrance"? There is no other reason why the writer of the Book of Jubilees should have proposed four days of remembrance rather than one, and attached such importance to them.

Another passage in the Book of Jubilees may be associated with this controversy. Abraham, we are told, sat up "through the night of the new moon of the seventh month to observe the stars from the evening till the morning in order to see what would be the character of the year in regard to rains."[21] In this type of book, incidents are not invented except with a particular purpose. This story seems intended to tell us that the year's rainfall is determined on Rosh ha-Shanah rather than on Sukkot.

At any rate, there is evidence in what has been said of a profound disagreement between Pharisees and Sadducees in regard to the meaning of Sukkot. For the Pharisees it was the season of sacrifice, prayer and water-rites; for the Sadducees it was the feast of ingathering and nothing more.

But, the reader will ask, did the farmers not need rain? Why then should the Sadducees who stood in such close relations with them, object to a rain ceremony? The answer is not far to seek. The Sadducees, taught by their priestly leaders, looked primarily to the service of the Day of Atonement for the year's blessings. They believed that if the service of the Day of Atonement was properly carried through, God would grant all His blessings to His people. They approached the Sukkot festival full of joy at the season of ingathering and strong in their faith that on the Day of Atonement the High Priest had won for them blessings for the year. They could not share the feeling with which the parched population of Jerusalem approached the festival that was the forerunner of the blessed rains. Hence they opposed the innovation.

B. The Date of Shabuot*

One of the most famous sectarian controversies is concerned with the date of Shabuot (Pentecost). The Pharisees observed Shabuot on the fiftieth day after the first day of Passover; the Sadducees on the seventh Sunday after the Passover week. Since all agreed that biblical law fixed the festival for the fiftieth day after the sacrifice of the first sheaf of barley cut from the fields, there was a corresponding disagreement as to the time of that offering. The Pharisees asserted that it should be made on the second day of Passover, the Sadducees on the Sunday of the Passover week.

On the surface, nothing could be more trivial than such a controversy. The biblical verses in Leviticus which give the provisions of the law are concededly ambiguous.[22] They provide that the first barley shall be cut and sacrificed on the morrow after the "*sabbath*," but the word may mean either the weekly Sabbath or the Passover festival. But if nothing more were involved in the issue than this, established custom or scholarly exegesis could certainly have solved the problem in early times. The difficulty lay rather in the implications of the date question. The Phari-

* Cf. Supplement, pp. 641-654.

sees gave Shabuot a fixed day because, they said, it commemorated the Sinaitic theophany which occurred on the
fiftieth day after the Exodus. The Sadducees denied that
the festival had any historical allusion or that the date of
the revelation was known.[23]

The identification of Shabuot with the season of Revelation, not mentioned indeed in Scripture, was yet made in
early times. Though the first talmudic sages who refer to
it flourished in the second century C.E., they merely transmitted a much older tradition.[24] The oldest portions of the
liturgy know Shabuot as the "day of the giving of our
Torah" and, what is perhaps more important, the Book of
Jubilees, composed early in the Maccabean age, recognizes
the historical background of the festival.[25]

Most significant of all, however, is the fact that a passage
in Joshua which, however late, must be pre-Maccabean,
and the Septuagint (ca. 300 B.C.E.) give support to the
Pharisaic teaching. The Book of Joshua clearly fixes the
time when the new grain may be eaten as the second day
of Passover. Speaking of the Israelites who entered Canaan
on the tenth day of the first month, four days before
Passover, it says: "And they did eat of the produce of the
land on the morrow after the passover, unleavened cakes
and parched corn, in the selfsame day. And the manna
ceased on the morrow, after they had eaten of the produce
of the land" (Josh. 5.11).

Moreover, the same interpretation of the passage in
Leviticus is also found in the Septuagint which substitutes
for the phrase, "the morrow of the sabbath," "the morrow
of the first day of Passover" (Lev. 23.15).

By removing the ambiguity of the passage in Leviticus,
the Septuagint as well as the Book of Joshua adopt the view

later pressed so vigorously by the Pharisees, and by implication indicate that the controversy regarding the date and significance of Shabuot had already arisen.[26]

Why did the Pharisees and their predecessors attach such importance to the historical significance of Shabuot? Because, since they were essentially town plebeians, it had no meaning for them otherwise. Ezekiel, for instance, who either did not know or did not accept this explanation of Shabuot, ignores the festival altogether and omits it from his calendar.[27]

For the farmers of the Maccabean age, Shabuot could serve as the harvest festival, as it did for their ancestors of the Davidic and Solomonic days. The joy of the harvest filled them with the desire for the festival. And the seventh week after Passover was about the time of the wheat harvest.

The inhabitant of Jerusalem was not indifferent to the question of the harvest. But he viewed the harvest from a distance; he had not ploughed; he had not watched the stalks; nor had he waited for it. If Shabuot was to have any significance for him and above all for his children, he had to find some meaning for it other than its agricultural associations.

The Pharisaic leaders, scholars and scribes that they were, had doubtless long wondered why the Sinaitic theophany, which alone gave meaning to the Exodus, was not celebrated by any festival. The birth of Israel as a nation was marked by Passover. Was it possible that the incident which had established Israel as a divine people would be passed over in silence?

The Pharisees' comparative divorce from agriculture and their interest in the Law thus combined to suggest the

association of Shabuot with the revelation on Sinai, just as
similar conditions in urban America have practically transformed Thanksgiving Day into an historical festival celebrating the landing of the Pilgrim Fathers. But this reinterpretation necessarily gave the festival a fixed date. The
Sadducees, with their rural background, could see no reason
for the new tradition. They found no authority for it in
Scripture and denounced it as pure imagination.

C. THE DAY OF ATONEMENT*

From their own point of view, perhaps the most important
and solemn difference between Pharisees and the Sadducees
concerned the ritual of the high-priestly service on the Day
of Atonement. The Law required that on that day the High
Priest should enter the Holy of Holies, the sacred compartment which otherwise remained closed throughout the year.
Within its dark walls, where Solomon had prayed that the
divine Presence might manifest itself, the High Priest
offered incense before the Lord. The controversy centers,
as usual, about what seems at first a most insignificant
detail of the ceremony.

The Sadducees maintained that the fire should be put
upon the incense in the outer hall and that the priest should
enter the mysterious darkness with the sweet-smelling smoke
before him, whereas the Pharisees held, on the contrary,
that the incense had to be kindled in the holy chamber
itself.[28]

Such significance did the Pharisees attach to this detail
that when they were in power, they compelled the High
Priest, who was generally a Sadducee, to take an oath that
he would perform the ceremony in accordance with their

* Cf. Supplement, pp. 654-660.

ruling.[29] The question is, however, how had they developed an opinion in the matter? This was not a popular custom like the water-drawing or the observance of Shabuot, in regard to which different communities were likely to develop varying ideas. The High Priests had always been patricians and had presumably worked out a ritual for their own guidance as they understood the biblical commandment. Did the Pharisees interfere merely for the sake of change and to display their power?

The Sadducean custom is, as a matter of fact, no less perplexing than the Pharisaic objection to it, for the simple reading of the Bible supports the contention of the Pharisees. In describing the ritual, the Levitical law says: "And he shall take a censer full of coals of fire from off the altar before the Lord, and his hands full of sweet incense beaten small, and bring it within the veil. And he shall put the incense upon the fire before the Lord" (Lev. 16.12). There is no ambiguity to the order. The priest brings the fire and the incense within the veil separately, into the holy compartment and there "puts the incense upon the fire."[30] Why did the High Priests disobey the express word of the Scriptures in a matter of such solemnity and sacred privilege?

To Professor Jacob Z. Lauterbach belongs the merit of having explained the principles underlying the strange controversy between the ancient sects.[31] The High Priest, who was about to enter the Holy of Holies alone in the darkness to minister at the Rock on which God was supposed to reveal Himself, was in mortal terror, brave though he might otherwise be. He could not forget the ominous warning of Scripture which, after describing the details of the ritual, adds "that he may not die." The Talmud tells us that the High Priest was forbidden to prolong his stay in the chamber

lest he terrify the congregation waiting in the outer courts
with beating hearts for his return from the dangerous visit.[32]
If the anxiety of the bystanders was so great, what must
have been that of the chief participant. He was fearful of
a wrong step and most fearful lest, on entering the dark
vault, he see before him the vision of the Deity whom none
may look upon and live. We can thus readily understand
how a timid High Priest would take it upon himself to try
to put the incense on the fire outside the chamber so as to
protect himself by a smoke-screen from whatever was to be
seen within. The Sadducees, as the party of the aristocrats
from which the High Priests came, were guided in their
interpretation of the law solely by the actual custom. At
first they considered the deviation permitted and finally
they declared it mandatory.

To the Pharisees, none of whom ever had to pass through
the ordeal of this lonely visit and sacrifice, it seemed wrong
to disobey the express word of God; the more especially
because the motive was unworthy, and one of superstitious
terror. According to their conception of God, He was not to
be seen at all and if He chose to make manifest a vision to
the High Priest it would be for life and not for death. The
high-priestly device was inexcusable—legally, because it
violated the written word, and theologically because it involved the crudest anthropomorphism.

The custom approved by the Sadducees must have come
into vogue before the Maccabean Rebellion. After that
period, the prestige of the Law became so great and the
respect in which it was held by everyone in all its minutiae
was so complete that not the slightest degree of deviation
could have been inaugurated. Had the Pharisaic custom
been followed in pre-Maccabean times, it would have had

the double sanction of writ and precedent, which could hardly have been overcome by the stress of superstition. It follows therefore that the protective device of the High Priests must have been invented and established generations before the Maccabean Rebellion. It came down from the past, side by side with the Scripture itself, the actual practice serving as commentary to the written word. We must also assume that throughout this time the plebeian scholars continued their opposition to the established form, contending that the order prescribed in the Bible was obligatory and that the High Priests were breaking the law. When the inchoate plebeian opposition became solidified in a Pharisaic party, the issue became partisan and sectarian and gained in bitterness in proportion as the matter discussed became sacred and exalted.

D. The Ritual of the Red Heifer*

A fourth sectarian controversy, based on the opposing interests of plebeians and patricians, concerned the ritual of the red heifer.

This ceremony was one of the most picturesque of the high-priestly functions. So highly was it regarded that, although Scripture provides that it be performed by one of the subordinate priests—Eleazar, not Aaron, is designated for it—yet the High Priests arrogated it to themselves.[33] According to rabbinic tradition, only seven of these heifers were sacrificed during the entire period of the Second Commonwealth and we know that, after the fall of the Temple, the last ashes were preserved by the Jews with great care and were still used as late as the third century.[34]

* Cf. Supplement, pp. 661-692.

The purpose of this strange observance was to purify anyone who had come in contact with a dead body. According to the Levitical law, such a person was to be considered impure for seven days. In order that he might be ritually clean at the expiration of that time, he had to be sprinkled during the period with water in which were mixed ashes of the red heifer.[35] The heifer, the ashes of which were to be used for this purpose, was carefully selected and watched from birth lest any blemish make her unfit for use. She could become contaminated easily; if she knew the yoke or if she grew two black hairs, she ceased to be fit for sacrifice. There was much ado about the place of slaughter and burning, about the manner of leading her there and about the care of the ashes, to prevent contamination.

The controversy between the Pharisees and the Sadducees was about a detail in the observance. The law required that the priest who prepared the red heifer be Levitically pure; but what was meant by "pure"?

If a man touched the carcass of a dead animal, he was, according to Leviticus 11.28, "unclean until the even." The verse says nothing about the necessity of bathing. On the other hand, we are told somewhat later that if anyone touches a person "that hath the issue," he must "bathe himself in water, and be unclean until the even" (Lev. 15.7). The same law applies to a man who has had sexual intercourse (Lev. 15.16). The rule was made uniform by early exegesis which seems to have required a ritual bath for all manner of impurity that lasted "till even."

The scriptural verses imply that the effect of the bath comes only with nightfall and that till then the person remains in the status of impurity. The Pharisees, however, maintained that this was not the correct interpretation of the Law. They insisted that the bath (*tebilah*) served to mitigate the impurity, though it did not completely remove it. The person who has bathed might not enter the Temple nor eat of the sacrifices or even of the heave-offering (*terumah*) but he might come into the "camp." He ceased to spread impurity among others and might therefore take part in the communal life.[36] He might eat of the tithes, the degree of holiness of which was less than that of the heave-offering. Finally, if he were a priest, he might take part in the sacrifice of the red heifer, which was carried out on the Mount of Olives[37] although, since he was unable to enter the Temple, he could not take part in any other sacrifice.

The Sadducees denied that a man who had "bathed from his impurity" but "upon whom the sun had not set" (that is, who was still within the first day of his impurity) could sacrifice the red heifer. They maintained that only a priest who was entirely pure, who had bathed from his impurity, if he had any, and had waited till the setting of the sun for complete purification could offer the sacrifice.[38]

It would seem that the controversy centers around a matter of unimportant ritual detail, but for the Pharisees it was apparently of great consequence. So insistent were they on the correctness of their views that they would compel the High Priest who was about to perform the ceremony to enter into a state of impurity, so that he might have to bathe, and then, by performing the sacrifice before the setting of the sun, testify to his acceptance of their interpretation.[39]

Commentators on the Mishna find some difficulty in explaining the strange perversity of the Pharisees.[40] For what could possibly be gained by rendering impure a priest who was pure? All agreed that a pure priest could perform the sacrifice legally. There was some question—and in view of the literal meaning of the biblical verses, serious question—whether a man who had bathed after his defilement but was still within the day of it could offer the sacrifice. Since the red heifer was sacrificed only about once in a half-century, no great harm could have resulted if its performance were delayed until the High Priest could perform it in a manner to satisfy the most exacting. But granted that the Pharisees were certain that their interpretation was correct, why should they compel a pure High Priest to defile himself? This astonishing obstinacy is hardly in keeping with the urbanity for which Josephus praises them.

We are further told that a certain High Priest, Ishmael ben Phiabi, accidentally prepared the red heifer in a state of complete purity. The Pharisees, who had neglected to make him impure, insisted that the ashes, prepared with such diligence and at such cost, be strewn and wasted and that another heifer be prepared in accordance with their lenient views.[41] And then there is the story of R. Johanan ben Zakkai, the man of peace and quiet, disciple of the great compromiser Hillel, who nevertheless lost all his usual tolerance when he found that the High Priest of his day was preparing to sacrifice the red heifer without previous defilement. "My lord High Priest," he said to him, "how much the high-priesthood becomes you! Will you not step in and bathe only once before performing the sacrifice?" The High Priest, moved by these kindly words, proceeded to bathe although, being quite pure, it was not necessary. As the priest returned, R. Johanan, still dissatisfied, approached him and nipped his ear in such a way as to make him a man with a "physical blemish" and unfit to perform any priestly service.[42] That R. Johanan should thus resort to physical force to prevent a practice which the Pharisees did not consider objectionable but merely unnecessary, seems incredible if we suppose that the matter rested on nothing more than a scholastic controversy.

But a consideration of the plebeian status of the Pharisees, throws a new light on the entire situation. The laws of impurity, which applied only to frequenters of the Temple, did not fall heavily upon the agriculturists. None of them made themselves pure except at the festival periods when they came to the Temple as pilgrims. Nor did the laws fall severely upon the priesthood, who, living at the Temple, could avoid contamination. They did bear hard on the inhabitants of Jerusalem. Artisans and traders, they sold wine and grain for use at sacrificial meals, vessels for the preparation of meals, priestly apparel, and other necessities of life. In order not to defile their wares, they had to remain in a state of purity. Moreover, many of them doubtless ate of the second tithe which the farmers, in accordance with the Law, brought to Jerusalem during the greater part of the year. In defilement, they were forbidden this holy food. A citizen of Jerusalem who found that he was impure with a major impurity—which meant, it must be remembered, not only when he had happened to touch an unclean vessel or attend a funeral but also when he had been with his wife—was literally barred from his own home. If he used a knife in a state of impurity, the knife became impure and would thereafter render impure any food with which it came in contact. If he touched an earthenware vessel or stove, it became incurably impure. The neighbors with whom he shared the stove would thus not let him approach it. In fact, he himself would not dare to draw near it, for if the stove became impure, the people who came to Jerusalem for the festivals would be compelled to seek food and lodging elsewhere.

One of the most important Pharisaic interpretations of the Law sought to remedy the difficulty by declaring that when a man had bathed after a major impurity he still remained unclean until evening—in accordance with the literal word of Scripture—yet not in the original sense of being able to impart impurity to household utensils, but in the lesser degree of merely being barred from the Temple and sacrificial meat.

This is the Pharisaic conception of *tebul yom*, a man who has bathed (*tabal*) from impurity but has not yet ended the day for which he is condemned to Levitical uncleanliness.

This law did not affect the country people at all, since they did not observe the laws of purity in their homes. During the Passover week, they could easily remain in a state of complete purity. Nor were the priests, the backbone of the Sadducean party, affected by it. They were still barred from the Temple and from the *terumah* until the sun had set on the day of their impurity. As for their contact with the lay population of Jerusalem, they must have accepted the Pharisaic ruling, since all the lay population of Jerusalem lived by it. To have rejected it would have meant starving themselves and making the Temple services impossible. This is apart from what Josephus and the Talmud tell us of the power of the Pharisaic populace to impose its will upon the Sadducean nobility and priesthood.[43]

Only at the ceremony of the red heifer were the Sadducean priests embarrassed by the Pharisaic ruling. They had accepted the Pharisaic Shabuot as a Temple holiday.

They offered incense on the Day of Atonement in accordance with Pharisaic teachings. In these matters there was a clear variation of custom. However, where their views were more stringent than those of their opponents, they thought it unreasonable that they should be compelled to act against their conscience. They found no warrant for the underlying conception of *tebul yom* in Scripture and it seemed to them that it had been purposely created to meet a difficulty in observing the Law. Moreover, a conscientious Sadducee could not agree readily to what he considered a defilement of the ashes of the red heifer, for that would render the ashes ineffective and nullify all future purifications performed with them.

The Pharisees could not agree to the Sadducean requirement that the priest officiating at the red heifer ceremonial be completely pure. The sacrifice was performed not in the Temple but on the Mount of Olives, and the only justification for absolute purity would have been a rejection of the Pharisaic doctrine of *tebul yom*. But how could the urban Pharisees abandon a teaching which alone made it possible for them to live a normal life?

The Pharisaic opposition to the Sadducean severity was thus not a matter of perversity at all. It was a question of clear necessity. In a Jerusalem which had become a large metropolis, it was impossible without some mitigating interpretation to maintain a law according to which the larger part of the population was defiled daily. The only logical arrangement was the one proposed by the Pharisees which resulted in a widespread custom of bathing each morning to wash away any impurity. This custom we find exemplified in Judith (12.8) who bathed each morning while she was in the camp of the enemy, where she was unable to avoid touching impure vessels and other utensils. The advantages which this interpretation gave to the plebeian merchant of Jerusalem were such that he could not surrender them. The only occasion when he was called upon to defend his doctrine was at the ceremony of the red heifer and it was then that he insisted upon the acceptance of his interpretation.

E. THE IMPURITY OF METALS*

"On one occasion," the Talmud tells us, "the *menorah* (the candelabrum in the Temple) had to be purified. The Sadducees who saw the procedure mocked, saying, 'Look at the Pharisees who are about to bathe the orb of the sun!' "[44]

Neither the Talmud nor the writers on the subject have any definite record of a controversy that would have justified the Sadducees in laughing at the Pharisaic lustration of the temple candelabrum. Merely to remark that the Pharisees were more stringent in their observance of Levitical purity than the Sadducees does not assist us much, for we know that in some respects the Sadducees were more rigorous.[45]

The story is, however, illuminated by the tradition handed down in the Jerusalem as well as the Babylonian Talmud, that "Simeon ben Shattah decreed that the laws of impurity should apply also to utensils made of metal."[46] We are further informed that he was also the sponsor for a decree bringing glassware under the laws of impurity.[47] We might suppose a priori that the Sadducees would refuse to accept a decree of Simeon ben Shattah (ca. 75 B.C.E.), especially when, even according to him, it was not based

* Cf. Supplement, pp. 693-694.

on biblical law or precedent but was merely an order of the Sanhedrin which he controlled. All doubt about the matter is removed by the incident we have just cited. The Sadducees laughed at the Pharisaic purification of the Menorah because they held that being made of metal, it could not become Levitically impure.

What were the conditions that lay behind this controversy?

The Scriptures in their various regulations about ritual purity speak of utensils made of wood, hides, cloth, and clay.[48] There are no provisions regarding metallic household articles. The reason for this is simple. In early times Jews did not use metal articles in their houses. The Temple, and perhaps the King, had gold, iron, and bronze dishes of various types, but not the rest of the people. Metal was expensive, and household arrangements in ancient Judea were primitive. As time passed, the richer classes probably provided themselves with such luxuries as knives and metal cups. Ultimately even glass, the most expensive of all articles in Judea, was used by some of the nobility. But among the artisan and trading masses all these remained unknown.[49]

Since the Scriptures made no express provision for the impurity of glass and metal utensils, they were touched by their owners, even in a state of impurity, without compunction and without lustration. The plebeians could see no reason for giving such special immunity to these utensils of luxury. Their view was not without support in the Torah, for in Numbers 31.22 the rule is laid down, "Howbeit the gold, and the silver, the brass, the iron, the tin, and the lead, every thing that may abide the fire, ye shall make to go through the fire, and it shall be clean; nevertheless it shall be purified with the water of sprinkling; and all that

abideth not the fire ye shall make to go through the water."
The patricians presumably held that purification was required only under the special conditions discussed in the
passage, namely, for vessels captured in war with the
heathen. They declined to extend the rule to metalware in
general.

The controversy regarding the matter had begun long
before the origin of the Pharisaic party. Even during the
turmoil of the Maccabean Wars, the plebeian sages, led by
Jose ben Joezer and Jose ben Johanan, decreed impurity
for glassware. Such a step would hardly have been taken
in the midst of unsettled conditions had not the issue been
raised and contested in earlier times. No special regulation
was made concerning metal goods, for it was held that they
were included in the biblical provision. Eighty years later,
however, when the Pharisees attained full power in the
state under Queen Salome, they not only reaffirmed the
impurity of glass, but issued a similar decree against metalware. The decree was opposed by the Sadducees who
regarded it as an innovation pointed against themselves.

F. The Sabbath Lights*

A special series of controversies arose from differences
concerning the Sabbath. The Sabbath, during the Second
Commonwealth, became the foremost institution in Judaism, as sacred in its way as the Temple itself. More than
once Jerusalem was taken without resistance because its
soldiers refused to fight on the Sabbath day.[50] Authentic
records tell us that in "the days of the Greeks," a man was
executed for riding on a horse in violation of the Sabbath.[51]
The Book of Jubilees (50.8 ff.) enumerates some fifteen

* Cf. Supplement, p. 660.

activities which it considers violations of the Sabbath punishable by death, and the Mishna classifies the prohibited acts under no less than thirty-nine heads.[52]

Disagreement about the rules governing the Sabbath observance of necessity tended to become factional and bitter. It was doubtless thus that a violent controversy arose about the beautiful custom of kindling Sabbath lights. Geiger was the first to suggest that the Sadducees forbade the use of fire on the Sabbath, and his view is now generally accepted.[53] The Pharisees, on the contrary, maintained that kindling the lights on the Sabbath eve was not merely permitted, but an absolute command. They declared it the foremost duty and privilege of the Jewish woman, and their rabbinic disciples devoted a whole chapter in the Mishna to the rules concerning the wick and oils to be used.

We may be certain that this controversy did not arise from a disagreement among exegetes as to the meaning of the verse: "Ye shall kindle no fire throughout your habitations upon the sabbath day" (Ex. 35.3). Customs create exegesis, not exegesis customs. Particularly was this true in ancient times when customs were naturally expressions of the popular soul and resisted artificial or arbitrary imposition.

A more probable explanation of this difference between the sects is that it arose naturally from the everyday conditions prevailing in ancient Judea, which made the use of fire on the Sabbath superfluous for patrician farmers and absolutely essential for plebeians, especially those who lived in Jerusalem.

It will be remembered that the patrician farmers of Judea had their estates mainly in the lowland of the coastal plain or about Jericho, whereas the plebeians were confined to the highlands. Now, as anyone who has traveled in the Holy Land knows, there is a sharp difference in temperature between the plains and the hills during the rainy winter season. Jericho is always tropical, and the coastal plain, too, is warm even in December and January, when the cold in Jerusalem is distinctly uncomfortable.[54]

The Bible tells how, in ancient times, King Jehoiakim had a special winter house in which he sat "in the ninth month" with the hearth fire burning before him, while the dire prophecies of Jeremiah were being read to him (Jer. 36.22). As late as the Passover season (the beginning of April) there was a fire burning in the home of the High Priest at which Peter warmed himself.[55] Likewise, in early autumn, on the Day of Atonement (the end of September), the waters in Jerusalem were so cold that heated irons were lowered into them to remove the chill when the High Priest underwent the five required ritual baths.[56]

At no season was artificial heat required in the lowlands. Fire was used there only to prepare food. Since cooking on the Sabbath was prohibited, the prosperous farmer of the valleys ushered in the holy day by extinguishing all his fires at sunset on Friday. The highland peasant and the native of Jerusalem, shivering in the chill of winter rain, could not indulge in this observance. They would not kindle a fire on the Sabbath, but neither would they extinguish the fires which were already burning. The lowland farmer became so addicted to his custom that he regarded fire as tabu on the Sabbath and, even when he removed to Jerusalem, his conscience would not let him avail himself of the plebeian leniency in this respect. As a matter of fact, if he had chosen to yield to the demands of the rigorous climate, class fashion—always the most tyrannical of masters—would have kept him from doing so. The ancient

Judean patrician coming to Jerusalem could no more reconcile himself to the use of fire on the Sabbath than the modern colonial official, called to govern a tropical country, can discard ceremonial evening clothes at dinner.

Moreover, among the plebeians of Jerusalem, fire was needed not only for heat but also for light. This use was practically unknown in the country, either on the hills or in the valleys. The Judean peasants, like their fellow-farmers of all times and all regions, were doubtless in the habit of going to sleep immediately after dark. There was nothing else to do. Public gatherings or festivities were not easily arranged at night, since travel was difficult, and even social visiting was done preferably by day. It was far otherwise in Jerusalem and other large towns. The Mishna, doubtless recording an urban practice, tells us that on Friday nights a teacher may read with his pupils by candle-light.[57] We know that at least on one occasion the children of R. Gamaliel came home from a banquet after midnight.[58] The Passover celebration among the plebeians generally lasted till late in the evening, frequently till midnight, and sometimes later.[59] We are told that R. Meir (and probably others) were accustomed to deliver lectures on Sabbath eve.[60] The Mishna contemplates the possibility of a person reading the *Shema'* as late as midnight. It is interesting to note that R. Eliezer b. Hyrcanus, a native of the country, opposed this rule and limited the time to the end of the first watch.[61]

The difference in habit between city and country inevitably affected the methods of welcoming Queen Sabbath. The Judean peasant, not knowing what to do with his Friday night leisure and being accustomed to early hours, went to bed soon after the Sabbath fell. The city-dweller, on the other hand, prepared to spend the evening visiting his friends, listening to a learned lecture or reviewing the weekly portion of the Pentateuch for the next morning's public reading. His last work on the weekday was to kindle lights for the Sabbath day. As time went on, the ushering in of the Sabbath, which had become associated for one group of people with the extinguishing of what they knew to be the week-day fire, was marked by the other with the kindling of what they recognized as Sabbath lights.

Since it was established by the plebeians of Jerusalem, the custom was accepted as a Pharisaic ceremony and thus made its way into many rural hamlets where it could not have been indigenous. Still, some resistance to it must have continued for centuries after the Pharisees had won apparent control of the whole Jewish community, for, during the seventh century, the ancient tabu against the use of fire was resurrected by the Karaites and made one of the fundamentals of their schismatic faith. They could hardly have invented the prohibition; nor could they have discovered it in extant literature. They must have found it current in some of the backward settlements which still clung to the ancient practice of the lowland peasants.

The rules regarding the Sabbath apply with equal force to the Day of Atonement; hence the difference in practice concerning the use of light and fire on the Sabbath extended also to that solemn festival. But, while the peasants of Judea and Galilee readily accepted the plebeian ruling for the Sabbath, their awe for *Yom ha-Kippurim* prevented them from violating their ancestral habits on that day. In many Pharisaic communities, therefore, the lights would be kindled on Friday evening but not on the eve of the Day of Atonement. The distinction is recorded in the Mishna:

"In localities where it is customary to kindle the lights for the Day of Atonement, they are kindled; where it is customary not to kindle them, they are not kindled."[62] Perforce the rabbinic authorities recognized the right of the local group to decide against the majority practice. This tolerance, however, did not extend to the Sabbath lights which had become universal among the plebeians and had developed into a subject of sectarian controversy.

As generations passed and children grew up who remembered the delight of well-lit Sabbath homes, the natural beginnings of the custom of kindling Sabbath lights were forgotten in the reverence for their beauty and splendor. To kindle the lights became one of the highest privileges of Jewish wifehood and the tenderest memories of a Jewish child go back to the picture of his mother, standing before her Sabbath lights, transfigured by the spiritual joy of the oncoming Sabbath.

G. The Merging of Households on the Sabbath (*'Erub*)*

Professor Jeremias tells how on the occasion of his first visit to Jerusalem many years ago, before electricity and telephones had become common, he was amazed to find strange wires drawn about various parts of the city.

"Are you so advanced that you have electric connections here?" he asked.

He was informed, however, that the wires were connected not with modern science but with ancient ritual.[63] They were needed to enable Jews to carry burdens on the Sabbath from house to house within certain districts. This interesting custom was the subject of a bitter sectarian controversy between Pharisee and Sadducee.

* Cf. Supplement, pp. 718 ff.

The controversy arose out of the attempt of ancient Jewish Law to suppress commercial traffic on the Sabbath. To accomplish this, it forbade the transfer of goods from place to place on the holy day. Both jurists and people more easily understood a prohibition against the tangible act of carrying a burden than against the legal concepts of purchase and sale. Hence, when Nehemiah found peddlars, peasants and Tyrian fishermen bringing their wares into Jerusalem for marketing on the Sabbath, he denounced not their commercial traffic but their bearing "all manner of burdens" (Neh. 13.15). The unknown prophet, whose words were incorporated in the seventeenth chapter of Jeremiah, also inveighs against those who carry a "burden on the Sabbath day," and "bring it in by the gates of Jerusalem" (17.21). He adds, however: "Neither carry forth a burden out of your houses on the Sabbath day, neither do ye any work; but hallow ye the Sabbath day, as I commanded your fathers." There was thus established a norm against taking anything into or out of a house on the Sabbath.

For the purposes of the Law the whole of a man's private estate was considered his house, so that the farmers and city patricians had no difficulty in bringing food or other necessities from court or garden into the house or vice versa. The plebeian, however, who lived in the crowded slums of Jerusalem, where one court was shared by several families, found the observance of the Law very difficult. In the little cubicles where the poor dwelt, there was not even room for their meager household utensils. Food had to be left in the court; water had to be brought from the common cistern; yet a literal interpretation of the Law regarded carrying either into the house as a violation of the Sabbath.

To meet this difficulty, the plebeians began to merge their several households into a single large unit for the Sabbath. They would prepare their meals and eat them together, and consider themselves a single family. This made it possible for them to carry things not only from their various houses into the common court but from one house to another during the Sabbath day.

Gradually, the common meal, which was frequently inconvenient to arrange, became a merely formal supplement to the regular breakfasts and dinners which were taken at home. In the end, all that was left of this custom was a special loaf of bread, kneaded from flour contributed by each family in the court; a potential meal which was never eaten at all. In this manner, the rigorous law was fully circumvented and adjusted. Actual sale on the Sabbath and the significant transfer of property remained forbidden, but the personal hardships involved in the prohibition were overcome.

The aristocrats, however, living in spacious homes or on large country estates, had never felt the weight of the original law. They were quite satisfied with the prohibition and saw no reason for evading it. What appeared to the plebeian as a natural adjustment of the Law was in the eyes of the patrician a monstrous fiction invented to flout it. He denied that a mere formal merger of households permitted the inhabitants of a court or alley to transfer goods from one house to another. So important was the arrangement for the life and well-being of the plebeians, however, that they declared the denial itself to be schismatic and heretical. In this manner arose the controversy concerning the validity of the 'erub (the formal or fictional merging of households).[64]

In later times, the principle of the *'erub* was extended, and it became customary to "merge" not only the households using the same court but the courts which opened into a single lane. In the final development of the institution, whole villages and even cities were "merged" into a single "household", enabling people to carry their burdens on the Sabbath within the limits of the locality without hindrance. In order to bring these larger units within the Law, it was necessary to surround them with a symbolic "wall" which ultimately became reduced to a wire stretched around the city boundaries. These wires can be seen in many European towns and are put up every Friday to make possible the "merging of the households" on the Sabbath. It was these wires which Professor Jeremias was so astonished to see in Jerusalem.

H. The Rights of Daughters as Heirs*

The social differences between the sects, which so deeply affected their attitude toward ritual, were reflected with equal clarity in their interpretations of the Civil Law. But whereas the ceremonial customs of the Sadducees were practically all inherited from their rural ancestors, the juristic decisions rendered by their judges were fixed during their experience as patricians in Jerusalem. Such questions as the rights of daughters to share in their parents' property, or of the punishment of false witnesses, or of the responsibility of masters for damages done by their slaves, were not issues on which *popular* class traditions could develop. Controversies arose regarding them only as the judges drawn from the opposing groups found themselves interpreting the Law in different manners. Hence the controversies between the sects in questions of Civil Law have

* Cf. Supplement, pp. 694-696.

about them a clear and recognized awareness of opposing class interests which is lacking in the more natural disagreements regarding ceremonial observances.

While in each case of disagreement on questions of Civil Law, we can see how the patrician interest clashed with that of the plebeians, the Sadducees were encouraged in espousing their class views in this field by the fact that they generally had the support of the patrician-controlled Roman Law.[65]

Both aspects of the Sadducean argument, the dominating class interest and the influence of Roman Law, are clearly exemplified in the controversy regarding the rights of daughters to inherit.[66]

As is well known, biblical Law recognizes sons as primary heirs; daughters inherit property only where there are no sons (Num. 27.8). It was assumed from the beginning that this precedence of brothers over sisters descended also to their sons; so that, if a man died while his father was alive, his sons took his place as next of kin, and were given precedence over any female relative.

The question arose, however, whether this rule applied also to the daughters of a son. If, for instance, the genealogical table was as follows:

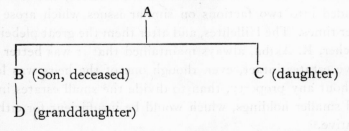

i. e., if B died while his father was alive, did D, his daughter, inherit his rights of priority over his sister, C?

Logically, it would seem that, even from the point of view of the ancients, who had such deep respect for masculinity, little could be said in favor of granting D the whole of her grandfather's property and disinheriting C. Certainly a man's child should not be set aside in favor of his grandchild, when they were both of the same sex. And, indeed, the Sadducees did maintain that in such a case the daughter and granddaughter divided the property equally.

The Pharisees, however, insisted that the granddaughter inherited all her father's rights and was the sole heir. This view, which seems so contrary to the general tendency of the Pharisees toward the emancipation of women, becomes clear only when we analyze the social background against which it was formulated.

The issue of women's rights was not involved from the Pharisaic point of view; for both relatives were women. What was involved was the advisability of dividing property between heirs. The plebeians, whose estates were so small that they could hardly maintain a family in comfort, even with much effort, consistently opposed any rule which made for further division. This attitude of the plebeians was clearly demonstrated when the Pharisees, themselves, divided into two factions on similar issues which arose in later times. The Hillelites, and after them the great plebeian teacher, R. Akiba, always maintained that it was better to leave estates intact, even though one of the heirs was left without any property, than to divide the small estates into still smaller holdings, which would be insufficient for either relative.[67]

The patricians with their larger and more productive estates did not have to choose between the painful alternatives, and were at liberty to bestow equal rights on the daughter and the granddaughter.

It should be noted, perhaps, that even according to Pharisaic law, the daughter was not left without support. A clear provision of the Pharisaic law declared that un-married daughters were to remain in their father's house after his death, and were to be supported by his heirs— whoever those might be—until they were married.[68] More-over, the plebeians did not regard it as humiliating or shameful for a woman to support herself. The daughter, who was denied the privilege of inheritance, was not an outcast; she simply shared the status of the daughters of many plebeian scribes, who had no property at all. If she did not wish to be maintained in her father's house after his death, she could find work and earn her livelihood. Among the patricians and provincials, who regarded the self-sufficient woman as an anomaly, if not worse, it seemed better to maintain the daughter in even the most pre-carious existence on a landed estate, rather than to thrust her into the world of work and commerce.

That the issue of daughter versus granddaughter was quite dissociated from that of feminist rights, becomes evident from a consideration of another controversy between the plebeians and the patricians regarding inheritance. If a man died, leaving sons and daughters, and the estate was inadequate to provide a means of livelihood for the sons and also to maintain the daughters until their marriage, the plebeians say: "Let the daughters be maintained, even if the sons are driven to beg." But Admon, a patrician judge, insisted, "Am I to lose my rights because I am a male?" His opinion was that the sons' rights of inheritance took precedence over the daughters' rights to maintenance.

The controversy between the sects reappeared in the discussion of the rights of daughters to inherit their mothers' property. Since the biblical Law speaks only of a man's estate, the patricians, led by the famous priest-scholar, Zechariah ben ha-Kazzab, said that an estate left by a woman should be divided equally between sons and daughters; his plebeian opponents denied this.[69]

While the element of class interest was doubtless the primary motive for the patrician interpretation of the law of inheritance, there can be no doubt that the Sadducees were strengthened in their view by the fact that Roman Law, in this as in some other matters, tended to side with them.

I. The Law of False Witnesses.*

The only instance in which the Pharisees are known to have demanded a harsher interpretation of the Law than the Sadducees was that of false witnesses. Biblical Law, like that of the Sumerians and the Code of Hammurabi,[70] provided that false witnesses should suffer the penalty they tried to inflict on their neighbor (Deut. 19.19). The Sadducees held that this rule applied only when the accused person had actually suffered injury through the testimony of the false witnesses. The Pharisees maintained, however, that the crime of the false witnesses was complete when judgment was issued in accordance with their testimony. Whether the sentence was actually executed did not affect their status.[71]

* Cf. Supplement, pp. 696-698.

The departure of the Pharisees from their ordinary leniency of interpretation can be explained only in terms of the social need. They were obviously convinced that in this instance they could not afford to indulge their inclination to be merciful. The whole structure of Jewish judicial procedure was based on the reliability of witnesses. It was cruelty to the whole group to permit anyone who tried to shake this foundation of the state to escape deserved penalties.

The Sadducees would doubtless have agreed with them regarding the importance of this social need. But they could not accept the Pharisaic principle that the witnesses had committed a punishable act in simply giving testimony. They regarded the *lex talionis* as properly applied to false witnesses who, in accordance with the general primitive practice, had also acted as executioners.[72] They were willing to extend it to cases where the Court, following later procedure, had appointed an executioner whom they, with their vague ideas of personality,[73] could still regard as the agent of the witnesses. But when the accused had suffered no physical injury, either through the witnesses or someone delegated to act for them, how could the witnesses be punished?

The answer of the Pharisees to this was, of course, that the witnesses were punished for a crime against the state, that of giving false testimony, and not for a wrong to an individual.[74] In order to understand this, however, the Sadducees would have had to admit that so abstract a matter as giving testimony was an act, in the juridical sense of the word. This they could not do. It was in vain that the Pharisees pointed out that Scripture expressly states, in connection with the law of evidence, that the false witness is to be punished for the wrong he *intended* to do to his brother (Deut. 19.19). The Sadducees held that intention alone was not enough; physical injury must accompany it before the Court could take action.[75]

The issue between the sects apparently arose in connection with an incident which has been recorded. A man who had given testimony in a murder case was proven to have been a false witness; and fortunately this discovery was made before the person against whom he had testified had been executed. Thereupon a court, headed by Simeon ben Shattah himself, executed the false witness. Such an innovation was this at the time that not only the Sadducees, but Judah ben Tabbai, the leader of the patrician faction of the Pharisees, vigorously protested. "May I not see the consolation," Judah is said to have cried out, "if you have not shed innocent blood!"[76]

Nevertheless Simeon's view prevailed among the Pharisees, and became part of the legal heritage of the whole Order. It continued however to be opposed by the Sadducees.

In this instance, again, we note that the Sadducean interpretation of the Law, based doubtless on Israelitish precedent, coincided entirely with the early Roman rule on the subject. There can be little doubt that this support of foreign precedent played an important rôle in the resistance which the Sadducees offered to the acceptance of Simeon ben Shattah's ruling.[77]

VIII. THE DOCTRINE OF THE RESURRECTION AND IMMORTALITY*

The fiercest of all the conflicts between Pharisee and Sadducee concerned the doctrine of the resurrection, for in it the class conflict was most explicitly formulated.

Crushed under the heel of the oppressor and exploiter, the artisan and trader of Jerusalem in the fourth century B.C.E. sought compensation in an ideal world beyond the grave, where all human inequalities would be leveled down before the overwhelming power of God. The bitterer his lot in this world, the more passionately he clung to his hopes of the next. An abstract immortality might satisfy the philosopher; the hungry slum-dweller of Jerusalem could be comforted by nothing less than the Egyptian and Persian doctrine of physical resurrection and restitution.[1]

The expectation that the struggles of the world would culminate in a glorious Messianic Age, ushering in peace and tranquillity reminiscent of Adam's Paradise, had long been prominent in Israel's thought; and this offered an excellent background for the new faith.[2] Several passages in the Second Isaiah seem to indicate that already he had been thinking in terms of the resurrection;[3] but it remained for a later prophet, the author of Isaiah, chapters 24–27, to avow the belief clearly and explicitly.

"Thy dead shall live, my dead bodies shall arise—
Awake and sing, ye that dwell in the dust—
For Thy dew is as the dew of light,
And the earth shall bring to life the shades" (26.19).

* Cf. Supplement, pp. 742-753.

But this doctrine had been so long and so pointedly ignored among the Jews that the introduction of it might well have appeared to be defection to foreign worship. Moreover, appealing as a future life might seem, the belief in it was derived from animism, ancestor worship, and other primitive errors which were hated and despised by the Jewish religious teachers. Throughout the duration of the First Commonwealth they had struggled against its infiltration from Egypt and had on the whole succeeded in keeping Jewish faith free from the taint both of the resurrection and of the superstitions associated with it.[4] But by the fifth century B.C.E. the peril of idolatry had almost disappeared in Jerusalem, and there was less reason for objection to a doctrine which in itself had so much that was pure, inspiring and morally helpful. It was inertia rather than religious policy which opposed the new article of faith; even after such "radicals" as the author of Isaiah 26 had spoken, official Judaism still regarded the belief in the resurrection with strong suspicion.

We may, however, see a possible concession in the Torah itself, where the Egyptian practice of embalming is accepted with approval for both Jacob and Joseph.[5] True, the resurrection is not even mentioned in this connection. But in Egyptian thought the preservation of the body was a necessary preparation for its ultimate quickening. Conscious opposition to the doctrine of the resurrection would surely not be compatible with the ascription of this practice to the revered patriarchs.

But while we have these scattered and indirect allusions to the resurrection in earlier writers, the first picture of a revivified world is given by the inaugurators of the Enoch literature, who are supposed to have lived about the year

200 B.C.E., shortly before Antiochus Epiphanes initiated his unsuccessful effort forcibly to Hellenize the Jews.

> "And no mortal is permitted to touch this tree of delicious fragrance till the great day of judgment, when He shall avenge and bring everything to its consummation forever; this tree, I say, will [then] be given to the righteous and humble. By its fruit, life will be given to the elect; it will be transplanted to the north, to the holy place, to the temple of the Lord, the Eternal King. Then will they rejoice with joy and be glad: they will enter Thy holy habitation: the fragrance thereof will be in their limbs, and they will live a long life on earth, such as their fathers have lived: and in their days no sorrow or pain or trouble or calamity will affect them" (Enoch 25.5–7, R. H. Charles' translation).

The apocalyptist was himself doubtless one of the "humble" of whom he speaks so affectionately. But he uses that term not as we do, to indicate the affectation of the mighty who put on "meekness" as a social amenity. The humility which he has in mind is not a virtue but a condition. The word " *anavim*" which was certainly the original rendered by the English "humble," came like its English equivalent, to mean "pious," "saintly," and "meek," because it signified the unprotesting, non-resisting, unambitious, lowly, the social opposites of the wealthy, who find it so difficult to enter the kingdom of heaven.

It was this aspect of the Jewish doctrine of the resurrection—its democracy—which gives it more than theological importance; and which indeed prepared the way for its spread throughout the world. Egyptian immortality was to be attained through power. The Pharaoh, the princes and the nobility not only possessed this world, but by costly burial arrangements they could ensure their return from death itself. Such a perpetuation of the wrongs of the mundane world would have aroused little enthusiasm in Jerusalem's market place; and, indeed, it is altogether probable that the resistance to it explains in large part the failure of the earlier Israelite and Judaite teachers to recognize the larger spiritual potentialities of the teaching of the resurrection. Only when the doctrine was presented as one of salvation for the righteous, be they rich or poor, Jew or Gentile, noble or plebeian, did the masses of Jerusalem become converted to it.

While, however, the poor of the fourth century B.C.E. and later times sought solace in the new faith, the patricians felt no impulse to abandon the traditional negation of future life. The patricians were not content with monopolizing this life; they even begrudged the poor another and better life beyond the grave. To assert the truth of the resurrection was to them nothing less than heresy, a recession from a standpoint to which prophetic Judaism had steadfastly adhered through almost a millennium, and an acceptance of the foreign influence of Egypt and of Zoroaster.

It is not among those who have enjoyed the triumphs of this world that we should look for preoccupation with the consolations of the next. It is an almost universal feature of religious history that the longing for another and better life to come was confined, in its strongest forms, to those who had been the victims of life as it is here. This was not less true among the Jews than among others.

The cleavage between the plebeian artisans and traders of Jerusalem and their wealthy neighbors was sharpened by the maturer concept of personality and the individual which was becoming current in the market place. The rural and aristocratic families and clans were held together as units by well remembered traditions, and above all by the property, nominally held by the father but actually the means of support to the whole group—wives, children, slaves and retainers. The members of the family lived, worked, prospered and suffered together. Their interests were inextricably interwoven, and, as everywhere, mutual interdependence gave rise to a sense of solidarity unknown in other circles. The family of Bathyra, for instance, acted as a unit in its interpretation of the Law; the high-priestly families were powerful clans, the individuals of which were merely organs of the general group. Such clan-consciousness was altogether lacking among the poorer classes, where there was no common property or tradition to unite the members of the family. On the contrary, the city was full of divisive forces tending to disrupt the family unit. Wife and children could earn their livelihood without the assistance of husband and father; they made friendships of their own, and tended to become independent in their judgments, thoughts and desires. Sociologists have long noted this disruptive effect of city life on the primitive family, but it is important to remember that the centrifugal force was especially strong among the laborers and tradesmen, and rather weak among the patricians, who in ancient times, as today, laid great stress on genealogy and family associations.[6]

True, the tendency toward the cult of the individual had shown itself early in Israel, but it was limited to the property-less groups, and was continually opposed by the land-owning patricians. The story of the argument between Abraham

and God concerning the fate of Sodom is a case in point.
"That be far from Thee," says Abraham, "to do after this
manner, to slay the righteous with the wicked, that so the
righteous shall be as the wicked, that be far from Thee;
shall not the Judge of all the earth do justly?" (Gen. 18.25).
The point of the story is lost, and the vehemence of Abraham
remains inexplicable, unless we bear in mind that Abraham
is here inveighing against a definite moral and theological
concept—the tribal feud, or the vendetta. The principle
was even more clearly expressed in Deuteronomy, where the
slaying of children for the sins of their father was explicitly
forbidden (24.16), and where we are told that God's wrath
descends from father to son only *for His enemies* (7.10), that
is, as the Talmud correctly understands, when the sons
imitate their fathers' wickedness.[7] In another passage of the
Torah, the defense of individual responsibility is attributed
to Moses. When God threatens to destroy Israel for the sins
of Korah, Moses asks Him in accents which ring through the
ages, "Shall one man sin, and wilt Thou be wroth with all
the congregation?" (Num. 16.22). A special notation is
made, in that connection, of the fact that the sons of Korah
were *not* punished when their father was destroyed (ibid.
26.12). Nevertheless when Amaziah put this rule into practice by sparing the children of the murderers of his father,
he made an indelible impression on the memory of the
people (II Kings 14.6). Men's thoughts had to be completely revolutionized before they became conscious of their
own ego. Even Jeremiah, prophet as he was, but coming
from the fields of Anathoth, assimilated the new doctrine
only by steps; it was not until Ezekiel's maturity that the
principle received its full and final formulation.

No sooner, however, had this been done, than the question of individual reward and punishment, hardly mentioned before Ezekiel's day, became a burning issue. If the individual rather than the group is the unit of moral responsibility, why do the wicked prosper and the righteous suffer? Isaiah had not asked the question, for individual prosperity or adversity were irrelevant in the social scheme as a whole. Jeremiah in his later years had struggled with it and had come to no definite conclusion.[8] The writers of Job could not escape the problem, which flowed inescapably from Ezekiel's theology.

The doctrine of the resurrection offered a full solution to the difficulty and was altogether in the spirit of the individualism which prompted it. The individual is not an indistinguishable part of the community; he is an immortal being, for whom, if he has merited it, there waits another and happier life when God shall say the word.

The plebeian artisan and trader was thus doubly prepared for the doctrine of the resurrection, by his tendency to respect the individual and by his overpowering impulse to believe in some place where the world was in moral balance. To these factors was added the continual contact with Persian and Egyptian traders and travelers.[9] The rural farmers naturally escaped this influence, and even the city patricians were partly immune to it.

We must not overlook, of course, the powerful effect of the natural piety of the plebeians on their willingness to accept the belief in the resurrection. It seemed to the religious teachers patent common sense that God would not forsake the righteous even after death. The idea that all mankind would find its permanent and ultimate home

in a shadowy Sheol must have horrified the intelligent
thinkers of this group, once they had rid themselves of the
inherited prejudice in its favor. But this piety and intellectual outlook were both, as we shall see,[10] far more fully
developed among the city plebeians than among the aristocrats. They strengthened the influences which were making
for the spread of the new doctrine; they could not bring it
to any new section of the populace.

Yet such was the opposition to the new faith that it could
hardly have won acceptance without the special assistance
of other circumstances. The plebeian writers of Enoch who
preached it were more than matched by the great patrician
teachers who denied it. Foremost among these opponents
of the doctrine of the resurrection was Ben Sira (ca. 200
B.C.E.), himself a scion of aristocracy, who had, like many
others in different ages, chosen to associate himself with
the suppressed classes rather than with his own peers.[11]
He became a scholar and teacher, opposed to the Hellenism
of his day, and generally sympathetic to the Hasideans.
But as frequently occurs with patrician leaders of plebeian
groups, he could not altogether enter into the soul of the
oppressed whom he wished to lead. He sympathized with
them, and like his great master, the High Priest Simeon
the Righteous, gave wider currency to some of their pro-
nouncements. But in fundamental matters his early breed-
ing, with its ingrained bias, inevitably asserted itself. The
teaching of the resurrection must have been particularly
repugnant to him. The prophets, most of the psalmists, the
writers of the main body of Job, had denied it; yet it was
making its way into Judaism. The plebeian acceptance of
the doctrine seemed to him as assimilationist as the Hellenistic pastimes and affectations of the aristocrats.

So we find him saying with explicitness not found elsewhere:

"For when a man dieth, he inheriteth
Worm and maggot, lice and creeping things" (Ecclus. 10.11).
"For what pleasure hath God in all that perish in Hades,
in place of those who live and give Him praise?
Thanksgiving perisheth from the dead as from one that is not" (17.27).
"Fear not death, it is thy destiny;
Remember that the former and the latter share it with thee" (41.3).

Another Hasidean teacher, Antigonus of Socho, whose Hellenized name gives evidence that he, like Ben Sira, was one of those who had renounced the privileges of their aristocratic heritage and thrown in their lot with the despised plebeians, tried to remove the burning issue from theological discussion. He appealed to the principle of virtue for virtue's sake, enunciating it with a vigor and dignity which, as Toy remarks, is quite without parallel "in the Old Testament or the New Testament."[12] "Be not," he taught, "like servants who obey their master in the hope of receiving reward."[13] In the cautious ambiguity of the words, we still can see, as did the later sages, the denial of the doctrine of resurrection. The sage does not denounce it as heresy. He simply holds that its spread would interfere with the highest morality of "virtue for virtue's sake."

Whatever this politic evasion may have done to dull the edge of the controversy in the time of Antigonus and imme-

diately after, its effect was completely wiped out in the
turmoil of the Jewish resistance to the armed tyranny of
Antiochus Epiphanes, distinguished as the first of a long
line of religious persecutors of Judaism. The assimilationist
movement among the Jews was too slow for him; in his
efforts to hasten the consummation, he actually became
the unconscious and unwilling instrument of their salvation.
The listless and passive opposition to Hellenism, which had
been initiated by Simeon the Righteous, Antigonus of
Socho, Ben Sira and others, would in all probability have
failed to catch up with the natural influence of environment; it was suddenly stimulated into furious zeal. Jewish
piety had, until this point, been contemptuously ignored by
the conqueror; it now became punishable with death. The
bodies of the "criminals" remained unburied; synagogues
were burned. The scrolls of the Law were desecrated and
destroyed. Thousands of Jews, forbidden to practice their
ancient customs and observances, fled to the paleolithic
caves which abound in the land. The rage of the tyrant
sought them out even there.

As they were faced with extinction and did not dare to
anticipate the incredible victory which ultimately came, the
vague and incipient suspicion of the Hasideans that their
kingdom was not of this world, crystallized into rigid belief.
It was now clear to them that all must perish before better
times would come. The doctrine of the resurrection which
had been held by a few eccentrics and progressives spread
to ever wider circles. The writer of the Book of Daniel
asserted it proudly and assured the dying martyrs that they
would be called back to life eternal, while their oppressors
also would be revived, but for everlasting derision and
contempt.[14]

That the writer of Daniel was an inhabitant of Jerusalem, hailing from plebeian rather than patrician circles, is implicit in the text. The sin which fills up the measure of Nebuchadnezzar's wickedness and brings about his expulsion from among men was not of the kind which could ever have awakened either the astonishment or resentment of an oriental noble. Arrogance was so proper to an aristocrat as actually to escape his attention. And the man who denounced it in the great king could be addressing himself only to the lowly. "The king spoke and said: 'Is not this great Babylon, which I have built for a royal dwelling-place by the might of my power, and for the glory of my majesty?' While the word was in the king's mouth, there fell a voice from heaven: 'O king Nebuchadnezzar, to thee it is spoken: the kingdom is departed from thee'" (Dan. 4.27). In his prayers Daniel speaks continuously of Jerusalem rather than of the whole land. "O Lord, according to all Thy righteousness, let Thine anger and Thy fury, I pray Thee, be turned away from Thy city, Jerusalem, . . . and Thy people are become a reproach to all that are round about us" (9.16). And then again, "O Lord, hear, O Lord, forgive, O Lord, attend and do, defer not for Thine own sake, O my God, because Thy name is called upon Thy city and Thy people" (ibid. 19). He advises Nebuchadnezzar to save himself from impending doom, not by ritual and prayer such as a patrician might recommend, but by almsgiving, the virtue peculiarly dear to the plebeian (4.24).

All remaining doubt that the plebeians were the first adherents in Israel to the doctrine of resurrection must be set at rest by a study of the actual events of the war. The Hasideans were joined in their resistance to Antiochus by the distinguished priestly family of Mattathias of Modin. In slaying the Jew who was about to offer an idolatrous sacrifice and the Syrian officer who was superintending the ceremony, the aged Mattathias raised the standard of revolt. These priests combined in themselves religious zeal with great worldly ability and a hypnotic power of leadership. They were not the men to endure present oppression and persecution in the prospect of other-worldly restitution. Such was the contagious effect of their example that for a time they overcame even the passivity of the Hasideans, rousing them out of their dreams of consolation to an active assertion of their rights. The assassination of the apostate and of the royal agent was the first blow in a bitter war, which was not to end before the Syrian power in Judea had been destroyed. Certain Hasideans who, having fled to the wilderness, were attacked on the Sabbath by Syrian soldiers, permitted themselves to be cut down in cold blood, rather than violate the sacred day. "And Mattathias and his friends knew it, and they mourned over them exceedingly. And one said to another, If we all do as our brethren have done, and fight not against the Gentiles for our lives and our ordinances, they will now quickly destroy us from off the earth. And they took counsel on that day saying, Whosoever shall come against us to battle on the Sabbath day, let us fight against him, and we shall in no wise die as our brethren died in the secret places" (I Macc. 1.39–41). To the modern mind this decision seems to be the simplest common sense; to the Hasidean it meant a moral revolution. The thousand pietists who yielded themselves up to Syrian attackers were under no delusion as to the fate which awaited them. They had fled to the mountains in order to practice what was forbidden in the cities; their offense was punishable with death. But, filled with the conviction of individual resurrection and regarding this world as nothing more than a prelude to a greater and finer life, they faced their executioners calmly and perhaps even cheerfully. The Hasmoneans who, under pressure of necessity, were prepared to make a radical alteration in the interpretation of the Sabbath law, were men of a different stamp. They were warriors and diplomats, planning victory in this world, instead of dreaming of compensation in the next.

Two mutually opposing ideals were momentarily united in the rush of victory. But the forces of life continued, year in, year out, to recreate those mutually hostile social and religious forms which could never find ultimate reconciliation. The Hasidean saints, overwhelmed by the boldness of the Hasmonean priests, were ready to forget for a time what their class and experience represented. But life does not forget. Gradually the cleavage between the plebeian followers and the patrician leaders reasserted itself. Some Hasideans broke away when Jonathan continued the war after autonomy had been won. Others still remained loyal; but their descendants were ultimately forced to withdraw when King John Hyrkan openly broke with them.

The divergence was the same; it expressed itself in new names. The Sadducees who rallied about the Hasmonean House vehemently denied the resurrection, while the Pharisees, drawn essentially from among the descendants of the earlier plebeians, as vehemently continued to affirm it. The victory lay with the Pharisees. By their faith in the life beyond death they won adherents throughout the Jewish world. The Jews of the diaspora were almost altogether

Pharisaic; and in Palestine the Sadducees were reduced to a few noble families.[15]

The rural farmers, among whom urban individualism had made no inroads, were yet won to the soothing belief in human immortality. No matter how much the peasant might be lost in his family and his clan, he was easily brought to an understanding of his own ego by the plebeian teacher who came from Jerusalem. The doctrine of salvation, through which Christianity was destined ultimately to conquer the whole Roman Empire, was the means whereby the Pharisee won the plebeians, at least of Judea, to himself. But the Sadducee could not yield. His negation of the doctrine was not merely agnostic; it was religious, based, as we have seen, on prophetic tradition. On the other hand, with each war and each martyrdom, the Pharisaic devotion to the new belief became more passionate, so that the Mishna regards it as a cardinal teaching of Judaism and condemns the dissenter to loss of future life.[16]

The Pharisees would not permit anyone denying it to recite public prayers in their synagogues, and to make certain of correct belief, they inserted at the beginning of their main service an avowal of it.

"Thou art mighty, feeding the quick, quickening the dead. Blessed art thou, O Lord, who dost quicken the dead."[17]

With the passing of years, the Pharisees, now more sophisticated, accepted the Greek philosophic doctrine of immortal souls, which renders belief in bodily resurrection superfluous and unnecessary. Yet such had been the struggle for the teaching of resurrection that it could no longer be forgotten. They continued to profess the older faith in a renewed world peopled with the revived dead, and at the same time denied that man can truly be said to die. The logical contradiction involved remained a puzzling and disturbing factor in rabbinic theology, and also in Christianity which is—in this respect—derived from it.

IX. THE ANGELS*

The social forces which, between the years 400 and 100 B.C.E., revolutionized the Jewish doctrine of the hereafter, also gave rise to a new angelology totally different from that of pre-exilic religion.[1] Michael, Gabriel, Raphael, and the host of other winged creatures, whose names fill the pages of Pharisaic, rabbinic and Christian writings, were quite unknown to the early biblical records. Human in almost every aspect of life, in desire, passion, ambition, and even in form and susceptibility to temptation, they had nothing in common with the impersonal "angel of the Lord" who figures so prominently in the patriarchal tales of Genesis. He was a manifestation of God, without will or character, altogether incapable of willfulness or disobedience, and existing only as representative of his Master. They, somewhat after the manner of the Olympian gods and goddesses, combined in themselves the moral frailty of man with the physical strength of deity. The Creator had endowed them with enormous power, immortal life and incomparably quick motion; whether they used these gifts to serve Him or to rebel against Him lay in their own choice. The true analogue in the later theology to the patriarchal "angel of the Lord," was the "Divine Presence" (*Shekinah*) of rabbinic Judaism and in a sense the "Holy Ghost" of Christianity; nothing but the name unites this "angel" with the "watchers," "holy ones" and other semi-divine beings of Pharisaism and its derivative doctrines.

* Cf. Supplement, pp. 744, 751-753.

Childish as the whole concept of angels may seem in the sophistication of an industrial age, its varied forms were essential to the happiness and spiritual adjustment of many generations. In fact, the belief in them may serve as an index to the growth of the Jewish mind as it emerged slowly from early faltering monotheism to the comparative maturity of Pharisaism and Rabbinism.

In the most primitive biblical records, God Himself is described in bold anthropomorphisms. He walks through the Garden in the cool of the day (Gen. 3.8); He descends from heaven to see the tower which the men of Shinar are building (ibid. 11.5); He is described as fearing that man, grown wise, may also obtain eternal life and become the equal of Himself (ibid. 3.22). In the dawn of prophetic religion, these tales were no longer taken literally; yet, imbedded in the consciousness of the people, they could not be completely eradicated. Hence the "angel of the Lord" is substituted for God in various passages. Neither the writer nor the reader attached any clear meaning to the periphrasis, but it soothed the pious ear to impute physical appearance to an "angel" rather than to the Deity. Similar devices were invented, centuries later, when the translators of Scripture sought to conceal the anthropomorphisms which biblical writers had retained. In the Aramaic version, otherwise slavishly literal, not God, but the "Word of the Lord," walks in the Garden of Eden (Gen. 3.8). The vivid Hebrew text says that when Noah entered the ark, "The Lord shut him in" (ibid. 7.16). But the Aramaic prefers the more vague, theological expression: "And the Lord protected him with His word." The Scriptures say bluntly, "And the Lord repented Him that He had made man on the earth" (ibid. 6.6). But the translator, recoiling from the imputation of fickleness to God, renders the verse: "And the Lord repented in *His Word* that he had made man." Theologians have untiringly sought to impress metaphysical reality on these pious circumlocutions. Treatises have been written on the *Memra* (word) of the humble Aramaic translators. The nature of the "angel of the Lord" is still a fertile subject for discussion and controversy among exegetes. Yet the obvious fact is that no contemporary reader was misled by the terms, angel, word, Divine Presence, Divine Glory, or Holy Spirit. Writers and speakers used them not to convey meaning, but to soften the harshness of bold imagery, just as modern government officials in difficult situations make a feint of hiding their identities behind fictitious "spokesmen." Such is the human passion for self-delusion that what cannot be said without offense of the principal may frequently be attributed without harm to the agent.

The invention of such an "angel of the Lord" was the easier in an age which had no clear conception of self or individuality. In a sense almost incomprehensible to us a servant was considered part of his master, a child of its parents, a wife of her husband.[2] An owner's responsibility for depredations committed by his ox did not arise merely from possible negligence, but was explained by identifying the beast with the master himself. Hence partial restitution had to be made for damages done by a tame animal (Ex. 21.35). A vicious ox could be tried in court together with his master and might be sentenced to death. The owner too was declared guilty of death, but ransom might be permitted him (Ex. 21.29 ff.). The children of a maid-servant belonged to her mistress in almost a physical sense.

Sarah beseeches Abraham to take her maid, Hagar, as second wife, that "I shall be builded up through her" (Gen. 16.2). Likewise Rachel, being barren, gives her handmaid, Bilhah, to Jacob, "and she may bear upon my knees, and I also may be builded up through her" (ibid. 30.3). When Judah's oldest son dies childless, the second son is commanded to cohabit with the widow, so as to raise offspring for his dead brother. "But Onan knew that the seed would not be his; and it came to pass, when he went in unto his brother's wife, that he spilled it on the ground, lest he should give seed to his brother" (ibid. 38.9). Paternity no more than motherhood was physical and individual; the personalities of the brothers were confused like those of mistress and servant.

Among people of this psychological immaturity, the term "angel" could be used to suggest a being altogether dependent on God, having no will or desire of his own, and yet partly capable of independent action and appearance.

Rising monotheism found the "angel" a convenient substitute for the *numina* or spirits and gods of mythology. Just as the medieval Christians transformed local gods into saints and evil spirits, so the ancient Israelites, yielding to prophetic monotheism, saved their beloved ancestral myths by attributing them to "angels." A more sophisticated age might have objected to such further confusion, but the Hebrews were easily contented in matters of abstract theology. They remained as vague about God and the angels as were the Greeks about Apollo and the sun or Alpheus and his river. Even today we accept with equanimity the continual identification of agents with principals and secretaries with employers. Our ancestors, living before the days of radical individualism and philosophical theologies, were still less aware of any fiction in such a merger of personalities. They could speak of angels in the same context, now as separate from God, now as identical with Him, with no more concern about the metaphysics involved than is Shaw's theatrical audience when he calls out before it the disembodied spirit of Joan of Arc.

The fascinating narrative of God's visit to Abraham offers an excellent illustration of this. Abraham sitting in the door of his tent, in the heat of the day, lifts up his eyes and sees "three men standing over against him" (Gen. 18.2). He is under no misapprehension regarding the true nature of these guests; he realizes at once that they are representatives of a single Divine Being. He shows this by addressing them first in the singular, collectively, as it were, and then in the plural, as he thinks of their individual, physical needs. "My Lord," he says, "if now I have found favor in thy sight, pass not away, I pray thee, from thy servant. Let now a little water be fetched, and wash your feet, and recline yourselves under the tree."

The disconcerting change of number is not to be explained by the usual critical devices of emendation or division of documents. No reasonable text student would justify the wanton change of all the grammatical forms in the second verse to make them correspond to the singular used in the beginning. Nor is it a happier solution of the problem to cut the obviously uniform story into two halves, deriving each from a separate source. But the difficulty is not at all inherent; it arises only from an effort to impose modern categories of thought on an author to whom they are quite foreign. As in the story of Jacob wrestling with the angel (Gen. 32.25), we have in this theophany a monotheistic parallel to a tale, in which the superhuman power was not an angel, but a *numen* or god. Some commentators have recognized this, but they have failed to draw the reasonable inference that the purpose of including the story in the Pentateuch is to reconcile the current legend with monotheistic doctrine. The narrator instead of challenging the ancient story, accepts its essentials, but removes its mythological overtones. Abraham did indeed see three men; but they were not gods; they were only angels or messengers of the One God, who at this time chose to manifest Himself through them. Why should not God manifest Himself through three angels rather than one? The skillful author emphasizes this point, by attributing to Abraham the grammatically awkward, but psychologically natural, use of singular and plural forms in the same brief sentence. The Patriarch, astonished by his great visitor, begs Him not to pass by; and then thinking of the three individuals, he speaks of them as separate from one another. So we say, "man is" or "men are" mortal, changing naturally from singular to plural as we think of the species or the persons composing it. An individualistic age, oppressed by its conception of personality, might find it difficult to envisage God descending to earth as more than one being. But the ancient, accustomed from birth to regard his tribe as a single unit, expressing its personality in an eponym, its alliances in legendary marriages, and its divisions in genealogical tables, had no such trouble.[3]

It may seem to us that if Abraham recognized the divinity of his visitors, there was no special merit in his liberality toward them. Who would not, after all, be hospitable to God and His angels? Wherein lay the sharp contrast, obviously intended by Scripture, between the generosity

of Abraham and the baseness of Sodom, if he knew his
guests and the Sodomites did not?

But, paradoxically, only a generation of diminished faith
could suppose that a saint would act differently toward
divine angels than toward fellow-men. Like an orphaned
child, who imagines that if he had a mother he would give
her all his love and duty, so we, living in an age of shaken
faith, suppose that given unquestioning belief, the world's
moral problem would be solved. The man of antiquity
knew better. Absolutely convinced as he was of God's
existence, power, and omniscience, he yet found it impossible to escape from sin. Aware that he was always in the
presence of God whether or not God appeared to him, he
was continually yielding to one temptation or another and
consequently knew directly and intuitively what we must
learn from patient study and science, namely, that moral
backsliding results not from intellectual scepticism alone,
but frequently from deeper impulses against which the
mind itself is helpless. The Cains, the Sodomites, the
Nabals, and the Absaloms, the men of the Deluge and the
men of the Tower, like the Davids and the Solomons, were
all convinced theists, as our ancestors recognized. But
knowing their Master, they either rebelled against Him or
suffered temporary lapses of loyalty. The oppressor and
betrayer acted not from heresy or ignorance, but from
willfulness and arrogance. It is only in modern times that
the self-centered and the cynical cover themselves with the
borrowed masque of metaphysical agnosticism; among our
ancestors, injustice and immorality, perhaps more common
than today, lacked the metaphysical and anti-theological
accoutrements with which a "little philosophy" has now
provided them.

High merit therefore attached among the ancients to those who, convinced like their fellows of God's being, were more gentle, pious and just. In giving the angels cordial greeting, Abraham was acting as he might have done to any other traveler. The stranger was under the special protection of God; to treat him with kindness was to recognize the divine authority, just as to be cruel to him was to flout it. Abraham's courtesy and liberality were not a whit the less noteworthy because they happened to be extended to God's messengers; just as his willingness to sacrifice Isaac was none the less heroic because it was made at the express behest of God.

The confusion of persons, begun in the story of Abraham's theophany, is continued in the story of the angels after they turn to Sodom. Abraham "stood yet before the Lord. And Abraham drew near, and said: 'Wilt Thou indeed sweep away the righteous with the wicked?'" (Gen. 18.22 ff.). The question is addressed not to the angels, but to God Himself, perhaps as manifested in the third angel, who did not go to Sodom. In Sodom the angels appear once more both as independent beings and as spokesmen for the Deity. "And when the morning arose, then the angels hastened Lot, saying: 'Arise, take thy wife, and thy two daughters that are here; lest thou be swept away in the iniquity of the city.' But he lingered; the men laid hold upon his hand, and upon the hand of his wife, and upon the hand of his two daughters; the Lord being merciful unto him. And they brought him forth and set him without the city. And it came to pass, when they had brought him forth abroad that he said: 'Escape for thy life; look not behind thee, neither stay thou in all the Plain; escape to the mountain, lest thou be swept away.' And Lot said unto *them*: 'Oh, not so, *my lord*; behold now, *thy* servant hath found grace in *thy* sight, and *thou* hast magnified *thy* mercy, which *thou* hast shown unto me in saving my life; and I cannot escape to the mountain, lest some evil overtake me and I die. Behold now, this city is near to flee unto, and it is a little one; oh, let me escape thither—is it not a little one?—and my soul shall live.' And *he* said unto him: 'See, *I* have accepted thee concerning this thing also, that *I* will not overthrow the city of which thou hast spoken' " (Gen. 19.15 ff.).

The talmudic Sages who, like some later exegetes, seek to force logical analysis on the simple story, are astounded at the arrogance of the angel's speech,[4] for according to later theology, it lay not with him but with God to spare or destroy. The biblical writer was not aware of any wrong, for the angel is here speaking not for himself, but for his Master, of whose personality he is but part.

Throughout the early scriptural records we find the same vague delineation of God and angels. At the sacrifice of Isaac, the "angel of the Lord" calls from heaven and says, "By Myself have I sworn, saith the Lord, because thou hast done this thing, and hast not withheld thy son, thine only son, that in blessing I will bless thee" (Gen. 22.15 ff.).

God's appearance to Moses in the burning bush is described in these words: "And the angel of the Lord appeared unto him in a flame of fire out of the midst of a bush; . . . and when the Lord saw that he turned aside to see, God called unto him from the midst of the bush, and said: 'Moses, Moses' . . . . Moreover He said: 'I am the God of thy father, the God of Abraham, the God of Isaac, and the God of Jacob' " (Ex. 3.2 ff.).

Hagar, comforted by the angel who was sent to her, "called the name of YHWH who spoke to her, Thou art a God of seeing" (Gen. 16.13). One of the oldest sections of the Book of Judges tells us that "an angel of the Lord came up from Gilgal to Bochim. And he said: '. . . I made you go up out of Egypt, and have brought you unto the land which I swore unto your fathers'" (2.1).

So completely did the ancient Hebrew disregard the angel's personal existence that he gave him no identifying name. He was the "angel of the Lord" and nothing more. Fearful lest angelology revert to polytheism, the monotheists insisted on this anonymity emphatically and vigorously. They twice remind us in Scripture that the angels are impersonal or, to use their language, nameless (Gen. 29.30; Judg. 13.18). Both Jacob and Manoah asked the names of the angels who appeared to them, and neither obtains a satisfactory answer. Another passage expresses the same thought by telling us that the angel bears the name of God "in him" (Ex. 23.21).

The use of the name as signifying personality is common among primitive tribes. The Scriptures themselves tell how the whole life of Abraham and Sarah was altered through the change of their names. Sarai was sterile; Sarah would be fruitful. Abram could father only the wild Ishmael; Abraham would be ancestor to Israel (Gen. 17.5, 15). Jacob became Israel not through his own announcement or through a judicial order, but by a decree of God Himself (ibid. 32.28). He was recreated, as it were. The levirate marriage derived its meaning according to Deuteronomic law from the rule that the child born of it "shall succeed in the name of his brother that is dead" (Deut. 25.6). This does not mean, as we might suppose from some translations, that the child must be called *after* his deceased uncle or merely that he inherited his uncle's property. He became, rather, as we have already noticed in the story of Judah, the son of the deceased uncle by posthumous adoption (Gen. 38.8). So persistent is the conception of the name as equivalent to personality that to this day it is customary among observant Jews to change the name of one who is dangerously ill.[5] R. Meir (ca. 150 C.E.) would judge people's characters from their names;[6] and as late a source as the *Book of the Pious* (thirteenth century) tells us, "A name may cause evil or good. The names of some people inevitably lead to greatness, as it is written, 'And may there be called in them my name and the name of my fathers, Abraham and Isaac.' " In the same book readers are warned not to visit sick namesakes, lest the death destined for their friend be transferred to them.[7] Among the soul's terrors after death, the cabalists enumerate amnesia, the inability to identify itself by name; and many a Jew still endeavors to save himself from this possible calamity by reciting, at the end of his prayers, a verse from Scripture beginning with the first letter of his name and ending with its last letter.[8]

These random examples, taken from various times and places, indicate how enduring and pervasive has been the traditional identification of name and individuality. We can now readily see why the early writers of Scripture, endeavoring beyond all else to protect their monotheistic teaching, stress the absolute anonymity and impersonality of the angels. But to advancing monotheism even nameless angels seemed too great a concession to mythology. This was especially true among the increasingly influential and articulate plebeians who recoiled from the concept of animate and intelligent beings without a personality of their own. The angels of theology were in their eyes heavenly analogues of the slaves of human society. Passionately devoted to freedom, they could not impute to God the slave-holding which they considered an imperfection in human society. Driven thus to choose between conscious and immortal equals of the Deity, which would have been poly-theism, and the equally objectionable monotheism with impersonal servants, the prophets, from Hosea in the eighth century to Zechariah at the end of the sixth, all avoid the mention of angels. Isaiah does indeed describe the birdlike seraphs who hover around God's throne (6.6), and Ezekiel the animate Wheels and Beasts of His magnificent Chariot (1.5 ff.). But since these were not human in form, their subjection was ethically unobjectionable. Ezekiel also twice speaks of "men" acting as divine intermediaries (10.2; 40.3), but significantly declines to denominate them angels. Clearly the religious teachers of the period felt that the concept itself, invented as a compromise with the more primitive mythology, should be forgotten. This was all the easier inasmuch as the later prophetic following was almost entirely plebeian and largely urban, concentrated in Jeru-salem. Such a community was removed from the "groves" and rural life, which were foci for tales of *elim* and *numina*. For them the "angel" had outlived his *raison d'être*, and was readily consigned to oblivion.[9]

After the deportation to Babylonia, the prophetic teach-ing in regard to angels as in other matters ceased to be uni-form. Exposed to a new world with new ideas, a new culture, and new problems, the exiles and their descendants inevitably developed different concepts from those current among their brethren and cousins whom Nebuchadnezzar had left behind in Palestine. Institutions which in Palestine ap-peared neutral or assimilatory because they were common to all the inhabitants, assumed in the foreign Babylonian environment, where they were unknown to the general population, the status of covenants between God and His chosen people. The Sabbath, circumcision and the sacrificial system, the observance of which the Palestinian prophets had taken for granted as part of the country's cultural life and involving no superior piety, became symbols of identification with the Jewish community and of resistance to assimilation.[10] Hence the wide difference between Jeremiah and Ezekiel in their attitude toward the ceremonial law, the priests, the Temple and the sacrifices. Jeremiah is always critical of the institutions and their observance; Ezekiel insists on their value and importance. Somewhat similarly the concept of angels from which Jeremiah and his contemporaries recoiled, lest they give unintentional encouragement to legends about *elim* and *numina*, was restored to Jewish theology in Babylonia. While in Palestine an individualized angel might be regarded as a concession to rural mythology, in Babylonia he was essential as a reinterpretation of the good and evil spirits of current national thought. Just as the earliest Israelitish thinkers had invented the "angel of the Lord" to replace the legendary *numina*, so their Babylonian successors needed the concept in a developed form as a substitute for the genii of their new neighbors. Older prophets like Ezekiel who had been born and reared in Palestine were hesitant and cautious regarding the revitalized notion; they avoided the dangerous and forbidden word *malak* (angel) and spoke of mediating "men" (*ish*).[11] But the younger teachers, who had never known any civilization but that of their native Babylonia, freely developed a new angelology without fear or care for the forgotten issues of another land and earlier days.

During the century after Cyrus' decree (538–ca. 430 B.C.E.), the continual influx of these teachers from Babylonia into Palestine brought the new doctrine to the ancient soil. But the Judaites whom Nebuchadnezzar had left behind on their native hills and who had remained loyal to ancient prophetic teaching through half a century of foreign domination, could not accept the alien doctrine. Hence we find throughout the Persian and Greek periods two parallel streams of thought in Palestine, the one continually developing the new angelology, the other as consistently rejecting it. The difference associated itself with other disagreements till the two antagonistic groups culminated the one in Pharisaism, the other in Sadducism.

Among the prophets who returned from Babylonia to Palestine, the foremost was Zechariah,[12] who in the years 520–516 B.C.E. urged the members of the new commonwealth to carry out the plan of building the Temple. For the first time in the history of literary prophecy, we have in him a teacher who receives God's word not directly but through an intermediary angel. The "angel who speaks to me" is a continual concept in his teaching.[13] He is the first in Jewish literature to mention Satan, the angel of evil, who clearly replaced for him the Zoroastrian Ahriman. He hears Satan complain to God of Joshua, the High Priest, and rejoices at the reprimand with which the baseless charges are received (3.2). Some decades later, the nameless apocalyptist of Isaiah 24–27, the prophet who for the first time suggests a future resurrection (26.19), speaks of a judgment day over angels as well as over men. "And it shall come to pass in that day, that the Lord will punish the host of the high heaven on high, and the kings of earth upon the earth" (24.21).

There is little in common between these sinful, fallible creatures and the mysterious impersonal strangers who appear to Abraham, Jacob and Manoah. These new angels are not "spokesmen" for God, but His courtiers and ministers. They worship and praise Him; they make official obeisance to Him; they tremblingly await His mighty nod; and are each prepared to carry out His imperious will, whether to slay or heal, to bind or loose, to guard or destroy. In short, the angelology postulates a Divine Court in heaven similar to that of the Great King on earth. Obviously the Jews living under Persian rule, animated by the same sensitivity which made them call their God "King of the kings of kings,"[14] to contrast Him with the Persian ruler who was but a "king of kings," also endowed Him with a retinue suitable to His foremost rank, exceeding in power and glamor anything visible on earth. The Jew whose self-respect was wounded when he thought of his dispersed and weak people, of his tiny and dependent Commonwealth—an insignificant portion of the vast stretches of the Persian Empire—consoled himself with the thoughts of his God's endless might.

Originating in the life of Babylonia, this picture remained a consolation to the plebeian of the restored Jerusalem. The children and grandchildren of the returning exiles were driven by the inexorable demands of human self-respect to enlarge and broaden the canvas, filling in its details and making vivid its colors.

Given this magnificent imagery, the Jewish cobbler could sit at his awl in Jerusalem, as in Babylon or Ecbatana, and listen with unperturbed patience and inner contempt to the derision heaped on him by Persian or Greek: for he had a secret in which they had no part; they served a passing power, he an eternal God. Their king had thousands, perhaps myriads, of soldiers, all of them mortal; but his Ruler had innumerable phalanxes of immortal angels. He could suffer with all the poise of an unrecognized prince, treated basely for the moment, but soon to be elevated into glory by his Father's emissaries.

The vision, so enticing to the plebeian artisan, could hardly be as pleasing to the patrician landowner, who was himself part of the government. The High Priest, at ease in the Temple and in his palace, needed no imagined Kingdom of God to save his self-respect. Only those at the bottom of the social ladder have to find their escape in dreams and visions; those who ascend a few rungs can expand their suppressed ego by a momentary glance at the many beneath them. The meanest Persian or Greek soldier shared in the glories of Xerxes or Alexander and found in that superiority full repayment for his own debasement. And similarly the Jewish official who received some recognition from the alien rule, and the patrician priest or landowner who played the part of a little king in his own domain, found life in this world entirely to his liking. Angelology like the resurrection was a deep-seated psychological need of the market place and the shop; the mansion and the palace were hesitant to accept it.

While the plebeian teacher traced the origin of his consoling doctrine to the prophet Zechariah, the patrician found equal authority for his vehement negation of angels not only in pre-exilic prophecy, but in Deutero-Isaiah and his followers. The Babylonian exiles had restored the forgotten angels, and even endowed them with the new gifts of personality and individuality. But the Palestinian prophets had remained loyal to the doctrines of Amos,

Isaiah, Micah and Jeremiah. Like these great preachers,
Deutero-Isaiah never mentions the angels; neither does
Haggai, the contemporary co-worker of Zechariah. Both of
these prophets, it can be shown, were Palestinian natives,
and were thus free from Babylonian influence.[15] They were
not satisfied to be silent on the subject; they actively
opposed the Babylonian innovation. Deutero-Isaiah does
not speak of angels, but quite pointedly uses the word
malak, by which they had been designated, for prophets.
It is as if he would say, the divine messengers of whom
our ancient authorities speak are not the Gabriels and
Michaels with whom the Babylonian Jews identify them,
but human prophets. Thus he cries out:

"Who is blind but My servant,
    Or deaf, but the messenger (*malak*) whom I send"
    (42.19).

And again:

"That confirmeth the word of His servant,
    And performeth the counsel of His messengers" (44.26),

once more using *malak* for prophet.

This might be taken as mere rhetoric, did we not find a
more emphatic, almost polemical, statement on the subject
in Haggai, where one of the prophecies is introduced with
the words, "Then said Haggai the *malak* of the Lord, as
malak of the Lord" (1.13). When we bear in mind that at
that very time Zechariah was attributing his inspiration to
a mediating *malak*, the contrast, clearly intended, makes
the otherwise redundant and unintelligible phrase
significant.

The controversy is dramatized in the Book of Job, where

the hero does not once mention the angels, although his friends refer to them frequently.[16]

Further traces of controversy on this subject in the meager records preserved from the Second Commonwealth are abundant, though somehow they have escaped observation and correlation. In addition to Deutero-Isaiah and Haggai, already mentioned, Ben Sira and the writer of the Book of Esther among the authors of this period, apparently negate the existence of the angels, whereas Malachi and the writers of Chronicles, Enoch, Tobit, Daniel, the Book of Jubilees, and the Testament of the Twelve Patriarchs, affirm it.[17]

Of the composite works, like Psalms and Proverbs, the doctrine is affirmed in some sections and denied in others.[18] For instance, in Psalms 34, 78, 91, 103 and 104, the angels play an important rôle; elsewhere they remain unmentioned though some reference to them could readily be expected.

As with regard to the resurrection, Ben Sira is outspoken and propagandist where his predecessors condemn by mere silence. The belief in Satan outrages him most.

"When the fool curseth Satan,
    He curseth his own soul" (21.27).

There is no angelic force outside of man to draw him to sin, for "God created man from the beginning and placed him in the hands of his inclination (*yezer*); if thou desirest thou canst keep the commandment" (15.14).

In direct opposition to these denials, the writers of Enoch not only assert the existence of the angels, but declare those who deny them heretics. "And this is the second Similitude concerning those who deny the name of the dwelling of the *holy ones* and the Lord of spirits. They will not ascend into the heaven, and on earth they will not come" (Enoch 45.1). The writer of the Testaments of the Twelve Patriarchs is even more emphatic: "Become not, my children," he makes Asher say, "like the men of Sodom which knew not the angels of the Lord and perished forever" (7.1). To this Pharisaic writer it seemed that the main sin of the Sodomites was not the inhospitality which Scripture imputed to them, nor yet the perversion of justice of which the talmudic sages accuse them,[19] but their heretical refusal to recognize the angels who came to them!

We cannot here enter into a sociological analysis of the books in which the angels are mentioned and those which ignore them. But even a cursory examination reveals the highly significant fact that the writers asserting the resurrection all believe in angels: Daniel, Enoch, the Testaments of the Twelve Patriarchs, and, we may add, the Apocalypse in Isaiah 24–27. Of the other books, the plebeian origin of Zechariah with his definite and artisan images; of Job, with its ringing cry for human equality and the rights of the oppressed; of Chronicles, with its untiring assertion of the rights of the Levites, the lower plebeian clergy, as opposed to the Aaronids, is obvious. (The Book of Jubilees is indeed in a class by itself. Its author, a Sadducean, perhaps a priestly aristocrat, is an obvious seeker for compromise between the sects. He accepts Pharisaic angelology and even immortality, but would have his followers forgo the belief in resurrection, which was the fundamental issue between the rival sects.[20])

Of the books opposing angelology, the patrician origin of Ben Sira, the ardent opponent also of the teaching of resurrection, need not be argued. Joel's ritualism as well as the whole tone of his prophecy with its manifest sympathy for priests and farmers, stamp him as country bred and patrician. We have but to compare his call to repentance through fasting and prayer with Malachi's demand for justice to the poor, to see that they derived from diametrically opposed social strata.[21] The vivid and detailed description of court life in the Book of Esther, as well as its combination of ceremonialism with worldliness, which will be discussed more fully below,[22] leave little doubt of its aristocratic origin. We have arrayed against each other two groups of writers; the one priestly and aristocratic, denying the angels; the other, plebeian and Levitical, continually and vehemently asserting their existence.[23]

This accords fully with the fact, recorded in the Acts of the Apostles (23.8), that in later times the Sadducees, following as usual the traditions of wealth and aristocracy, opposed the doctrine of angels, while the Pharisees defended it. "For the Sadducees say that there is no Resurrection, neither angel nor spirit; while the Pharisees confess both." The source is admittedly late, but the information it contains cannot, therefore, be impugned. No Greek writer could have invented such a controversy between the sects. We must understand, of course, that the Sadducean negation of angelology was not complete. They accepted the Scriptures; and the earliest records of the Pentateuch mention the "angel of the Lord." But, inheriting the patrician teachings of their forefathers, the Sadducees denied the elaborate angelology which finds its expression in Zechariah, Job, Tobit, the Enoch Literature, the Book of Jubilees and the Testaments of the Twelve Patriarchs.

Pharisaic angelology, as consoling to believers as the doctrine of resurrection, was less adapted for missionary purposes. The rich farmer could be persuaded of the value of resurrection; he was enticed by immortality even if it had to be shared by his "inferiors." But he saw no reason for assigning personality to the slaves of the heavenly court. He could think of the angels as related to God, as his own servants were related to him; they were part of him. Hence there was not the unanimity among the neo-Pharisees of the country regarding angels which we find regarding resurrection. Yet, the Essenes, who were essentially plebeian farmers of the Judean highlands, did accept it and, according to Josephus, had a secret tradition regarding "angels."[24]

It is true that neither Josephus nor the rabbinic sources mention the controversy between the Pharisees and the Sadducees regarding angels. Yet this silence cannot militate against the authenticity of the record in the Book of Acts. Josephus was writing for Greeks rather than for Jews, and may have found difficulty in reconstructing the issue in terms of the Stoic, Epicurean and Pythagorean philosophies which he tries to impose on the Jewish sects. For the same reason, he says nothing about the violent conflicts between the Sadducees and the Pharisees regarding such matters as water-libations and laws of impurity.

The rabbinic records of the ancient controversies are altogether too meager to give any validity to an *argumentum e silentio*. They tell us nothing of the conflict regarding Divine Providence which was fundamental to the whole teaching of the Pharisees, nor do they clearly explain the disagreement about the Oral Law.

But there was a special reason for the silence of the sages about this controversy: they had ceased to be a unit affirming the Pharisaic position. As Pharisaism absorbed into itself the larger part of the nation, including a majority of the provincials, the dispute about the angels was carried over into its midst. The new semi-patrician Pharisees, brought from farm and palatial home to the leadership of the plebeian movement, could not adjust themselves to the ordinary doctrine. Either they followed their fathers in continuing to reject it, or they put upon it an interpretation which their poorer colleagues considered blasphemous. The result was a medley of opinion, which leaves the rabbinic doctrine of angels the least clear in the whole of talmudic theology. R. Ishmael, for instance, in two important controversies expressed his disbelief in individual angels, such as the older Pharisees had postulated. Both controversies deal with the interpretation of verses in the Psalter. R. Akiba (ca. 120 C.E.), like all modern commentators, holds that the verse, "Man did eat the bread of the Mighty" (Ps. 78.25), refers to the angels. When the interpretation was reported to his colleague, R. Ishmael, he said, "Go out and say to Akiba, You are in error! Do angels eat? The verse speaks only of the food which is absorbed into all of man's limbs."[25] To force the biblical words into his interpretation, R. Ishmael changes the vowels in the received text. Surely no one, least of all R. Ishmael, who prided himself on his literalism and logical interpretation, would do such violence to the traditional reading if he did not feel an important issue was at stake. R. Ishmael simply could not believe that the Psalmist described the angels as eating bread; the picture was too anthropomorphic. But R. Akiba found it altogether natural and in consonance with what he, and many another scholar, believed. When we consider that R. Ishmael was a descendant of a priestly family, and one of the foremost of talmudic aristocrats, as well as the founder of a school noted for its patrician leanings, while R. Akiba rose to learning from humble sheep-tending and was the leading and most extreme exponent of plebeian doctrine, we realize the significance of this controversy.

The same dogmatic controversy reappears in the discussion of Psalm 104.12, where the author, describing the wild-life of Palestine, turns from the quadrupeds to the winged species and sings: "Beside them dwell the fowl of the heaven, from among the branches they sing." R. Akiba, more anxious to verify his theology than to indulge his taste for poetry, takes the "fowl of the heaven" to mean "the angels of service." But R. Ishmael, insisting on a literal interpretation of the verse, since this time it suits his purposes, maintains that the Psalmist speaks of "the birds who dwell in the trees, and who continually utter the praise of God."[26]

Within the school of R. Akiba, but only slightly influenced by him, sat the great patrician teacher of the next generation, R. Simeon ben Yohai. Like R. Ishmael, he was passionately opposed to the belief in humanized angels. In his brusque manner, he would curse those who, relying on the sixth chapter of Genesis, spoke of sins between the "sons of God" and the daughters of men.[27] The verse refers to the "sons of the judges," he held.

In another passage, R. Simeon unhesitatingly sweeps away the whole structure which two centuries of mystic speculation had built up about the Heavenly Chariot in Ezekiel's vision. From Hillel onward the plebeian scholars had woven a great web of secret teaching about the Heavenly Chariot, its living Wheels, and its conscious Beasts. "R. Johanan ben Zakkai had received the tradition from Hillel; R. Joshua ben Hananya from R. Johanan ben Zakkai,"[28] each of the three being the most noted plebeian teacher of his day. But R. Simeon ben Yohai, standing firm on traditional patrician ground, says: "The Patriarchs, they are the Chariot." In other words, he denies that there is any field for the whispered mysteries or that the Beast and Wheels are anything but figures of speech. They are prophetic visions allegorizing the ancestors of Israel.[29]

While the views of R. Ishmael and R. Simeon prove conclusively that a number of patrician and semi-patrician teachers denied the fantastic angelology as forcibly as had the Sadducees of earlier days, there was a group of rural teachers who not only accepted the doctrine of angels, but imagined them in such human form as even the plebeians could not accept. This was altogether natural, for the difficulty of the provincial sages lay in the fact that they could not, like the plebeians, conceive of immaterial spirit. Their simple common-sense minds yearned for the concrete and the touchable; and recoiled from the abstract and purely intellectual.

R. Judah ben Bathyra, one of their foremost representatives, describes Adam sitting in the Garden of Eden and angels standing about "roasting his meat, cooling his wine," and doing for him all other menial service.[30] R. Pappias, the rural teacher who shocked the more cultured sages by locking his wife in the house when he left it, not even permitting her to converse with male relatives,[31] interpreted the verse: "Behold the man is become as one of us" (Gen. 3.22), in absolute literalness. "He was like unto the angels of service," R. Pappias says. R. Akiba, hearing this exegesis, cried out, "Stop, Pappias. The Scriptures mean only that man was like to the angels in that God placed before him two ways, one of life and one of death, and he chose that of death."[32] In other words, man's divinity consists in his freedom of will and not in his combination of material form and intellect.

R. Meir, who in other respects tended to agree with R. Simeon, held a diametrically different view regarding the angels. "When God appeared against the Egyptians," he says, "He came surrounded by nine thousand myriads of angels of destruction; some of them angels of trembling, some of them angels of fright, some of them angels of hail and some of them angels of fire, so that whoever sees them is overcome with terror."[33] R. Eliezer ben Hyrcanus paints a similar picture of God at the Red Sea, surrounded by hosts of material angels.[34] R. Nathan the Babylonian, the close friend and colleague of R. Meir, says that Moses, cleansed of the food in his entrails, was "like unto the angels, implying that the divine beings differ from man not in their lack of material form, but in their freedom from the necessity of food.

R. Ishmael himself came to accept this view in the course of time. He interpreted the verse, "Ye shall not make with Me—gods of silver, or gods of gold, ye shall not make unto you" (Ex. 20.20), as follows: "Ye shall not make the form of any of My servants who wait on Me above: neither the forms of angels, nor the forms of Wheels, nor the forms of Cherubim."[35]

The anthropomorphic conception of the angels reached its highest development in the apocalyptic literature,[36] especially the Book of Jubilees, which actually describes some angels as circumcised.[37] The authoritative talmudic teachers recoiled with horror from such fantasies. They could not, however, reject the doctrine of anthropomorphic angels altogether; and in their wavering between the conceptions of non-personal and personal intermediaries between God and man, they tended to reverse and contradict themselves. Because of this it is impossible to define "a rabbinic conception of angelology." But there can be little doubt that the subject was earnestly discussed in rabbinic schools; and that some of them had definite and pronounced views on the whole subject. R. Judah the Patriarch, for instance, in his Mishna, zealously omitted all references to mediating beings even when they were mentioned in the statements which he incorporated into his text.[38]

Such censorship, taken together with the forceful statements of R. Ishmael and R. Simeon, seems to establish the fact that even as late as the second and the third centuries C.E. a heated discussion about the reality and the form of the angels was being conducted in the academies. The controversy, originally purely social, had now become academic and intellectual; yet it still retained some signs of its earliest economic class origin.

X. THE SIMPLE LIFE

According to Josephus one of the foremost characteristics of the Pharisees was that "they lived meanly and despised delicacies in diet."[1] This report is amply confirmed by the rabbinic record, which preserves the taunt of the Sadducees, "The Pharisees are bound by tradition to deny themselves the pleasures of this world; yet in the future world they will also have nothing."[2]

It has usually been assumed that both Josephus and the Talmud refer to the poverty of the Pharisees, which prevented them from indulging in the luxury of the upper classes. But we know that not all the Pharisees were poor; and, quite aside from that, the records present the Pharisaic attitude as a matter of principle. The Sadducean taunt would lose all its meaning, if the Pharisees had no choice about their mode of life; and even Josephus would hardly say that they "despised delicacies in diet," if he meant that they could not afford good food.

The controversy becomes fully intelligible, however, in the light of the earlier struggles between the plebeians and the patricians. Hundreds of years before the rise of Pharisaism, the plebeians had already inveighed against the use of luxuries by their opponents; and we may be sure that in those early days, as well as in the second century B.C.E., the patricians replied with sardonic taunts of one form or another. Indeed we can trace the struggle between the groups on this question back to the very entrance of the Hebrews into Canaan.[3] The nomads who broke into the settled country and found themselves in the presence of its richer and more highly developed civilization, were by no means ready to abandon their old life in favor of the new. Dire need had compelled these nomads to forsake the traditional homes of their ancestors in the wilderness and to seek partial means of support from agriculture. But like the Nabataeans of Diodorus, they still considered it degrading and impious to build houses and cities, to plant vines and trees, to wear ornaments of gold and silver, to ride on horses and to possess chariots.[4] They could not believe that their God would delight in a well-built Temple; or that He would permit Himself to be represented in statues of stone,[5] or wood, or gold; or that He would accept rich offerings in preference to those which they were accustomed to give Him. As they adapted themselves to the soil, some of them forgot these purist doctrines; yet among those who remained in the stony Judean highlands and in the pastoral lands of Transjordan there was a majority who retained the ancient tradition. They ascribed the building of the first cities in history to the fratricide Cain (Gen. 4.17) and the arrogant men of Shinar, who wanted to make themselves a name (ibid. 11.4). They considered it a superior merit in Jacob that "he was a simple man, dwelling in tents," while his brother, Esau, combined in himself the wickedness of the primordial hunter and the civilized agriculturist (ibid. 25.27). Long after these nomads had been settled in Palestine, they continued to abstain from the gold and silver nose rings which were the pride of the Canaanite patricians, and for centuries insisted on retaining the characteristic long, uncut hair, which was the mark of their highland peasantry.[6]

These tabus against innocent luxuries were explained in

various ways. It was said that Jacob had ordered his children to surrender their golden ornaments so as to be purified from the contamination of idolatry (Gen. 35.4); and also that the Israelites had used their ornaments to make the Golden Calf in Sinai (Ex. 32.3).[7] But the objection to them was, doubtless, more fundamental than either incident would indicate; the possession of nose rings and other jewels was a sign of patricianship and a deviation from the purity and simplicity of nomadic plebeian life.

It was quite natural that the Israelites should encourage the development of a group who were especially devoted to the old forms. They were called Nazirites, and were expressly forbidden to cut their hair or drink wine (Num. 6.2 ff.). Like Engidu, of the Gilgamesh epic, who lived in peace with the beasts and knew nothing of "land or people," they were to wear their hair "like women," letting "it grow like wheat."[8]

Even people who did not accept this tradition as a normal rule of life, submitted to it in moments of crises, as on the eve of battle. Just as they refrained from sex-life during war, because "God walketh in the midst of thy camp" (Deut. 23.15; I Sam. 21.6; II Sam. 11.11);[9] so they let their hair grow as a sign of superior holiness and purity. So widespread was this custom that long hair became, among the Israelites as among certain pre-Mohammedan Arabs, the first signals of approaching war. "When men let grow their hair in Israel," sings Deborah, "when the people offer themselves willingly, bless ye the Lord" (Judg. 5.2). Of those who lived this superior life also in times of peace, some bound themselves to it by special vows; others were bound to it from birth by their parents. Such pre-natal vows were especially common among barren women who begged God for children whom they might give to Him (Judg. 13.7; I Sam. 1.11, 28).

The plebeian purists reserved their most severe condemnation, however, for the use of horses. In Palestine as in Attica,[10] this efficient and expensive animal was possessed only by the gentry of the low country; the peasants of the highlands joined the nomads in declaring themselves not only unable, but also unwilling, to have them. The Book of Deuteronomy (17.16) actually forbids the king to own many horses, and explains that in order to acquire them it might be necessary to offer mercenary troops to Egypt in exchange. In practice, however, the ownership of horses was opposed even when there was no such danger. When David captured seventeen hundred horses from Zobah, he did not take them; he houghed all but one hundred of them (II Sam. 8.4). It was evidence of the apostasy of both King Solomon and King Ahab that they built up a cavalry.[11] The Psalmist (20.8) declares that a horseman tends to put his trust in his steed rather than God; and one of the latest of the prophets made a lasting impression on future imaginative apocalyptists by declaring that the Messiah would come riding on an ass (Zech. 9.9).

It was natural that the God who hated every manifestation of wealth should oppose the erection of costly temples. Long after the people had settled in houses, the Ark of the Covenant still was placed "behind the curtain," the traditional tent of the wilderness (II Sam. 7.2). And indeed it is only such a sanctuary that is permitted in the Pentateuch (Ex. 26.1 ff.). When David, rising in wealth, proposed to Nathan, the prophet, the establishment of a built sanctuary, the prophet replied in the name of God that this could not be done (ibid. 7.5 ff.). The altars built by the plebeians for the worship of God were of earth; when stone was used, it was unhewn (Ex. 20.21 f.). It is curious to note that when King Solomon was building the Temple, in violation of the desert tradition, he yet felt bound to respect this rule. He had to use hewn stones, of course; but he resorted to the legal fiction of having them prepared at the quarry so that "there was neither hammer, nor axe nor any tool of iron heard in the house, while it was in building" (I Kings 6.7).

There were, however, some Hebrews who, becoming acclimatized to the country, adopted the "manner of the Canaanites." They were to be found especially among the patricians who had gained a foothold in the fertile lowland. It was they who built the temple at Gilgal, called Ha-Pesilim or "The Hewn Images," doubtless from the fact that there were stone Images of YHWH established there. It was to this sanctuary that Ehud, the early Benjaminite warrior (in whose territory Gilgal was included) resorted before making his attack on Eglon, King of Moab, oppressor of Israel (Judg. 3.19). And what is historically far more significant, it was at this sanctuary that Saul—also a Benjaminite—chose to announce his kingdom (I Sam. 13.7).[12] To understand all that is implied in this statement, we must remember that Saul was selected as King by Samuel who, realizing that the popular demand for a royal leader could not be resisted, decided at least to make the selection himself. He thought he had chosen carefully and wisely when he picked the young warrior-peasant. What must have been Samuel's chagrin when he discovered that Saul's first royal act was to gather his forces at Gilgal and offer sacrifices there, at the sanctuary of the patricians, where

God was represented in the form so hateful to plebeian, nomad tradition. It is this background which explains Samuel's delay in coming to Gilgal, and also his vehement denunciation of Saul for having offered the sacrifice (ibid. 13.4 ff.). It is in vain that subsequent editors, trying to reconcile the traditions surrounding Gilgal with those of plebeian Hebraism, make Samuel call the meeting at Gilgal (ibid. 11. 14). The discrepancy between the editor's interpolation and the original story is too great to be mistaken.

It was a similar sign of defection from God when Jeroboam, the plebeian worker, whom Ahijah of Shiloh, imitating Samuel's rôle as king-maker, had placed on the throne of Israel, transformed the ancient shrine of Beth-el, which had consisted of only a rock on which libations of oil were poured (Gen. 28.18), into a great temple with a golden heifer as representative of YHWH (I Kings 12.29).

So eminent an aristocrat as Isaiah identifies luxury with idol-worship. In denouncing the sins of Jerusalem, he enumerates not only her social and religious delinquencies, but gives a whole list of ornaments worn by its maidens (3.18 ff.). Together with the increase in the number of idols, he laments the fact that "their land also is full of silver and gold, neither is there any end of their treasures" (2.7). He can see no ideal future for the land until the people return to the life of the simplest peasantry, with a diet of milk and honey. "And it shall come to pass in that day, that a man shall rear a young cow, and two sheep; and it shall come to pass, for the abundance of milk that they shall give, he shall eat curd; for curd and honey shall every one eat that is left in the midst of the land" (7.21). The places which grew a thousand vines would be left for briers and thorns, and the hills which were being covered with grain-fields would be reserved "for the sending forth of oxen and for the treading of sheep" (7.25).

Even before him, Hosea had announced that the ideal age of the world would be a return to that of the wilderness. "Therefore, behold I will allure her, and bring her into the wilderness, and speak tenderly unto her. And I will give her her vineyards from thence, and the valley of Achor for a door of hope; and she shall respond there, as in the days of her youth, and as in the day when she came up out of the land of Egypt" (2.16 f.).

This basic difference between the ancient plebeians and patricians led, as we have already seen, to the schismatic issue regarding the water-libations. But there were other differences, which for special reasons did not become partisan. One of them concerned the use of oil, which, common among all classes in Galilee,[13] was considered a luxury in Judea. Indeed, Josephus records that the Essenes regarded the use of oil as a "defilement," and that when one of them was anointed with it against his will, he immediately wiped it off.[14] Even among the talmudic sages, it was considered "improper for a scholar to walk about with ointment" in his hair.[15] When a woman poured some oil on the head of Jesus, when he was in Jerusalem, her action aroused indignation among many, who said, "Why was this waste of ointment made?" But Jesus, hailing from Galilee, saw nothing inappropriate in her action (Mk. 14.4).[16]

The general Pharisaic objection to such use of oil made necessary a special regulation to permit the Galilean members of the sect to "pour out channels of wine and oil before brides and bridegrooms."[17] Many members of the Pharisaic order considered the custom Amoritic and pagan; but the majority refused to forbid it. Indeed it is recorded that when the children of Gamaliel the Patriarch, came to Cabul, they permitted their hosts to pour out such channels of oil and wine in their honor.[18]

Far more serious than this objection to the use of oil was the protest of the plebeians against the extravagant banquets of the patricians and provincials. The so-called Zadokite Document, dating from the beginning of the first century B.C.E., denounced gluttony as one of the sins of the contemporary Sadducees.[19] But, as we have seen, the writer of the Assumption of Moses, about a hundred years later, found that it was rampant also among the patrician Pharisees, the Shammaites, of his day.[20]

It is this view which R. Akiba, the most outspoken of the plebeian leaders, expressed when he said, "Poverty is as becoming to Israel as a red strap on the neck of a white horse";[21] and when he declared further that "all the prophets complained to God of the silver and gold which He caused Israel to bring forth from Egypt."[22] A century before him, Hillel, the organizer of the plebeian faction of the Pharisees, had put the same thought somewhat differently when he said, "The more flesh, the more worms; the more property, the more anxiety."[23] "This is the way which is suitable for the study of the Torah," a later teacher remarked, "a morsel of bread with salt shalt thou eat, and water by measure shalt thou drink, thou shalt sleep upon the ground, and live a life of trouble the while thou toilest in the Torah. If thou doest thus, happy shalt thou be, and it shall be well with thee."[24]

By its very nature the struggle for the simple life had to be renewed in each generation. Fashions change, new discoveries are made, new delicacies are invented; and each of them has to be weighed in the balance to determine whether it belongs to the realm of the necessary or the superfluous. A thousand years after the disappearance of Pharisaism as a separate sect, the struggle between patricians and plebeians led to the enactment of new sumptuary laws in the European ghettos, rivaling those which were established, for similar reasons, in the larger communities of the day.[25]

XI. PROVIDENCE, DETERMINISM AND
FREE WILL

Among the important sectarian issues of his day, Josephus mentions the belief in Fate, with regard to which he identifies three views. The Sadducees, according to him, were absolute free willists, denying "Fate and saying there is no such thing." Diametrically opposed to them were the Essenes who held, he says, that all things are determined and that man is given no choice whatever. Between the two extreme doctrines was that of the Pharisees who maintained that "some actions, but not all, are the work of Fate; and that regarding some of them it is in our power to decide whether or not they shall come to pass."[1] It is the purpose of this chapter to show that the Sadducean attitude was natural to the patricians of Jerusalem and was traditional among them from an early time; that the Pharisaic view was equally inherent in the life of the urban plebeians and was found among them since the seventh century B.C.E.; and that the teaching of the Essenes was nothing but the simple piety of the ancient fellah, undisturbed by metropolitan sophistication.

In his analysis Josephus identifies Fatalism with the doctrine of Divine Providence, using the concepts interchangeably. He intended, doubtless, in this manner to clarify the subject for the Greek reader. But, as usual, oversimplification and forced parallelism resulted in mystification, so that subsequent generations were only misled and confused by Josephus' definitions. In fact, it seems that Josephus himself ultimately became muddled and his successive interpretations are partly contradictory. This was inevitable. A philosopher may be able to formulate his ideas on so complex and difficult a subject in a brief statement. But the underlying reactions of a whole social stratum could hardly become sufficiently precise or explicit for short, logical propositions. The people were aware of certain "feelings" on the subject; they carried about certain concepts; but it would have been too much to ask definitive dogmas of their untrained minds. This was particularly true of the ancient Jew, whose thinkers—not to speak of the masses—avoided, whenever possible, abstruse thought and ideas. Only when we have entered into the spirit of the ancient classes and sects and reconstructed their natural response to their environment, can we follow what Josephus is trying to tell us in his abstract and prolix phrases.

Like all primitive men, the ancient Israelite who lived about 1000 B.C.E. was completely unaware of his ego. Not only, as we have already seen, did he lose his identity in his clan or tribe; he was not even aware that his thoughts or ideas were his own. Everything came to him from God. If David took it into his sinful head to violate ancient tradition and count the people, the evil temptation was divine. "The anger of the Lord was kindled against Israel," says the ancient historian, "and He moved David against them, saying: 'Go, number Israel and Judah'" (II Sam. 24.1). It did not shock the readers of Kings to be told that God sent an evil and lying spirit to lure Ahab to his defeat in Ramoth-Gilead (I Kings 22.21). Elijah was uttering no blasphemy in the ears of his contemporaries, though he gave immeasurable trouble to all subsequent commentators, when he said to God: " 'Hear me, O Lord, hear me, that this people may know that Thou, Lord, art God, for *Thou didst turn their heart backward*' " (I Kings 18.37).

In the Torah itself, we find recorded God's promise to Moses that He will harden Pharaoh's heart to prevent his escaping the plagues through premature yielding (e. g. Ex. 7.3). Isaiah hears without surprise God's command: "Make the heart of this people fat, and make their ears heavy, and shut their eyes; lest they, seeing with their eyes, and hearing with their ears, and understanding with their heart, return, and be healed" (Isa. 6.10).

Such ideas were as natural to primitive men as to children. It did not occur to them that man himself was the author of his thoughts and inclinations. Yet they punished people for doing wrong. Never having conceived of intention as separate from act, they did not reckon with it. If one of them hurt himself against a stone, he was ready to strike it; just as Xerxes was prepared to beat the Hellespont for sinking his ships. Transferring, like all men, their own emotions to God, our ancestors considered it likely that God would punish transgressors for their action, without making any inquiry into the intention behind the deed.[2] Since the notion of human responsibility and the significance of inwardness was yet unrecognized, children were punished for the sins of their parents without theological or moral qualm.[3] Their personal innocence did not matter; for punishment was still emotional, not rational. An ox which gored a man would be stoned to death, not slaughtered (Ex. 21.28). Its destruction was intended not to prevent recurrence of the injury, but as vengeance for its misdeeds.

Indeed, in England of the twelfth century, it was still the rule that a man was guilty of homicide unless he could swear that he had done nothing whereby the dead man

was brought "further from life, or nearer to death."[4] "If,"
says an eminent authority, "once it be granted that a man's
death was caused by the act of another, then the other is
liable, no matter what may have been his intentions or his
motives."[5] If by mischance a man fell from a tree and
killed another, the victim's kinsman might, if he chose,
climb a tree and fall on the murderer![6] Indeed, if a person
gave his sword to a smith to be sharpened, and it was used
by the latter to kill someone, it were better for the owner
not to receive the implement, for he would bring a "bane"
into his house, and become responsible for its misdeeds. In
fact, the famous jurist, Bracton, sets down the rule: "If a
man by misadventure is crushed or drowned or otherwise
slain, let hue and cry at once be raised; but in such a case
there is no need to make pursuit from field to field and vill
to vill; for the malefactor has been caught, to wit, the
bane,"[7] or instrument of death—the boat, the cart, or the
beam. The conception that *Reum non facit nisi mens rea*,
which Augustine had tried to introduce from the later
Jewish-Christian tradition into Western thought, was still
far from acceptance.

We can hardly conceive of such naïveté and simplicity;
yet during a war we are ourselves not particularly careful
to save the innocent from suffering with the guilty. When
mobs become infuriated, they readily sink back into the
mental stage which was universal some thousands of years
ago, and many a person has been lynched who could not
judicially be punished. In fact, our punitive acts, rational-
ized as they are, frequently bear the stamp of vengeance on
them. Many of us still think it peculiar that prisoners should
be treated like ordinary men and women, and believe it

helpful—all criminologists to the contrary notwithstanding—
to brutalize their spirits yet more by repaying crime with
cruelty. Though we know in our hearts that crime is a
social disease for which it is as absurd to seek vengeance
from the afflicted individual as it was to beat the sick and
the insane, we continue to subject the wretch who trans-
gresses our laws to refinements of pain and humiliation.
Let us then be sympathetic to our less enlightened forefathers who followed their instincts without the inhibitions
which thousands of years of religion, philosophy and art
have imposed upon us.

It was an epoch-making event in the history of civilization when the Lawgiver declared that a betrothed woman
who was a victim of rape should not be executed with her
assailant. What seems to us patent common sense is argued
by the Legislator with a prolixity which shows the strength
of the opposing tradition: "But unto the damsel thou shalt
do nothing; there is in the damsel no sin worthy of death;
for as when a man riseth against his neighbour and slayeth
him, so is this matter. For he found her in the field; and
the betrothed damsel cried, and there was none to save
her" (Deut. 22.26).

These notions tended to persist in peasant life. The
farmer is so completely dependent on God for everything,
that he naturally attributes to Him even his desires and
wants. By his own work he can achieve little; it is God
who has to protect him from plagues, floods, droughts and
locusts. In his unsophistication the Palestinian peasant
never stopped to theorize about the reasons for suffering
or divine punishment. It was sufficient explanation of evil
to say that the "anger of God was kindled." How this

anger had arisen, whether it had moral justification, whether
the punishment it implied was deserved, did not particularly
concern his simple mind.

But as cities developed, new ideas began to gain ground
among the people. Both the rich men who moved to the
town for the sake of society and the poor who came there
in search of work, soon became aware not only of their
individuality, but also of their mentality. The farmer's
success depended altogether on nature and God; the city
man's, largely on his skill and cunning. The great landowner who derived his income from rents now entered
political and diplomatic life; he engaged in large commerce;
he had to deal with crafty artisans and merchants. Even
more than he, did the plebeian, working in his shop or
trading in the market, learn the fundamental distinction
between promise and performance, between fact and report.
The town bred the flatterer and the hypocrite, in whom,
as by electrolysis, deed was separated from intention. The
smooth-tongued merchant discovered the dissociation in
himself, and even the wealthy patricians were not all too
simple to grasp it.

The antithesis between act and pretense was even more
readily noticed by new arrivals in the city. The natives
of the metropolis grew up in the atmosphere of deception,
and many of them took no more notice of it than of the
physical air which they breathed. But a farmer, fresh from
the redolent country, was struck—if he was at all observant
—by the sharp contrast between word and meaning. Jeremiah[8] was the first among the prophets to stress the importance of inwardness and "speaking the truth in one's heart."
In his theology, God not only examines human action, but
He tries "the reins and the heart" (13.3: 17.10; 20.12).

We may be sure that many another farmer, brought to the city not to be a messenger of God but to wait at Court, also noticed the artifice and falsehood of the market place, and came thereby to a new understanding of the human mind. As soon as the distinction between intention and accident was made, the whole doctrine of sin and punishment, both human and divine, had to be revolutionized. Theology could no longer attribute to God the origin of sin without freeing man from the burden of punishment.

The patricians in Jerusalem found little difficulty in this problem. The same urban conditions which had raised it also provided the answer. Masters of the land, they came to regard themselves as "self-made." They had become in a measure independent of such petty matters as good harvest, sufficient rain, and safety from locusts. No matter how the country might suffer, their needs were provided. Inevitably such men came to think, in spite of the warning of the Deuteronomist, "My power and the might of my hand hath gotten me this wealth" (Deut. 8.17). Jeremiah knew the man who "maketh flesh his arm, and whose heart departeth from the Lord" (17.5). Long before, the Legislator had considered it an act of righteousness in Abraham that unlike the patrician he "believed in the Lord," and trusted His promise (Gen. 15.6). When Isaiah promised Ahaz safety from his enemies and offered a divine sign, the King contemptuously replied: "I will not ask, neither will I try the Lord" (Isa. 7.12). It was this attitude which predominated among the princes generally, so that when preparations for war were being made, Isaiah could properly complain: "And ye have also seen the breaches of the city of David that they were many and ye gathered together the waters of the lower pool . . . Ye also made a ditch between the two walls for the water of the old pool. But ye have not looked to the Maker thereof, neither had ye respect for Him that fashioned it long ago" (Isa. 22.9 ff.).

The plebeians of the city could not grant the claim of the patrician that wisdom and success are from man, himself. Liberated from the rural doctrine of absolute determination as they were, they yet denied that human prudence determines a person's fortune. Their own poverty demonstrated this to them; for they could not admit that they were the victims of their folly. They were thus caught in a paradox, which held them for centuries. Their ill fortune, which they could not attribute to themselves, was clear evidence of the power of Fate; yet their awareness of their ego, induced by city life, made them conscious of free will. This paradox is evident in the teaching of the prophets, the plebeians of the Second Commonwealth, and the Pharisees.

None of the pre-exilic prophets is clear regarding this question. Isaiah apparently adheres to the ancient rural teaching of the divine origin of human decisions; Jeremiah wavers; and Ezekiel, the most outspoken of all individualists, proclaims God the source of delusion as well as of truth.[9]

In the Book of Deuteronomy an attempt is made to clarify the issue. God places good and evil before man, so that man has complete freedom of choice in the moral field (11.26; 30.15, 19). But man's success in mundane affairs is achieved not through his "power and the might of his hand," for it is God who gives him "power to get wealth" (8.18).

This compromise doctrine has remained dominant in Jewish theology practically until our own day. Yet before it came to be explicitly recognized, Jewish thought was to undergo a long and complicated development, which can only be appreciated after a study of several later biblical and Apocryphal books. We shall consider them in the following order: Proverbs, Esther, Judith, Ben Sira, Lamentations Chapter 3, Chronicles, Job, Ecclesiastes, and the Psalms of the Persian Period.

A. The Book of Proverbs

The Book of Proverbs is really a collection of eight small tracts on conduct. They are separated from one another by special headings, so that the division is not a mere literary hypothesis but an established fact. The booklets were all concededly put into their present form during the Second Commonwealth. But it is altogether probable that the individual apothegms were coined, and a beginning of some of the collections made, hundreds of years earlier.

Two traditions are discernible in each of these little booklets: one patrician, the other plebeian. It is characteristic of the magnanimity and liberalism of the Hasideans and Pharisees that they absorbed both streams of thought into their literature; yet this ultimate merger must not be permitted to conceal the fact of the original separation, and even opposition, of the teachings. The patrician proverbs urge the pupil to be wise, cautious, thrifty, and self-reliant. Its teachings can be duplicated from the Babylonian Proverbs, the Story of Ahikar, and the Babylonian Job, as well as from such Egyptian works as the Wisdom of Amen-em-ope, and the Wisdom of Ani. But what is peculiar to the Jewish Wisdom literature is the plebeian tradition which is

found side by side with that of the patricians. Among no
other people of antiquity, so far as we know, did the landless
plebeians attain the state of culture they reached in Judea;
and, hence, nowhere else do we find an ethical tradition
based on purely plebeian ideals of faith, endurance and
reliance on God.[10] In the younger booklets, the two streams
of thought are still easily separated by the methods of
literary criticism. In the older booklets they have become
fused, and we can only detect the different traditions by the
contents of the apothegms. Because of this fact, it will be
most convenient to open the discussion of Proverbs with its
youngest portion, chapters 1–9.[11]

Several commentators have pointed out that the larger
part of this small treatise implies a background of affluence.[12]
The author addresses himself to a young man, obviously
the child of rich parents. He is able to help his friends
through gifts or by going surety for them (3.28; 6.1). The
women who seek to entice him are of the wealthiest classes:
"I have decked my couch with coverlets, with striped cloths
of the yarn of Egypt. I have perfumed my bed with myrrh,
aloes and cinnamon. Come, let us take our fill of love until
the morning; let us solace ourselves with loves. For my
husband is not at home, he is gone on a long journey; he
hath taken the bag of money with him; he will come home
at the full moon" (7.10–20). In accosting this youth,
Wisdom, herself, must assay her value in terms of money:
"My fruit is better than gold, yea than fine gold; and my
produce than choice silver" (8.19). The picture is patently
taken from patrician life; the child of Jerusalem's slums was
in no danger of the temptations against which the writer
warns and would have been overwhelmed rather than
stimulated by the rewards offered.

But the "wisdom" inculcated in the treatise is quite secular and non-religious. In those parts of it which are basic and original, there is hardly a reference to the fear of God, and none to the love of Him. The youth is warned against evil companions who must ultimately lead him to destruction (1.15); he is urged to follow wisdom because "length of days is in her right hand; in her left are riches and honour" (3.16); he is asked to emulate the diligence of the ant (6.6), and to avoid above all the sins of slothfulness and laziness. Wicked women should be shunned because angry husbands take fearful vengeance on betrayers (6.29). There is no attempt made to place the sanctity of the home and the ideal of chastity on any higher plane than that of material self-interest. No virtue save diligence and thrift is inculcated; and the folly of going surety for a friend is, by implication at least, condemned (6.1).

Here and there this materialistic tone is interrupted by higher ethical and religious considerations. But the passages containing them have, on purely literary grounds, already been shown to be interpolations by a "Hasidean" editor. They are all foreign to the text and generally not only oppose its spirit, but disturb its continuity. Thus at the very beginning of the book, in chapter 2, we read:

1. "My son, if thou wilt hear my words,
   And lay up my commandments with thee,
2. So that thou make thine ear attend unto wisdom,
   And thy heart incline to discernment;
3. Yea, if thou call for understanding,
   And lift up thy voice for discernment;
4. If thou seek her as silver,
   And search for her as for hid treasures;

5. *Then shalt thou understand the fear of the Lord,*
    And find the knowledge of God.
6. *For the Lord giveth wisdom,*
    Out of His mouth cometh knowledge and discernment;
7. *He layeth up sound wisdom for the upright,*
    He is a shield to them that walk in integrity;
8. *That He may guard the paths of justice,*
    And preserve the way of His godly ones.
9. Then shalt thou understand righteousness and justice,
    And equity, yea, every good path."

It is fairly obvious that the real apodosis to the condition set forth in the first four verses, begins with verse 9. If thou search after wisdom, thou shalt understand righteousness and judgment. As the text stands before us, there are two conclusions, the one secular, the other pietistic. But there can be no doubt that the pietistic and not the secular apodosis came from the interpolator. For while there is some formal connection between verse 5 and what precedes, the remainder is purely religious exhortation, altogether foreign to the spirit of what went before. If "the Lord giveth wisdom," as verse 6 assures us, why insist on study? If "He may guard the paths of justice and preserve the way of His godly ones," the prudent thing would be to seek not wisdom, but saintliness. This is indeed what the glossator is trying to teach, but it is quite alien to the spirit of the book to which, after a manner of a parasite, he attaches himself.

Similarly, though perhaps somewhat less obviously, the verse, "The fear of the Lord is the beginning of knowledge," in the first chapter of the book, is an isolated spark of religious teaching in the midst of a cold environment of pure secularism. The author is giving the purpose of the book:

5. "That the wise man may hear, and increase in learning,
   And the man of understanding may attain unto wise
       counsels;
6. To understand a proverb, and a figure;
   The words of the wise, and their dark sayings.
7. *The fear of the Lord is the beginning of knowledge;*
   But the foolish despise wisdom and discipline.
8. Hear, my son, the instruction of thy father,
   And forsake not the teaching of thy mother."

At the beginning of chapter 3, personified Wisdom speaks, calling the youth to her and promising her usual rewards:

1. "My son, forget not my teaching;
   But let thy heart keep my commandments;
2. For length of days, and years of life,
   And peace, will they add to thee.
3. Let not kindness and truth forsake thee;
   Bind them about thy neck,
   Write them upon the tables of thy heart;
4. So shalt thou find grace and good favour
   In the sight of God and man."

The motif of material success in this exhortation is unmistakable. The basis for morals is wisdom; the sanction of wisdom is success. It is the laws of wisdom, rather than those of God, which the author urges: they, not the Sinaitic commandments, give long life and peace. Even to find grace in the eyes of God, it is necessary to follow prudence rather than piety. The *Hasid* is unable to brook this teaching and interrupts with one of his interpolations:

5. "Trust in the Lord with all thy heart,
   And lean not upon thine own understanding.
6. In all thy ways acknowledge Him,
   And He will direct thy paths.
7. Be not wise in thine own eyes;
   Fear the Lord, and depart from evil;
8. It shall be health to thy navel,
   And marrow to thy bones.
9. Honour the Lord with thy substance,
   And with the first-fruits of thine increase;
10. So shall thy barns be filled with plenty,
    And thy vats shall overflow with new wine.
11. My son, despise not the chastening of the Lord,
    Neither spurn thou His correction;
12. For whom the Lord loveth He correcteth,
    Even as a father the son in whom he delighteth."

The interpolator's ideal is not prudence at all, but faith and obedience to God. He warns the young man not to be "wise in thine own eyes." To be successful is not the highest good at all, according to him; to suffer may be a sign of divine love and, therefore, better and superior.

Throughout Proverbs, the opposing philosophies of patrician and plebeian appear in this curious juxtaposition. The following random examples, culled from different parts, illustrate the patrician philosophy:

1. "He becometh poor that dealeth with a slack hand;
   But the hand of the diligent maketh rich" (10.4).
2. "The rich man's wealth is his strong city;
   The ruin of the poor is their poverty" (10.15).

3. "The hand of the diligent shall bear rule;
   But the slothful shall be under tribute" (12.24).

4. "The soul of the sluggard desireth and hath nothing;
   But the soul of the diligent shall be abundantly gratified" (13.4).

5. "The ransom of a man's life are his riches;
   But the poor heareth no threatening" (13.8).

6. "The poor is hated even of his own neighbour;
   But the rich hath many friends" (14.20).

7. "The crown of the wise is their riches;
   But the folly of fools remaineth folly" (14.24).

8. "A man void of understanding is he that striketh hands,
   And becometh surety in the presence of his neighbour" (17.18).

9. "The rich man's wealth is his strong city,
   And as a high wall in his own conceit" (18.11).

10. "Wealth addeth many friends;
    But as for the poor, his friend separateth himself from him" (19.4).

11. "Luxury is not seemly for a fool;
    Much less for a servant to have rule over princes" (19.10).

12. "The rich ruleth over the poor,
    And the borrower is servant to the lender" (22.7).

13. "He that tilleth his ground shall have plenty of bread;
    But he that followeth after vain things shall have poverty enough" (28.19).

It is altogether incredible that the groups or individuals from whom are derived these mundane and materialistic teachings could also bring forth the following pietistic maxims so contradictory to them in spirit:

1. "Treasures of wickedness profit nothing;
   But righteousness delivereth from death" (10.2).

2. "The Lord will not suffer the soul of the righteous
   to famish;
   But He thrusteth away the desire of the wicked"
   (10.3).

3. "The blessing of the Lord it maketh rich,
   And toil addeth nothing thereto" (10.22).

4. "He that trusteth in his riches shall fall;
   But the righteous shall flourish as foliage" (11.28).

5. "The eyes of the Lord are in every place,
   Keeping watch upon the evil and the good" (15.3).

6. "The nether-world and Destruction are before the
   Lord,
   How much more then the hearts of the children of
   men!" (15.11).

7. "The preparations of the heart are man's,
   But the answer of the tongue is from the Lord" (16.1).

8. "Better is a little with righteousness
   Than great revenues with injustice" (16.8).

9. "The name of the Lord is a strong tower:
   The righteous runneth into it, and is set up on
   high" (18.10).

10. "There are many devices in a man's heart;
    But the counsel of the Lord, that shall stand" (19.21).

11. "The king's heart is in the hand of the Lord as the
    watercourses:
    He turneth it whithersoever He will" (21.1).

12. "A man's goings are of the Lord;
    How then can man look to his way?" (20.24).
13. "Every way of a man is right in his own eyes;
    But the Lord weigheth the hearts" (21.2).

The booklets (10.1–22.16, and chapters 25–29) from which these sayings are taken are the oldest parts of Proverbs. Continuous interpolation and addition have so fused the two traditions in these works that literary criticism is no longer of use. But it is noteworthy that in each of these sections the patrician proverbs predominate in the first half, and the plebeian proverbs toward the end. Guided by an intuitive recognition of this and also by differences in literary form, Toy suggested the division of each section into two separate treatises.[13] While this suggestion cannot be accepted, for plebeian, pietistic proverbs occur also in the first parts of each section, its proposal indicates the soundness of the distinction between the two groups of teachings.

The present condition of these two booklets makes it altogether probable, however, that their original, patrician nuclei, were several centuries older than the final compilation of the Book of Proverbs. Such an hypothesis would allow ample time for the intrusion of the later plebeian supplements and their interweaving into the very warp and woof of the original material. It would also explain the curious ascription of chapters 25–29 to the "men of Hezekiah" (ca. 720 B.C.E.) which, as Gressmann[14] has shrewdly observed, cannot be altogether meaningless.

In the younger parts of the book, however, the division of the two philosophies is still as unobscured as in the first nine chapters. The Wisdom of Agur ben Yakeh, contained in the thirtieth chapter, is altogether plebeian. He opens his work by denying any association with the usual aristocratic Wisdom teachers.

"Surely I am more brutish, unlike a man,
And have not the understanding of a man;
And I have not learned wisdom,
That I should have the knowledge of the Holy One"
(30.2–3).

Unlike the official Wisdom writer, this author recognizes the existence of angels,[15] thus fixing definitely his plebeian status. He continues:

"Every word of God is tried;
He is a shield unto them that take refuge in Him . . .
Two things have I asked of Thee,
Deny me them not before I die!
Remove far from me falsehood and lies;
Give me neither poverty nor riches;
Feed me with mine allotted bread;
Lest I be full, and deny, and say: 'Who is the Lord?'
Or lest I be poor, and steal,
And profane the name of my God" (30.5–9).

The difference between these teachings and those about wealth being a tower of strength, need not be stressed. The writer is a plebeian pietist and democrat, fearful equally of sin and riches. Can we then be astonished that he says:

"Slander not a servant unto his master,
Lest he curse thee, and thou be found guilty" (30.10).

Thinking of the oppressor, he remarks:

"There is a generation, O how lofty are their eyes!
And their eye-lids are lifted up.
There is a generation whose teeth are as swords, and
   their great teeth as knives,
To devour the poor from off the earth, and the needy
   from among men" (30.13–14).

The democratic teachings of Agur are followed by maxims diametrically opposed to them:

"For three things the earth doth quake,
And four which it cannot endure:
For a servant when he reigneth;
And a churl when he is filled with food;
For an odious woman when she is married;
And a handmaid that is heir to her mistress" (30.21 ff.).

We expect from what we have already seen that the author of this supplement should have high regard for diligence and energy. And so indeed he has:

"There are four which are little upon the earth,
But they are exceeding wise:
The ants are a people not strong,
Yet they provide their food in the summer . . .
The locusts have no king,
Yet they go forth all of them by bands" (30.24 ff.).

It is now generally held that the booklet included in Proverbs 22.17–24.22 is based on Egyptian source material.[16] Its predominantly patrician tone cannot therefore be used as direct evidence for social conditions in Palestine. Nevertheless the Palestinian teachers clearly sought in the foreign works only doctrines which were acceptable to them. We may therefore take it that it was a patrician who brought into Scripture the apothegm:

> "Seest thou a man diligent in his business? he shall stand
>   before kings;
> He shall not stand before mean men" (22.29).

The child whom the teacher addresses may have the opportunity of dining with the governor and must be taught the imitation court etiquette there in use:

> "When thou sittest to eat with a ruler,
> Consider well him that is before thee;
> And put a knife to thy throat,
> If thou be a man given to appetite" (23.1–2).

True to the principles of his caste, this ethicist cannot inculcate virtue without supplying a practical reason for it. Self-denial is meaningless to him. A good act must have its reward—or it will be imprudent. Unashamedly he says:

> "Remove not the ancient landmark;
> And enter not into the fields of the fatherless;
> For their Redeemer is strong;
> He will plead their cause with thee" (23.10–11).
> "Rejoice not when thine enemy falleth,
> And let not thy heart be glad when he stumbleth;
> Lest the Lord see it, and it displease Him,
> And He turn away His wrath from him" (24.17 ff.).

This is altogether in the spirit of that other patrician writer, who teaches:

> "If thine enemy be hungry, give him bread to eat,
> And if he be thirsty, give him water to drink;
> For thou wilt heap coals of fire upon his head,
> And the Lord will reward thee" (25.21 ff.).

The mundane practicality of the maxims is no more amazing than their denial of the spiritual inwardness which was so fundamental to the plebeian teaching of the day. Could these proverbs have come from the circles which believed that:

"The spirit of man is the lamp of the Lord,
Searching all the inward parts" (20.27)?

Yet even in this small patrician treatise, the plebeian glossator has left his marks. In the introduction to it which reads:

"Incline thine ear, and hear the words of the wise,
And apply thy heart unto my knowledge.
For it is a pleasant thing if thou keep them within thee;
Let them be established altogether upon thy lips
(22.17–18),"

the writer significantly adds,

"That thy trust may be in the Lord."

Recognizing the kinship between the patrician teaching of many proverbs and the Sadducism against which they were still struggling, some sages wished to exclude the book from the canon. They said, "Its words contradict one another."[17] Later teachers cited as an example of this inconsistency the juxtaposition of the two verses, "Answer the fool according to his folly," and "Answer not the fool according to his folly."[18] But we may be certain that so slight and obvious a contradiction would hardly have called forth a movement to discredit the book. The inner conflict in the teachings of Proverbs is more profound and complete. It reaches down to the whole of its theology and ethics. And because the sages noticed that much of it contradicted the plebeian teachings of faith and trust to which they as Pharisees were committed, they felt that it had no place in Scripture.

B. Esther and Judith

But Proverbs is not the only biblical book in which the ethics of the patricians is reflected and which some scholars, for that reason, sought to exclude from the canon. There was similar opposition to the Book of Esther,[19] for it, too, emanates from patrician circles and gives expression to contemporary upper class philosophy. The author is at home in the palaces and at the banquets of the rich, he knows their manners, their whims, and their habits. He gives a vivid and detailed portrayal of Court life such as would be impossible for one who had never seen even its dim reflection in the satrap's palace in Jerusalem. But above all, the avowed purpose of the book indicates the patrician origin of its author. For apparently he is trying to establish, or to make more popular, the observance of Purim in the capital. He expressly tells us that "the Jews of the villages, that dwell in the unwalled towns, make the fourteenth day of the month Adar a day of gladness and feasting and a good day, and of sending portions one to another" (9.19). There is nothing in these words to indicate that in his day Jerusalem already knew Purim as a holiday; on the contrary, the author is arguing for the *establishment* of the custom.[20] He is a ritualist, to whom fasting, sackcloth, and ashes are essential when trouble looms. But the idea of prayer to God does not occur to his hero or heroine. He describes what appears to a religious-minded reader a most miraculous intervention of God in human affairs in terms of purely human motives, cunning action and good fortune.

Neither the name of God nor His angels appear once in the whole narrative. The author approves wholeheartedly of Mordecai's priggishness in refusing to obey the royal decree and bend the knee to Haman. The later sages, unable to enter into the mind of such a person, supposed that Haman carried an idol with him; so that Mordecai was prevented by religious scruple from paying him homage.[21] But the author of the book is altogether unaware of this. On the contrary, Mordecai is himself named after a Babylonian god, as Esther is after Astarte. Unlike Daniel, she makes no effort, so far as the story goes, to limit her diet to ritually permitted foods. The author relates without any sense of shock or pain the "elevation" of the Jewish girl to the harem of Ahasuerus.[22] For him, as for the Sadducees of a later day, national bias was not proof against social aspiration; and the honor of a king's bed outweighed the disgrace of heathen contamination.

The contrast between the patrician and the plebeian psychologies is made very clear when we compare the Book of Esther with the almost contemporary novel of Judith. In that story, too, salvation comes to Israel through a woman's charms; yet how differently the heroines pursue their tasks and how differently the tales are told. The book of Judith is as clearly a product of a humble scribe, as Esther is of wealthy nobility. The scene is laid in the Judean hill-country, the land of the poorer peasantry; Judith is not, like Mordecai and Esther, a member of the patrician tribe of Benjamin, but of the weakened remnant of Simeon. She is described as wealthy to make her piety and self-mortification the more remarkable; but the author takes care to say that her affluence came to her from her husband, and not from her parents. Like all other plebeian writers, the author is certain that God is especially interested in the poor; He is the "God of the afflicted, the helper of the oppressed, an upholder of the weak, a protector of the forlorn, a savior of them that are without hope" (9.11).

Unlike Esther, again, Judith does not partake of the forbidden food of the general into whose camp she goes. She takes along her own meat and, like Daniel, avoids both heathen wine and bread. She escapes the contamination of heathen dalliance, and each morning cleanses herself from the unavoidable defilement of pagan propinquity. Like Esther, she fasts; but unlike the Queen, she prays to God for help, and recognizes that while she may be an instrument, safety comes only from Him. "Smite by the deceit of my lips the servant with the prince, and the prince with the servant; break down their stateliness by the hand of a woman. For Thy power standeth not in multitude, nor Thy might in strong men" (ibid.). Speaking to the leaders of her people she reminds them that the Lord "hath power to defend us in such time as He will or to destroy us before the face of our enemies" (8.15). And finally she says to them, with full plebeian resignation to the Divine Will: "The Lord doth scourge them that come near unto Him to admonish them" (8.27).

And when the deed is accomplished and Judith returns to her people with the head of the hated Holophernes, they give thanks not to her, the agent, but to God, the principal. "And all the people were amazed and bowed down and worshipped God, and said with one accord, Blessed art Thou, O our God, which hast this day brought to nought the enemies of Thy people" (13.16). Yet Judith's part in the victory over Holophernes was far greater and more courageous than that of Esther in the discomfiture of

Haman. Esther's was assisted by a series of fortunate coincidences: Mordecai had overheard the plot against the king; the king happened to be sleepless on the night when Haman came to petition for Mordecai's head; she found grace in the royal eye as she stood unbidden in the court before his throne. Judith is guided throughout her work by common sense; she relies on no miracles and is aided by none. Yet both she and her people attribute her success to God, whereas the writer of Esther cannot find sufficient words of praise for her and Mordecai, though of themselves they could hardly have achieved anything. The writer of Judith must have been aware of this sharp contrast, and perhaps intended it. He may have wished to show, among other things, how the Hasideans interpreted the normal working of the world, and how God saves us through what we regard as our own judgment and activity.

Seen against the foil of the rival story, the Book of Esther confirms all the more effectively the other evidence of the lack of true religious spirit and trust in God among the pre-Maccabean nobility. With their own Wisdom writers and with the later Sadducees, these patrician landowners believed not in piety and devotion, but in prudence and achievement. Because such ideals were widely fostered, the plebeians were compelled to insist the more strongly on their own doctrines of faith and trust.

C. BEN SIRA

Ben Sira was probably a contemporary of the writer of Esther, and no less than he, a patrician. We have already seen how he agrees with the patricians in denying resurrection and the existence of angels. It is significant that in the truly aristocratic manner of the day he despises trade and craftsmanship. Like Hosea, he believed that all merchants are swindlers.

> "Hardly shall the merchant keep himself from wrong-
> doing,
> And a huckster will not be acquitted of sin.
> Many have sinned for the sake of gain;
> And he that seeketh to multiply [gain] turneth away
> his eye.
> A nail sticketh fast between the joinings of stones,
> And sin will thrust itself between buyer and seller"
> (26.29–27.2).

Of the husbandman and the laborer, he says:

> "How can he become wise, that holdeth the goad,
> And glorieth in brandishing the lance?
> Who leadeth cattle and turneth about oxen,
> And whose discourse is with bullocks . . .
> Likewise the maker of carving and cunning device,
> Who by night as by day hath no rest;
> Who engraveth signet engravings,
> And whose art it is to make variety of design . . .
> So also the smith that sitteth by the furnace,
> And regardeth the weighty vessels . . .
> Likewise the potter who sitteth at his wheel,
> And driveth the vessel with the soles of his feet . . .
> All these are deft with their hands,
> And each is wise in his handiwork.
> Without them a city cannot be inhabited,
> And wherever they dwell they hunger not.

But they shall not be inquired of for public counsel,
And in the assembly they shall enjoy no precedence"
(38.25–33).

How distant are these teachings from that of the Legislator
who regarded the builders of the tabernacle and the weavers
of its curtains as "filled with the spirit of God!"[23] And how
harshly these patrician dicta must have fallen on the ears
of the contemporary Hillels and Joshua ben Hananyas who,
laboring all day in their smithery and workshop, devoted
their evenings and Sabbaths to study.

Ben Sira's philosophy is, of course, no longer purely
patrician. Living when the Book of Proverbs had already
received its present form, he regarded himself as a collector
of ancient wisdom and tried to reconcile the incongruities
and contradictions he found therein. He says of himself:

"I, indeed, came last of all,
   As one that gleaneth after the grape-gatherers;
   I advanced by the blessing of God,
   And filled my winepress as a grape-gatherer" (33.16).

Yet fundamentally his sympathies are those of his class.
No less than the patricians of a former age does he insist on
the virtues of dilligence and prudence:

"Be not boastful with thy tongue,
   Nor slack and negligent in thy work" (4.29).
"The rich man laboreth to gather riches,
   And when he resteth, it is to partake of delights.
   The poor man toileth for the needs of his house,
   And if he rest he becometh needy" (31.3–4).

"A rich man, when he is shaken, is supported by a friend,
But the poor man, when he is shaken, is thrust away
    by a friend . . .
When the rich man speaketh, all keep silence
And they extol his intelligence to the clouds.
When the poor man speaketh: 'Who is this?' say they;
And if he stumble they will assist his overthrow" (13.21).

Somewhat after the manner of a later Talmudist explaining contradictions in Scripture, he tries to harmonize the opposing maxims of Proverbs, all of which for him are true and inspired. Since the Proverbs both forbid and command going surety for a neighbor, Ben Sira solves the problem by saying:

"Lend not to a man that is mightier than thou,
And if thou lend, thou art as one that loseth.
Be not surety for one that is more excellent than thou,
And if thou become surety thou art as one that payeth"
    (8.12).

Disagreeing with the patrician proverb, he definitely respects wisdom beyond wealth, and makes its attainment life's principal purpose:

"There is a poor man that is honored on account of his
    wisdom
And there is he that is honored on account of his
    wealth.
He that is honored in his poverty — how much more
    in his wealth!
And he that is despicable in his wealth — how much
    more in his poverty!

The wisdom of the poor man lifteth up his head.
And causeth him to sit among princes" (10.30—11.1).

He recognizes the dangers of over-diligence:

"My son, why multiply thus business,
Seeing that he who is in haste to increase shall not be
unpunished."

Yet, he continues:

"My son, if thou dost not run, thou shalt not attain,
And if thou seekest not, thou shalt not find" (11.11).

It is characteristic of Ben Sira's Pharisaic grandson who translated the book into Greek, that he should render the last two lines (which we fortunately possess in the original form both in the Hebrew text and in the Syriac translation) as follows:

"My son, if thou runnest, thou shalt not attain,
And if thou seekest, thou shalt not escape."

With the same freedom he had changed Ben Sira's denial of a future world into a Pharisaic affirmation of it. Ben Sira, as now recovered in the original Hebrew, says:

"Humble thy pride greatly,
For the expectation of man is worms" (7.17).

His grandson, who had become a Pharisee, translates:

"Humble thy soul greatly,
For the punishment of the ungodly is *fire and worms*."

The most philosophical of all the patrician teachers, Ben Sira necessarily draws each proposition to its logical conclusion, and states with propagandist clarity what is merely implied by his fellows. He insists on freedom of the will, which he thinks is compromised by the plebeian teaching. The belief that evil as well as good originated with God seems to him sheer blasphemy.

"Say not: 'From God is my transgression,'
For that which He hateth made He not;
Say not: 'He made me to stumble,'
For there is no need of evil men.
Evil and abomination doth the Lord hate,
And He doth not let it come nigh to them that fear Him,
God created man from the beginning
And placed him in the hand of his inclination;
If thou desirest, thou canst keep the commandment,
And it is wisdom to do His good pleasure . . .
Life and death are before man,
That which he desireth shall be given him . . .
He commandeth no man to sin,
Nor giveth strength to men of lies" (15.11 ff.).

Here Ben Sira touches the weak point of the plebeian doctrine, its compromise with regard to human freedom. By making man's decisions altogether dependent on God, it reduced human choice to nothingness; that it yet insisted that man was free was simply a paradox, which Ben Sira cannot accept.

It is not a contradiction in Ben Sira's teaching that he attributes the origin of sin in the world to Eve's eating of the forbidden fruit. That exercise of free will was the first fall of man. With that transgression, not only sin, but death entered into the world.

"From a woman did sin originate,
And because of her we all must die" (25.24).

In Ben Sira's patrician circles, as we have already seen, the principle of individual responsibility was not yet absolutely recognized. It seemed altogether probable to him that children would be punished for their parents and that the human race had incurred death through Eve's dereliction But the verse is not, as has been supposed by some commentators, a denial of human freedom. Man is still able to choose good and evil; but no matter how good he may be, he is tainted with the sin of his first parent.

XII. THE PLEBEIAN PARADOX

A. The Third Chapter of Lamentations

While the patricians were thus constructing a materialist philosophy, their views were challenged at every step by the contemporary plebeians, who were fast moving toward organization as Hasideans.

The doctrine which Ben Sira so completely rejects was given its most forceful and vigorous exposition by a contemporary psalmist, the writer of what has become the third chapter of Lamentations. This beautiful, didactic poem came to be attributed to Jeremiah, but its author was clearly a plebeian of the third century B.C.E. He was a man who had suffered much, he had seen "affliction by the rod of His wrath," he had been caused to walk "in darkness and not in light."

"He hath made me to dwell in dark places,
As those that have been long dead . . .
He hath caused the arrows of His quiver
To enter into my reins.
I am become a derision to all my people,
And their song all the day" (3.6 ff.).

Having introduced himself to us in these words, the author explains how he found comfort and consolation in his unswerving faith:

"This I recall to my mind,
Therefore have I hope.
Surely the Lord's mercies are not consumed,

226

Surely His compassions fail not.
They are new every morning;
Great is Thy faithfulness.
'The Lord is my portion,' saith my soul;
'Therefore will I hope in Him' . . .
For the Lord will not cast off forever.
For though He cause grief, yet will He have compassion
According to the multitude of His mercies.
For He doth not afflict willingly,
Nor grieve the children of men.
To crush under foot
All the prisoners of the earth,
To turn aside the right of a man
Before the face of the Most High,
To subvert a man in his cause,
The Lord approveth not.
Who is he that saith, and it cometh to pass,
When the Lord commandeth it not?
Out of the mouth of the Most High proceedeth not
Evil and good?" (Lam. 3.21–24, 31–38).

This confession of plebeian faith is altogether worthy of
the Hasidean glossator to Proverbs; the efficacy of human
endeavor is completely denied—all is in the hands of God.
The evil of the oppressor comes not from him, but from
God. As the Hasidean Proverb has it:

"The Lord hath made everything for His own purpose,
 Yea, even the wicked for the day of evil" (Prov. 16.4).

There is no freedom of the will in Ben Sira's sense; and
it is absurd to seek safety by begging of princes. Salvation
is in God, and in Him alone.

B. CHRONICLES

It was in this spirit that the Chronicler, living about the same time, proceeded to rewrite the whole of Jewish history. A Levite, and hence an ecclesiastical plebeian, he fills his book with the philosophy of trust in God.[1] For him the gravest sin is lack of faith. He is no longer concerned, like the compiler of the Book of Kings, with the evil of idol-worship. In his day that had practically disappeared from Israel. So the "wicked" kings are for him not men who served Baal, but who relied on themselves. Arrogance, not idolatry, brought on—in his opinion—the destruction of the Jewish state. The good king Asa, about to meet a vastly outnumbering host of Ethiopians, prays to God: "Lord, there is none beside Thee to help, between the mighty and him that hath no strength; help us, O Lord our God; for we rely on Thee, and in Thy name are we come against this multitude" (II Chron. 14.10). When some time later, the same King Asa was attacked by the King of Israel, he turned not to the God who had delivered him from the Ethiopians in answer to his prayer, but entered into dip-lomatic arrangements with the Arameans. Whereupon, a prophet says to him: "Because thou hast relied on the King of Aram, and hast not relied on the Lord thy God, therefore is the host of the king of Aram escaped out of thy hand. Were not the Ethiopians and the Lubim a huge host, with chariots and horsemen exceeding many? yet, because thou didst rely on the Lord, He delivered them into thy hand. For the eyes of the Lord run to and fro throughout the whole earth, to show Himself strong in the behalf of those whose heart is whole toward Him. Herein hast thou done foolishly; for from henceforth thou shalt have wars" (ibid. 16.7–9).

Asa's son, King Jehoshaphat, had similar experiences. Attacked by a huge army of Moabites and Ammonites, he prayed: "Our God, wilt Thou not execute judgment on them? for we have no might against this great multitude that cometh against us; neither know we what to do; but our eyes are upon Thee" (ibid. 20.12). Jehoshaphat was, of course, victorious in this battle, but toward the end of his reign he entered into a joint shipping enterprise with King Ahaziah of Israel, and in punishment for this dereliction, the vessels "were broken" and did not reach their destination (ibid. 37).

David is made to pray in these words: "Thine, O Lord, is the greatness, and the power, and the glory, and the victory, and the majesty . . . But who am I, and what is my people, that we should be able to offer so willingly after this sort? for all things come of Thee, and of Thine own have we given Thee . . . O Lord, the God of Abraham, of Isaac and of Israel, our fathers, keep this for ever, even the imagination (*yezer*) of the thoughts of the heart of Thy people, and direct their heart unto Thee; and give unto Solomon my son a whole heart, to keep Thy commandments, Thy testimonies, and Thy statutes, and to do all these things, and to build the palace, for which I have made provision" (I Chron. 29.11–19).

The Chronicler makes one concession to contemporary objection to attributing evil to God; he blames it on Satan. Whereas the earlier writer of Samuel had said that "the anger of the Lord was kindled against Israel, and He moved David against them, saying: 'Go, number Israel and

Judah' " (II Sam. 24.1), the Chronicler records rather: "And Satan stood up against Israel, and moved David to number Israel" (I Chron. 21.1). The Chronicler was not alone in the teaching; the writer of Enoch, living shortly afterward, declares: "Man was created exactly like the angels to the intent that he should continue righteous and pure," but one of the angels or satans "instructed mankind in writing with ink and paper, and thereby many have sinned from eternity to eternity and until this day" (69.9-11).

C. Job

To retain the point of view of the Chronicler, the plebeian had to possess deep faith and complete freedom from any sense of class inferiority. If he judged life by his external sense-impressions rather than by his spiritual intuition, he, of course, soon discovered the righteous forsaken and their children in want of bread. Indeed, there must have been hundreds who saw bitter want in their own homes, but who, lacking the spiritual power of mighty saints, were not sufficiently humble to admit that their pain was a result of impiety or an expression of divine love. There thus arose a group among the plebeians who, denying free will like the others, also denied Providence. They admitted that man cannot improve his condition through prudence, but they considered piety equally futile. They were the Palestinian forerunners of our modern Haeckels, the Jewish equivalents of the Athenian cynics. They accepted the world like the other plebeians, but sullenly, and angrily, or, at best, derisively, rather than serenely and in good humor.

The Book of Job has preserved for us a running debate between these cynics and the believers. Projected into the land of Uz, among the patriarchal nomad chieftains of the desert, the work yet bears the ineradicable marks of its origin in Jerusalem of the fourth century B.C.E. Behind the shifting curtains of Arab sheiks, we can discern the cunning faces and expressive gestures of Jerusalem traders, arguing in tones and cadences far more suitable to metropolitan sophistication than to pastoral simplicity. Though the language of both Job and his companions is skillfully colored with Arabisms, and though he is declared to be the owner of large herds of sheep, cattle, she-asses, and camels, but of no land, yet he has a good deal to say about silver and gold, about hired men and purchasers, about judges who sit in the gate, and the oppressors of the widow and the orphan.

Job and his friends agree in their sympathy for the plebeians and their opposition to the powerful. Among the virtues of the grave, Job discovers human equality:

"The small and the great are there alike;
And the servant is free from his master" (3.19).

A strange sentiment indeed in the mouth of a Bedouin chief, no matter how righteous; but altogether natural for a plebeian living in the Jerusalem of the Second Commonwealth. Among the virtues for which this pseudo-nomad claims credit is his kindness toward his slaves and his recognition of their equality with him.

"If I did despise the cause of my man-servant,
Or of my maid-servant when they contended with me—
What then shall I do when God riseth up?

And when He remembereth, what shall I answer Him?
Did not He that made me in the womb make him?
And did not One fashion us in the womb?" (31.13 ff.).

But if these words did not emanate from a contemporary
of Moses or the patriarchs, neither did they come from any
man of wealth, unless like some of the prophets he broke
with his class and sided with the oppressed. The patrician
of Jerusalem was no more ready than the slave-holder of
modern times to be told that he and his chattel were both
equal before God.

The friends of Job are equally emphatic. Eliphaz, the
oldest of them, praises God because:

"He saveth from the sword of their mouth,
Even the needy from the hand of the mighty.
So the poor hath hope,
And iniquity stoppeth her mouth" (5.15 ff.).

A little later Zophar, denouncing the wicked and prophesying
their destruction, says:

"That which he laboured for shall he give back, and shall
    not swallow it down;
According to the substance that he hath gotten, he
    shall not rejoice.
For he hath oppressed and forsaken the poor;
He hath violently taken away a house, and he shall not
    build it up" (20.18 ff.).

The continued and iterated protest against injustice, which
becomes one of the main motifs of the book, marks it as a
product of the plebeian mind. Neither Job nor his opponents
in the debate have anything in common with the Wisdom
teachers and their ideal of prudence and success, or Ben

Sira and his insistence on human freedom of choice. Widely as these pietists disagree among themselves, thrift, diligence, and cleverness never occur to them as ethical ideals. Their debate centers about Plan versus Accident; it is not, as in Proverbs, Prudence versus Piety. Job's friends are at one with the Chronicler, the writer of the third chapter of Lamentations, and the Hasidean glossator to the Proverbs, in holding that God will reward the righteous and protect them. Goodness alone is worthwhile. Opposing them, Job paints a world without any righteous ruler, left to the control of chance or worse, the wicked swallowing up the righteous, and never being called to account for it.

Job is clearly speaking not merely for the author, but for a whole philosophic group among the plebeians. When Eliphaz advises them to pray to God, they blasphemously reply: "If the scourge slay suddenly, He will mock at the calamity of the guiltless. The earth is given into the hand of the wicked; he covereth the faces of the judges thereof" (9.23). To Bildad's assurance that "God will not cast away an innocent man, neither will He uphold the evil-doers" (8.20), Job responds, "I shall be condemned; why then do I labour in vain? If I wash myself with water, and make my hands never so clean; yet shalt Thou plunge me in the ditch, and mine own clothes shall abhor me" (9.29 ff.). Zophar, the youngest of the friends, tries to persuade Job that "if thou set thy heart aright, and stretch out thy hands toward Him—if iniquity be in thy hand, put it far away, and let not unrighteousness dwell in thy tents— surely then shalt thou lift up thy face without spot; yea, thou shalt be stedfast, and shalt not fear" (11.13 ff.). But Job points out that "the tents of robbers prosper, and they that provoke God are secure" (12.6). And so the argument continues through some thirty chapters. The friends continually claim that righteousness has its rewards, and Job points to the adversity of the good and the happiness of the sinful.

Both groups were obviously deeply influenced by Persian environment and theology. Job's picture of God is simply an infinite Ahriman. He accepts the Zoroastrian teaching of an evil force, but sees no evidence of any Ahura Mazda to counteract, much less to control, it.

The book presumably ended, in its original form, with the victory of Job, being a pamphlet issued in defense of the sceptic teaching. This is evident from the sentence, "The words of Job are ended," with which the discussion between him and his friends closes. Job had the last word, and his disputants had to withdraw from the field. But later pietists could not take this view of the argument and added two appendices to refute Job. The one is ascribed to Elihu, a person not mentioned previously in the book but who sat listening to the argument and now injected his own ideas into it. His refutation of Job is merely a less able and eloquent repetition of the arguments of the three friends who spoke first. On a far higher plane, both in literary form and in intellectual content, stands the final refutation ascribed to God Himself, speaking to Job "out of the storm." The argument of these chapters is also slightly adumbrated in the discussion with the friends, but not pressed. It is that God is indeed just, but in a manner which is beyond man's understanding. The righteous may indeed suffer and the wicked prosper; but this does not impugn the truth of God or His justice, for both are beyond human comprehension. The faith of the sophisticated pietist is that God will give man not necessarily what he wants, but what is in truth good for him.

Dissatisfied with this, a final redactor transformed the whole spirit of the book from a philosophic discussion into a pious novel. He altered the prologue so as to attribute Job's troubles to the machinations of Satan, and added an epilogue to supply the "happy ending," in which Job's fortunes are once more reversed, and he receives in double measure all the goods he has lost. With these changes the book became a truly religious work, teaching faith in God, and fit for admission to the biblical canon.

D. KOHELETH (ECCLESIASTES)

But the philosophic group of cynical plebeians did not disappear with the transformation of their masterpiece. About the year 200 B.C.E., another of their number attempted an equally pointed and eloquent and perhaps more constructive, though far briefer, criticism of both the dominant Wisdom and pietistic systems of ethics and theology. Like the rest of the controversial literature, his work, Koheleth, suffered much at the hands of glossators and interpolators, yet the original can be recovered by the usual methods of literary criticism and stands out as a work distinguished in thought and style, and giving forcible and vivid presentation to the ideals of the sceptic plebeian school.

The book, attributed to King Solomon, has frequently been described as the work of a rich man. The basis for this is the writer's own statement that he possessed fields and vineyards, men-servants and maid-servants, flocks of sheep and cattle, and silver and gold, "more also than all that were before me over Jerusalem" (1.16). It is indeed strange, however, that critics who so readily deny the ascription of the book to Solomon should take this masquerade seriously. Obviously a writer disguising himself as Israel's wealthiest king would speak of his vast possessions; but poverty no less than wealth can hide in the raiment of royalty. The writer's weariness and his contempt for affluence are in fact characteristic not of the aging rich, but rather of the philosopher's vision of them.

There is ample positive evidence of its plebeian origin in the book. Like Job, it protests vigorously against social injustice. "I returned," says the author, "and considered all the oppressions that are done under the sun; and behold the tears of such as were oppressed, and they had no comforter; and on the side of their oppressors there was power, and they had no comforter" (4.1). "Moreover I saw under the sun, in the place of justice, that wickedness was there; and in the place of righteousness, that wickedness was there" (3.16).

The teachings of the book are altogether contrary to those natural to patricians and advanced by them in the works we have considered. The search after wisdom is folly, "for in much wisdom is much vexation; and he that increaseth knowledge increaseth sorrow" (1.18). But so also is the attempt to be virtuous, for "there is a righteous man that perisheth in his righteousness, and there is a wicked man that prolongeth his life in his evil-doing" (7.15). Everything happens through chance, the wise and the foolish, the wicked and the righteous are equally exposed to it, "as the fishes that are taken in an evil net" (9.12). "All things come alike to all; there is one event to the righteous and to the wicked; to the good and to the clean and to the unclean; to him that sacrificeth and to him that sacrificeth not; as is the good, so the sinner, and he that sweareth, as he that feareth an oath. There is an evil in all that is done under the sun, and there is one event unto all; yea also the heart of the sons of men is full of evil, and madness is in their heart while they live, and after that they go to the dead" (9.2 ff.). Diligence, which the patrician teachers so much praised, is the worst of follies. "What profit hath he that worketh in that he laboureth?" (3.9) "The race is not to the swift, nor the battle to the strong, neither yet bread to the wise, nor yet riches to the man of understanding, nor yet favour to men of skill; but time and chance happeneth to them all" (9.11). "And I hated all my labour wherein I laboured under the sun, seeing that I must leave it unto the man that shall be after me. And who knoweth whether he will be a wise man or a fool? yet he will have rule over all my labour wherein I have laboured, and wherein I have shown myself wise under the sun" (2.18).

The bitter polemic spares neither the pious nor the wise. There is nothing good under the sun save eating and drinking and enjoying the passing scene. "Man hath no pre-eminence above a beast; for all is vanity . . . Who knoweth the spirit of man whether it goeth upward, and the spirit of the beast whether it goeth downward to the earth?" (3.19 ff.). Achievement, virtue, thrift, goodness—none of them are effective and none justify sacrifice.

The spirit permeating this book is thus identical with that of Job himself, and emanates doubtless from the same sceptical, cynical, plebeian circle. Both of the groups attacked in the work, the patricians and the pietists, added anti-toxic glosses to it. These glosses are readily separable, so different are they in tone and manner from the rest of the book. The glosses generally occur where the original writer is most emphatic in his scepticism and cynicism. Thus, Koheleth passionately confesses that after striving for a whole lifetime, he found that "all was vanity and a striving after wind, and there was no profit under the sun," and the glossator at once replies, in the manner of a critical annotator, "Then I saw that wisdom excelleth folly, as far as light excelleth darkness. The wise man, his eyes are in his head; but the fool walketh in darkness" (2.11 ff.). The very form of the verse is that of the usual Wisdom apothegm.

Somewhat later in the book, Koheleth says: "Again, I considered all labour and all excelling in work, that is man's rivalry with his neighbour. This also is vanity and striving after wind." The glossator thereupon remarks:

> "The fool foldeth his hands together,
> And eateth his own flesh" (4.5).

As emphatically as any Wisdom writer, this glossator announces his firm faith in riches and possessions:

> "Wisdom is good with an inheritance,
> Yea, a profit to them that see the sun" (7.11).
> "By slothfulness the rafters sink in;
> And through idleness of the hands the house leaketh" (10.18).

He believes unequivocally in diligence and hard work, not only for the masses but also for princes:

> "Woe to thee, O land, when thy king is a boy,
> And thy princes feast in the morning!
> Happy art thou, O land, when thy king is a free man,
> And thy princes eat in due season" (10.16).

No wonder that he loses all patience with his author, who perversely says, in disparagement of labor:

"Whoso quarrieth stones shall be hurt therewith;
And he that cleaveth wood is endangered thereby"
(10.9 ff.).

This taunt at his philosophy incenses the glossator; forgetting his usual calm, he retorts in most unphilosophic deprecation of the mentality of the principal writer:

"If the iron be blunt,
And one do not whet the edge,
Then must he put to more strength,
But wisdom is profitable to direct" (10.10).

But neither would the pietist of the school and class which had produced the third chapter of Lamentations, the Chronicles, the Hasidean Proverbs, and the additions to Job, remain silent in the face of the attack on his teaching. With characteristic audacity, he gives each argument of Koheleth a Hasidean turn, which all but conceals the original heresy. So cleverly are the new ideas woven into the old that sometimes it is hard to extricate them. Koheleth denies the value of human progress and achievement, saying: "That which is hath been long ago, and that which is to be hath already been." The pietist apparently accepts the statement, adding only the qualification, "And God seeketh that which is pursued" (3.15).

When Koheleth cynically remarks that "no man hath power over the wind to retain the wind; neither hath he power over the day of death;" the pietist simply reminds us, "neither shall wickedness deliver him that is given to it" (8.8). The original book ends with the advice: "Rejoice,

O young man, in thy youth; and let thy heart cheer thee in
the days of thy youth, and walk in the ways of thy heart,
and in the sight of thine eyes" (11.9); sentiments, of course,
equally hostile to the pious and the prudent. But the Hasid,
as in Job, takes the last word, and adds, with a shaking
index finger, "But know thou, that for all these things God
will bring thee into judgment" (11.9). Replying to the
author's expressed doubt regarding man's spirit, whether
it really ascends on high, the Hasid continues, after a vivid
description of old age and its weakness,

"And the dust returneth to the earth as it was,
And the spirit returneth unto God who gave it" (12.7).

The present book of Koheleth thus appears, under critical
examination, to be a symposium of all the three dominant
philosophies of its day. With its glosses properly labeled,
it alone might serve, small as it is, to provide us with a clear
picture of the opposing forces which within a century were
destined to rend Israel into two bitterly hostile and mutually
irreconcilable camps.

E. THE PSALMS

Written in the tense atmosphere of pre-Maccabean Jerusalem, the Psalms of the Persian and Greek periods, no less
than the Wisdom and historical literature, are strongly
partisan; signals, as it were, of the approaching storm. The
Psalms are indeed all alike in their prayerful mood; and
may appear to the superficial reader at one in their complete
faith and reliance on God. But closer scrutiny reveals
profound differences, corresponding to those dividing the
patrician and plebeian maxims in Proverbs.[2]

Like Job and Koheleth, most of the psalms are an irrepressible welling forth of the plebeian spirit which, no longer able to endure the crushing weight and darkness of subterranean existence, broke out magnificently into the bright sunshine of a divine world. Not the priests of the higher clergy, but the subordinate Levites, were the singers in the Temple. And it is not the aristocratic families of Jedaiah and Joiarib, but the humble guilds of Korah and Asaf to whom the psalms are accredited. Even those psalms which were composed outside the Temple were most frequently of plebeian origin. They were written by learned scribes and scholars, such as were far more frequent among the traders and shopkeepers than among the nobility. Hence the larger part of the Psalter is in close sympathy with the plebeian teaching. The few patrician hymns serve merely as a foil to contrast with the far more numerous works of the plebeians. This is doubtless how it came to pass that this ancient work has served for so many centuries as a solace to aching hearts. The apparel of sorrow changes; the soul's anguish remains the same.

Some of the Psalms still mirror for us the spiritual conflict through which the Judean of the third century B.C.E. passed as he was torn hither and thither by opposing schools of thought. Perhaps the most moving of this group is Psalm 73.

"But as for me, my feet were almost gone,
    My steps had well nigh slipped.
    For I was envious at the arrogant,
    When I saw the prosperity of the wicked.
    For there are no pangs at their death,
    And their body is sound.

In the trouble of man they are not;
Neither are they plagued like men.
Therefore pride is as a chain about their neck;
Violence covereth them as a garment . . .
And they say: 'How doth God know?
And is there knowledge in the Most High?' . . ,
Surely in vain have I cleansed my heart,
And washed my hands in innocency;
For all the day have I been plagued,
And my chastisement came every morning" (2–14).

Two reflections save the poet from the brink of scepticism.
He discovers that the wicked do not always prosper:

"Surely Thou settest them in slippery places;
Thou hurlest them down to utter ruin.
How are they become a desolation in a moment!
They are wholly consumed by terrors" (18–19).

But a nobler and more significant thought turns his mind
from this vengeful mood. He realizes suddenly that his own
unhappiness is altogether unwarranted:

"But I was brutish and ignorant;
I was as a beast before Thee.
Nevertheless I am continually with Thee;
Thou holdest my right hand . . .
Whom have I in heaven but Thee?
And beside Thee I desire none upon earth.
My flesh and my heart faileth,
But God is the rock of my heart and my portion for
     ever" (22–26).

Not all the plebeians had to struggle through doubt to
arrive at faith. Like the Hasidean glossator to Proverbs,

some of the psalmists are unshakably convinced that the reward of virtue is happiness. Such a poet was the author of Psalm 37, in which occur the most emphatic assertions of pietist faith to be found in the Scriptures:

"Fret not thyself because of evil-doers,
  Neither be thou envious against them that work unrighteousness.
For they shall soon wither like the grass,
And fade as the green herb.
Trust in the Lord and do good;
Dwell in the land, and cherish faithfulness.
So shalt thou delight thyself in the Lord;
And He shall give thee the petitions of thy heart.
Commit thy way unto the Lord;
Trust also in Him, and He will bring it to pass . . . "
  (1–5).

Like the Hasid teacher of Proverbs, he maintains:

"Better is a little that the righteous hath
  Than the abundance of many wicked.
For the arms of the wicked shall be broken;
But the Lord upholdeth the righteous" (16–17).

He holds that human actions are largely determined by God.

"It is of the Lord that a man's goings are established;
And He delighteth in his way" (23).

The same teaching is found again in the beautiful Psalm 33:

"A king is not saved by the multitude of a host;
A mighty man is not delivered by great strength.
A horse is a vain thing for safety;
Neither doth it afford escape by its great strength.

Behold, the eye of the Lord is toward them that fear Him,
Toward them that wait for His mercy" (16–18).

But God's power is not merely in saving men from evil;
He looks into their inward parts and knows all their thoughts.
The wicked delude themselves with the notion:

". . . The Lord will not see,
Neither will the God of Jacob give heed" (94.7).

But the psalmist asks them:

"Consider, ye brutish among the people;
And ye fools, when will ye understand?
He that planted the ear, shall He not hear?
He that formed the eye, shall He not see?" (94.8–9).

Perhaps the psalmist is here protesting particularly against
a secularized and worldly priesthood, in whom sanctity has
become mere sanctimoniousness, and piety is supplanted by
power, for he says:

"Shall the seat of wickedness have fellowship with Thee,
Which frameth mischief by statute?
They gather themselves together against the soul of
the righteous,
And condemn innocent blood" (20–21).

Two of the psalmists explicitly deny human freedom of
choice and pray to God that they may repent and be brought
back to Him. One of them prays:

"Behold, Thou desirest truth in the inward parts;
Make me, therefore, to know wisdom in mine inmost
heart . . .
Create me a clean heart, O God;
And renew a stedfast spirit within" (51.8–12).

That he was a plebeian and not a patrician follows from his violent attack on the Temple service, which was so especially revered among the nobility:

> "O Lord, open Thou my lips;
> And my mouth shall declare Thy praise.
> For Thou delightest not in sacrifice, else would I give it;
> Thou hast no pleasure in burnt-offering.
> The sacrifices of God are a broken spirit;
> A broken and a contrite heart, O God, Thou wilt not
>   despise" (51.17–19).

The argus-eyed glossator could not permit this anti-ecclesiastical sentiment to pass without comment, and so he adds, as though the original words applied only to the exile when there was no temple:

> "Do good in Thy favour unto Zion;
> Build Thou the walls of Jerusalem.
> Then wilt Thou delight in the sacrifices of righteousness,
>   in burnt-offering and whole offering;
> Then will they offer bullocks upon Thine altar" (20–21).

A similar denial of free will occurs in Psalm 86. The author of that prayer is confessedly a plebeian:

> "Incline Thine ear, O Lord, and answer me;
> For I am poor and needy . . .
> In the day of my trouble I call upon Thee;
> For Thou wilt answer me . . .
> O God, the proud are risen up against me,
> And the company of violent men have sought after
>   my soul,
> And have not set Thee before them" (1–14).

He asks for divine mercy, but especially:

"Teach me, O Lord, Thy way, that I may walk in Thy
truth;
Make one my heart to fear Thy name" (11).

It may seem to us altogether natural that one should pray
to God for a righteous heart and for understanding; we do
so continually in formal worship, without considering that
we are thereby denying freedom of choice. But what has
become trite and commonplace to us through the usage of
two millennia, was meant in bald literalness by the ancient
poet. When he asked God to "make his heart one to fear
the Divine Name," he really believed that virtue emanates,
together with wickedness, from God alone. We never find
such a conception in patrician works; but it is consistent
with the system of thought developed by the plebeians,
inherited from them by the Pharisees, and taken over from
the Pharisees by both rabbinic Judaism and Christianity.

Priestly psalms, like later Sadducean philosophy, are not
marked by positive affirmations or definite negations, but
by their strange omissions. The doctrines of diligence, thrift,
and success would hardly have been appropriate in any
prayer. Yet Psalms 93, and 94–99, a group which obviously
belongs together, extolling the already existent theocracy
of the Second Commonwealth and the beauty of the Temple,
are clearly the work of either priests or men of priestly
sympathies; men to whom the existing social order appears
glorious and utterly without flaw. Since the High Priest
is Judea's foremost citizen, the Lord, whom he represents,
has already come into His Kingdom. It is impossible to
catch the full spirit of self-satisfaction and patrician jollity
running through these poems without reading the whole of

them. Yet it may be well to cite a few verses whose significance is especially to be noted:

"The Lord reigneth; He is clothed in majesty;
The Lord is clothed, He hath girded Himself with
    strength;
Yea, the world is established, that it cannot be moved.
Thy throne is established of old;
Thou art from everlasting . . . " (93.1–2).

O come, let us sing unto the Lord;
Let us shout for joy to the Rock of our salvation.
Let us come before His presence with thanksgiving,
Let us shout for joy unto Him with psalms . . .
O come, let us bow down and bend the knee;
Let us kneel before the Lord our Maker;
For He is our God,
And we are the people of His pasture, and the flock of
    His hand" (95.1–7).

"O sing unto the Lord a new song;
Sing unto the Lord, all the earth.
Sing unto the Lord, bless His name;
Proclaim His salvation from day to day . . .
Say among the nations: 'The Lord reigneth.'
The world also is established that it cannot be
    moved . . .
Let the sea roar, and the fulness thereof;
Let the field exult, and all that is therein;
Then shall all the trees of the wood sing for joy
Before the Lord, for He is come;
For He is come to judge the earth;
He will judge the world with righteousness,
And the peoples in His faithfulness" (96.1–13).

It is noteworthy that judgment hangs over the pagan peoples, but not apparently over the oppressors in Israel. This becomes even more evident in the following psalm:

> "The Lord reigneth; let the earth rejoice;
> Let the multitude of isles be glad . . .
> Ashamed be all they that serve graven images,
> That boast themselves of things of nought;
> Bow down to Him, all ye gods . . .
> Zion heard and was glad,
> And the daughters of Judah rejoiced;
> Because of Thy judgments, O Lord.
> For Thou, Lord, art most high above all the earth;
> Thou art exalted far above all gods" (97.1–9).

A Hasidean glossator here interrupts with these verses, altogether alien to the spirit of the poem, and in no way integrated with it, even in form:

> "O ye that love the Lord, hate evil;
> He preserveth the soul of all his pious saints [Hasidim];
> He delivereth them out of the hand of the wicked.
> Light is sown for the righteous,
> And gladness for the upright in heart.
> Be glad in the Lord, ye righteous;
> And give thanks to His holy name" (10 ff.).

The fundamental motif of the collection continues in the following two psalms: joy in the Kingdom of God and exultation over all the heathen. Once only does a new thought occur, and this serves to show the priestly interest of the author. In Psalm 99, he says:

"Moses and Aaron among His priests,
And Samuel among them that called upon His name,
Did call upon the Lord, and He answered them" (99.6).

Glosses, like those which have been indicated, are probably as frequent in the Psalms as in Proverbs or Koheleth. But in short poems, it is not always easy to prove that they are intrusions, and the mere difference in intellectual outlook cannot itself justify excision. Sometimes, however, we are fortunate in the possession of purely literary evidence to strengthen the suspicions aroused by differences in ethical and theological ideas. Psalm 136, which is based on the first twelve verses of Psalm 135 (merely adding the response: "For His mercy endureth for ever"), contains at the end four verses to which there is nothing corresponding in the preceding psalm. These verses are, characteristically, plebeian, in contrast to the rest which is essentially patrician and nationalist:

"Who remembered us in our low estate,
    For His mercy endureth forever;
And hath delivered us from our adversaries,
    For His mercy endureth forever;
Who giveth food to all flesh,
    For His mercy endureth forever.
O give thanks to the God of Heaven,
    For His mercy endureth forever."

Without these additional strophes the Psalm contains 22 verses, which were doubtless intended to correspond to the number of letters in the Hebrew alphabet. The interpolation of the four additional verses destroys the correspondence.

The addition of the Hasidean gloss only helps to emphasize the patrician character of the remainder of the psalm. Somewhat like the writer of Esther, the psalmist gloats over the destruction of the heathen:

"To Him that smote Egypt in their first-born . . .
And brought out Israel from among them . . .
With a strong hand, and with an outstretched arm . . .
To Him who divided the Red Sea in sunder . . .
And made Israel to pass through the midst of it . . .
But overthrew Pharaoh and his host in the Red Sea . . .
To Him that led His people through the wilderness . . .
To Him that smote great kings . . .
And slew mighty kings . . . .
Sihon, King of the Amorites . . .
And Og, King of Bashan . . . " (136.10–20).

Not a word in praise of God, the Lawgiver; no suggestion of thanks for the miracle of the manna. The writer's mind is fixed on war and he revels in the thought of Israel's ancient victories.

F. The Maccabean Age and After

The Maccabean victories put an end to plebeian cynicism and heresy, and encouraged both the pietists and the Wisdom teachers. The marvelous deliverance of Israel from the Syrian yoke justified all the glorious prophecies of the past. The Jobs and the Koheleths could no longer claim that the world was governed by Accident or Evil; for all had seen the salvation of the Lord. Yet the comparison of the Books of Esther and Judith have already given us an insight into the varying interpretations put on the most natural events by the rival groups of patricians and plebeians. The patrician was always ready to emphasize the human element in achievement; the plebeian, the divine. The Hasid needed no supernatural cataclysm to reveal to him the finger of God; he saw it in everyday occurrences. His own ingenuity, when it succeeded, seemed to him a divine miracle. The patrician, on the other hand, took credit even for fortuitous coincidence. Hence the patrician gave the Hasmonean generalship and diplomacy an unduly large share in the unexpected victory of the Judeans, whereas the plebeian denied them any merit whatever. The bitterness of the struggle between faith in Prudence and faith in Providence was thus not at all mitigated when the harassed Judeans finally achieved independence; on the contrary, it was increased.

The Sadducees, followers of the Hasmoneans and descendants of the pre-Maccabean patricians, insisted, as Josephus correctly informs us, that achievement is not a matter of fortune, fate or Divine Grace, but rather of sheer human prudence and diligence. Opposing them, the Pharisees taught faith in God, holding that all things are from Him. Yet, at the same time, they could not deny human free will, which lay at the basis of their doctrine of responsibility for sin. Thus they maintained both teachings without succeeding entirely in reconciling them.

The Testaments of the Twelve Patriarchs, a plebeian work generally dated about 100 B.C.E., attributes sin to the machinations of hostile spirits (T. Reuben 2.2; 3.3 ff.; T. Simeon 2.7; 3.1; T. Judah 16.1; T. Dan 1.6; T. Gad 1.9; 3.1). Yet it holds that man can escape the allurements of these satans through prayer and caution; and it insists that man can choose between the "two ways" which have been set before him (T. Asher 1.5). The contemporary writer of the Book of Jubilees, endeavoring to reconcile Pharisaism with Sadducism, adopts the plebeian teaching of "Providence plus Freedom" without reservation. Man's future is preordained, and is engraved on heavenly tablets. "And the judgment of all is ordained and written on the heavenly tablets in righteousness—even the judgment of all who depart from the path which is ordained for them to walk in; and if they walk not therein, judgment is written down for every creature and for every kind" (5.13). A century later the same idea was expressed by the Pharisaic author of the Psalms of Solomon. He maintains that

"Our works are subject to our own choice and power,
    To do right or wrong in the work of our hands;
    And in Thy righteousness Thou visitest the sons of
        men" (9.7).

Yet the oppressor can accomplish nothing without the will of God, it is He who gives him power over the righteous:

"For no man taketh spoil from a mighty man,
    Who then can take aught of all that Thou has made
        except Thou, Thyself, givest.
    For man and his portion lie before Thee in balance,
    He cannot add to, so as to enlarge, what has been
        prescribed by Thee" (5.4 ff.).

Ethicists rather than metaphysicians, the Pharisees found the combination of the two opposing formulae convenient and helpful. If a man tried to further his material interests by ordinary methods of prudence, the Pharisee smiled at his naïveté in thinking that he could achieve success without the aid of God. "There is no wisdom, nor counsel, nor

understanding, in opposition to the Lord." Human judgment itself was but an instrument in the hands of God.
But if anyone tried to draw the conclusion that man was not
responsible for his acts, the Pharisee insisted that he was.
In the words of R. Akiba: "All is foreseen, but freedom is
granted."[3]

Josephus tries to explain this paradox in a wordy passage,
which really adds nothing to R. Akiba's terse apothegm.
Josephus says: "While they [the Pharisees] hold that all
things are done by Fate, they do not deny the freedom of
men to act as they see fit. Their notion is that it has pleased
God to create such a temperament whereby what He wills is
done, yet so that the choice is given men to pursue vice or
virtue."[4]

In another passage, written at an earlier time, Josephus
had offered a simpler explanation of the difficulty inherent
in the Pharisaic view. He there says: "The Pharisees
ascribe everything to Fate and to God; yet they maintain
that it lies principally with man to do what is right or otherwise; although Fate shares in every action."[5] This interpretation, too, has its talmudic parallel in the dictum: "All
is in the hands of God, save the fear of God."[6]

But neither the ingenuity of the Talmud nor the prolixity
of Josephus could resolve the difficult puzzle which still
persists as a perplexing problem until this day. We shall
probably never know—at least not till man has evolved
far beyond his present capacities—whether the paradox is
inherent in the mind at a certain stage in its development,
or in the universe itself. Looking at himself from within,
the ancient plebeian of Jerusalem, like his successor in the
modern industrial world, saw his acts proceeding from
personal volition and choice. But then rising out of himself

and gazing back, with the objectivity which he used to
scrutinize his neighbor, he discovered how little in his life
was a matter of decision and how much of pure chance.
Heredity, environment, family connections, physical appearance, accidental injuries and escapes, seemed to play a
determining part in human life. The paradox to which the
Pharisee cleaved thus seemed as natural to him as the air
he breathed; he could not tell, any more than we can, how
much of it represented objective reality and how much sub-
jective delusion. Prophetic vision or mephitic nightmare,
it was inescapable. His comparative poverty prevented him
from admitting the principle that "if you wish it you can be
successful"; and on the other hand, his freedom from clan,
family, and tribal connections, left his ego exposed, incapable of hiding under the protecting covers of a social group.

Among the provincials outside of Jerusalem, the whole
problem never arose. There the individual still lay hidden
in the womb of his clan, not even desiring to be born. The
conception of human freedom was naturally alien to a people
who did not yet recognize their ego.

Among the poorer farmers of the Judean hills arose the
order of Essenes who, according to Josephus, were scattered
over the country in small communistic groups, tended
together their little farms, and asked from the earth nothing
more than enough to sustain life. These Essenes had been
won away from their rural complacency by Pharisaic teachers, but like many pupils they had gone beyond their masters,
carrying the received doctrine to its logical conclusion. They
found the doctrine of determinism which they had received
in their country communities, natural and logical. Being
unworried by the individualism of the metropolitan Phari-

sees, they could assert without any qualification that "fate determines all things and that nought befalls man but what is according to its determination."[7]

As the Pharisaic Order spread among the people of Judea and counted within itself all "but the wealthiest" nobles, it was inevitable that it should divide on the question of determinism, as on the question of angels. The forces which had made the pre-Maccabean patricians and the Sadducees believe in human effort, operated also among the Pharisees when they developed a patrician wing. The whole Pharisaic Order accepted as a matter of course the doctrine of faith and Divine Providence. But they disagreed regarding the manner in which Providence operates in human life. The plebeian Pharisees insisted that the future is not in man's hands to change, either through prudence or through piety. Man must be willing to entrust it entirely to God's mercies. The patrician faction of the Order held that while human prudence, such as the Sadducees depended on, might fail, piety was an effective means of changing one's fortunes, and that even foresight had its place in the ethical life. To strengthen their position, the plebeians developed into a fundamental principle of their faction the ancient teaching of the merit of the fathers (*zekut abot*), which seemed necessarily to imply the pre-determination of man's fate.[8] The patricians, rejecting the principle, pointed to the many biblical passages which explicitly denied that the virtue of ancestors can help descendants. The oldest recorded controversy on the subject, among the Pharisees, is that between the two leading scholars of the middle of the first century B.C.E., Shemayah and Abtalyon. Shemayah insists that the Red Sea was opened before the Israelites in reward for the faith which Abraham displayed; Abtalyon, the patrician, maintains that the miracle was caused by the merit of the Israelites themselves.[9]

It is altogether probable that this controversy regarding the ancient history of their people was associated with different policies of these scholars toward contemporary events;[10] and that it is recorded for that reason. Nevertheless the positions which they take are entirely in accord with the traditional theologies of their classes.

This is evident from a study of the teaching of the later patrician sages. A hundred years after Shemayah and Abtalyon, Akabiah ben Mahalalel, the foremost Pharisaic patrician of his day, when asked by his son for a recommendation to the other sages, answered, in what seems to have been a maxim, "Thy deeds will bring thee near, and thy deeds will remove thee."[11]

In the following generation, R. Eliezer ben Hyrcanus and R. Joshua ben Hananya discussed the application of the principle to national policy. R. Eliezer maintained that "if the people of Israel repent and do good deeds they will be redeemed, otherwise they will not be redeemed."[12] Joshua insisted that they would be redeemed in either event. But, as usual, it remained for the scholars of the next generation, R. Akiba and R. Ishmael, to formulate the opposing doctrines into philosophical ideas. R. Akiba said, "A father determines the fate of his son in five respects: in regard to beauty, strength, riches, wisdom, and longevity." This was denied by his colleagues, who would only agree that the child's fate depended on his father during minority. "Where have you seen," R. Akiba asked them, "a person who was blind when he was a minor and suddenly gained his sight at puberty?"[13] Yet this would naturally happen frequently if children suffered for their parents' sins during their minority, but were freed from the incubus when they reached their majority.

As the schools of Ishmael and Akiba developed, they continued their controversy regarding the doctrine of *Zekut Abot*, and the *midrashim* which emanate from the rival schools have perpetuated the difference in their explanations of a whole series of biblical verses.[14]

On the other hand, R. Akiba was compelled to defend the traditional plebeian paradox of Providence plus Freedom against the provincials who, accepting the principle of Providence, were inclined to limit the scope of human choice even in ethics. The leader of these was the Galilean sage, Simeon ben Azzai, Akiba's son-in-law. He taught that "freedom is granted only in the sense of the verse, 'So far as concerneth the scorners, He addeth to their scorn; but unto the righteous, He giveth grace' " (Prov. 3.34). The verse implies that if a man desires to study the Torah a little, he will be given opportunity to study it much; if he desires to forget even a little of it, he will be made to forget much more.[15] Putting the same thought more succinctly, he said: "The reward of observance is that it leads to more observance; the punishment of sin, that it leads to further sin."[16] With even greater emphasis, he denied the effectiveness of piety or prudence on man's life. "By thy name," he said, "shalt thou be called; in thy place shalt thou be seated; and thine own shall be given thee. No man can touch that which is prepared for his fellow; and no kingdom can take a hair's breadth of what is destined for its neighbor."[17]

Akiba admitted the power of habit, but could not see how that affected his doctrine of freedom in the moral sphere. "The attraction of sin," he said, "is at first as feeble as a spider's thread; but ultimately it becomes as powerful as a ship's cable."[18]

In agreement with this teaching, Simeon ben Zoma, Akiba's younger colleague, remarked, "Who is strong? He who rules his passions (*yezer*)."[19]

While the plebeians disagreed among themselves regarding the place of free will in their system, there was one subject regarding which they had no doubt—the futility of prudence, and hence of anxiety. Of their great sage, Hillel, it is recorded that on one occasion, returning to his native city, he saw a large crowd massed in the market place, uttering painful and pathetic cries. It was obvious that some accident had occurred, and Hillel's companions were anxious for the safety of their families. The saint alone retained his equanimity. "I know that there is nothing wrong in my home," he quietly remarked to his followers. And with that assurance he proceeded into the city to inquire after the cause of the commotion.[20]

The tale is probably legendary, but it illustrates what those who invented it, the disciples of Hillel, regarded as the ideal response to danger. Hillel would have been lacking in true faith, had he, noticing the disturbance, feared for his own wife and children. When he had left he had entrusted them to the care of God. To display any anxiety was to suspect the Guardian. Accidents might indeed occur, but only to those who lacked full trust.

Desiring to give expression to his faith, Hillel would never prepare for the Sabbath till Friday. "God is to be blessed each day," he would say, "for the day's goods." But Shammai, his patrician opponent, laying less stress on the teaching of trustfulness in God than on the ritual observance of the Sabbath, "spent all his life in preparing for the Sabbath. If he came across a goodly animal, he would say, this will be for the Sabbath. If next day he found a better one, he would say, this will be for the Sabbath, and he would consume the first on the weekday. So that all his life he was continually enjoying the Sabbath."[21] This was not merely a personal idiosyncrasy, but a principle of his faction. It is recorded in the name of Hananiah ben Hezekiah ben Gorion, a patrician leader of the last Temple days, that he considered the procedure a biblical commandment. "Remember the Sabbath day to keep it holy," means, "Remember it from the beginning of the week."[22]

Several generations after Hillel, the teaching of his school was summed up by R. Eleazar ben Azariah (ca. 100 C.E.) in these words: "Whoever has sufficient food for the day and says, 'What shall I eat tomorrow?' is lacking in faith."[23]

But this doctrine was by no means accepted by the patrician sages. During the Hadrianic persecutions, the famous R. Hanina ben Teradyon used to defy the Roman authorities by reading the Torah in public. A great patrician teacher, R. Joseph ben Kismah, meeting him, warned him against impending danger. "Do you not know," said he, "that this nation [the Romans] has been given dominion from Heaven? They have destroyed the Temple, and slain the pious, and slaughtered the nobles, and yet they are existing! Yet I hear that you publicly read the Law, in violation of their decrees!" "God will have mercy," piously answered R. Hanina. Whereupon R. Jose answered in tones altogether suitable to the Wisdom teachers, "I am talking common sense to you, and you say, 'God will have mercy.' I shall be surprised if they do not burn you together with the scroll."[24] And so indeed it happened.

Even in the school of R. Akiba, we find R. Meir, the sage who so frequently expresses patrician ideas, denying Providence in individual human life. "God," he says, "is like a judge who spreads a curtain before him and knows not what proceeds without."[25] The earnest protest of R. Meir's colleagues against this heresy shows that it was meant seriously, and that R. Meir, in the second century of the Common Era, actually held views akin to those defended by the patricians for six centuries before him.

While these meager records would not of themselves justify any generalizations regarding conflicts within the rabbinic circles, taken together with the other evidence which has been adduced for earlier differences between patricians and plebeians, they leave no doubt that the old conflict persisted even within the Pharisaic group. The issue appears only rarely in the rabbinic works, because the piety of the sages softened the native self-confidence and arrogance of the wealthy among them. And whatever expression regarding prudence was given in patrician doctrine, was lost by succeeding generations who chose to preserve out of the past only that which they regarded as helpful and constructive.

XIII. THE ORAL LAW

"The Pharisees," says Josephus, "have delivered to the people by tradition from their fathers a great many observances which are not written in the law of Moses; and for that reason the Sadducean group reject them, saying that only those observances are obligatory which are in the written word, but that those derived from the tradition of the forefathers need not be kept."[1]

This prolix statement simply confirms the talmudic record that the Sadducees rejected the Oral Law, which the Pharisees held equally authoritative with the Written Law. But it tells us nothing about the origin and nature of the traditions which constituted the Oral Law. Why should the Sadducees have rejected them? And whence did the Pharisees derive them? The answer to these questions must be sought in the development of Jewish legal institutions during the Second Commonwealth, and shows that the issue of the Oral Law, like those of resurrection, angelology, and Divine Providence, was fundamentally social and economic rather than academic and theological.

In pre-exilic Judah, questions of ritual law appear to have been settled by the priests, while civil and criminal litigation was brought before the elders of the city. This, at any rate, is the arrangement set up in the Torah which, however, makes the priests of the main sanctuary in Jerusalem a supreme court in all matters of dispute, whether they concern bodily injury, physical damage, or religious ceremonial.[2] During the exile, however, the priests and the elders were no longer free to devote themselves to this form of public service. The elders ceased to be the leisured patrician sheiks they had been in their homeland; the priests no longer could get their sustenance from the table of the Lord. The new prayer worship which was established in the exiled community provided for some of the priests and prophets, but most of them had to turn to gainful occupation for a livelihood. It was quite natural that some of them should seek to combine with their religious functions the genteel occupation of the scribe, the public secretary and notary.[2] The same conditions which in the Middle Ages brought about such close relations between clerk and cleric, operated also in Babylonia a millennium and a half earlier. The *sofer* knew not merely how to write, but also what to write. Just as the carpenter was also architect, mathematician, and teacher of his craft, so the writer was author, composer, penman, and instructor. In days when writing was used only for important affairs, to commemorate historical incidents, to transact business, to teach ethics, and to perpetuate law, the public amanuensis was necessarily a religious and legal functionary.[3]

More learned in the inherited literature of his people than his fellows, the professional scribe was called upon, in the absence of priest or prophet, to read the Law or the ancient prophetic writings. So that while on the one hand the minister tended to become the notary, on the other, the notary tended to become a minister. Readers who are conversant with the administration of religious affairs in new Jewish settlements like those of rural America and the British colonies, will find a parallel in the attempts which are frequently made to combine the usual duties of the traditional rabbi with those of other public officials, like the pedagogue and the *hazzan* (the reader of the prayers in the synagogue). In medieval Germany the duty of reading the service was almost universally associated with the religious guidance of the community; men like Rabbenu Gershom (ca. 1000 C.E.), R. Meir of Rothenburg (ca. 1250 C.E.), R. Israel Isserlein (ca. 1400 C.E.), and R. Jacob Molin (ca. 1500 C.E.) were almost as famous for their rendition of the prayers as for their scholarship and erudition. Somewhat similarly the ancient Judaites in Babylonia were forced by the sheer pressure of economy to merge the two callings of minister and scribe.

When the Judaites returned to Palestine the development was apparently accelerated by what appears to have been a purely fortuitous circumstance. Ezra, who arrived in Palestine in 457 B.C.E. protected by letters from the Great King, put himself at the head of the teachers of Law. The fact that he held a recognized government position, and was formally entitled *Sofer Data*[4] (Scribe or Secretary for Jewish Law) raised the status of all his colleagues who dealt with the Torah. This, combined with the influence of Egypt, where the scribe was held in high esteem, prevented the institution, which had proven so useful in Babylonia, from disappearing.

The trained scribes continued to serve as teachers and synagogue leaders, the more especially because of the effort being made to replace the ancient village altar of provincial Judea with the synagogue. Where no priest or prophet could be found, the scribe was needed in the reëstablished homeland, as he had been in Babylonia, as synagogue functionary.

Since the primary vocation of the scribe had been to make copies of the Law, he naturally became its most exact master. The father who wished his son to understand the mysteries of the divine revelation and who felt himself incompetent to teach him, necessarily apprenticed him to one of these erudite copyist-teachers. Centuries later it was still usual in Palestine to describe a liberal education as instruction in "writing."[5] The pen was the key to learning, if not to power.

Thus the calling of the scribe, which had provided an escape to the priesthood in Babylonia, became its rival in the new commonwealth. The priest could no longer claim, as his predecessor in the First Commonwealth had done, the sole mastery of the Law; there were laymen who excelled him. While he was concerned only with that part of the Torah which dealt with the Temple and the sacrifices, the scribe knew the whole of it. Free alike from the burdens of wealth and of grinding toil, he could devote himself without interruption to the study of the Torah. The priest's time was taken up with service at the Temple, attention to business, contact with friendly farmers, and dutiful attendance on his superiors, but the poor plebeian scholar-scribe did his daily stint, ate his meager fare, and proceeded to his book. Without any ability, therefore, to challenge the power or prestige of the priesthood, the scribe yet had the authority which always attaches sooner or later to exact knowledge.

But the rivalry of priest and scribe was not merely professional, like that of allopath and homoeopath, it was also social. The wealth which accrued to the priest made him the spokesman of the patrician and upper middle class groups; the scribe remained a humble plebeian. After all he was a mere craftsman, living in a community where craftsmen were regarded as little better than paupers. No father who could raise his child to inherit his farm would train him to the vocation of a copyist. This may seem strange to us, because in our days the urban secretary is so much more affluent than the average peasant. We may also wonder that the priest, who derived most of his income from free will offerings, never felt himself humiliated, while the scribe who was paid for his work was a member of a degraded calling. But the priest received his dues from God, and not from man; he was a member of a high and exclusive caste. In his tribe he combined the advantages of family relationship and of trade unionism, to both of which he added the enormous advantages of religious sanction. The scribe had no such protection. His calling was open to every mendicant; it was without the buttress of either kinship, occupational restriction, or ceremonial qualification. The social stigma which thus attached to the calling drove from it all who by chance did attain any measure of affluence, so that its plebeian character was perpetually reaffirmed.

The interpretations of the Law given respectively by priest and scribe were necessarily colored by their diametrically opposed social connections. The priest in his decisions followed the patrician precedents and sympathies of the Temple, the scribe the inherited ideas of his plebeian class. But the power of the patrician in the state and of the priest in the Temple made the decisions of the latter authoritative; those of the plebeian scribe were at best a tolerated deviation.

Before the Maccabean revolt, Pentecost was certainly observed at the Temple on Sunday, the plebeian opposition notwithstanding; the High Priest performed the ceremonies on the Day of Atonement as he, and not the rabble, pleased; the crowds, pouring water on the altar during Sukkot and marching with their willow-branches, were tolerated rather than encouraged. The plebeian artisan and trader presumably desisted from work on *his* Pentecost, but that was a private matter; the national festival was that of the Temple which was ruled by the patricians. The priest did not need to concern himself with any distinction between the Written Law and the Oral Interpretation; in official circles his explanations were accepted as the true meaning of the written record.

The plebeian scribe, on the other hand, convinced that his ideas were correct and corresponded to the true will of God, had no choice but to transmit them orally to his disciples and followers as the authoritative explanation of Scripture. Asked inevitably how he knew that he, and not the priests at the Temple, was right, he could only point to the ancestral tradition. But the warrant of his teacher was not enough, unless he added that it went back to older authorities, and ultimately to the inspired prophets themselves. In its final form the doctrine held that the plebeian traditions antedated even the prophets, having been revealed to Moses as a divine commentary on the written code.[6]

The Oral Law thus became a platform of articulate, plebeian protest against the official interpretation of the Written Law. The patricians rejected it because it consisted wholly of teachings which emanated from the plebeian interests and needs and were disavowed by the Temple priests— the spokesmen of the patricians. But they not only denied the validity of the plebeian deductions, they were at times tempted even to suppress them. Rejected and persecuted, the scribe was no longer content with the oral traditions which were a repository of plebeian ideas; he read into the Law new applications of the old principles even when the literal meaning of the text was against him. He became in a real sense the successor of the urban plebeian prophets of the First Commonwealth. Indeed, he went beyond them, for while the prophets of the First Commonwealth had continually inveighed against the aggression of the powerful, their criticisms had been based on nothing more objective than an intuitive sense of social justice. Powerful though this had been, it needed a system of juridical decisions to implement it. The rapacious landowners who, according to Isaiah (5.8), seized the property of the small farmer, acted, we may be certain, in absolute conformity with the existing civil law. They did not hire brigands or bandits to dislodge their victims; they resorted to the more "civilized" and orderly processes of loan, court action, and foreclosure. Yet these legal forms did not shield them from the prophet's wrath, for he was interested not in the means employed, but in the ends achieved.

The urban plebeian could not rest quiescent under this oppression by the patrician. The plebeian was passive and resigned, but he had to give scope to his mind and his imagination, which were always asking of him what he would do if he were in power. The Torah was, for him, an ideal and divine instrument of government; if injustice prevailed under its supposed rule, it was the student's duty to show how God's word was being misinterpreted, misunderstood, and misapplied.

This involved the adjustment of the Written Law and its further development. In dealing with the Torah, the plebeian, quite unconsciously, was faced with the dilemma of choosing between loyalty to the letter, which for all its humane interests was yet fixed and unbending, and the spirit, which was dynamic and living.

Biblical Law, for instance, gave parents greater power over their children than plebeian ideals of the fourth and third century B.C.E. considered just. Deuteronomy (21.16, 18) had taken away from the father the right of summary execution without due process of law, and had limited the possibility of disinheritance. Leviticus (25.44) had further abolished the sale of girls into slavery. Yet both sons and daughters remained the property of the father; the son's work belonged to his parent, and the daughter, no longer offered for sale as a slave, still carried, as a purchasable wife, some of the stigma of her earlier status.

Some time during the Second Commonwealth, plebeian law met this situation by limiting the whole biblical Law concerning sons and daughters to children under the age of puberty. There is no warrant whatever for this interpretation in Scripture. But it seemed common sense to the plebeian, and he presumed that it must be true.[7]

Two early Maccabean works, the Testaments of the Twelve Patriarchs and the Book of Jubilees,[8] imply this interpretation of the law. Both of them give Dinah's age at the time of her seduction by Shechem, the son of Hamor, as twelve years. The meaning of this is clear; the seduction of girls over twelve is not criminally punishable, for they have the right to give themselves to the man of their choice. To us of a changed world, such "emancipation" of womanhood may seem rather extreme, but the ancients, dealing with fetters of a Written Law, were not given any alternative. If they wished to free woman from subjection to man, they were compelled to place on her heavy responsibilities in tender years. Fortunately oriental maidens mature both mentally and physically much earlier than occidentals, and the twelve-year-old girl of the East was far more sophisticated and understanding than the child of a modern occidental metropolis.

Though we have no record of any controversy regarding this reform, we may assume that so radical a departure from ancient custom was not readily accepted by the patricians. In fact, the emphasis on the law in contemporary literature implies resistance to it. If this is true, the interpretation remained for centuries idealist aspiration, rather than accepted legislation. It was part of the plebeian platform to be made practical law when the opportunity should present itself.

Further examples of the democratic aspirations of the plebeians which became incorporated into the Oral Law will be given in the next chapter. But some of the regulations which the plebeians proposed emanated not from any social need, but were based, so far as we can see, on research into Scripture. For the plebeian was driven to develop his Oral Law in response not only to the pressing demands of daily life, but also to the inner longing for intellectual activity, which has already been described.

Animated as he was by love of the Torah and joy in it, is it any wonder that the student ransacked the text for new truths? He was fascinated by apparent inconsistencies, redundancies, and ambiguities, knowing that there must be some hidden significance in them, for "the law of the Lord is perfect" (Ps. 19.8).

The patrician, whose human energies found other outlets than study and whose mind had not become speculative and studious, had less interest in the solutions or the discoveries. The momentous problems of seeming contradictions and apparent superfluities left him unruffled and unworried. Fully accepting the divinity of the Torah, he doubtless felt what a great patrician teacher of later generations expressed in the words: "The Torah speaks in the language of men."[9]

A. The Tithes

Among the many apparent contradictions between various parts of the Torah, perhaps the most glaring is that which concerns the law of tithes. Deuteronomy specifically provides that the tenth part of all produce shall be taken to Jerusalem and consumed there. "Thou shalt surely tithe all the increase of thy seed, that which is brought forth in the field year by year. And thou shalt eat before the Lord thy God, in the place which He shall choose to cause His name to dwell there, the tithe of thy corn, of thy wine, of thine oil, and the firstlings of thy herd and of thy flock" (14.22–23). The Lawgiver, recognizing that the owner may not be able to consume the tithe in the course of a short visit to the capital, urges that it be shared with the Levite, the stranger, the fatherless and the widow (ibid. 29). But in Numbers (18.21) we are told, "And unto the children of Levi, behold, I have given all the tithe in Israel for an inheritance, in return for their service which they serve, even the service of the tent of meeting." The tithe is thus to be given to the Levites, to be used freely, save that they must surrender ten percent of their income, in turn, to the priests (Num. 18.26). To reconcile these opposing statements was a challenging task from which plebeian ingenuity could not withdraw.

The patricians, particularly those who lived at a distance from Jerusalem, apparently solved the problem in their own way, quite satisfactorily to themselves. They held that only one tithe had to be offered; it was brought into the treasure-house at Jerusalem, there to be divided among the deserving Levites, and to be eaten within the vicinity of the Temple. This procedure is assumed in Malachi, Nehemiah, and Chronicles.[10] Since most of the farmers could not possibly visit Jerusalem each year, they felt themselves free from the obligation of any payment whatever. Malachi protests against this laxity and demands the tithe, no less than the heave-offering:

> "Will a man rob God?
> Yet ye rob Me.
> But ye say: 'Wherein have we robbed Thee?'
> In tithes and heave offerings . . .
> Bring ye the whole tithe into the store-house,
> That there may be food in My house,
> And try Me now herewith,
> Saith the Lord of hosts,
> If I will not open to you the windows of heaven,
> And pour out a blessing,
> That there shall be more than sufficiency" (3.8 ff.).

Neither the prophet nor any other writer of the period makes any demand for the fulfillment of both the Deuteronomic law and that of Numbers. There is no instance where in addition to giving the Levitical tithe, the owners bring another for their own use in the capital. It was apparently held that the Levitical tithe, eaten in the "House of God," satisfied the requirements both of Numbers and Deuteronomy.

But the militant plebeians were not satisfied with this compromise. For them the tithes of Numbers and Deuteronomy were not identical, but supplementary. A first tithe had to be given to the Levite, and then a second tithe was to be brought by the farmer into Jerusalem for his own use. We may imagine how few adherents this interpretation, involving practically a tax of twenty percent on all agricultural products, found among the farmers and the patrician landowners. The Levites were naturally all in favor of it, for it allowed them to eat their tithe anywhere in Palestine, and not necessarily in the Temple. It was similarly approved, doubtless, by the traders of Jerusalem, who welcomed the additional custom the law of the second tithe brought to their doors. For Deuteronomy (14.25) provides specifically that the farmer, unable to transfer his produce to Jerusalem, may exchange it for money, and spend it in the capital.

The plebeian Chronicler, whose primary interest is the Levites, is silent about the second tithe, though he vigorously presses the Levitical claim to the first. Doubtless he despaired of persuading the bulk of Judea's rural population, who were unwilling to pay one tithe to the Levite, to set aside a second tithe for a visit to the sanctuary. But the author of Tobit,[11] writing about 200 B.C.E., that is, long before the organization of the Pharisaic party, is witness to the antiquity of the plebeian ruling, requiring both tithes.

B. WASHING THE HANDS*

An apparent contradiction in Scripture was the foundation for the complicated law of tithes; an equally difficult redundancy led to the establishment of the system of hand-washings which was destined in later ages to give the Jews so much security from disease, at the same time that it exposed them

* Cf. Supplement, pp. 718 ff.

to even graver peril from their enemies. The Jew, trained to wash his hands before prayer, before eating, and on numerous other occasions, appears to have been comparatively immune from certain pestilential ravages like the Black Death. His neighbors, unacquainted with the virtues of superior cleanliness, associated his comparative immunity with Satan and supposed that the Jew poisoned their wells, practiced black arts, or otherwise acted to destroy the general population. The consequence was that having escaped the plague, the Jew perished by the sword. The plebeian scholars who invented the ablutions could hardly have foreseen these momentous consequences which were destined to flow from their simple innovations. They were primarily interested in this instance not in reform, but in the application and interpretation of a biblical text, which seemed to them especially significant. Scribes, as so many of them were by vocation, the repetition of words in Scripture worried them more than other readers and students. So that while an inclination toward cleanliness may have affected their interpretation of Scripture, it remained hidden and subconscious. In the forefront of their thought, as of their argument, was the concern with the biblical redundancy.

In the Scriptures, Moses is commanded to set up in the tabernacle a "laver of brass"—"And thou shalt put it between the tent of meeting and the altar and thou shalt put water therein; and Aaron and his sons shall wash their hands and their feet thereat; when they go into the tent of meeting they shall wash with water, that they die not; or when they come near to the altar to minister, to cause an offering made by fire to smoke unto the Lord; so they shall wash their hands and their feet, that they die not" (Ex. 30.18 ff.).

The prolixity and periphrasis of this passage, contrasting so sharply with the directness and clarity of most Pentateuchal legislation, apparently disturbed the early scribes. They noticed that "washing" is commanded thrice, and came to the conclusion, altogether reasonable once their premises are granted, that three ablutions are intended by the Lawgiver. The priest entering the Temple courts must bathe, approaching the altar he must wash his hands and feet, and then leaving it he must wash his hands and feet again.

Both the Testaments of the Twelve Patriarchs and the older Testament of Levi cite this rule, which is also quoted in the Book of Jubilees.[12] While none of these sources is, so far as we can tell, pre-Maccabean, the tradition, found in all of them, must be considerably older than they. Had it been of patrician origin, it must have been accepted by the priests without question. The necessity of stressing it, during the reign of John Hyrkan, shows that the priests resisted it, and hence that it was of plebeian origin.

It may at first seem strange that the plebeians should be so absorbed in the question of *priestly* cleanliness, but a little consideration will clarify this difficulty. The priests, like other patricians, purified themselves only when they had to come to the Temple. Divided into twenty-four families, each of which served only two weeks in the year, most of them continued impure during the greater part of the time. Even in talmudic times, it was an everyday experience to see the priests who had been impure all day, returning at nightfall from the bath which they had taken to permit them to eat the heave-offering.[13] Four centuries earlier, the Chronicler had maintained that "the Levites were more upright of heart to purify themselves than the priests" (II Chron. 29.34). He was, indeed, not an unbiased witness, yet he would hardly have dared to publish what was contrary to common experience. It was but natural, for the plebeians, fearing the impurity of the priests, to ask them to bathe on entering the Temple. This would at least mitigate the effects of a possible contamination. The rule was thus established: "No man may enter the Temple courts, even if he be pure, without immersing himself in water."[14]

But this ritual immersion could not relieve the priest of the expressly commanded ablution of the hands and feet. That still had to be done, after the bath, as he approached the altar. After the sacrifice, he had to cleanse his hands and feet from the sacrificial blood, and it was natural to apply to this ablution the final injunction of Scripture regarding the matter.

Perhaps the plebeian scholar was the more moved to insist on the ablutions after the sacrifice, because for him, as a layman, the primitive identification of the holy with the forbidden was still real. The priest who ate the sacrificial meat and the heave-offering could not attach to them the complete, extra-mundane sanctity, which the rest of the population associated with them. The priest could see why he should wash his hands, and even bathe, before sacrificing; but he could see no reason for washing away the holy meat or blood when he had completed the service. He intended to remain in his state of acquired holiness all the day. But the Pharisaic scribe considered it a derogation of the holy things that the priest should use the hands which had come into contact with them for secular and profane work.[15]

When Queen Salome brought the Pharisees into power (ca. 76 B.C.E.), these ablutions became part of the regular

Temple ritual. But now that their prescriptions had been accepted, the Pharisees gradually forgot the controversy which had surrounded them. There was no longer any need to hand them down as part of the Oral Law. The young priests imitated the observances of their fathers, and regarded them as part of the Written Law. The lay teacher, left free to give his whole attention to other controversies, soon forgot those in which he had been victorious, and certainly preserved no record of the arguments by which he had vanquished his opponents. Hence it came about that the later Pharisees and sages no longer recalled the exegetical bases for the rule requiring the repeated ablutions of the priests. In fact, these later scholars could not even state the principle which was involved in the ancient controversy, and encountered difficulty in explaining the practices which they had themselves initiated. Had not the Testaments of the Patriarchs and the Book of Jubilees with their earlier record come to light in our own time, we should still be unable to explain the origin of many customs and rites which now appear unquestionably to be based on the early plebeian principle.

Among the customs which the sages were unable to explain because they had forgotten the early plebeian insistence on the double washing, before and after sacrifice, was the ritual of the Day of Atonement. The High Priest, it is recorded, would bathe five times on that day, and wash his hands and feet ten times. The Mishna and Talmud are at a loss to explain these numerous and apparently unnecessary ablutions. But the discovery of the original plebeian and Pharisaic prescription for Temple services explains it completely. The High Priest had five sacred functions to perform on the Day of Atonement: the daily morning sacrifice, the ceremony of atonement in the Holy of Holies, the sin-offering of rams for himself and for the people, the second entry into the Holy of Holies to remove the vessels in which the incense had been left, and finally the regular daily after-noon offering. Each of these had to be preceded, in accord-ance with the usual ritual, by a bath and washing the hands and feet, and was followed by washing the hands and feet. Our present knowledge of the original prescriptions of the plebeians, inherited by them from the Pharisees, make the reason for this complicated ceremonial clear. Without it, the ceremonial is altogether inexplicable.

Another Temple regulation of Pharisaic origin was that specifying the twelve species of evergreen trees to be used for fuel on the altar. This rule, too, ceased to be part of the transmitted Oral Law as soon as it became adopted practice. It is unmentioned in the Talmud; only the Book of Jubilees and the Testaments of the Twelve Patriarchs record it.[16]

Nothing better indicates the true nature of the Oral Law as a compendium of protest and ideal legislation than this disappearance of a norm concerning which there no longer was a controversy. Those parts of the Pharisaic platform which still were challenged either officially by Temple author-ities, or unofficially by the Sadducees in their private practice, continued to be taught in the schools as Oral Law. But where a rule had been accepted and was no longer sub-ject to debate, the Pharisees left its perpetuation to practice rather than to precept.

The sages were themselves aware that much had thus disappeared out of the Oral Law. In their usual way, they project these omissions into antiquity, and say that "many laws were forgotten during the period of mourning for Moses,"[17] and on other similar occasions.

Among the customs which emanated from the ritual of washing hands before and after sacrifice, was that prescribing similar washing before and after each meal. No longer aware of the significance attaching to the original Temple custom, the sages were naturally at a loss to explain its derivative in their own daily life. They supposed that "King Solomon established the washing of the hands."[18]

This, of course, means nothing more than that they could not recall the authority by whom the ablutions had been introduced. But authentic traditions, preserved in rabbinic literature, prove that the priests regarded the eating of heave-offering (*terumah*) as a divine service. When, for instance, R. Tarfon, who was a priest, was once absent from the academy, he explained to R. Gamaliel II that he had been engaged in "priestly worship." "You talk riddles," R. Gamaliel said to him. "Is there any ministry for the priests, now that the Temple is in ruins?" "I was eating the heave-offering," R. Tarfon replied, "and we consider that like the Temple service itself."[19] Holding the use of their priestly food in this high regard, the priests naturally transferred to it the ablutions which were required for the actual sacrifice at the altar.[20] They thus became accustomed to wash their hands both before the meals and after them. From the priests the custom passed to the more rigorously observant laymen, who liked to believe that any table can become like the table of the Lord.

Closely associated with the ablutions after the sacrifices and the sacred meals, was the peculiar rule requiring similar washing after contact with a holy scroll. Just as the Pharisees required the priest to wash away the holiness of the sacrificial meat and the heave-offering before using his hands for mundane affairs, so they washed their own hands after touching a sacred book, to prevent the contamination of the holy with the profane. The Sadducean priests who had been compelled to accept the principle of hand-washing after sacrifice, challenged the rule when applied to the scrolls. The Mishna records the following discussion on the matter: "The Sadducees said to the Pharisees, 'We complain of you, Pharisees, for you say that the Holy Writings defile the hands; while the works of Homer do not defile the hands.'" But R. Johanan ben Zakkai, acting as spokesman for the Pharisees, pointed out that according to biblical Law "the bones of an ass are pure, while the bones of Johanan the High Priest are impure." To this the Sadducees responded: "The impurity of bones is an index to our reverence for them; it is intended to prevent a man from using the bones of his father and mother for spoons." "If that is so," R. Johanan ben Zakkai said, "the Holy Writings are also declared impure because of our reverence for them; while the books of Homer, which we do not revere, are not impure."[21]

The Sadducees succeeded in establishing their practice at the Temple, so that it became a fixed rule that "the Scroll of the Sanctuary does not defile the hands."[22] Outside of the Temple, they had to yield to the Pharisaic interpretation of the Law. Perhaps the Pharisees were the more determined to carry their point in this matter because they wanted, through it, to show that the study of the Torah is a means of approaching God, and that it was as important as the sacrificial worship.

The origin of the Oral Law in the interpretations of the plebeian scholars was still recognized in the early talmudic sources, which term its provisions as "words of the scribes." But in their day, the scholar had ceased to be associated with the tasks of an amanuensis, and the word *sofer* was used for him only in an applied sense. Yet so powerful had been the influence of these early copyist-teachers on the development of the Law, that the original term continued to be used, both within and outside Pharisaic circles. The Gospel writers speak continuously of the "scribes and the Pharisees" as a single group, for the scribes were nothing more than the scholars and philosophers of the Pharisaic sect.

and considerable sums were carried over in the treasury
from one year to another. When the Temple was destroyed,
the Romans ... ... business,
declined to absorb the tax they never appropriated it.

XIV. REVERENCE FOR MAN*

The mordant hunger for equality with the patrician, which drove the Pharisee to the dogmas of resurrection, angelology, and determinism, also led to a *legal* controversy between him and the Sadducees. Characteristically, the quarrel involved not civil or property rights, but Temple usage. The Temple's foremost source of revenue was an annual tax of half a shekel (about half a dollar), which all Jews, whether in Palestine or in the diaspora, gladly paid. The Bible (Ex. 30.1 ff.) demands this contribution only during a census, but actually it was given year by year. The sum asked was so small, and the desire for association with the national worship so great, that Jews throughout the world enthusiastically sent their half-shekels to the treasury of the sanctuary. On the first of Adar, a month before the beginning of the Jewish ecclesiastical year, "announcements were made concerning the *shekalim*."[1] On the Sabbath preceding this announcement, the portion of the Torah dealing with the custom was read in all the synagogues.[2] The story told in the Book of Kings of Joash's reforms in the Temple supervision was appropriately chosen as prophetic reading. Such fascination did the institution have for the people that the special Sabbath of *shekalim* is still observed by reading these scriptural citations, and is further marked in many synagogues by the recitation of additional prayers composed for the occasion. In ancient times the funds collected were so large that they were more than sufficient to cover the cost of the national worship,

* Cf. Supplement, pp. 708-716, 720-724.

and considerable sums were carried over in the treasury
from one year to another.[3] When the Temple was destroyed,
the Romans with their incomparable sense of business,
declined to abolish the tax: they merely appropriated it.

The plebeians had always been especially interested in
this fund because it symbolized the equality of all Israel
before God. Whatever other gifts the rich might give to
the sanctuary, they were not a farthing above the poorest in
the "heave-offering of the chamber" (as the treasury of
the *shekalim* came to be called). "The rich shall not give
more, and the poor shall not give less than half a shekel,
when they give the offering of the Lord, to make atonement
for your souls," commands the Torah (Ex. 30.15). The
masses were consequently especially anxious that this fund
and no other should be used to pay for the daily sacrifices
in the Temple. The great plebeian document, which established this tax as an annual contribution (Neh. 10.38 ff.),
specifically provides that it shall be used "for the service of
the house of our God, for the showbread, and for the continual meal-offering, and for the continual burnt-offering, of
the sabbaths, of the new moons, for the appointed seasons,
and for the holy things, and for the sin-offerings to make
atonement for Israel, and for all the work of the house of our
God" (Neh. 10.33). Purchased from the funds of this treasury, the daily sacrifice became not only nominally but in
reality the public offering of the whole people to their God.
To the plebeian, who rarely could afford to give his own
sacrifice to the Temple, this was an important point, which
he continually stressed. The patricians however could not
appreciate his sensitiveness in the matter. Whether the
daily sacrifice was bought from the particular coins which
had been collected throughout the world or from some other

funds, seemed to them a trivial question, unworthy of discussion.

Following this line of reasoning, the patricians permitted the public sacrifice to be contributed voluntarily by rich individuals. The plebeians, and after them the Pharisees, denied that a sacrifice made by a private person could possibly be called a "public offering."

The controversy continued for centuries until the Pharisees, coming into power about 76 B.C.E., finally carried their principle into practice. The victory was so important in their eyes that they established an annual half-holiday to commemorate it.[4]

In another instance, however, the devotion of the Pharisees to the principle of human equality led them to a juridically indefensible position. The question involved was the liability of an owner for damages committed by his slave without his knowledge. The Sadducees held the master responsible for his slave as he would be for his ox; the Pharisees denied this and left the injured person without redress.[5]

The Pharisaic rule would have worked obvious injustice in any slave-holding community. If the master is freed from responsibility for damage done by his slave, all motive for exercising discipline over him with regard to such depredations disappears. The slave, who has no personal responsibility, is left free to ruin anyone against whom he may bear a grudge. The patricians — who were owners of slaves — could not possibly accept this Pharisaic doctrine, which indeed could only have arisen among plebeians, for whom the whole question was theoretical.

But just because the Pharisees were without interest in the practical application of this rule, it afforded them an excellent opportunity for the expression of their abstract principle. Ordinarily, they would have hesitated to sacrifice definite social need to mere metaphysical notions. But since they owned no slaves, they were free from the usual judicial inhibitions, and could readily indulge their tendency to make the slave's personality equal with that of the free man.

The Sadducees are reported to have said to the Pharisees in the discussion of this question: "If I am responsible for damage done by my ox and my ass, although I have no obligation with regard to any ceremonial observances by them, how much more must I be responsible for the damage done by my men-servants or maid-servants, since I am obliged to arrange for their observance of the ceremonial law." To this the Pharisees replied: "No, you may rightly make a master responsible for damage done by his ox or his ass, since these animals have no mind. But how can you make the master responsible for damage done by the man-servant or maid-servant, who have minds of their own?"[6]

The argument shows plainly that the Pharisees based their rule on the recognition of the moral responsibility of sentient beings. The slave has a mind of his own; to make the master answerable for him is a derogation of the principle of human responsibility. Their respect for the dignity of man as *homo sapiens* made it impossible for them to countenance a law which made one man answerable for another's deeds. To compare the slave to an ox or an ass was in itself a judicial insult: the one was human, the other a chattel.

The Sadducees were unsympathetic to the principle of human equality involved in the metaphysics of the Pharisees, and at the same time were keenly aware of the social dangers involved for their class in the adoption of the proposed law.

Men of wealth, with large tracts of land exposed to depreda-
tion, they were indignant at a ruling which left them without redress against an unruly slave of their neighbor.

The significance of the controversy becomes even clearer
in the light of a conflict which later arose within Pharisaism
itself. When, during Herod's reign, Pharisaism became
practically coterminous with the Jewish people, its own
wealthier, rural faction found fault with another extremely
individualistic decision rendered by the dominant plebeian
group within the party. "If a man sends another to commit
murder, the agent is guilty," held the plebeian Pharisees,
"but the principal is innocent." Shammai, who was the
spokesman of the near-patricians in the party, said, "The
principal is guilty."[7] In this ruling, too, the plebeian view
is opposed to all principles of common-sense jurisprudence.
To free the accessory before the fact from all responsibility for misdeeds which arise from his evil influence is to
invite crime. But the plebeians were so permeated with
their belief in the individual and the moral responsibility
of man, that they were blinded to the inevitable social
consequences of their decisions.

Opposed to the Pharisaic doctrine of the individual, the
patricians upheld the principle of extended personality. Like
the Jews of much more primitive days, who had identified
the master with the servant, these rural teachers considered
the slave or the agent "the hand" of his principal. This led
the rural wing of the Pharisees, the Shammaites, to forbid
the employment of a pagan to work for a Jew on the Sabbath. If the Gentile labored as the agent of the Jew, it was
as though the Jew himself were violating the holy day's
rest. They carried this principle to such extremes that they
forbade selling goods to a Gentile, or loading his animals,

or lifting a burden on him, unless it was reasonably certain that he could arrive at his destination before the Sabbath. They would not send skins to be tanned, or clothes to be washed, by Gentiles, unless it was clear that the work would be completed by Friday.[8]

In the Temple, where the patrician priests were in full control, the principle of individual responsibility was unrecognized. If through error Temple property was used for profane purposes, not only the agent but also the principal was held responsible.[9] The later sages, codifying the Law as they found it crystallized in precedent, note this as an exception, which without knowledge of the social basis of the conflict involved, they are unable satisfactorily to explain.

Plebeian respect for man extended also to the criminal. The consequent leniency of the Pharisaic teachers in punishment became proverbial, and contrasted sharply with Sadducean severity.[10] In this humanitarianism, however, the Pharisees also went to extremes. The limitations which the plebeian faction among them put on evidence and procedure gradually tended to stultify the whole system of criminal law. One of their leaders, Johanan ben Zakkai, as a young judge rejected witnesses who disagreed in their description of the stems of the figs growing on the tree under which the crime was committed.[11] When the Romans deprived the Jews of criminal jurisdiction, the sages became yet more extreme in their now purely theoretical decisions. No longer apprehensive of any social evil growing out of their judgments, they felt free to carry all their plebeian principles to their logical and impractical conclusions. R. Tarfon and R. Akiba, two of their great teachers in the second century, said: "Had we been members of the Sanhedrin when it had the power of capital punishment, no man would ever have been executed by it."[12] A plebeian sage of the following generation, R. Jose, would not condemn a criminal to any punishment unless he had been specifically warned by the witnesses that his act was forbidden.[13] R. Simeon ben Gamaliel II who was fully plebeian in spirit, but yet took a judge's view of the law, remarked of R. Tarfon and R. Akiba's boast, "They would indeed have multiplied murders in Israel."[14] But the willingness of the sages to interfere with the judgment of man was a necessary corollary of their firm reliance on the judgment of God. R. Akiba was quite willing that a criminal should escape the penalties imposed by the human courts, for he believed firmly that the guilty would meet their fate at the hands of God. "If he escapes your hand, he shall not escape Mine," are the words which the sage's disciples attributed to God.[15] It was the duty of the court to punish those who were certainly guilty, but every shadow of doubt should be resolved in favor of the accused.

Leniency toward the criminal was further consonant with the doctrine of non-resistance to evil, which at this time became fundamental to plebeian thought. Among the earlier Pharisees, the teaching of submission and resignedness took the form of international pacifism. But as Pharisaism became more philosophical and reflective, the principle of non-resistance came to be applied also in private life. It could not be otherwise among a group who held firmly to the belief that all things are from God. The greater the faith in Providence, the more complete the submissiveness of the believer to all that came upon him.

When Hillel saw a dead body floating in the river he remarked: "Because thou didst drown others wast thou drowned; but in the end, they who drowned thee will yet meet their fate."[16] Following this principle, R. Joshua ben Korha sharply rebuked Eleazar, the son of his colleague, R. Simeon ben Yohai, when he accepted service in the Roman gendarmery. "Vinegar, child of wine, how long wilt thou hand over the people of God to the executioner?" he asked. "I am removing the thistles from the vineyards," the son of R. Simeon replied. "Let the Owner of the vineyard remove His own thistles," was the impractical reply of the saint, who could not brook violence even in punishment of the wicked.[17] When evil occurred, it was customary in these circles to say, "This also is for the best."[18] If a cow broke its leg, the peasant was taught to think, "For my good was the beast injured." R. Akiba, in whom the teachings of the class found most eloquent expression, said: "The verse, 'Thou shalt love the Lord thy God with all thy heart, and with all thy soul and with all thy might' means, thou must be grateful to Him whatever be the measure He mete out unto thee." "A person must bless God for evil no less than for good."[19]

There was nothing new in these maxims except the formulation. The prologue to Job had implied them all. No matter how great his suffering, Job would not open his mouth to complain, "Nor ascribed aught unseemly to God" (1.22). The ideal manner of meeting evil was to say as he did, "The Lord gave, the Lord hath taken away; blessed be the name of the Lord" (1.21).

Seen against this background, the teachings of early Christianity become more significant and coherent. "Thy will be done," is the premise, from which it follows, by plebeian logic, that "if any man sue thee at the law and take away thy coat, let him have thy cloak also. And whoever shall compel thee to go a mile with him, go with him twain."[20]

The principle of non-violence was, however, more than a logical corollary to natural plebeian doctrines. It was itself admirably fitted to the situation of the trader and the artisan. "The customer is always right," is a maxim of modern shop-keepers, which was in a way foreshadowed in the bazaars of ancient Jerusalem. The merchant soon learns that when abstract or even legal justice is on his side, it may often be to his interest to forgo the advantage. The more complete his patience, the more ready is he to speak softly; and the less prone he is to anger, the greater will be his ultimate reward. Having learned the lesson of patience in his shop, the plebeian carried the habit with him into home, syn-agogue, temple and court.

But why did not these city plebeians, without resorting to rebellion, enact in their Oral Law some protest against the exploitation of their class? Granted that their principles forbade them to right wrong by direct action, why did they exhaust their theoretical rebelliousness in theological, rather than economic, doctrines? Would not the energy which they used to foist on Judaism the doctrines of angels and resurrection have been better used to demand, at least in words, the reallocation of land according to Pentateuchal principles of equality?

The difficulty lay in the restraints which their loyalty to the Temple fastened on the urban plebeians. The traders and workers might resent the arrogance and oppression of the rich priests, but they could take no action against it, by word or deed. The outstanding position of the Temple, its complete monopoly of the sacrificial system, and the recurrent pilgrimages to it, had made Jerusalem a great city. The plebeians lived on the valuable morsels which fell to them from this great hierarchical table. They wept and sobbed in persecution, and dreamed of future freedom, but they durst not breathe a word of distrust or lift a finger of rebellion lest they themselves perish in the ruin of their exploiters.

Perhaps they did not become consciously aware of the peril, but made their decisions by the inner intuitions which so frequently dominate class movements. The plebeian in Jerusalem probably could not say explicitly why he did not demand of the priests immediate conformity with the biblical prescriptions forbidding them to own land. But he knew well that the major priests would sooner renounce the service at the Temple than their landed estates; and he also knew that these patricians supplied him with much of his custom and trade. A thoroughgoing change of the Temple priesthood would weaken the hold of the institution itself on the people, and would inevitably diminish the prestige of the metropolis. The more the plebeian pondered over the situation, the more completely convinced he must have become that he had much to lose in breaking his chains.

But so long as the priests were not driven from the soil, the utopian division of land on Pentateuchal principles was impossible. How could each Israelite be given his ancestral portion of the soil, when a goodly part of it was held by the priests, who theoretically had no right to it at all?

Yet there are indications that some groups did strive for the enforcement of the land laws. The claim of the lowland farmers to descent from the tribe of Benjamin who had originally possessed that country,[21] implies a recognition of tribal rights even in the Second Commonwealth. About the year 100 B.C.E., an apocryphal code was composed having at its core the reëstablishment of the Jubilee year. Presumably the author would not have thought of such a reform had not the proposal been seriously made by some interested groups. The Essenes and the sect of Damascus declined to take part in the Temple sacrifice so long as it was controlled by defiled and irreligious priests. But these movements were confined to eccentrics. The main body of plebeians, led by the scribes and Pharisees of the city, accepted the situation without murmur, and awaited patiently the coming of the Redeemer.

XV. THE PROPHETIC IDEAL OF
EQUALITY

The dogma of human equality to which the Pharisees adhered had come to them, like many of their other teachings and customs, from earlier plebeian sages of Jerusalem. But while the controversy about equality was confined in Pharisaism to a few esoteric issues, it had in earlier ages pervaded the whole social and religious life. The urban prophets of the First Commonwealth and their disciples in the Exile, were not bound by the economic shackles which prevented the Pharisees from giving full expression to their hatred of oligarchy and aristocracy. At first timidly, but with increasing boldness, these great teachers put forth the concept of a sacred Commonwealth of economically, politically, and socially equal citizens.

The social teaching of the prophets is not, however, as is popularly supposed, absolutely uniform. Only false prophets, who have personal motives to serve, say the sages, speak in full unison.[1] The true prophets, while in accord on general principles, differed in their detailed interpretation of them. People who read the Scriptures cursorily may be persuaded that they contain nothing but indictments of wealth and power. Actually they contain whole books whose authors were apparently unaware of any social struggle. This is true primarily of works emanating from rural districts where the primitive principle of status was unchallenged by either rich or poor. Having inherited their place in society from forgotten forbears, they took it for granted, and even in their hearts ventured not to utter complaints. They accepted their yoke as part of the natural order of the universe — like sickness and death.

Only in the large metropolitan center of Jerusalem and under its influence, among the plebeian shepherds of the Judean desert land, did the concept of individual freedom develop. In the city, a man's status was fixed not by previous generations, but in part at least, by his own efforts and good fortune. Working with his own hands and selling with his own cunning, he attained a sense of independence, which the peasant, bound to the soil like his ox, could never achieve. To be subject to a master seemed to the city man the lowest possible degradation. He might have little or much, but what he had was his own.[2]

Those shepherds who brought their beasts for sale in the market of Jerusalem were easily infected with this feeling of freedom and individuality. Their primitive clan and family organization was indeed essential so long as the country lacked a stable government able to protect property and repress violence. The constant peril from enemy and marauder to which an individual was exposed, could be warded off only by uncompromising clan solidarity. But under the ordered government of the later kingdom, when life and property were secure, and the goatherd on the hills of Judea was as safe as the tradesman in Jerusalem, clan and tribal organization insensibly melted away, and the individual came into his own.

As soon as the individual became conscious of himself, he also became conscious of discrimination against himself. The sheep-tender knew well where the real power of the state lay — in the hands of the landed patricians. The centuries of struggle between him and them had ended in

their complete victory: Abel, "the keeper of sheep," had
been slain by Cain, "the tiller of the ground." A goodly
part of the early Scripture is a reflection of the bitterness
engendered by this sense of defeat and frustration.

The first of the great literary prophets, Amos and Hosea,
illustrate this contrast between the farmer's ignorance of
any social conflict and the plebeian shepherd's keen awareness of it. From the very beginning of his message, Amos,
the shepherd-prophet, ruthlessly arraigns the men who "sell
the righteous for silver, and the needy for a pair of shoes."
They pant after the dust of the earth on the head of the
poor and turn aside the way of the humble (2.6–7). They
"lay themselves down beside every altar upon clothes taken
in pledge" (ibid. 8). "For they know not to do right, saith
the Lord, who store up violence and robbery in their
palaces" (3.10).

The prophet noticed all this precisely because he was a
child, not of the soil, but of the sheepfolds. He hailed from
Tekoa, that stony land, which to this day is unable to
provide its inhabitants with their daily needs.[3] In his youth
he had earned his livelihood by dressing "sycamore trees"
(7.14); and he had grown up to look after sheep and oxen.
He had, indeed, become a *noked*, an owner of flocks, and in
his own circles must have been considered well-to-do. He
could afford to travel about the country, and to despise the
ordinary material rewards of ancient prophecy (7.12). But
his plebeian sympathies were aroused, and with them his
desert indignation at the luxuries and profligacies of the
landowners.

The behavior of the aristocratic women, no less than
that of their husbands, stung the prophet's puritan soul.

Addressing the crowds of pilgrims who had assembled from their country places to worship at Beth-el, he denounced them with indignation, not unmixed, perhaps, with vindictiveness.

> "Hear ye this word, ye kine of Bashan,
>   That are in the mountain of Samaria,
>   That oppress the poor, that crush the needy,
>   That say unto their lords: 'Bring, that we may
>   feast!' "(4.1).
> "For I know how manifold are your transgressions,
>   And how mighty are your sins;
>   Ye that afflict the just, that take a ransom,
>   And that turn aside the needy in the gate" (5.12).

No such bitter invective against social injustice comes to us from Hosea, the peasant prophet of the fertile North. He reserves his anger and indignation for the ritual sin of Baal-worship, for the Ephraimite vice of drunkenness, and for duplicity, the cardinal social sin in the eyes of the provincial. We can trace, however, a development in the mind of this prophet as he grows out of his early village simplicity into his later metropolitan sophistication. The small book which he bequeathed to us consists of two separate parts so different from each other both in style and content that some writers have attributed them to different authors.[4] The first three chapters are largely autobiographical, telling the story of the prophet's tragic marriage, and containing his first prophecies; the last eleven chapters deal with his maturity when, coming into Samaria, he saw Israel as a nation against the background of international life.

Early in life this prophet, an undistinguished member of the YHWH following in the North, had married the daughter of Diblaim, an adherent of the Baal cult. What drew Hosea out of the obscurity of his life into the glare of contemporary public life (and subsequent world renown) was the behavior of his wife after their first child was born.[5] Finding herself no longer fertile then, Gomer followed the usual practice of her circle, resorting to the Baal temple for a cure, and gave herself to fellow-worshipers in the obscure sex ritual which her husband had always despised; for he, a follower of YHWH, had a deep-seated respect for monogamy and chastity. He named the girl who was born thereafter, *Lo-ruhamah*, "the unloved," and a later child *Lo-ammi*, "not my people."

His sufferings during his wife's waywardness brought Hosea into a keener understanding of Israel's sin in deserting God. The double injury he had suffered, as a man of piety and as a husband, made him hate the Baal and its worship with unmeasured vindictiveness. There was nothing left for him in life save to give himself altogether to the extermination of the miserable, humiliating superstition. But added to these emotional responses was his intellectual development under the stress of pain. If he, a man, was so wounded by Gomer's desertion, how poignant and immeasurable was God's disappointment in His people Israel, when they went astray? Suddenly he felt for God not merely reverence, awe, and fear—as he had been accustomed since childhood—but a deep love and sympathy, as for a great fellow-sufferer. He knew from the wretched despair of his own human heart what the Almighty was suffering, and the eloquence which this realization calls forth in the peasant rings in our ears across the ages with undiminished power. Passionate anger and, even more, passionate love; jealous hatred which wishes to destroy, and enduring

affection which seeks only to recall, play across his verses
in alternations of darkness and light.

"And I will not have compassion upon her children;
For they are the children of harlotry.
For their mother hath played the harlot,
She that conceived them hath done shamefully;
For she said: 'I will go after my lovers,
That give me my bread and my water,
My wool and my flax, mine oil and my drink.'
Therefore, behold, I will hedge up thy way with thorns,
And I will make a wall against her,
That she shall not find her paths.
And she shall run after her lovers, but she shall not
    overtake them,
And she shall seek them, but she shall not find them;
Then shall she say: 'I will go and return to my first
    husband;
For then was it better with me than now' "(2.6–9).

But forgetting a moment later this promise of hopeful
reunion, he reverts to his original anger, and attibutes to
God a fierce denunciation of Israel.

"And now will I uncover her shame in the sight of
    her lovers,
And none shall deliver her out of My hand.
I will also cause all her mirth to cease,
Her feasts, her new moons, and her sabbaths,
And all her appointed seasons.
And I will lay waste her vines and her fig-trees,
Whereof she hath said: 'These are my hire
That my lovers have given me' " (ibid. 12–14).

After a period of inner struggle, Hosea's love for his wife overcame his anger against her, and condoning her sin, he took her back into his home. "And I said unto her: 'Thou shalt sit solitary for me many days; thou shalt not play the harlot, and thou shalt not be any man's wife; nor will I be thine'" (3.3). The act of forgiveness seemed to Hosea a symbol of God's love for Israel. If he could not find it in his mortal heart to abandon the woman who had betrayed him, would the All-Merciful reject Israel forever because of their sins?

Throughout the prophecies of this period, we find no suggestion of any wrong in Israel other than that of idolatry. Not a word is said of oppressive wealth or suffering poverty. The prophet is not even aware of anything wicked in Israel's national policy, in its administration of justice, in the rapid succession of new kings. Like Jeremiah in the early days at Anathoth, Hosea so far is interested only in bringing the people back to the worship of YHWH.

Sooner or later, however, the great village prophets make their way into the metropolis. They may be driven by persecution of their townsmen, they may be attracted by the hope of sympathy from the more sophisticated and understanding city, or they may seek wider circles of influence. At all events, like Micah a few decades later and Jeremiah after a century, Hosea left his home and went to the center of the people's life. Presumably this was Samaria, though nothing is told us of that. But here another disillusionment was prepared for the unfortunate prophet. Like Jeremiah in Jerusalem, Hosea in Samaria found not less but more wickedness than in the village of his birth. His fellow-peasants might be superstitious idol-worshipers, but they were honest, straightforward, and direct. In the metropolis, even those who professed loyalty to YHWH, were corrupt at heart.

> "Hear the word of the Lord, ye children of Israel!
> For the Lord hath a controversy with the inhabitants
> of the land,
> Because there is no truth, nor mercy,
> Nor knowledge of God in the land.
> Swearing and lying, and killing, and stealing, and
> committing adultery!
> They break all bounds, and blood toucheth blood"
> (4.1–2).
> "They speak words,
> They swear falsely, they make covenants;
> Thus judgment springeth up as hemlock
> In the furrows of the field" (10.4).
> "Ye have plowed wickedness, ye have reaped iniquity,
> Ye have eaten the fruit of lies" (10.13).

He is stirred to fiercest anger by the complacency and self-righteousness of the men of Samaria:

> "And Ephraim said: 'Surely I am become rich,
> I have found me wealth;
> In all my labours they shall find in me
> No iniquity that were sin' " (12.9).

In the capital he addresses no longer the peasantry but the "house of the king" (5.1), and realizes the inherent godlessness of Israel's diplomacy. His peasant mind is particularly sensitive to the dishonesty of making contradictory treaties with various empires.

"And Ephraim is become like a silly dove, without
  understanding;
They call unto Egypt, they go to Assyria" (7.11).
"Ephraim striveth after wind, and followeth after the
  east wind;
All the day he multiplieth lies and desolation;
And they make a covenant with Assyria,
And oil is carried into Egypt" (12.2).

He realizes that the nation is corrupt at the top as well
as at the bottom, and he sees no hope for it.

"They make the king glad with their wickedness,
And the princes with their lies . . .
On the day of our king
The princes made him sick with the heat of wine . . .
They are all hot as an oven,
And devour their judges;
All their kings are fallen,
There is none among them that calleth unto Me"
  (7.3 ff.).

Throughout these bitter words, we find nothing at all
resembling Amos's call for justice and human equality.[6] It is
clear that even in the city, Hosea saw in wrong-doing
merely a formalistic deviation from the standards to which
he was accustomed; he had not yet come to see the evil of
exploitation of man by man. He speaks of the trader with
the provincial's undisguised contempt (12.8), and, like
another rural prophet of a later age, finds it particularly
despicable that men should worship idols, "the work of
craftsmen" (13.2; 8.6).[7] The implications of the phrase may
not be obvious to us, but can we imagine a smith or a
carpenter using it? Would he not be more likely to say, as

the psalmist does, "the work of men's hands?" (Ps. 115.4; 135.15; cf. also II Kings 19.18; 22.17; Isa. 37.19; contrast Jer. 10.3; Isa. 40.19, 20; 41.7; 44.12). But Hosea makes no effort to hide his contempt for the worker, any more than did Ben Sira, five centuries later.[8] And feeling no respect for the artisan, the prophet cannot envisage his life as a perpetual struggle against oppression, as Amos did.

We must not associate this difference between Amos and Hosea with the personal idiosyncracies or status of the prophets. None of the inspired teachers whose works have been preserved spoke from private bias. If Hosea was a landowner, Amos, too, as we have seen, was probably equally affluent. But the one had lived in an environment where there was no social struggle, the other where it was the most glaring fact.

How readily the literary prophets raised themselves out of their class in the face of the social conflict becomes clear when we turn to Isaiah, a leading aristocrat, who yet became the foremost tribune of the people. Though he was apparently far wealthier than Hosea, he entered whole-heartedly into the struggle between rich and poor, relentlessly condemning avarice, greed, and oppression. For aristocrat as he was, he lived in Jerusalem, and could see the social conflict in all its bitter ferocity.

Isaiah beholds the Lord, enthroned in the Temple, entering into judgment against the elders and princes of His people, and defending the oppressed poor:

"It is ye who have eaten up the vineyard;
The spoil of the poor is in your houses.
What mean ye that ye crush My people,
And grind the face of the poor?" (Isa. 3.14 ff.).

"Woe unto them that join house to house,
That lay field to field,
Till there be no room, and ye be made to dwell
Alone in the midst of the land!" (5.8).

He knows that all these injustices are performed with the show of legality; but for that reason he protests all the more vigorously against the iniquitous legislation:

"Woe unto them that decree unrighteous decrees,
And to the writers that write iniquity;
To turn aside the needy from judgment,
And to take away the right of the poor of My people.
That widows may be their spoil,
And that they may make the fatherless their prey!"
(10.1 ff.).

He hopes for the rise of a new king who will usher in a new order, not only of peace with the world, but of equality within the commonwealth:

"And there shall come forth a shoot out of the stock
of Jesse,
And a twig shall grow forth out of his roots. . . .
With righteousness shall he judge the poor,
And decide with equity for the humble of the land;
And he shall smite the land with the rod of his mouth
And with the breath of his lips shall he slay the
wicked" (11.1 ff.).[9]

The case of Jeremiah demonstrates even more clearly how necessary was the city environment to make the prophet realize the meaning of the social struggle and oppression. Jeremiah had spent his youth in his native Anathoth, and only after he had become a prophet did he remove to Jerusalem. In his present book the first four chapters belong to his early rural period; but beginning with the fifth chapter — as is indicated in the first verse, "Run to and fro in the streets of Jerusalem" — we have addresses delivered in the capital.[10] Comparing the two parts, we are amazed to find that the difference between them is almost as great as that between Hosea and Amos.

No sooner does the prophet begin to preach in the capital than he realizes that the land is weighted down by heavier sins than idolatry itself. He had come to Jerusalem for encouragement in his effort to purge the land of idols; he found that the "great ones" themselves were in need of moral rehabilitation.

> "For among My people are found wicked men;
>   They pry, as fowlers lie in wait;
>   They set a trap, they catch men.
>   As a cage is full of birds,
>   So are their houses full of deceit;
>   Therefore are they become great, and waxen rich;
>   They are waxen fat, they are become sleek;
>   Yea, they overpass in deeds of wickedness;
>   They plead not the cause, the cause of the fatherless,
>   That they might make it to prosper;
>   And the right of the needy do they not judge" (5.26 ff.).

> "Therefore will I give their wives unto others,
>   And their fields to them that shall possess them;
>   For from the least even unto the greatest
>   Everyone is greedy for gain,
>   From the prophet even unto the priest
>   Everyone dealeth falsely" (8.10 ff.).

"Thus saith the Lord;
Let not the wise man glory in his wisdom,
Neither let the mighty man glory in his might,
Let not the rich man glory in his riches;
But let him that glorieth, glory in this,
That he understandeth, and knoweth Me,
That I am the Lord who exercise mercy,
Justice, and righteousness, in the earth;
For in these things I delight,
Saith the Lord" (9.22 ff.).

When the king uses forced labor, the prophet cries out:
"Woe unto him that buildeth his house by un-
    righteousness,
And his chambers by injustice;
That useth his neighbour's service without wages,
And giveth him not his hire;
That saith: 'I will build me a wide house
And spacious chambers,'
And cutteth him out windows,
And it is ceiled with cedar, and painted with
    vermilion" (22.13).

The word, re'a, which Jeremiah uses for the humble
proletarian, implies much more than can be conveyed by
the English "neighbor," as it has been translated. It means
friend, comrade, colleague. It is the word used in the verse,
"Thou shalt love thy neighbour as thyself" (Lev. 19.18).
The prophet who, when he arrived in Jerusalem, still
distinguished the "great" from the lowly, now calls the
meanest laborer the "comrade" of the King.

During the siege of Jerusalem, the nobility, in their fear,
had undertaken to carry out the law which required them

to set their slaves free after six years of service. But when for some reason Nebuchadnezzar temporarily moved away from the city, the nobles immediately seized the freedmen and forced them back into slavery. Jeremiah, indignant at the double wickedness of oppression and fraud, thunders: "But ye turned and profaned My name, and caused every man his servant, and every man his handmaid, whom ye had let go free at their pleasure, to return; and ye brought them into subjection, to be unto you for servants and handmaids. Therefore, thus saith the Lord: Ye have not hearkened unto Me, to proclaim liberty, every man to his brother, and every man to his neighbour; behold, I proclaim for you a liberty, saith the Lord, unto the sword, unto the pestilence, and unto the famine" (34.16).

Here even the slave is called "brother" and "neighbor" to his master. Jeremiah has altogether outgrown the concept of fixed status for pigeon-holed human beings; all men are the equal children of God. This thought could not have come to him, inspired prophet though he was, in the peaceful fields of Anathoth. He had to see the raging fires of class warfare in Jerusalem before he realized the nature and the extent of the evils practiced on the weak by the strong.

The development of Jeremiah's mind through his stay at the capital casts light on another prophet, who lived almost a century before him, Micah of Mareshah. Like Jeremiah, Micah was a native of a small village who came to Jerusalem as a mature man. Only the first three out of the seven chapters of his book can with certainty be ascribed to him. But, as in Jeremiah, the first prophecy (contained in chapter 1) deals exclusively with the sin of idolatry, and the later ones (in chapters 2 and 3) are devoted with the same completeness to social justice. The example of

Jeremiah makes it altogether probable that the reason for this difference is that the first prophecy was delivered before, and the following two after, Micah came to Jerusalem.

The difference between rural blindness and urban sensitiveness to the social struggle is further illustrated by the contrast between two contemporaries of Jeremiah, Nahum the Elkoshite and Habakkuk. Nahum was definitely a provincial. Although Elkosh has not been positively identified, all historians agree in seeking it in the hinterland, at a distance from Jerusalem. This presumption of Nahum's country origin is confirmed by the rural imagery which he uses, as well as by the content of his message. His pictures are drawn from the Bashan, the Carmel, and the flower of Lebanon (1.4), from the overflowing stream (1.8), from the fig trees with first-ripe figs (3.12), from the canker-worm about to burst from its chrysalis (3.16), and the locusts and grasshoppers "which camp in the walls in the cold day, but when the sun ariseth they flee away, and their place is not known where they are" (3.17).

His conception of God is simple, primitive, unsophisticated, countrified. "The Lord is a jealous and avenging God, the Lord avengeth and is full of wrath; the Lord taketh vengeance on His adversaries, and He reserveth wrath for His enemies. The Lord is long-suffering, and great in power, and will by no means clear the guilty; the Lord, in the whirlwind and in the storm is His way, and the clouds are the dust of His feet" (1.2 ff.).

These words, it must be kept in mind, were spoken not in the infancy of the prophetic movement, about the ninth century B.C.E., but in the age of Jeremiah, when it had reached its full maturity and had definitely rejected the doctrine of divine vengeance with other anthropomorphisms. Neither Jeremiah nor Zephaniah ever speak of God as taking revenge on His enemies or as being jealous in any human sense.[11] The concepts are even further from Habakkuk, who, unlike his three contemporaries, was altogether alien to the country, having spent his childhood as well as his manhood in the metropolis.

Nahum's country origin explains and exculpates the brutality which he displays toward the enemies whom his imagination already sees vanquished and destroyed. He positively enjoys the vision of Nineveh suffering the humiliation and pain which she had frequently inflicted on others. With a lack of delicacy which would have astonished the better bred urban writers and speakers, he compares the demolished city to a princess taken into captivity. "Behold, I am against thee, saith the Lord of hosts, and I will uncover thy skirts upon thy face, and I will show the nations thy nakedness, and the kingdoms thy shame. And I will cast detestable things upon thee, and make thee vile" (3.5 ff.). So fascinated is he by this horrible picture, that he reverts to it again and again. "The gates of the rivers are opened, and the palace is dissolved. And the queen is uncovered, she is carried away, and her hand-maidens moan as with the voice of doves, tabering on their breasts" (2.7 f.). Neither his mind nor his pen recoils from these visions; he can even look upon the cruel death of infants without terrifying horror: "Yet she was carried away," he says of Ethiopia, "she went into captivity; her young children were also dashed in pieces at the head of all the streets. And they cast lots for her honourable men, and all her great men were bound in chains. Thou also shalt be drunken, thou shalt swoon" (3.10).

Predictions of evil are of course common among the prophets; but only among those of country origin do we find the enumeration of such horrible details.[12]

A village prophet, Nahum characteristically sees in Assyria a hated and cruel foe, but not an imperialistic oppressor. He denounces her unsparingly, and predicts destruction for her; but in all his vehement words, not a syllable escapes him to reproach her with tyrannical rule of her subjects. For the prophet is obviously too accustomed to exploitation of the weak by the strong for him to mention that as one of the charges in his indictment. Like Hosea, he takes the arrogance of the great for granted together with the oppression of the lowly. Assyria's treatment of her subject nations arouses in him as little comment as does the neighboring farmer's treatment of his wives, slaves, employees, and the smaller peasants. Since he felt no indignation against the powerful at home, he could not summon any anger for the same sins committed by the foreigner. He is conscious of deep hostility for the Mesopotamian Empire, but it is only because she is the enemy of God (1.11). The sins of which he finds her guilty are those which provoke the peasant in any large city: deceit, luxury, unchastity and concern with commerce.

"Woe to the bloody city! [he cries]
    It is full of lies and rapine" (3.1).
"Because of the multitude of the harlotries of the well-
        favoured harlot,
    The mistress of witchcraft,
    That selleth nations through her harlotries,
    And families through her witchcrafts" (3.4).

"Thou hast multiplied thy merchants above the stars
of heaven;
[They shall be as] the canker-worm that spreadeth
itself, and flieth away" (3.16).

Habakkuk was as urban as Nahum was rural. The
rabbinic sages — who in such matters are trustworthy
interpreters of the stylistic nuances of Scripture — infer this
from the silence of the Bible about his place of birth.
"Whenever the name of a prophet's city is omitted, it may
be presumed to have been Jerusalem,"[13] they remark. We
may further take it that the omission of his father's name
points to plebeian origin. These surmises are fully corrobo-
rated by his style, which lacks completely the richness and
earthiness characteristic of the provincial writers. Whereas
Nahum's messengers go up on the high hills to make their
announcements (2.1), Habakkuk takes his position on the
metropolitan watchtower (2.1). He hears the stone crying
from the well and the beam answering it out of the
timber (2.11).

He is amazed at the ruler

". . . . that buildeth a town with blood,
And establisheth a city by iniquity" (2.12).

In his sophisticated environment, seduction has become a
fine art, and there are those who give their neighbor to
drink, "that puttest thy venom thereto . . . . that thou
mayest look on their nakedness" (2.15). He is chagrined at
the evil suffered by the land, but mentions as correlative
with it that done "to the city and to all that dwell therein"
(2.17). There are no canker-worms or grasshoppers, nor
streams nor forests in his imagery.

In the crowded lanes of Jerusalem, men take on for him the appearance of "the fishes of the sea, and the creeping things, that have no ruler over them" (1.14). But his very description shows how foreign he is to the angler's occupation!

"They take up all of them with the angle,
    They catch them in their net,
    And gather them in their drag;
    Therefore, they rejoice and exult" (1.15).

It would indeed be a strange stream where fishing was so easy a task.[14]

Theologically, Habakkuk is as far in advance of his contemporaries, Jeremiah and Zephaniah, as Nahum is behind them. Not alone is his God without jealousy or vengeance, but "too pure of eyes to behold evil." He does not go forth into battle; on the contrary, "The Lord is in His holy Temple," yet, "Let all the earth keep silence before Him" (2.20). It is in urban sophistication, rather than in rural naïveté, that we must seek the origin of such an advanced conception of God.

Habakkuk is as fascinated by the social conflict as Isaiah himself. In his vision, the alien oppressor takes on the features and the form of the neighboring magnate. The struggle between the weak nations and the powerful empire corresponds exactly to that between the oppressed plebeian and the mighty patrician. The Chaldean, rising in the distance, will soon overrun Judea. As the prophet envisages this prospect, he asks himself concerning them, as he has asked himself a thousand times concerning exploiters nearer home, "By what right?"

So completely does he identify oppression in his native community with the tyranny of the stranger that we who live 2600 years later cannot altogether follow him, being uncertain in some passages of which tyrant he is speaking:

"How long, O Lord, shall I cry
And Thou wilt not hear?
I cry out to Thee of violence,
And Thou wilt not save.
Why dost Thou show me iniquity
And beholdest mischief?
And why are spoiling and violence before me?" (1.2–3).

"Thou that art of eyes too pure to behold evil,
And canst not look on mischief,
Wherefore lookest Thou, when they deal treacherously,
And holdest Thy peace, when the wicked swalloweth up
The man that is more righteous than he?" (1.13).

The fourth prophet of this period, Zephaniah, was, like Isaiah, a child of aristocracy, who had heeded the prophetic call to identify himself with the plebeians. His noble birth is attested by the singularly long genealogy given for him, tracing his lineage back four generations, to his great-great-grandfather, who bore the name of Hezekiah. The extraordinary mention of so distant a forbear leads to the suggestion that this particular Hezekiah may have been the king of that name. But whether Zephaniah was of the royal family or not, he was certainly a patrician. Following the tradition of true prophecy, he had identified himself with the masses of the people. He foresees a day of the Lord, when God will bring visitation on all the nobles and the sons of the King (1.8). With them will fall the whole patrician class who in his day, as in Isaiah's before him, and in those of the Hellenists and the Maccabees centuries later, said: "The Lord will not do good, neither will He do evil" (1.12). Lest we have any doubt of the social status of these ancient disclaimers of Providence, Zephaniah continues: "Therefore their wealth shall become a booty and their houses a desolation; yea, they shall build houses and not inhabit them, and they shall plant vineyards, but shall not drink the wine thereof" (1.13).

Living in Jerusalem, he sees the social conflict in all its horror.

> "Woe to her that is filthy and polluted,
>   To the oppressing city!
> She hearkened not to the voice,
> She received not correction;
> She trusted not in the Lord,
> She drew not near to her God.
> Her princes in the midst of her are roaring lions;
> Her judges are wolves of the desert,
> They leave not a bone for the morrow" (3.1 ff.).

His hope is in the meek and the humble. "Seek ye the Lord, all ye humble of the earth, that have executed His ordinance; seek righteousness, seek humility. It may be that ye shall be hid in the day of the Lord's anger" (2.3).

The Book of Ezekiel, which we must now consider, consists of two elements: an original nucleus and a later revision or enlargement.[15] The weight of evidence favors the theory that both parts are the work of the same writer; and it is on that postulate that the following analysis proceeds.

The argument would not, however, be materially altered were the contrary hypothesis, of a later editor or reviser, to be accepted. For the discussion is based primarily on parts of the book which are almost universally attributed to the prophet himself.

The personality and character of Ezekiel, as reconstructed through a sociological study of the book which bears his name, are both fascinating and transparent. A man of remarkable histrionic powers, he was, like many actors on less sublime stages, most self-revealing when he believed himself completely effaced and concealed. Behind the dramatics of faintings and attacks of dumbness, of prolonged inertness and visionary flights, which have deluded even some modern commentators into declaring him a psychopath or a clairvoyant, we discover in the ancient prophet, a man of singularly clear vision, carefully analyzed ideas, sober rationality, and rare moral, artistic, and intellectual gifts. He was an inspired genius, whose moving eloquence, vivid imagination, superb command of words, and almost incredible self-control, combined with his impressionable and highly retentive memory, keen eye for detail, uncanny ability to assimilate new ideas, and mathematical precision and power of schematic formulation, inevitably made him the leader of his generation. Like the earlier prophets, Ezekiel was uncompromisingly devoted to his ideals, stern and unyielding in his sense of justice, and fierce in his loyalty to the God and the traditions of his people. But when, after he had remained silent and motionless for days and even weeks, he broke forth into renewed prophetic utterance, the music of his voice and his language tore the hearts even of those who were utterly opposed to

him (33.31 ff.). His literary and oratorical tact in suggesting, obliquely yet unmistakably, situations which he
could not explicitly mention, mark him as a statesman as
well as an orator. Developing out of his youthful groping
into intellectual maturity, he courageously rejected some of
the ideas he had previously defended; created the most
original and complete theology the people of Israel had yet
seen; and brought the ideals which had been inchoate in
the works of half a dozen plebeian prophets into a climax
of masterful formulation.

The prophet who was to attain this influence and immortality, was born about the year 615 B.C.E.,[16] shortly after
the reformation of Josiah, in a small Palestinian hamlet
on one of the large estates belonging to his father, Buzi,
who was apparently a wealthy priest associated with the
Temple in Jerusalem.[17] There was little in Ezekiel's childhood surroundings to give promise of future distinction or
fame. In the natural course of events, it could only be
expected that the boy would inherit some of his father's
lands, and take his place at the great metropolitan sanctuary. But a series of national catastrophes tore the young
lad, together with thousands of others, out of the fate
which seemed to await them, and as far as Ezekiel was
concerned made him the center of the exiled Jewish community. Yet the influence of his provincial background is
apparent in all of Ezekiel's earlier prophecies; and in some
phases even of his maturer thought and activity. It was
his native village which supplied Ezekiel with his distinc-
tively rural imagery — the picture of Babylonia as a great
eagle, which carries off the top of the cedar (17.3 ff.); of
Egypt as a tall tree in the forest of the Lebanon (31.3 ff.);
of Judah as a lioness, the mother of two whelps, Jeconiah

and Zedekiah (19.2 ff.); or as a vine planted by many waters (19.10 ff.); or, finally deprived of both nobility and craftsmen through the exile of 597 B.C.E., as a vine branch of which both ends have been burned, and the middle too is singed (15.4 ff.). It was thence, too, that Ezekiel derived his peculiarly direct, almost coarse, diction and metaphor, surpassing anything to be found even in Hosea and Jeremiah. Both of those older, provincial prophets had described Israel as the faithless bride of God. But neither of them had approached the ferocity or unbridled freedom with which Ezekiel denounced what he calls his nation's adultery. He sees Israel as a new-born foundling, abandoned in the desert, wallowing in filth, naked, exposed, and ready to perish. God passed by her and took pity on her distress, saved her and took her into His home.

"Thy[18] navel was uncut,
Neither wast thou washed in water,
Thou wast not rubbed with salt,
Nor put in swaddling clothes—
No eye pitied thee,
To have compassion upon thee,
But thou wast cast into the open field
In the day when thou wast born.
When I passed by thee,
And saw thee wallowing in thy blood,
And I said unto thee, out of thy blood shalt thou live,
Grow like a blossom.
Thou didst grow and become great,
Thou camest unto maturity;
Thy breasts were fashioned
And thy hair was grown" (16.4 ff.).

Ezekiel's literary power is obvious even through the translation, which cannot, however, begin to do justice to the original. But we cannot imagine any of the metropolitan prophets, Isaiah, Zephaniah, or Habakkuk, using such language even in their most passionate moments. Ezekiel, however, proceeds, with growing boldness: "But thou didst trust in thy beauty, and play the harlot because of thy renown, and didst pour out thy harlotries on everyone that passed by. . . . thou hast built unto thee an eminent place, and hast made thee a lofty place in every street . . . . and hast made thy beauty an abomination, and opened thy feet to every one that passed by, and multiplied harlotries" (16.15 ff.).

Not satisfied with this horrifying address, Ezekiel returns to the theme again in chapter 23, and again gives details of Judah's lust and sin in words which would have fallen like blasphemy on the ears of the polished plebeians of Jerusalem.[19]

The same rural coarseness reappears in the repellent symbolism of chapter 4, verse 10, where Ezekiel describes himself as commanded by God to limit his food and drink as a symbol for the sufferings of the siege, and then continues: "And thou shalt eat it as barley cakes, and thou shalt bake it in their sight with dung that cometh out of man . . . . Then said I: 'Ah Lord God! behold , my soul hath not been polluted; for from my youth up even till now have I not eaten of that which dieth of itself, or is torn of beasts; neither came there abhorred flesh into my mouth.' Then He said unto me: 'See, I have given thee cow's dung for man's dung, and thou shalt prepare thy bread thereon.' "[20]

Like other provincials, Ezekiel could be both passionately harsh and passionately tender. The punishments he metes out to the sinful shock us by their terror; yet the same prophet hears God speak to him of his wife as "the delight of thine eyes" (24.16). Some commentators have found difficulty in understanding how a man who so serenely and unperturbedly foretells the gravest human misfortunes, could be so humanly affectionate in his family relations. But that was part of the rural, Palestinian psychology. It was no more strange that Ezekiel, fierce to his hearers, should think tenderly of his wife, than that R. Eliezer, who frightened all who came near him, should be a gentle dove to his little niece.[21]

It is not merely, however, Ezekiel's style, but also his mode of thought, which betrays his rural origin. Like Jeremiah[22] he felt a special tenderness for the northern kingdom of Israel. Living in country hamlets, in a region which was claimed by both north and south, these prophets could not develop the local patriotism which made others exclusively concerned with the fate of Judah and altogether neglectful of the older, and larger, land of Ephraim. No redemption which failed to provide for the Ten Tribes was acceptable to Ezekiel.[23] But more than that; he implicitly rejects the primacy of Jerusalem. The terms he uses of the Judaite capital could hardly come from one who believed in her sanctity. "Thine origin," he cries to the great metropolis, was "of the Canaanite; the Amorite was thy father, and thy mother was a Hittite" (16.3). He thinks with placid equanimity of the horrors of the siege which Jerusalem must undergo (4.1 ff.); and in a terrifying vision sees the angel about to destroy the men of the metropolis, beginning with the Temple itself (9.6 ff.). In fact, it is clear that in his early days, Ezekiel did not accept the doctrine of the centralization of worship. That is why he never upbraids the people for building local altars and provincial houses of worship. Indeed, so consistently does he avoid the subject that some writers have maintained that he could not have known the Book of Deuteronomy;[24] and that therefore that work must be exilic or even later. The fact, however, is that Ezekiel's trend of mind arose not from ignorance of the Deuteronomic Law, but from his rural upbringing.

An incident which left a deep scar on Ezekiel's sensitive, religious spirit, converted this indifference to the Temple and Jerusalem into frank and bitter hostility. It seems probable that soon after the year 604 B.C.E., when through the battle of Charchemish, Judah passed from the suzerainty of Egypt to that of Babylonia, Buzi took Ezekiel, then perhaps eleven or twelve years old, to the Temple in Jerusalem.[25] We may imagine with what excitement the future prophet looked forward to the sight of the sanctuary; how when he arrived at the Temple his eyes feasted on every detail of its structure and its ritual; how carefully he watched the ministration in which his father participated; and with what joy he imagined himself taking his place in the holy courts and at the altar. No wonder that having made a few such pilgrimages in his youth, he could ultimately draw a new plan of building and a new program of worship from memory. But alas it was not only the worship of God that he was to see and that was ever after to haunt his sensitive imagination. As his father led him through the Temple courts, he noticed within the gates of the structure, hidden from the sight of the crowds of people, the restored image of Astarte, the Mesopotamian love-goddess which Manasseh had erected many decades earlier, but which Josiah had destroyed.[26] Amazed at this apparition, he followed his father from room to room, discovering as he went continually more incredible symbols of idolatry. Here he found walls covered with images which in his haste he could not clearly identify, but which seemed to portray a number of animal forms, with a crowd of priests offering incense to them; there he discovered a group of women observing the Babylonian ritual of bewailing the god Tammuz; and finally, he arrived in a chamber where about twenty-five men stood with their backs to the Sacred Place, the Innermost Shrine, Israel's Holy of Holies, where God made His Presence manifest over the ancient Ark of the Tablets of Stone. They were looking to the east, in the direction of the Temple's main gate, worshiping the Sun, as it rose higher in the heavens (8.16 ff.).[27]

If his mother had been insulted before his eyes, Ezekiel could not have been more outraged. Little did his father realize what the experience meant to the child. He had been brought up to fear and love the God of Israel, and to consider defection from Him the gravest of sins. And here, in the very seat of His worship, in the House which was dedicated to Him, in dark, hidden chambers, Israel, the bride of God, was playing the harlot! Decades later, as a prophet in Babylonia, he reconstructed the scene, as vividly as though he were passing through it once again. He could identify the very places of these nefarious crimes, he could see the faces of the transgressing priests, he heard once again the voice of God calling for their destruction.

The truth was, of course, that Jehoiakim had introduced this peculiar, foreign ritual not willingly, but under compulsion. Like Ahaz and Manasseh before him, he had to submit to the worship of his suzerain. When he became the vassal of Nebuchadnezzar, it was inevitable that the Babylonian gods should be worshiped in his temple.[28] Fearful of the opposition of the prophetic party, which had become much stronger since the Reformation of Josiah, he had arranged, doubtless with the consent of the Babylonians, to have the service performed in secret. Even Jeremiah, ever watchful for any signs of apostasy, and a stern critic of the government, knew nothing of these proceedings. Had he had the slightest inkling of them, he would certainly have excoriated the Temple, its priests, and the rulers, even more harshly and ruthlessly than he did; and he would certainly have denounced explicitly and unequivocally the conspiracy of silence through which the forbidden ceremonies were concealed from the public. Not even the fear of the oppressor could justify foreign worship in the mind of the prophet. He was opposed to rebellion to save tribute, but he favored martyrdom for the sake of God. Knowing nothing, however, of this secret worship, Jeremiah makes no mention of it. The priests, who joined the king in arranging the ritual, were apparently satisfied that there was no alternative. They reconciled themselves to the inevitable, and calmed their conscience with the thought that after all the idolatrous forms were carried on without public knowledge, and therefore without effect on the people's religion. How could Buzi, who doubtless shared this opportunistic view, realize that Ezekiel, who walked by his side, could not accept it, and that his heart was breaking at what he saw. Too young to realize the true reason for the concealment, he thought the priests were trying to hide their nefarious conduct not from the people, but from God. Their wickedness was thus not only wanton, but insulting. In acts, if not in words, they were saying, "The Lord seeth us not, the Lord hath forsaken the land" (8.12). The precocious boy became convinced that the sanctuary had no future; it was doomed to destruction. No husband, however merciful he might be, would permit his house to be transformed into a brothel.

Then and there, we may believe, Ezekiel's fate was decided. He could never be a priest in this Temple, he would devote his life to exposing its nefarious iniquities. He could not be a minister at God's altar; he would be a prophet in His true service. His adolescent religiosity became a lifetime passion; a youthful idealism which nothing could transform into middle-aged opportunism.

Two other incidents of his early life probably left a lasting impression on Ezekiel's mind: his visits to Tyre and Egypt.[29] His father's wealth which enabled Ezekiel to become acquainted with such luxuries as costly jewels, imported linens, and fine silks, also provided him with the means of travel. An inland, Palestinian boy, he was overwhelmed by the sight of the Tyrian harbor and the Egyptian Nile. The huge, sea-going ships which lay at anchor, with their tall masts pointing heavenwards, and their vast, dazzlingly white sails spread out to the sun, seemed to him a personification of the island city, situated in the "heart of the sea," and enmeshing the ends of the earth in the web of its commerce. He envied and admired her; but with characteristic provincial suspicion of all traders,[30] he also feared her. When he thought of her as a person, instead of a ship, she took the form of the only

independent women he heard about — and was warned
against — in his native hamlet; the women hucksters, whom
the priests were forbidden to marry,[31] who were accused of
ostensibly selling goods and really offering their bodies.
Harlotry and traffic were synonymous to him. When he
came to Egypt, he saw that country, too, personified in its
fierce crocodiles, which with their terrifying jaws and their
elongated bodies, threatening peril to anyone approaching
them, move so slowly that they succeeded only in befouling
the waters.

> "Thou didst liken thyself unto a young lion of the nations;
> Whereas thou art as a dragon in the seas;
> And thou didst gush forth, with thy rivers,
> And didst trouble the waters with thy feet,
> And foul their rivers" (32.2 ff.).

The provincial mind, which reacted so impressionably to
the sights of foreign lands, revealed itself also in the early
theology of the prophet. While his conception of God was
superior to that of the idolatrous peasants among whom he
lived, it was definitely anthropomorphic. He paints bold
word images of the Divine Being, which must have worried
some of his purist hearers, no less than the similar descriptions by the saintly R. Pappias worried R. Akiba in the
second century C.E.[32] In his opening theophany, Ezekiel
reveals this characteristic of his thought. He sees the skies
open above him, and beholds the appearance, as it were,
of a man, "with brightness round about him, like the
sparkle of a flame, from the appearance of his loins upward;
and from the appearance of his loins downward it was
like the appearance of the bow which is in the cloud in
the day of the rain: such was the appearance of the likeness

of the glory of the Lord. And when I saw it, I fell upon my face, and I heard a voice of one that spoke."[33] Continuing in the same vein, he reports, "And He said unto me: 'Son of man, stand upon thy feet, and I will speak with thee.' And the spirit entered into me, and He spoke unto me, and set me upon my feet, ... 'Open thy mouth and eat that which I give unto thee.' And when I looked, behold, a hand was put forth unto me! and, lo, a roll of a book was therein; and He spread it before me, and it was written within and without; and there were written therein lamentations, and moaning, and woe" (1.5–2.10).

In chapter 8, he describes a similar vision of God. "And it came to pass in the sixth year, in the sixth month, in the fifth day of the month, as I sat in my house, and the elders of Judah sat before me, that the hand of the Lord God fell there upon me. Then I beheld, and lo, the appearance, as it were, of a man,[34] from the appearance of his loins and downward, fire; and from his loins and upward, as the appearance of brightness, as the colour of electrum. And the form of a hand was put forth and I was taken by a lock of my head; and a spirit . . . . brought me in the vision of God to Jerusalem."

Those whom these anthropomorphisms shock would do well to read some of the mystical works of the seventh century C.E., the *Book of Palaces*, and the *Measurement of the Height*,[35] where they will find, more than twelve centuries after Ezekiel, the same conception of God restated, even more boldly and in greater detail. Indeed when Maimonides declared that those who held anthropomorphic conceptions of God were heretics, R. Abraham ben David of Posquières remarked in a gloss, "Why did he call such a person heretic, when many who were *his betters and superiors* followed this thought!"[36] For the idea of God as a spiritual, non-material being did not at once permeate all the people of Judah. The metropolitan prophets grasped it; those, however, who were reared in the villages, loved God and knew Him, but the idea of a Great Abstraction was beyond them.

No less significant is the fact that until the end of his life Ezekiel continued to believe, with the simple provincials, that all human thoughts, good and evil, emanate from God. This is the more astonishing because in other respects, his conception of moral responsibility and the individual, in its ultimate form, was more advanced than that of any predecessor. But he had not, like Jeremiah, had the advantage of residence in Jerusalem; he had never grappled with the problem of urban hypocrisy;[37] he had never discovered the difference between rural directness and metropolitan disingenuousness; he knew nothing of Jeremiah's conception of God as probing the reins and the heart" (Jer. 11.20; 17.10); and so he never understood the meaning of intention in human activity. In one of the latest passages of his book, he still speaks of the false prophets as being lured to their sin by God Himself! "And when the prophet is enticed and speaketh a word, *I the Lord have enticed that prophet*, and I will stretch out My hand upon him, and will destroy him from the midst of My people Israel" (14.9).

His rural mentality is evident also in his ethics. In his early addresses he shares the normal provincial prophet's unawareness of any social conflict. His denunciations are confined to the sin of idol-worship; they never reach the problems of human relationship. The issues which concern him on the river Chebar are in no wise different from those of Jerusalem. He sees the Judaites as a single nation; and considers it altogether appropriate to inveigh in chapter after chapter against the transgressions which are being committed at a distance of four months' journey, on Mount Moriah. His utter indifference to the moral problems of his hearers has led Professor C. C. Torrey, one of the most brilliant and ingenious modern commentators on his book, to declare the whole work pseudepigraphic. But indeed it was not so. Ezekiel, the rural prophet, knew but one manner of loyalty to YHWH, being devoted to His sole worship; he knew but one sin, the worship of idols. Nothing else mattered.

With such an ideology, he naturally could not think of the Judaites as individuals, with separate moral problems, and subject to separate divine judgments. He had not yet arrived at the principle of the moral responsibility of the individual, which was to be his supreme contribution to world thought. The whole people sins as a unit, and is punished as a unit.

Just when Ezekiel underwent the transformation which made him "the watchman of the House of Israel," warning each person of his wrongdoing, and keenly conscious of individual responsibility, we cannot tell. Several influences, doubtless, coöperated in remaking his spiritual outlook. The first was almost certainly his advance into middle age. In his younger days, he was satisfied to pour out the feelings of his heart in song, without asking himself whether his words were achieving their desired effect. It did not occur to him that the crowds who gathered to listen to him remained unaffected by his ideas. He was altogether unconscious of the fact that his power lay not in persuasive argument, but in the magnetic quality of his voice, his speech, and his histrionics. He saw people weep, and he thought that they were converted; he heard their applause, and fancied that they were convinced. Only as decades passed, and he could detect no perceptible change in their manner of life, did the truth dawn upon him. "And as for thee, son of man, the children of thy people that talk of thee by the walls and in the doors of the houses, and speak one to another, every one to his brother, saying: 'Come, I pray you, and hear what is the word that cometh forth from the Lord; and come unto thee as the people cometh, and sit before thee as My people, and hear thy words, *but do them not* — for with their mouth they show much love, but their heart goeth after their covetousness; and lo, thou art unto them as a love song of one that hath a pleasant voice, and can play well on an instrument; so they hear thy words, but they do them not—when this cometh to pass—behold, it cometh — then shall they know that a prophet hath been among them" (33.30 ff.).

This charge of futility against his earlier life was not altogether justified; it was simply a reaction from his earlier optimism. The fact that people were not transformed by his words, did not mean that he was speaking in a vacuum. He had helped to prevent their assimilation into the Babylonian environment, and had thus saved them from the fate which overtook the Ten Tribes who were exiled to Media. Speaking as a member of Judah's ecclesiastic, land-owning aristocracy, he had been able to influence many whom the plebeian prophets could not reach at all. But this negative significance of his work was, of course, imperceptible to Ezekiel; it can only be discerned in the perspective of later, comparative history. Perhaps it was when he approached his fortieth year (about 580 B.C.E.), shortly after the final destruction of Jerusalem, that he found himself sunk in deep pessimism. What seemed a lifetime of effort had produced no visible results; he could expect people to follow him only when his predictions would be confirmed. But that would be long after his death, when vindications would be useless.

And yet the vigorous mind would not surrender. Weary of his poetic muse, he would try another instrument. He ceased to be the poet, and became the rhetorician.

He no longer sang, he spoke; he refused to entertain, he would only exhort. Those who wanted to be amused with clever rhythms and beautiful metaphors could go elsewhere; he would speak directly, pointedly, and clearly, in emphatic prose, repeating himself when necessary, straining after no oratorical or literary effects, giving the people only his unvarnished ideas. He even went over the material he had already written down, and added prose supplements and revisions to his earlier poetic utterances. From the point of view of the historian, this change of style was most fortunate, for it enables us to distinguish the later prophecies, revisions, and supplementary notes, from the original poems, and thus to follow Ezekiel's spiritual and intellectual development from the beginning until the end.[38]

Ezekiel's new preference for the prose style was, however, symptomatic of deeper changes in the whole character of the man. He had not merely grown older in years, he was richer in experience. Rationalize the situation as he might, the fact was that he turned his back on poetry because he had himself become prosaic, interested less in giving vent to his inner fire and delivering his message than in achieving results and leading people. The doctrines which he preached at this period of his life prove this. They reflect not only more mature reasoning than those of his youth, but an essentially different type of mind.

What had happened is of profound interest to the psychologist as well as to the student of Scripture. When Ezekiel had come to Babylonia among the exiles of the year 597 B.C.E., he had found himself, like the other exiles, utterly destitute. Neither his priestly prerogatives nor his landed estates were of any use to him in a land where there was no Jewish temple and where he could collect no rentals from his Judaite property. How did he maintain himself? He was not yet a prophet; and even when he became one, it is altogether improbable that he received any emoluments from that office. His book leaves us no room for doubt; he became a craftsman. As part of his vocation, he learned the art of engraving a city on brick after the manner of the Babylonians (4.1); he knew how to portray a siege on this map of clay (ibid.); he trained himself to the utmost precision in weights and measures (4.10; 5.1); and could even construct in his mind the complicated machinery of the Divine Chariot (ch. 1, etc.), and the architectural intricacies of the future Temple (ch. 40 ff.). The use of such technical symbols and imagery can have but one meaning; the land-owning priest of Palestine had become an artisan.

The associations into which his vocation led him would inevitably have affected Ezekiel's conception of his task. The development was hastened, however, by the social traditions of the prophetic group to which he adhered.

As will presently be demonstrated, this group consisted primarily of urban plebeians, the former artisans and traders of Jerusalem's market place. Ezekiel's association with them, rather than with the "false," patriotic, provincial prophets, who were sending letters even from distant Babylonia to incite the Judaites to renewed war, was originally a pure accident — the result of his devotion to God and his mistrust of the Temple and its ecclesiastics. But having once joined them and led them, he became gradually converted to their views, not merely with regard to the principal issue of the day — the relation of Judah to Babylonia — but also with regard to such questions as anthropomorphic description of God, the doctrine of individual responsibility, and social justice. Like other converts of middle age,[39] Ezekiel became an extremist member of the faction he had joined, feeling free to break away completely from the traditions which bound even that group and to carry their ideas to their logical conclusion.

He now declared that the individual, not the nation, was the proper focus of prophetic activity. Turning his back on everything he had said from the beginning of his prophetic activity, he described the prophet as a watchman, who is responsible for the safety of the city, in the sense that he must keep secure the life of each of its inhabitants (3.17 f.; 33.1 ff.). When anyone commits a sin, it becomes the duty of the watchman to warn him, in order that he may return to righteousness. God desires not to punish the wicked, Ezekiel now assures us, but to bring them back to the good life (33.11). To those who recalled that for many years Ezekiel had failed to carry out what he now declared his foremost duty, he explains that God had forbidden him to

act the part of the prophet. The people through their sins
had forfeited his guidance (3.26).

But if under normal conditions the individual and his
fate are the prophet's primary concern, that must be
because God punishes and rewards individuals, rather than
people. Nationalist and family ties thus cease to have
significance. A righteous man can save neither his son nor
his daughter; the soul that sinneth, it shall die (18.4).
Indeed, he went so far as to say that though "Noah, Daniel,
and Job" (three of the foremost saints) were in a city which
was threatened with danger, "they should deliver but their
own souls by their righteousness" (14.14).[40] Their justice
and their mercy would be of no avail to their fellow-
townsmen, for each man and woman and child must be
saved by individual merit.

With this high conception of the individual, Ezekiel
brought back into prophecy the plebeian sensitiveness to
social injustice. The oppression of the weak by the strong
is as much apostasy from God as the worship of idols or
the refusal to observe proper ceremonials. The great
iniquity of Jerusalem was not, he now holds, her waywardness from God, but the ethical wrong-doing of which
the plebeian prophets had spoken so often. "Behold, the
princes of Israel, everyone according to his might, have
been in thee to shed blood. In thee have they made light
of father and mother; in the midst of thee have they dealt
by oppression with the stranger; in thee have they wronged
the fatherless and the widow . . . . In thee, have been tale-
bearers to shed blood; and in thee have they eaten upon
the mountains; in the midst of thee they have committed
lewdness . . . . In thee have they taken gifts to shed blood;
thou hast taken interest and increase, and thou hast greedily

gained of thy neighbours by oppression, and hast forgotten
Me, saith the Lord God" (22.6 ff.).

In another passage he is equally emphatic and powerful:
"If a man be just, and do that which is lawful and right,
and hath not eaten upon the mountains, neither hath he
lifted up his eyes to the idols of the house of Israel, neither
hath defiled his neighbour's wife, neither hath he come
near to a woman in her impurity; and hath not wronged
any, but hath restored his pledge for a debt, hath taken
nought by robbery, hath given his bread to the hungry, and
hath covered the naked with a garment; he that hath not
given forth upon interest, neither hath taken any increase,
that hath withdrawn his hand from iniquity, hath executed
true justice between man and man, hath walked in My
statutes, and hath kept Mine ordinances, to deal truly; he
is just, he shall surely live, saith the Lord God" (18.5 ff.).

It is significant that he regards as the culminating sin
of Sodom not inhospitality — for which the Book of
Genesis indicts her[41] — but arrogance and perversion of
justice. "Behold," he cried, "this was the iniquity of thy
sister, Sodom" (16.49). Clearly in these lines Ezekiel had
in mind the evils which he saw in the city in which he
lived. The anger which he was pouring forth against
Sodom was intended, as so frequently in plebeian prophecy,
for nearer and more contemporary wrong-doers.

In one of his greatest prophecies he inveighs against the
"shepherds of Israel," the leaders of the destroyed Judaite
Commonwealth. "Woe unto the shepherds of Israel that
have fed themselves! Should not the shepherd feed the
sheep? Ye did eat the fat, and ye clothed you with the wool,
ye killed the fatlings; yet ye fed not the sheep. The weak
have ye not strengthened, neither have ye healed that

which was sick, neither have ye bound up that which was broken, neither have ye brought back that which was driven away, neither have ye sought that which was lost; but with force have ye ruled over them and with rigour" (34.2 ff.). In a second passage, he returns to his invective against the powerful with a somewhat different picture: "And as for you, O My flock, thus saith the Lord God: Behold, I judge between cattle and cattle, even the rams and the he-goats. Seemeth it a small thing unto you to have fed upon the good pasture, but ye must tread down with your feet the residue of your pasture? And to have drunk of the settled waters, but ye must foul the residue with your feet? And as for My sheep, they eat that which ye have trodden with your feet, and they drink that which ye have fouled with your feet . . . . Because ye thrust with side and with shoulder, and push all the weak with your horns, till ye have scattered them abroad; therefore will I save My flock, and they shall no more be a prey; and I will judge between cattle and cattle" (34.17 ff.).

Advancing beyond anything taught by the prophets before him, Ezekiel now declares all men equal. Revising his book, he invented the term "son of man" for God's address to him,[42] to signify that even the divine messenger appears before his Master only as one of the multitude. The territories which in his final eschatological vision he divides among the twelve tribes are to be exactly equal. With his usual mathematical precision he insists that they will extend in parallel longitudinal strips across the country from east to west, with a central section set aside for the Temple and the priests. Not only the tribes, but also the individuals composing them, are to be treated with absolute equality. In order to achieve this, the returning tribes would be equal numerically, as well as territorially. Hence he reports, "Thus saith the Lord God: This shall be the border, whereby ye shall divide the land for inheritance according to the twelve tribes of Israel, Joseph receiving two portions. And ye shall inherit it, *one as well as another*, concerning which I lifted up My hand to give it unto your fathers" (47.13). The ideal Commonwealth is no longer to have a King, but a prince (*Nasi*), to whom a special estate is assigned. "It shall be to him for a possession in Israel, and My princes shall no more wrong My people; but they shall give the land to the house of Israel according to their tribes" (45.8).

The mechanistic, arithmetical approach to all of life's problems, which led Ezekiel to use technician's metaphors and symbols, and to arrange the future Commonwealth into a cubistic pattern, suggesting the worker in wood, was carried over into his peculiarly schematic doctrine of reward and punishment. The repenting sinner will be forgiven, but if a man do righteousness all his life and sin at the end, "none of his righteous deeds that he hath done shall be remembered; for his trespass that he trespassed, and for his sin that he hath sinned, for them shall he die" (18.24). On the other hand a man may be wicked all his life and repent at the end, and then "none of his transgressions that he hath committed shall be remembered against him" (18.22). "Yet ye say," continues Ezekiel, "the way of the Lord is not equal. Hear now, O house of Israel: Is it My way that is not equal? Is it not your ways that are unequal?" (18.25) The Hebrew expression which we render in English by "equal" or "straight" is taken from carpentry!

His mature conception of God became as urban, lofty, sophisticated, and spiritual, as it had been provincial and anthropomorphic. To conceal the realistic picture of the Deity which he had drawn and published in his first prophecy, he had recourse to a curious device. He surrounded the original verses with a much larger supplement, in which they are all but lost. He created a vast and intricate "Heavenly Chariot," with "beasts" and "wheels" moving in various directions, and making an overwhelming picture on the mind as it tries to grasp the complicated, intentionally unintelligible structure. After years of life in Babylonia, he no longer saw the Divine Presence manifest itself through the opening of the heavens, but as "coming from the north," where the Babylonians placed their deities.[43]

The prophet now accepted also the principle of the centralization of worship. The restored Temple was to be built, not indeed in Jerusalem, but in a new city, located nearer the center of the land. But it would be the sole sanctuary. In order to reconcile his early prophecies with this new doctrine, Ezekiel again had recourse to an amazingly clever device — he dated his prophecy by Josiah's reformation![44] What could be better evidence of his acceptance of Josiah's principles than making their promulgation the beginning of an era. Yet it is impossible to believe that this date was original. The ancient Israelites never, so far as we know, counted their years from specific historical events. The only exceptions to this rule are a few obviously post-exilic passages like I Kings 6.1, which date later events from the Exodus. But not even prophetic extravagance could place Josiah's reformation in the same class with the birth of Israel as a people. More than that, all of the other prophecies in the book are dated either by the years of Jehoiachin's reign,[45] or by the beginning of the Exile.

Why should the first prophecy be dated by the reformation, except to indicate the importance of that epoch-making event to the prophet?

Ezekiel's career was drawing to its close when in the year 562 B.C.E. Amil-Marduk, the biblical Evil-merodach, came to the throne of Babylonia and suddenly inspired the Judaites with new Messianic hopes of a speedy return to their homeland. But before the Babylonian ruler could carry out any beneficent plans toward Judah, he was deposed and slain, and Nergal-Shar-Usur, spiritual heir of Nebuchadnezzar, came to the throne, putting an end to all expectations of immediate return.

These frustrated expectations made Ezekiel more critical of Babylonia than he had been in the earlier decades of the exile. In his original prophecies he spoke of the Chaldeans with unconcealed admiration, and was intensely devoted to them. He predicted only victories for them, against Jerusalem, against Tyre, against Egypt. But the disappointment of the hopes aroused by Amil-Marduk made the Judaites bitter, and in the last prophecies of Ezekiel a new note of hostility to Babylonia appears. Naturally this enmity had to be well concealed, but it is not difficult to recognize it through the thin disguise with which the prophet covers it. Other teachers living in Palestine and wishing to predict Babylonia's imminent downfall, resorted to a simple cipher. They used the Hebrew alphabet backward, so to speak, writing the last letter, *Tau*, for the first, *Aleph*, *Shin* for *Bet*, *Resh* for *Gimmel*, and so forth. *Babel* thus became *Sheshach*, and *Kasdim* (the Chaldeans) were called *Leb-kamai*.[46] But such a cipher was possible only in the outlying provinces and in rural communities, where the preacher was safe from denunciation and betrayal. In Babylonia, where the number of delators must have been considerable, such an obvious cipher would have afforded little protection. Ezekiel resorts to a subtler, less artificial, but equally effective method. He pours forth his anger not against Babylonia, but against Tyre and Egypt. But the sins which he chooses to denounce in those distant monarchies were those which to any Judaite, particularly a plebeian, would seem to be particularly characteristic of Babylonia herself: pride, self-will, haughtiness and arrogance.

"Thus saith the Lord God:
Because thy heart is lifted up,
And thou hast said: I am a God,
I sit in the seat of God,
In the heart of the seas;
Yet thou art man and not God,
Though thou didst set thy heart as the heart of God —
Behold, thou art wiser than Daniel!
There is no secret that they can hide from thee!
By thy wisdom and thy discernment
Thou hast gotten thee riches;
And hast gotten gold and silver
Into thy treasures;
In thy great wisdom by thy traffic,
Hast thou increased thy riches,
And thy heart is lifted up because of thy riches —
Therefore thus saith the Lord God:
Because thou hast set thy heart
As the heart of God;
Therefore, behold, I will bring strangers upon thee,

The terrible of the nations;
And they shall draw their swords against the beauty
    of thy wisdom,
And they shall defile thy brightness" (28.1 ff.).

Can we doubt that the Judaites who had suffered so
grievously at the hands of Babylonia, and so little at the
hands of Tyre, were keeping Nebuchadnezzar in mind
throughout the whole passage? There was no need of interpretation, and no danger of decipherment. Ostensibly
Ezekiel was speaking with vehemence of Babylonia's
enemies and rebellious subjects. But all his Judaite hearers
knew that the prophet's heart was bursting with rage not
against the Phoenician who had left Judah in peace, but
against the tyrant whose conquering armies had pillaged
the land, devastated the capital, burned the Temple,
slaughtered innocents, violated virgins, and enslaved men.
The prophet cautiously inserts into the midst of his tirade
the verse "in the heart of the seas"; but that is an obvious
decoy. Remove the phrase — in Hebrew but two words —
and the discourse applies with unerring accuracy to
Babylonia. It was the great King of Babylon, not poor
Hiram of Tyre, who placed himself in the seat of the gods,
whose heart had been lifted up because of his riches, who
had thought of himself, "I am a God."[47]

When, turning from Tyre to Egypt, Ezekiel prophesies
its doom at the hands of the Chaldeans, we still know that
his indignation against Pharaoh is a case of transference.
He is giving vent to long suppressed bitterness and finding a
suitable object for it in the Nile Kingdom, which serves but
as effigy for its rival on the Euphrates.

To the beautiful poem about Egypt he had composed in his youth, he adds the prosaic remarks: "Therefore thus saith the Lord, God: because thou art exalted in stature, and he hath set his top among the thick boughs, and his heart is lifted up in his height; I do even deliver him into the hand of the mighty one of the nations; he shall surely deal with him; I do drive him out according to his wickedness" (31.10 ff.).

The passionate complaint against Egyptian pride transforms the whole of the older poem from an attack on Pharaoh into an equally powerful, but far more subtle, denunciation of Babylonia. What, indeed, could the prophet on the Tigris know of Egyptian haughtiness or suffer because of it? It was the nearer, Babylonian pride and arrogance which called forth his anger and his bitterness.

The most powerful of Ezekiel's later prophecies against Babylonia occurs in the mystifying predictions about "Gog, the land of Magog." That the true significance of this prophecy should have remained hidden is the stranger since the cipher is comparatively simple.[48] There was no nation called Magog in Ezekiel's day. There had been such a tribe in ancient times and it is numbered among the descendants of Japhet (Gen. 10.2). But it had never become important and the possibility that such a people would attain world dominion was infinitely remote. What then did Ezekiel have in mind when he foresaw the day when "Gog would come into the land of Israel." A moment's reflection will explain it. Write Magog backwards in Hebrew (*Gagam*) and substitute for each letter the one preceding it in the Hebrew alphabet, and it becomes *Babel*, Babylonia. To save himself further from detection, the prophet associates with Magog a number of Japhethite and

Hamite nations ("Persia, Ethiopia and Put with them"), and then proceeds to say: "It shall come to pass in that day, that things shall come into thy mind, and thou shalt devise an evil device; and thou shalt say: I will go up against the land of unwalled villages; I will come upon them that are at quiet, that dwell safely, all of them dwelling without walls, and having neither bars nor gates; to take spoil and to take the prey; to turn thy hand against the waste places, that are now inhabited, and against the people that are gathered out of the nations, that have gotten cattle and goods, that dwell in the middle of the earth.... *And it shall come to pass in that day when Gog shall come against the land of Israel,* saith the Lord God, that My fury shall arise up in My nostrils.... And I will call for a sword against him throughout all my mountains, saith the Lord God.... And I will plead against him with pestilence and with blood and I will cause to rain upon him and upon his bands, and upon the many peoples that are with him, an overflowing shower, and great hail-stones, fire, and brimstone" (38.10 ff.). The idea that Ezekiel simply built up this apocalyptic vision of an unknown people who will rule the earth and meet their doom in Palestine only for his amusement, seems preposterous. When he spoke of a nation ruling the earth, he and everyone who heard him thought at once of Nebuchadnezzar. Cover the image in other garments as he might, his people knew that he was foretelling a second Babylonian invasion of Palestine, whose cities would be unwalled, and whose people would be undefended. And then, God would appear to destroy the foe and avenge the insult that He had suffered with His people in the destruction of 586. "Thus will I magnify Myself, and sanctify Myself, and I will make Myself known in the eyes of many nations; and they shall know that I am the Lord" (38.23).

The prophet, using these strange ciphers, succeeded in carrying his thought to his hearers without exposing himself to any danger from traducers. No Babylonian official could possibly understand how Ezekiel, prophesying the doom of Babylonia's enemies, was really gloating over her own destruction. It would have seemed incredible and far-fetched; since, of course, the Babylonians could not regard themselves as the incarnation of Arrogance. Perhaps a modern reader, who has never had to suffer oppression and to stifle protest, will find it equally difficult to believe that the audience followed the mental trend of the prophet without previous understanding of the ciphers used. But when the minds of the hearer and speaker are in absolute harmony, little effort is required to bring images from one to the other. A mere suggestion is sufficient. What we, at the distance of thousands of years, can arrive at only after patient and careful study, the simplest hearer understood as soon as the sound was uttered. So also centuries after Ezekiel, the rabbinic sages frequently used Pharaoh, Haman, Bileam, Edom, Amalek, Assyria, Babylonia and other forgotten persons and peoples as effigies for their persecutors.[49] They even dared insert in their prayers a petition for the destruction of the Kingdom of Arrogance, without fear that the true significance of it would be understood.[50] Almost within our own time, in the Russia of the Czars, itinerant preachers would portray in the synagogues the doom of Israel's enemies; and while the names they repeated were always biblical and rabbinic — Pharaoh, Sennacherib, Nebuchadnezzar, Antiochus and Hadrian — the passion behind the words was directed at the tyrant of St. Petersburg.[51] The oppressed of the world must always find some way to give vent to their pains. And just as in the fortress of St. Peter and St. Paul the prisoners who had never communicated with each other by word of mouth soon learned to interpret the taps made on the walls by their fellows in neighboring cells and were thus enabled to carry on conversations with them;[52] just as in the South, the slaves managed to carry information from one to another during the Civil War,[53] so that they were always informed of its progress without the help of their masters; so the Jews, both ancient and modern, smarting under their oppressors, found some outlet for their anguish in uttering against forgotten enemies the bitterness which they felt toward the present oppressor.

In Ezekiel's classless society, urban prophecy finds its fit culmination. It was a natural product of the exile, where new beginnings had to be made and no old tradition had to be considered. The prophet who had been reared in Babylonia could see how utterly irrelevant were all distinctions of caste and class. As in a dungeon or in the grave, prince and pauper, priest and squire, artisan and trader, giver and beggar, were equal and alike. Stripped of the insignia, not less than of the advantages of position, the proud descendants of kings and nobles stood quietly beside the meanest child of the slums and recognized his equality with them. The idea which had been germinating for centuries among the plebeians would now be grasped in its fullness and its entirety. For all his radicalism, the mature Ezekiel appears the obvious spiritual heir of Amos, Isaiah, Habakkuk and Jeremiah.

The patrician teaching which these plebeian groups so vigorously opposed found no expression in pre-exilic literature. No prophet who adopted it could have been immortalized in the canon. But its existence is implied by the ferocious attack which it evoked. We shall presently see that in the Second Commonwealth the Wisdom teachers and the Sadducees formulated the traditional attitude of their class into an ethical philosophy. But whether the earlier nobility pursued its goal consciously or instinctively, it certainly was a definite and powerful stratum of the population, which sought continuously to subject the others to itself.

There thus appears with regard to the doctrine of equality the same tripartite division of the nation which we already found in examining the teaching of Providence. The plebeians of the city and the shepherd class demanded equality; the patricians denied it; while the peasantry, both the rich gentry and the poorer farmers, were unaware of any struggle or difference.

The struggle between the various classes becomes more significant when seen against the background of the legislation of the Torah. The Pentateuch everywhere upholds the contention of the plebeians and the principle of human equality. It is this fact which makes the neutrality of the farmer and the opposition of the patrician particularly striking. Indeed, at the end of eight centuries, long after the Torah had become the recognized constitution of the land, we still find each party adhering to its own attitude and philosophy. The patrician was still struggling against equality and the farmer still retained his neutrality; while the plebeian alone carried on in the spirit of the Law. Only so far as the principle of human equality had been given definite expression in explicit norms, was it accepted by all. Yet to that extent the Torah did alleviate the condition of the oppressed and stay the hand of the exploiter and tyrant. Even more, in spite of selfish class interest, the patrician came to realize vaguely that he was setting himself against the spirit of the Law he revered, and many a time yielded to God when he would have resisted man.

XVI. THE ORIGIN OF THE PROPHETIC
DOCTRINE OF PEACE

Each of the three major social strata of the ancient
Judean Commonwealth had its own international policy.
To put the matter briefly, the farmer was an uncompromising nationalist; the urban plebeian, a liberal universalist;
and the court aristocrat, a perpetual opportunist.[1] The
history of the Jewish commonwealth from the tenth century
B.C.E. onward is a continuous demonstration of this truth,
which applied to the days of Isaiah no less than to those of
Malachi, and to the time of Ben Sira as well as to that of
the Pharisees and the later rabbis. The various attitudes
of each group were inevitable outgrowths of its spiritual
needs and economic necessities. Yet it is interesting to
note how logically they are correlated also with the various
abstract beliefs about God and the world which have been
described in preceding chapters. The farmer's nationalism
was as natural as his primitive doctrine of personality.
His faith that his personal fortunes were a matter of concern to the Deity strengthened and supported his nationalist
arrogance. The patrician, who denied any divine control
over the affairs of men and pursued with relentless avarice
his goal of mundane success, inevitably sought to make
capital out of every occurrence and combination of circumstances in public no less than in private life. Finally the
urban plebeian, whose sophisticated mind could not be
content with a denial of self, and who yet held his baser
impulses in check by a fine idealistic belief in God, was

naturally driven to pacifist universalism, in which all men were recognized as brothers.

The political cleavage was, however, also associated with a wide variation in form of worship between patrician, plebeian, and provincial. The masses of the country peasantry followed practices which were drawn in equal parts from the desert service of YHWH and the agricultural ritual of the Baal. Both were indigenous to the land, the one to the fertile valleys, the other to the stony hills and sandy wilderness. But the farmer would have rejected vigorously any attempt to introduce a foreign god, like those of Tyre, or Egypt, or Moab. On the other hand, the metropolitan patricians, headed by the King and the princes, worshiped in the Temple of YHWH in Jerusalem, but at the same time their hearts turned continually to the other gods of the neighboring countries. Their respect for the great nations always inclined them to seek solace also from the gods whom those peoples served. Like some modern men and women, in other aspects of life, they confused emancipation with faithlessness. Opposed to both these groups, were the plebeians of the city, who, as sophisticated as the nobility, were yet loyal to the God and customs of their forefathers. The social trichotomy thus cut across the whole spiritual life of the ancient Jew; to whatever corner of his thought one turned, one always found the threefold division between the patrician courtier, the plebeian worker and the rural peasant. In the present chapter and those immediately following, it is our purpose to show how these opposing doctrines affected, and were affected by, passing historical events.

Together with his respect for his own people the rural Judaite developed also a deep love for their customs and ceremonies. His traditional rites, festivals, and modes of worship were sacred beyond words. If he was a henotheist, and believed in other gods besides the God of Israel, he held them to be debased, mean and weak. No other country was like his own. All lands but Palestine were "unclean."[2] She was superior even in what appeared to be her faults. Thus, as late as the second century C.E., a rural sage tells us that among Palestine's advantages over Egypt are her hills. "For when you own a single acre in the plain, that is all you have. But if you own an acre on a hill, you have an acre on each slope—to the north, to the south, to the east, and to the west, as well as on the summit; so that the area of the land is quintupled!"[3]

The patriotism of the gentry was the more emphatic because they formed the military class.[4] We might suppose, a priori, that those who have to risk their lives in battle would be most loathe to engage in war. Yet historically, soldiers are the most hungry for it. Nor is this altogether strange. The avidity of the explorer for the frozen north, of the scientist for dangerous experiment, of the aviator for the unknown perils of the air, and of the pietist for martyrdom, show how little man really cares for life. When an adventure to the thought of which man is accustomed calls, all else is forgotten. Had this not been so, wars would, as William James recognized,[5] have ceased long ago. Since the ancient militia, like that of the Middle Ages, was drawn from the *anshe hayyil*, the country squires, the natural chauvinism of the class was sharpened and enhanced.

The farmer's taste for war was whetted by the rewards it offered him. As we have already noted, the new lands seized from weaker nations, the booty taken from the opposing armies or the unhappy civilians, the men and women captured in battle or siege, were divided among the warriors (cf. I Sam. 22.7; Jer. 37.12). The landowner might double his property, he could increase the number of his slaves, he could add a new face to his harem. The picture of victory drawn by the mother of Sisera belonged in truth to all ages:

"Are they not finding, are they not dividing the spoil?
A damsel, two damsels to every man;
To Sisera a spoil of dyed garments,
A spoil of dyed garments of embroidery,
The dyed garments of broidery for the neck of every spoiler?" (Judg. 5.30).

The only difference was that in later "civilized" times, lands and men slaves were more prized than women and embroidered garments.

The urban plebeians were as pacifist as the farmers were warlike.[6] The artisans and traders of Jerusalem had nothing to gain from victory and all to lose in defeat. Generals and soldiers proceeding to battle were apt to commandeer their goods or their cattle and even their services. Returning successful, their arrogance was increased and their power enhanced. During the course of war trade routes were deflected, foreign custom was driven to other centers, and the country's own commerce was minimized. Especially when Jerusalem had become the "gate of peoples," did the merchants begin to feel the heavy burdens of war. But even before that the interests of its traders lay in continued peace and quiet. Every long stretch of peace brought prosperity and growth to the city; war always brought about impoverishment.

These troubles, associated with any conflict, were incomparably aggravated if the army suffered defeat. For then the capital was besieged by the enemy and exposed to the ravages of famine, thirst, disease, and continuous, nerve-destroying battle. Trade was completely at an end, and, worst of all, there was before one the continual nightmare of victory for the besieger. Once a breach had been made in the wall, death became better than life for the citizens of the unhappy town. The besieging army, infuriated by delay, threw itself mercilessly on the inhabitants, sparing neither old nor young, man nor woman. Those who escaped death were carried off into exile or sold as slaves. Their wives were fortunate to be taken as handmaidens and concubines; they might be turned over to a life of infamy, rented out to any passer-by like a cow or a cart.[7] These terrors were all too vivid for the metropolitan trader; he heard too much about wars and how they were carried on to have any illusions about the fate in store for the vanquished. And well he knew his own people's weakness in comparison with the strength of the surrounding nations. The villager might really believe his people's army invincible. In his childish simplicity he might trust the bards who told him only of victories but never mentioned defeats. His complete trust in the God of Israel gave him additional courage and strength, for it never occurred to him that God might fail His people. The trader of Jerusalem knew the world better. He had met the men of other nations at the bazaars, and knew the strength of their armies and their resources. He had a more universalistic conception of God and realized that the Deity had no predilections among peoples. He saw the corruption at court, recognized the incompetence of kings and rulers, and understood the weakness of captains and generals. Terror and understanding combined to make the city plebeian a thoroughgoing pacifist who shrank from war above all evils, and who believed that "God could find no vessel holding greater blessing for Israel than peace."[8]

With all his internationalism and universalist sympathies the urban plebeian yet agreed with the farmer in his devotion to ancestral ceremonies. The union of the two ideals, which to many a modern may seem contradictory, is manifest in the whole history of the urban-plebeian group. Understanding fully the might and wisdom of other peoples, the artisan or trader of Jerusalem did not yet resign his judgment to them. Like all men he preferred the ways, manners and rites to which his childhood had accustomed him. The respect he gave to other peoples did not seem to him sufficient reason for adopting their civilization or culture. On the contrary, since he early became convinced that there was no hope of empire for his people, his patriotism expended itself altogether in a passion for their spiritual life. Thus he could never be persuaded to risk his life to extend his country's boundaries, yet we find him again and again a willing martyr for his traditions and his culture. To the contemporary farmer, as well as to the patrician, this attitude must have seemed paradoxical, like the association of freedom of choice with divine foreknowledge. But to the urban plebeian himself it seemed natural and logical. His love for his people had nothing to do with political boundaries or imperial designs; it was religious, spiritual and cultural. When their independence was at stake he worried not at all; when their Torah was threatened nothing was too precious to be offered in its defense.

Over and above these two groups, the warlike gentry and the pacifist metropolitans, rose the aristocracy of the Court. They shared the warlike passions of the gentry, but also the cool understanding of their plebeian fellow-citizens of Jerusalem. Many of them had been reared on their ancestral estates in the provinces; others had inherited rural prejudices from their fathers and grandfathers. We have already seen how their particular customs can in general be traced to country conditions. Closely allied to the peasants through ties of blood and of culture, they were also the commanders of the army. They enjoyed war with a relish, as a surgeon enjoys a difficult operation. But their desire for war was held in close check by information which the deluded peasantry did not share.

They were not, like the peasants, deceived regarding the strength of their own people or of its mighty neighbors. They knew that in any battle between tiny Judea and the powerful empires of Egypt, Assyria, Babylonia, or Rome, there could be no doubt of the ultimate issue. They had no desire to be taken from their luxurious palaces to a distant dungeon; and they could never be moved to risk an exchange of the dominion they exerted at home for the slavery which might await them elsewhere. Moreover, like the nobility of most small peoples, they developed a sincere admiration for the leaders of greater nations. Having no standard of excellence save power, they fawned on the strong as they bullied the weak. We have seen that they had no real faith. They believed in the existence of God but would have heartily subscribed to the blasphemy that

"God is on the side of the strongest battalions." Relying on their resources of material power and clever leadership, they were prepared to give battle only when they felt the chances of victory lay with them. At all other times they were as pacifist as the plebeians. In fact they went further than the plebeians. While the plebeians loved their people and its culture, the patricians having no such faith or loyalty became (when they were convinced of their nation's weakness) absolute assimilationists. Political quietism was not enough for them; they had to yield their very souls and spirits.

Generation after generation, the interplay of the three parties repeated itself. The surrounding enemies, the internal conditions, the political configuration of the land, the economic status of the whole people, changed. But so long as the three classes—country gentry, city plebeians, and court patricians—persisted, each maintained the same cultural and political position which it had held in earlier days.

The political struggle between the patricians and the plebeians probably arose long before the tenth century B.C.E. But our information for those early periods is too meager to become the basis for a generalization. It appears, however, that the shepherd clans which in the earliest days were certainly as warlike as the peasants, gradually lost their desire for battle.

Some interesting records of this love of peace are noticeable in the Torah. First among these, perhaps, is the remarkable transformation of the Cain-Abel story from a primitive war saga into a pacifist allegory.[9] The moral of the present story, which describes how Abel, the righteous shepherd, was slain by his wicked brother Cain, the peasant,

whom God thereupon condemned to wander homeless
about the earth, is clear. It is intended to inculcate tenderness and the hatred of violence. But this can be neither
the original form nor intent of the composer. The
Kenite or, more properly, Cainite tribe, whose eponymous
hero figures so prominently in the drama, was not agricultural but nomadic. It retained its unsettled habits
long after Israel and Judah had become organized nations;
in fact, it is this nomadic trait which the story explains
as punishment for the ancestral sin. How then does it
happen that the founder of the tribe is described in Scripture
as a farmer? The tortuous explanations offered by the
commentators avail us nothing; it is clear that the basic
myth has undergone inversion as well as conversion. Cain
could originally have stood for no other class than the
nomadic shepherds of the southern wilderness, and Abel,
his brother, was consequently the peasant. The Kenite
bards, to whom we owe the story in its simplest form,
pictured in it a raid by their tribe on a neighboring rural
settlement, which was utterly destroyed. Our accounts of
the Kenites show that they were fully capable of such
butchery. Their women no less than their men were handy
with implements of death. That demure lady, Jael, who,
inviting a fleeing general into her house, dashed his brains
out while he bent over a bowl of milk which she had handed
him, was a Kenite. The contemporary Israelites whom
this brutal assassination saved from a tyrant's power were
indeed grateful, and sang: "Blessed above women shall
Jael be, the wife of Heber the Kenite" (Judg. 5.24). But
we, being removed from the scene of her Amazonian operations by some thirty-two centuries, may beg leave to doubt
her dove-like gentleness or the pacifism of the tribe which

produced her. We can readily see how her fellow-tribesmen would recall with joy the day of their victory, when they fell—like the Danites of a later day—on an unsuspecting, peaceful community and utterly destroyed every member of it. That Cain murdered Abel seemed to them a cause for rejoicing rather than for penitence.

But the Hebrew shepherds who adopted the tale from the Kenites, their near neighbors and friends, reconstructed it to suit their pacifist notions. They could not believe that Cain, the murderer, was a shepherd like themselves. Having no feeling of special loyalty to the name, they insisted that Abel, the slain victim, was the shepherd, and that he had died at the hands of a farmer-brother. The reason for Cain's jealousy was, they said, that God had preferred Abel's offering of sheep to his own sacrifice of fruit. This last detail, which has so much puzzled the readers of the Scripture, is final proof of the shepherd origin of the transformed story. Smile as we may at the thought, the ancient shepherd truly believed that God preferred him to the peasant.[10] He recalled that Abraham, Isaac, Jacob, Moses and David had all been chosen from the shepherd group; Rachel was a shepherd lass, and so was Zipporah, the wife of Moses. High merit attached, in his opinion, to the occupation of sheep-tending; and it was altogether fitting that the first martyr in history should come from its midst.

In its attempt to inculcate the lesson of peace, the Torah intentionally employs a current tale to the morals of which it is diametrically opposed. Through this device it gains a double pedagogic advantage—it overcomes a social danger, and actually makes it serve a useful purpose. The poison is transformed into its own antidote. No one could hope to eradicate the memory of so popular a tale as that of Cain-Abel. The alternative—and a far better one—was to alter its fundamental character. It was with a similar double purpose in view that the writer of Scripture recast the polytheistic myth of Abraham's encounter with the three numina into a monotheistic picture of a divine theophany.[11] "The wood of the forest must be made the means of its being cut down."[12]

The history of the patriarchs is pervaded by the pacifist motif evident in the Cain-Abel allegory.[13] Abraham, Isaac, and Jacob never sought battle. Abraham waged war, as related in the fourteenth chapter of Genesis, against the kings who seized his nephew, but having freed him, the patriarch declined to accept any of the booty. Simeon and Levi did indeed destroy the city of Shechem, but their action was denounced by Jacob in his last blessing. Abraham actually made a covenant of peace with the Philistines, promising never to attack them. "And it came to pass at that time, that Abimelech and Phicol the captain of his host spoke unto Abraham, saying: 'God is with thee in all that thou doest. Now therefore swear unto me here by God that thou wilt not deal falsely with me, nor with my son, nor with my son's son; but according to the kindness that I have done unto thee, thou shalt do unto me, and to the land wherein thou hast sojourned.' And Abraham said: 'I will swear'" (Gen. 21.22 f.). To appreciate the full meaning of the story, the reader must remember that the Philistines were the most persistent enemies of the Israelites. From the day they landed on the west coast of Palestine (to which, by the way, they gave its name) until the end of the Commonwealth, they were almost always at war with the Judaites. The Israelitish monarchy was in part established to oppose united strength to the Philistine confederation, and David's prestige arose largely from his victories over the ancient enemies. As early as Samson's day, when intermarriage with Canaanites was not yet considered wicked, his parents objected to his taking to wife the daughter of "the uncircumcised" Philistines, who were so cruelly harassing their people. To declare that this people had been hospitable to Abraham and Isaac, and that a covenant of peace had been made between the two peoples, required courage and boldness.

The Torah further describes the Israelites, coming from Egypt, as pacifists. They waged no war which could possibly be avoided. Their claim to the land of Canaan is based not on force, but on God's promise to Abraham (Gen. 15.18). The land had been forfeited by its sinful inhabitants and was rightfully transferred to another people. Indeed, the Israelites were sent to Egypt for four hundred years until the measure of Amoritic wickedness might be full (ibid. v. 16). On their way to their land, the Israelites were opposed by the Transjordanian kings, Sihon and Og. They begged for the right of neutral passage. " 'Let me pass through thy land; we will not turn aside into field or into vineyard; we will not drink of the water of the wells; we will go by the king's highway until we have passed thy border' " (Num. 21.22). When Sihon and Og declined to permit them entry, Israel met them in battle.

But the pacifism of the fundamental law was as little accepted in the rural districts as its teaching of human equality. The first literary prophets who disagreed so widely in their attitude toward social conflict were equally opposed to each other in their conception of Israel and the other nations. What united them was their common enthusiasm for the God of Israel and their hatred of idols. But there was a great difference in the degree of their nationalist fervor. Amos was a universalist; he states his doctrine clearly and unequivocally. "Are ye not as the children of the Ethiopians unto Me, O children of Israel?" he asks, in the name of the Lord. "Have not I brought up Israel out of the land of Egypt, and the Philistines from Caphtor, and Aram from Kir?" (9.7). All peoples are equal before the Lord.

Amos opens his book with a significant arraignment of the nations of the world before the bar of Divine Justice. One by one he calls them and indicts them: Damascus, Philistia, Tyre, Edom, Ammon, Moab, and finally Israel and Judah, who by implication are no different from the others.

Hosea was altogether without any understanding of this universalism. Just as he was unaware of any social struggle between rich and poor, so he was blind to the fundamental equality of his own people with all others. He loved his people with a passion, still vibrant in cold print. The doom, which as a prophet of the angry and forsaken God he foretold for the nation, gave him the deepest anguish, as he described it. He was not, like Amos, the righteous judge; he was a helpless advocate who realized his client's iniquity.

"How shall I give thee up, Ephraim?
How shall I surrender thee, Israel?
How shall I make thee as Admah?
How shall I set thee as Zeboim?" (11.8).

"When Israel was a child, then I loved him,
And out of Egypt I called My son" (11.1).

"I found Israel like grapes in the wilderness,
I saw your fathers as the first-ripe in the fig-tree at
   her first season" (9.10).

Even when he prophesies doom, it is with a lump in his
throat, with tears ready to pour down his cheeks. We can
almost hear the repressed sob when he says:

"Shall I ransom them from the power of the nether-
   world?
Shall I redeem them from death?
Ho, thy plagues, O death!
Ho, thy destruction, O nether-world!
Repentance be hid from Mine eyes!" (13.14).

There is nothing in Amos to correspond to this struggle
between the passion for justice and the love of country. It
cannot be a mere coincidence that the two country prophets,
Hosea and Jeremiah, should also be the two in whom the
relation of God to Israel is most continually described as
marital. The prophets transferred to God Himself the deep
feeling which pervaded their hearts when they thought of
their people. Hosea was in fact typical of a whole line of
Jewish teachers who, reared in the country and feeling its
prejudices, had yet come under the influence of the plebeian
doctrine of God. In every generation we find in them a
curious admixture of conflicting ideologies and sympathies,
as they struggled to reconcile in themselves the heart of
the country with the intellect of the city.

But if such was the patriotic passion of the critical
prophet, how deep and engrossing must have been the
nationalism, how narrow the chauvinism, of his untutored
fellows on the farm?   After all, Hosea had been called

of the Lord and was the prophetic associate of plebeian pacifists. If the love of nation had such a powerful hold on him, how completely must it have enshrouded the country gentry, with their inexperience, their martial ambitions and their provincial contempt for aliens.

The varying ideologies of the two prophets Amos and Hosea thus indicate the existence in that early time of two distinct social philosophies: that of the pacifist plebeians and that of the nationalist provincials. Beyond both was that of the patricians, which never appears in prophecy, because it altogether lacked spiritual ideals. For it, we must turn not to the pages of inspired oratory but to the chronicles of historical events. Here we find the patricians most prominent, since the destiny of the land lay in their hands. The provincials also appear; but the plebeians, so important in prophecy, were at first, at least, of too little importance in politics to figure at all.

The different political views can be traced back almost to the beginning of Israel's settlement in Canaan, when for the first time the ancient distinction between patrician leaders and plebeian followers was translated into economic terms. In the wilderness, the clans had lived under a peculiar system of political autocracy and economic democracy. They were essentially communes, all of whose members were equal in the enjoyment of the clan's property and supplies. The sheik had indeed almost unlimited authority, but this was in no manner personal. He was merely the personification of the clan. He could give no special privileges to his sons and daughters; he could bequeath to them no disproportionate privileges in the clan's possessions; he could not free them from any of their clan obligations. So meager, indeed, were the possessions of these desert groups that any unequal division would have involved obvious and intense suffering, such as could only be inflicted in punishment for clear wrong-doing. Moreover, the constant danger from hostile neighbors and from the terrifying elements made the conception of individual possession a manifest absurdity. No one standing alone could live for more than a few days; how then could he think of himself as independent of his clansmen?

Such was the fundamental democracy of this tribal organization, that when the Hebrews entered Canaan, they reduced the division between upper and lower classes which they found there to the narrowest proportions. The sharp contrast between the palaces of the Canaanite rich and the hovels of their poor, disappears in the archaeological level of Israel's invasion; their big houses are smaller, and their small houses larger, than those of their Canaanite predecessors.

Yet in the course of time the new agricultural life combined with the example set by the ousted Canaanites to disrupt the primitive sense of clan solidarity, and with it the consciousness of equality among the members. The land was divided among the individual members of the clans, and immediately the family superseded the larger group as the unit of economic organization.[14] The patrician leaders now had their fields, as the plebeian followers had theirs. Failure of one's crop led to personal suffering which was in no wise shared by one's neighbor. Each man's fields descended from him to his children, fixing the amount of their supplies forever. When the clan went out to battle, the spoils were no longer taken into a common treasury for distribution as they might be needed. They were divided at once among the warriors; and it was altogether natural

that the patrician leaders of the armies should seize the
choice lands and slaves for themselves and their children.
This further widened the breach between leaders and
followers; it was not merely the sheik who held a place of
primacy in the community, but his family, his household,
and his estates. The ancient tradition could not, of course,
be altogether destroyed. The Israelitish community remained until the very end one of the most democratic in
the whole Orient. The King could be approached by the
meanest commoner;[15] and was subject to reproof by
individual subject as well as by assembled tribesmen. The
gathering of all the members of the tribe remained the
final legislative authority, whenever it was convoked.[16]
Nevertheless, it was obvious that the old chieftain-ruled
democracies had given way to a new oligarchy of powerful
patrician landowners.

Once a breach was created between patricians and
plebeians, it became part of the fundamental policy of the
upper class to widen it through new conquests and further
self-enrichment. Looking down from the hills of Judah and
Ephraim, which the Israelites already possessed, the
patricians saw stretched out before them a far goodlier
land, with luxuriant vineyards, rich cities, fine houses,
many chariots, quick horses, and innumerable slaves. They
could not restrain their hunger for this desirable morsel,
and could not persuade themselves that they had less right
to the rich spoils of this coastal plain than to the meager
returns of the hill country.

That the lowlands could be conquered only with the
help of the plebeians, who were gradually being submerged,
was obvious. The generals could march forth against their

enemies only if they were followed by devoted bands of passionate and deluded soldiers. The aim of the patrician thus became twofold: to whet the plebeian's appetite for war, without giving him more than a minimum of its spoils.[17]

There was only one difficulty in the way of the success of this plan: it was opposed by a group of people who considered riches an evil and covetousness rebellion against God. Their doctrine of the simple life, described in chapter 10, was irreconcilable with wars of aggrandizement. They showed the plebeians how their standard of living in the hills of Palestine was at least as high as that of their ancestors had been in the wilderness. To demand more was, in their opinion, sheer contumacy and apostasy.

These arguments may sound quite strange to us in the twentieth century, but they had a powerful effect on some of the ancient peasantry. They came to oppose war not because it might lead to ruin, but lest it bring enrichment; they feared victory no less than defeat. They recoiled from wealth as from idolatry; indeed, the two became inseparable in their untutored but inspired minds.

Even those plebeians, however, who could not follow the argument of the advocates of the simple life could be made to understand that they had little to gain from following the patricians into battle. That was so simple a fact that even the simplest could comprehend it. There thus grew up two factions in ancient Israel: one patrician, militarist, and expansionist; the other plebeian, quietist, and opposed to all aggression. Through factors which have been described in the previous chapters,[18] the first became identified with the assimilationist worship of the Baal, the second with the prophetic loyalty to the God of Israel.

The issue did not reach critical proportions so long as the opponents of the Israelites were the Canaanites, whom they had been dispossessing from the beginning. It entered a new stage, when the tribes, having suppressed the intervening Canaanite groups, found themselves face to face with another enemy, the Philistines, who had settled on the southwestern coast of the land shortly after the Israelites had crossed the Jordan.

The conflict which ensued between the two peoples was not easily decided; it lasted in its full virulence for more than a hundred years. The Hebrews had the advantages of preponderant numbers and the strategic bases in their hills; the Philistines, those of superior equipment, better organization, and war on their own soil. The Samson legend preserves a vivid recollection of the beginnings of the protracted war.[19] The patricians, anxious to fan the national spirit of the Israelites into a consuming hatred for their opponents, resorted to every trick of propaganda. The character, worship, and personal habits of the lowland strangers were maligned. The Philistines were declared to be mean and treacherous, as well as weak and stupid (Judg. 14.18; 16.1 ff.). Their god, Dagon, became a butt for mocking wits (I Sam. 5.4); and their failure to adopt the universal Palestinian custom of circumcision was declared a sufficient reason against intermarriage with them (Judg. 14.3).

Little could be achieved, however, until the patricians obtained the assistance of the priests of Shiloh, the foremost sanctuary of the Ephraimites, then the leading tribe in Israel. This highland shrine had originally, like that of Beth-el, doubtless been devoted to the plebeian ideals of the simple life.[20] Two factors, however, tended to raise it to a preëminence dangerous to its traditions: the increasing prosperity of the Ephraimites, its worshipers; and the possession of the sacred Ark of Mosaic origin. In time, it surpassed in importance even the patrician temple at Gilgal; and it was then that it itself became the center of patrician worship and influence. The defection from tradition was marked, in the first instance, by the adoption of the pagan rite of vineyard dances and bride seizures during the autumnal vintage festival (Judg. 21.19) and apparently also of Canaanite fertility orgies, including the defilement of the "women that did service at the door of the tent of meeting" by the priests themselves (I Sam. 2.22). The priesthood, who thus fell away from the high ethical standards of their Levitical ancestors, were openly accused not only of Canaanite licentiousness, but of greed and avarice. Slave-owners like other patricians, the priests would send their servants to collect their portions of the sacrificial meat; and the servants refusing to accept the parts fixed by custom and tradition, threatened to use force if the priests' exorbitant demands were not met.[21]

The curious fact that the two latest priests of this Temple—Hofni and Phinehas—bore non-Hebraic names, completes the chain of evidence against them.[22] Like the Jasons and Menelauses of later days, they were not only secularized and patrician-minded,[23] but assimilationist, ashamed in their Hebrew sanctuary of their Hebrew language and their ancestral nomenclature, and anxious to imitate the "manner of Egypt and Canaan."

No wonder that these priests deserted the pacifist traditions of the plebeians and joined the patricians in their effort to seize new territory for Israel. When the conflict between Israel and the Philistines culminated in a fierce struggle at Aphek, near the northern end of the coastal plain, Hofni and Phinehas were ready not merely to join the armies of their people, but took the sacred Ark from its ancient shrine with them into the battle lines.

But neither the leadership of the warlike priests nor the presence of the sacred symbol could save the Israelites. The two-day battle cost them no less than thirty thousand lives; they were driven back in a wild rout, while the Ark of the Lord was captured and its priests were killed. The Philistines sweeping on in the wake of their great victory, burned the temple at Shiloh,[24] and established themselves as masters of the whole country.

The historian tells us little of the events which followed this crushing disaster. But, doubtless, the defeat of their armies, the death of their priests, the capture of the Ark, and the destruction of the sanctuary, must have made a deep impression on the people. The plebeian, anti-expansionist party which had almost ceased to exist, was revived, and insisted more vigorously than ever that Israel's defeat had been due to the betrayal of God by His priests, pointing to the setback as proof of their doctrine that God was opposed to the policy of aggression.

The influence of the plebeian group was further augmented through the rise of a new leader who expounded its principle with greater force and clarity than had any of his predecessors—the seer, Samuel. The meager records of his life and activity which have been preserved do not permit a complete reconstruction of his personality. Yet there can be no doubt that he was one of the foremost religious teachers Israel has produced. A highland Ephraimite by birth,[25] he was thoroughly imbued with the desert tradition of the simple life and the new shepherd doctrine of non-agression, and used the tremendous force of his personality and his keen statesmanly insight to further both causes. Indeed, his whole life may be regarded as an attempt to establish the two fundamental plebeian doctrines as the cornerstones of the Israelitish Commonwealth.

Apparently he was raised in the temple of Shiloh, as a Nazirite, who had been dedicated to God by his mother. When the temple of Shiloh was destroyed, he undertook to establish a new sanctuary for his tribe in Ramah. Such, however, was the prestige which he ultimately attained that he was called from time to time to preside also over the more ancient sanctuaries of Mizpah, Beth-el, and even Gilgal.[26] When his sons—named Abijah, "YHWH is my father" and Joel, "YHWH is God"—became old enough for priestly service, he placed them in the shrine of Beer-sheba, in the coastal plain.[27] His influence thus extended through a large part of the country.

While the Israelites, and particularly the tribe of Ephraim, remembered the crushing defeat they had suffered at Aphek, Samuel was their ideal leader. He brought them the inspiration of the God of their fathers, taught them to resist the Baal worship, and discouraged them from undertaking any wars even against their conquerors. But as he grew old, the seer discovered that a new generation had arisen about him, who refused to resign themselves to subjection to the Philistines. They listened with impatience to the seer's pacific doctrines.[28] So long as the Philistine governor ruled in Gibeah they would have nothing to do with the acceptance of the status quo. They considered the disaster which had befallen their people a direct result of disunion, and called for the organization of the Hebrew tribes under a military, rather than a religious, leader.

How far Samuel himself shared this feeling, it is impossible to say. The later of the two accounts of his activity, declares that he opposed the movement to appoint a King. But it is altogether probable, as has been maintained, that this tradition originated in circles which in subsequent generations looked back on the period of the Judges as a Golden Age, and considered the establishment of Israelite royalty a national misfortune.

Either, then, of his own initiative or driven by the force of public opinion, Samuel decided to seek a king to unify the Israelite tribes.[29] With unusual adroitness, he selected for the office not a fellow-tribesman, but a Benjaminite, a young warrior, who was a working farmer, not a patrician, and was definitely a member of the YHWH-following.[30] Such a person, Samuel must have felt certain, would insure the continued loyalty of the newly created state to the God of the fathers.

The appointment of a King over a united Israel[31] was the more significant because it ran counter to the Canaanite tendency of the period, which was to substitute oligarchy for monarchy, and independent city states for federated governments.

It is altogether probable that Samuel, having made his choice, confided his decision to Saul. At any rate, when the opportunity came, Saul was ready to seize it. The Ammonites attacked the city of Jabesh-gilead in Transjordan; and its inhabitants appealed to their brethren throughout Israel for aid. When the call came to Saul, he immediately announced his readiness to respond, and sent a summons for help to all the tribes. An army gathered about him, they crossed the Jordan, dealt the Ammonites a crushing defeat, and returned triumphantly to announce Saul as the new King.

As has already been observed, Saul's first act showed Samuel that he had made a mistake in his choice;[32] the new King chose the patrician shrine of Gilgal[33] as the place of his anointment, and did not even await Samuel's coming to inaugurate the sacrifice. There was no time for recrimination, however; the Philistines, hearing of the appointment of an Israelite King, were preparing to make battle against them. A fortunate chance gave Saul and his son, Jehonathan, another victory over the enemies of their people; and fully established the new kingdom.[34]

But it was soon obvious that Saul's choice of Gilgal as the shrine for anointment was no accidental error of judgment. The highland peasant was determined to please the patricians and to follow their policies, in order that he might win their recognition. He signalized his conversion to the patrician cause, by openly announcing his adherence to the Baal, the lowland agricultural God, whose very name was anathema to the prophets. He had called his first son, born before his accession to the throne, Jehonathan, "YHWH hath given"; but the two youngest, princes from the cradle, were named Ishbaal,[35] "the man of Baal," and Merib-baal (II Sam. 21.8), a name which was also given to Jehonathan's son (ibid. 4.4; 9.6).[36]

This was not all. Rejecting the whole of Samuel's doctrine of non-aggression, Saul slew many of the Gibeonites, a native people with whom the Israelites had an ancient treaty, and confiscated the Gibeonite lands for himself and his fellow-Benjaminites.[37] Then, having freed the country of the Philistine yoke, he pursued the enemy into their own territory, obtaining further estates for his retainers. As a result of these activities Gibeon became the center of the Benjaminite highland territory, while its lowland section extended far into the *shefelah*. Like many other conquerors, the Benjaminites transferred to their new lowland estates the names of the villages from which they had come, and have thus perpetuated the record of their raid on the Philistines.[38]

These unexpected developments took Samuel by surprise; yet he was unwilling to admit that he had committed an error. He continued his efforts to win the King back to the plebeian prophetic cause; and sometimes Samuel appeared to be making headway. Saul agreed to suppress the necromancers, although he himself believed in their power (I Sam. 28.9). And finally he was even persuaded to desist from his war against the Philistines, and to undertake an expedition against the Amalekite nomads who were harassing the Judaite shepherds. The King and the prophet both intended, doubtless, to utilize this occasion to renew the alliance between the throne and the prophetic following, in general, and the tribe of Judah, in particular.[39] The event, however, proved Saul's undoing. He was completely victorious over the Amalekites, it is true. But his inability to understand Samuel's point of view regarding the war created a permanent breach between the two men. Samuel considered the expedition against the Amalekites not a war of conquest, like those which Saul had undertaken against the Philistines, but "a war of the Lord" to protect His people from unjust attack. The booty taken in such a struggle was holy; to use it for profane purposes was a sacrilege. It was *herem*, tabu, fit only for destruction "before the Lord."[40] Such wanton annihilation of booty was entirely in accord with the prophetic spirit, which feared enrichment even more than war, but it was quite foreign to the mentality of Saul. Blind to this conception of the battle, the King seized the possessions of the Amalekites, and divided them among his men, reserving only a few as hecatombs for the Lord.

Samuel's dismay when he heard of these proceedings can hardly be exaggerated. The King had once more violated his trust; but this time more shamelessly than ever before. He had undertaken the expedition against the Amalekites at the instance of Samuel; he had used it *to wean the Judaite shepherds away from Samuel's doctrines.* By offering the people part of the booty which had been taken from the Philistines, he had dramatically demonstrated the real significance of a war of conquest, and had endeavored, at least, to make them less willing to listen to the prophetic teachings of self-abnegation.

It is only when we realize the enormity of Saul's betrayal that we can understand the vehemence of Samuel's anger. The prophet who had patiently borne Saul's adoption of the patrician militaristic policies, his conversion to Baal, and his expansionist wars in Philistia, was outraged when the "holy war" was made an occasion for forbidden enrichment. Samuel had intended his *herem* to be a suppression of what we might call "war profits"—a faltering, and primitive, if cruel, step toward ultimate pacifism; he could not endure the frustration of the effort.

It was probably soon after this incident that Saul realized the futility of his efforts to establish a permanent dynasty in Israel. He had lost the support of the prophetic group; the patricians were his masters, not his servants. Able general as he was and, in some respects, astute leader, he was altogether inadequate for the task to which he had been called. Perhaps no one could have succeeded better. The establishment of a throne among powerful patrician leaders, who had become accustomed to oligarchic rule, required genius of the rarest order. But Saul was singularly lacking in the basic elements of character necessary for even partial achievement of his aims. He had no gift for political organization or for appeal to mass enthusiasm. The people admired him and were grateful to him; he did not know how to make them love him. The consciousness of his failure, joined to the anxieties of office, threw the former peasant into despondency.

To brighten his melancholy, young David was brought to Court. He was a member of the powerful family of Jesse of Bethlehem, Judah, and may have been sent as a pledge of the tribe's loyalty. From the first David captivated all who came in contact with him. He soothed the king's temper; became the most intimate friend of Jonathan, the heir apparent; and won the love of Michal, one of the princesses.[41] Saul, however, was not destined to enjoy his company long. The young man's military skill and courage amazed his elders; and the King soon realized that the pleasing minstrel might readily become a dangerous rival. The plebeian shepherds of the Judaite highlands were far from contented with Saul's rule; what more natural than that they should try to place their own tribesman on the throne of Israel, or at least to secede under his leadership from the Israelite federation?

The sequel is well known. Suspicion created the evil it feared. Saul made an attempt on David's life; David fled to the wilderness of Judah, where he became the leader of an outlaw band; the King, infuriated by this development, seized Ahimelech, the priest of Nob, who had given

David some food during his flight, and slaughtered Ahimelech and all his fellow-priests; Ebiathar, the son of the martyred Ahimelech, naturally fled to David for refuge, giving the outlaw the prestige of ecclesiastical sanction. David's own tribesmen, the Judaites, however, far from sympathizing with him, resented his exactions and tried to betray him to the King; one of the few rich landowners of the neighborhood, Nabal, actually resisted David's demands. Nabal would have paid with his life for this temerity, had not Abigail, his courageous, quick-thinking wife, realized their danger and hastened to appease the outlaws with suitable gifts. When shortly thereafter her husband died, she became David's wife, bringing him sufficient property to make him a patrician in his own right. Nevertheless, fearing Saul more than ever, David had to flee from the land and seek shelter with the Philistines, the traditional enemies of his people.

Meanwhile, Saul, freed from the restraining influence of Samuel, had given himself over entirely to an anti-Philistine, expansionist, patrician policy. The protracted struggle culminated in a second battle at Aphek, and once again Israel met with a crushing defeat. Saul and three of his sons were killed; the Israelitish army was driven back into the valley of Jezreel and even across the Jordan. The efforts of a lifetime had been wasted; Israel was once more vassal to the Philistines.

Fortunately for David, the Philistine generals had declined to permit him to participate in the battle, and had thus saved him from choosing between treason to his people and betrayal of his hosts. When the war was over, he was free to accept the kingship of the tribe of Judah, which was at once offered him. Apparently even the patricians of that tribe, who had resented his exactions as an outlaw, saw that he had become too powerful to resist and that it was better to have him as friend than as enemy. The rest of the tribes were under the direct rule of the Philistines, who appointed a governor with his home in Gibeah, Saul's capital. Only across the Jordan, did Abner, Saul's general, manage to set up a petty government for his master's sole remaining son, Ishbaal.

Both Ishbaal and David were, of course, vassals of the Philistines, who permitted them to reign, because they preferred a divided to a united Israel. The Philistines did not even interfere when Abner and his army crossed the Jordan and invested Gibeon, in the territory of Benjamin, where many of the exiled Benjaminites had their estates. David, however, who had been hoping to establish his rule over all Cisjordan, at once sent his army against Abner. David's followers were victorious and the kingdom of Ishbaal remained limited to the small territory across the Jordan.

The patrician leaders of Benjamin, Ephraim, and the other agricultural tribes to the north were now placed in a dilemma. To accept as their King the former Judaite shepherd, who had made war against Saul, become a leader of brigands, and entered into an alliance with the Philistines, was certainly humiliating. But there was only one alternative: continued vassalage to the Philistines. There was no possibility of breaking the Philistine yoke without David's help. There was no other military leader who could match his ability; and the coöperation of the Judaites, whom he controlled, was essential to any important warlike undertaking.

One man was especially disturbed by the situation:

Abner, Saul's cousin, and former general of the Israelitish army. His personal relationship to Ishbaal, his resentment of David's activities, and his sentimental attachment to the memory of Saul made the acceptance of the Judaite King particularly difficult for Abner. Yet two private considerations moved him, more than anyone else, to seek unity and peace: his desire to return to his estates in the land of Benjamin, and his ambition to regain the command of a united Israelitish army. If only he could bring himself to support David's claim to the throne, he could certainly obtain as a reward his old office — the second most distinguished in the kingdom. Indeed, David could find no better way of assuring the loyalty of Saul's former followers, and the northern tribes in general, than by offering this important place in the government to one who represented them.

The tension of this inner conflict between loyalty and ambition made Abner morose and irritable. His anger burst into fury, however, when Ishbaal upbraided him for having taken one of Saul's concubines. Throughout the east, such an act was considered seditious. But Ishbaal could hardly afford to alienate Abner, whose creature he was. The trivial incident decided his fate. Abner entered into negotiations with David and became intermediary between him and the northern patricians.

Abner had, however, left out of account the one person who, after David, was most concerned with these plans— the nephew and general-in-chief of the Judaite King, Joab, a man equally distinguished by almost Odyssean craft and boldness and total lack of scruple. Though nothing was told Joab of the purpose of Abner's visit, he had little difficulty in penetrating its meaning and was determined to defend

himself at all costs. As Abner left David on his way to
complete the arrangement with the heads of the northern
tribes, Joab waylaid and murdered him, on the pretext that
he had slain Asael, Joab's brother, in one of the battles
between the followers of Ishbaal and David.

The death of Abner was as fatal to Ishbaal as his continued life might have been. Not only did David recite a
moving eulogy over the fallen general, but he observed
personal mourning for him as for a near relative. "So all
the people, and all Israel understood that day that it was
not of the king to slay Abner the son of Ner" (II Sam. 3.37).
David's position with the patricians of Israel was thus not
at all weakened. On the contrary, everybody realized that
with Abner dead, Ishbaal could not long retain the rule of
his kingdom.

Within a short time, two ambitious Benjaminites, seeking
David's favor, crossed the Jordan, entered Ishbaal's room,
and murdered him. When they brought his head to David,
expecting a reward, he greeted them with furious anger and
ordered them executed. Nevertheless, the event brought
the tribes of Israel to his feet. Utterly leaderless, their
elders came to Hebron and proclaimed him king of the
united nation.

The new King was Saul's equal in personal strength,
courage and attractiveness. In addition he was a sweet
singer and a gifted poet. But above all he was a rare strat-
egist, an able general, a clever administrator, with a shrewd
understanding of the popular mind, as well as a deep affection for the masses, and democratic pleasure in mingling
with them. His intuitive tact proved invaluable to him in
the early days when the question of his succession hung in
the balance. The message he sent to the men of Jabesh-

gilead, thanking them for their piety, when they risked their lives to give burial to the bodies of Saul and his children; his mourning for Saul and then for Abner; his punishment of Ishbaal's assassins, won the hearts of all his subjects. It would be absurd to condemn these acts as mere hypocrisy. So masterful and moving a poem as the elegy over Saul and Jonathan, which most scholars accept as genuine,[42] could hardly be the product of dissimulation and pretended emotion. The truth is, doubtless, that David was a man of both deep feeling and unusual histrionic powers. Perhaps he himself could not have told how much of his grief for Saul was genuine, and how much intended "for effect." But whatever their psychological origin, his actions had the desired result — they brought him to the throne of a united people.

He achieved the union not merely of the tribes but also of the classes within them. The prophetic party hailed him as its own true son, the descendant of the shepherd clans, the opponent of the renegade Saul. The patricians saw in David a deliverer from the yoke of the oppressing Philistine. What his policy would be when the yoke was removed and the time for further conquest came, no one asked for the moment.

But David was not at all deceived by this acclaim. His native insight was supplemented by the valuable experience he had gained in the court of Saul and as leader of an outlaw band. He knew that the patricians had used Saul to advance their own interests; and David realized that they had accepted him as the lesser of two evils. If his kingdom was to be established, he needed a new patricianship—one of his own creation. He could achieve this aim only through the development of the commerce of Jerusalem, enriching some of the plebeians who became its traders.[43] This policy both he and his son, Solomon, pursued throughout their reigns.

In other simpler respects, David, too, favored the plebeians. He was utterly democratic, mingling freely with his subjects in their festivities, deigning even to don a light linen tunic, barely concealing the body, such as other celebrants wore on festive occasions. His closest friends were chosen from among the prophets; indeed, Nathan, the prophet, was apparently one of his chief counselors. David restored the Ark of the Lord to its ancient position of prominence; desisted from the erection of a formal temple when the prophet opposed the plan and declared his preference for the traditional tent-sanctuary;[44] his first children after his accession to the throne were named Abishalom, "My father is peace"; Adonijah, "YHWH is my Lord"; and Shefatiah, "YHWH is judge."[45]

Curiously the ease with which people approached David won him their love without losing him their respect. During the many years of his leadership of an outlaw band, he had mastered the technique of gaining both veneration and affection; of being democratic and at the same time commanding obedience. His wife, Michal, the daughter of Saul, could not, however, understand this. She reproved him for what she considered lack of princely dignity, only to receive the sharp rejoinder: "Before the Lord, who chose me above thy father, and above all his house, to appoint me prince over the people of the Lord, over Israel, before the Lord will I make merry. And I will be yet more vile than thus, and will be base in mine own sight; and with the handmaids whom thou hast spoken of, with them will I get me honour" (II Sam. 6.21).

Ebiathar, who had shared his sufferings and dangers for so many years, was elevated to the priesthood. But David was far too wary a king to entrust the highest ecclesiastical office to one person and to permit the establishment of a priestly dynasty which might rival his own. The priestly honors were divided between Ebiathar, Zadok, and finally also the "sons of David."[46]

His first problem was naturally the liberation of the land from the Philistines. When this had been accomplished,[47] he broke completely with the patricians who had controlled Saul. The King treated the Canaanites, whose lands the aristocrats coveted, with remarkable leniency, and yielded to the demand of the Gibeonites for seven members of Saul's family, whom they executed in vengeance for the evil that late king had done them (II Sam. 21.1 ff.). When he conquered the Jebusites, he permitted them to retain their lands, and even insisted on paying for the plot which he needed for his proposed sanctuary (ibid. 24.24). He apparently adopted the policy which had become traditional among the southern tribes, Judah and Simeon, of relying on assimilation to solve the problem of the antagonism between Israelites and natives.[48]

His relations with the Tyrians were especially friendly. He hired their artisans to build his cedar palace, and planned, doubtless, to rely on them in the erection of his sanctuary, had that proposal been carried out. There was no reason for conflict with this people. He could not compete for their sea-trade; and, on the other hand, he needed their help in obtaining foreign markets for the products of his country.

Yet David was not a true follower of prophecy.[49] He had no real love for peace and the simple life. His policy toward the Canaanites and the Philistines was dictated by a definitely mundane consideration, namely his desire to defeat the patricians through the establishment of a dominating trading community in his capital.

From some points of view, he might have preferred to establish his capital nearer the center of the country than Jerusalem was. But it was essential to his plans that he remain near the tribe of Judah, on whose loyalty he thought he could depend. The boundary between that tribe and Benjamin was thus the northern limit to which he could go. On the other hand, except for its geographical eccentricity, Jerusalem was admirably well placed for the capital of the Kingdom. It was an almost impregnable fortress; its climate was temperate and salubrious; it had an ancient tradition as a sacred city; it had been newly conquered, and thus belonged to none of the tribes. It lacked but one necessity, water. But, of course, David could not have anticipated the brilliant future which awaited his capital, and the enormous population it would have to maintain from the few springs and cisterns with which it was provided.

In order to establish Jerusalem and its commercial groups on a firm basis, David resorted to conquests — not, however, in Philistia, but in Transjordan, where he could obtain an abundance of copper, and where he could seize the great desert trade routes. Both the Arabah and Aram-zobah were famous for their mines, and control of them was essential for the commercial revolution which the king projected. The seizure of the Arabah was necessary to open the road to the Gulf of Akaba, with the possibility of developing a southern sea-trade.

Following this policy, David seized on various pretexts

to make war on all the Transjordanian nations. Whether it be true that the King of Ammon was mad enough to insult the messengers whom David had sent to him to express sympathy on the death of his father, we can no longer tell (II Sam. 10.1 ff.). Perhaps they were instructed to make suggestions to the new King which provoked his resentment and insulting treatment. At any rate, David lost no time in using the supposed affront as an occasion for war and reducing Ammon to a province of Israel. The same policy was followed with regard to the Edomites, the Moabites, and the people of Aram-zobah. Even Damascus was conquered, and placed under the control of an Israelite governor (ibid. 8.6).

The tribute exacted from these defeated peoples enriched the national treasury and built up the commercial prestige of Jerusalem. The old patrician group obtained nothing, and neither did the plebeians. Only those who settled in Jerusalem received any reward at all; they found a new opportunity for work and trade in the growing city.

The disciples of Samuel did not at once realize the full significance of David's activity. The change from the older policy of patrician aggressiveness to the newer policy of commercial expansion had been too abrupt. They doubtless considered the attack on Edom unjustified, and could only point to the ancient tradition which describes Esau as a bluff, but good brother, as a reason for leaving his descendants in peace. Esau had had Jacob at his mercy, and yet had spared him (Gen. 33.4 ff.); would it not behoove Israel to act with similar generosity toward Esau's descendants? Lot, the ancestor of Ammon and Moab, had parted from Abraham in great friendship (ibid. 13.11) and was a man of fine, hospitable instincts (ibid. 19.1 ff.), in spite of his crude manners. The Arameans were of Abraham's family; Abraham, Isaac, and Jacob, had sought their wives among them.

Yet these suggestions did not take the form of any strong protest against the Davidic policy. The plebeians saw that their opponents, the patricians, were not growing in strength, and waited for the result of David's activity before rendering final judgment.

But the patricians, both of Judah and of the other tribes, were under no illusions regarding the probable outcome of David's wars. They had carried a heavy burden during the wars, supplying men and means, but they had received nothing in return. The number of their slaves did not increase, their estates were not extended, the patricians were in no way enriched.

The dissatisfaction which resulted from this new policy would alone have shaken David's throne. Combined with it, however, was a graver peril arising from his own family, for David's excellence in every aspect of public life was outweighed by his weakness as a father. The sordid tale of his unfortunate family life has been immortalized in the remarkably objective, yet profoundly moving history contained in the Second Book of Samuel. Amnon, David's oldest son and his heir-apparent, inheriting his father's passionate nature, had violated Tamar, his half-sister. Her shame had been avenged by Absalom, who was her full brother, and incidentally was next to Amnon in the line of succession. Fearing David's wrath, Absalom fled, but ultimately returned, and was forgiven. Realizing, however, that David would probably not permit him to inherit the throne, the wily young man undertook to seize it by force. He easily won the ear of the dissatisfied patricians, both of Judah and the other tribes, and when he announced himself as King in Hebron, the ancient capital of Judah, he had a sufficiently large following to drive David from Jerusalem. The King, however, escaped across the Jordan, where his policy had won all of Saul's former friends over to his side. When Absalom pursued him, a battle resulted in which the prince was killed and his army defeated.

This did not, however, end the resistance to David. The patricians of the various tribes, left without a candidate for the throne, were still unprepared to submit to the King. Only after prolonged negotiations in which David appealed to his blood kinship with the Judaites, and promised Amasa, who had been the leader of the rebel armies, the chief generalship in place of Joab, was David able to return to Jerusalem.

Yet the North remained unreconciled. Sheba, son of Bichri, a Benjaminite, proposed that the kingship be abolished altogether and the earlier tribal amphictyony reëstablished. "We have no portion in David," he cried, "neither have we inheritance in the son of Jesse; every man to his tents, O Israel" (II Sam. 20.1). David, keeping his promise, sent Amasa out to gather an army against Sheba. Whether through negligence or inability, Amasa was delayed, and David was compelled to turn for aid to his nephew Abishai, the brother of Joab. Abishai and Joab came up with Amasa in Gibeon, slew him, and taking charge of the army pursued the rebels. Finally Sheba was entrapped in the city of Abel of Beth-maacah, where he was slain.

So completely had the rebels been vanquished that when David died, a short time later, the kingship passed to his son, Solomon, without any difficulty.

Solomon lacked David's military skill, and Benaiah ben Jehoiada, who was his general-in-chief, was no substitute for Joab. Not only were they unable to enhance the Davidic empire, they could not even hold it together. One of the vassals of the King of Zobah, whom David had conquered, had fled to the desert and become a bandit leader. He now conquered Damascus and established a kingdom there which was to rival, and at times to control, that of Israel. Hadad the Edomite, who had fled to Egypt when David seized his country, returned and gained control of the mountains with their rich copper mines; only the valley of the Arabah with its port at Ezion-geber remained under the control of the Israelites.

In spite of these losses, the domain over which Solomon ruled was extensive, and he was able to pursue David's mercantile policies further and actually to establish Jerusalem as a great trading center. The annual income of his government is put at no less than six hundred and sixty talents of gold, the equivalent in weight of about thirty-five millions of dollars (1935). Even if this figure represents not the average, but an unusually prosperous year, it still indicates an extraordinary change in Palestinian economy since the days of Saul. The country had ceased to be purely agricultural and pastoral; it had become largely commercial.

The expanding trade required new capital; and in order to obtain this, Solomon sold a strip of land in Galilee to the Phoenicians for one hundred and twenty talents of gold (a little more than six millions of dollars). With these moneys, he could undertake the vast building operations which made his reign so memorable: the royal palace and the Temple in Jerusalem, the fortifications of Beth-horon and Gezer, as well as those of the capital, and the stables for his horses in Lachish, Gezer, Megiddo, and Taanach.

These activities could not, however, be maintained merely through the profits of foreign trade and the sale of a strip of land. Heavy taxes were laid on the people, and large numbers of them were drafted for labor in the quarries and in the timberland. The men put in charge of the corvée and the collection of taxes were frequently plebeians. We know that at least one, Jeroboam, who was in charge of the Ephraimite corvée, was the son of a poor widow, who began his governmental service as a laborer in the fortifications of Jerusalem (I Kings 11.26). Solomon recognized his ability and appointed him overseer of all the workers of his tribe. It is significant, doubtless, that most of the governors of the various districts are called by patronymics rather than by their personal names (ibid. 4.9 ff.). It is clear that Solomon was consciously carrying out the plans which David had laid for the establishment of a new metropolitan officialdom, raised from the plebeian groups.[50]

Solomon's many marriages were intended to confirm treaty arrangements and to stimulate trade. That he had to permit these foreign princesses to worship their own gods was a light matter with the new King, who apparently did not hesitate even to worship Melkart, the god of Tyre, when he visited that city (ibid. 11.5).

By the end of Solomon's reign, Jerusalem controlled Judah and the South. The new aristocracy was sufficiently powerful to prevent the older patricians from rebelling against Solomon or his successor, as their ancestors under Absalom had rebelled against David. But the metropolis of the south could not control the northern tribes, where the patricians were all-powerful and dissatisfied. Forced labor, heavy taxes, and the centralization of government were innovations which brought them no benefit. The splendor of Solomon's capital interested the former oligarchs but little; they were keenly aware, however, of the sacrifices which they had to make to maintain it.

Joined with them in opposition to the new economy were plebeians of the hill country. They were as opposed to Solomon's luxurious buildings as they had been to those of the earlier patricians. The importation of horses still seemed to the plebeians unforgivable apostasy.[51] When in addition Solomon permitted his wives to conduct heathen worship in Jerusalem, the plebeians were amazed. It did not occur to them that this was part of international courtesy; their God was a jealous God who could not brook idol worship. Thus the building of the Temple, far from winning the plebeian YHWH worshipers to Solomon, actually estranged them from him.

The truth was, of course, that Solomon's mercantile patricianship was fully as assimilationist, opportunist and militarist (when that policy paid) as the old agricultural oligarchy had been. There was only this difference; the horizons of the new nobility were wider. Instead of adopting the manners of the neighboring Canaanites, they went for their patterns to distant Tyre, Egypt, and Mesopotamia.

The plebeians realized at last that they had been deceived. What many of them had considered the acceptance of their policy of the simple life, was far more dangerous than the older patrician policy had been. Whatever might have been true of David, who had already become an almost legendary figure, Solomon was as ambitious for increased wealth and power as any anti-Philistine, patrician landowner had ever been. The period of the Judges, with all its chaos, disorganization, tribal power, and patrician leadership, now appeared to have been a golden age. The establishment of the Kingdom seemed an error, and it was generally asserted that Samuel had acquiesced in it under compulsion and against his better judgment.[52]

Discontent led to sedition even during Solomon's lifetime. Jeroboam son of Nebat, whom the King had raised from the ranks to the command of the Ephraimitic corvée, rebelled, and received the support of Ahijah of Shiloh, an Ephraimitic prophet. Solomon's quick action prevented the rebellion from making any headway, and Jeroboam had to flee to Egypt. When, however, the King died, the opposition to the Davidic dynasty and its policy expressed itself more forcefully. An assembly of the northern tribes gathered at Shechem, one of their most ancient sanctuaries, and fixed the terms on which, alone, they would accept Rehoboam, the son of Solomon, as their King. Rehoboam, badly advised, refused to make any concessions, and the Assembly, instead of ratifying his appointment, rejected him utterly. "What portion have we in David!" they cried, echoing the words of Sheba son of Bichri, "neither have we inheritance in the son of Jesse; to your tents, O Israel; now see to thine own house, David" (I Kings 12.16). These words imply a determination to return to the oligarchic tribal government of the period of the Judges, and doubtless that was in the minds of the rebels. But Jeroboam, hearing of the unrest, returned from Egypt and managed to obtain his election as King of the northern tribes. Judah, and the tribe of Simeon which had practically merged with it, remained loyal to Rehoboam.

Neither of the two kingdoms could carry on the imperial-istic activity of David and Solomon. Judah, which con-tained the growing metropolis of Jerusalem, was too small and too poor. In territory it was about a third that of the northern kingdom; the disproportion in wealth and fertility was even greater. A large part of the country was covered by arid desert and by stony highlands which were scarcely more fertile. There was no possibility that the tiny state would be able to hold David's Transjordanian conquests in subjection. Cut off from essential supplies of copper, which it was receiving from these provinces, as well as from the taxes and agricultural products which the northern hinter-land was providing, the metropolis of David and Solomon could remain nothing more than an overgrown village, far too large for the state it controlled.

The northern kingdom was almost equally impotent. It had not yet risen out of the agricultural civilization which had been typical of all Israel but two generations earlier. The commercial revolution of David and Solomon, which had built up the metropolis of Jerusalem with its urban life, had affected the outlying districts only by increasing their burdens of government. In addition, local and tribal patriotism were powerful and were destined to defeat every effort to establish a permanent national throne. At best the new King, like Saul before him, could be only a puppet in the hands of the tribal patricians.

Once more the plebeian prophets who, in their anger at David's imperialism had fomented the rebellion, discovered that they had only exchanged one set of opportunist masters for another. Their fear of Solomonic luxury had been founded on sound intuition; but the results of the rebellion were bound to be disastrous from their point of view.

Jeroboam's first acts showed that he had broken with them and that Ahijah's fate was to resemble that of Samuel. Violating all the principles of prophetic religion and succumbing entirely to the influence of patrician assimilation, the new King set up golden bullocks as representations of God in the shrines of Beth-el and Dan.[53] He rebuilt the ancient Canaanite sanctuary in Shechem on a more elaborate basis and apparently established there also a visible image of God.[54]

His foreign policy was equally patrician. He turned his back on Transjordan with its copper mines, and resumed the war against the Philistines which had been interrupted for two generations.

A touching incident proves that at heart Jeroboam was still a follower of the prophets, and that his anti-prophetic activity was not of his own choosing. When his son fell ill, he sent his wife *in disguise* to consult the prophet who had first stimulated his ambition, Ahijah of Shiloh. That stern moralist recognized the poor Queen and predicted the child's death, which occurred even before she could return home (I Kings 14.2 ff.).

The division of the kingdom involved not merely apostasy, but subjection and vassalage. The Egyptians, who had controlled Palestine before the advent of the Israelites, had watched the progress of David's empire with increasing irritation and hunger for control. Although Solomon was related to their court by marriage, they had offered asylum to his enemies; and when the tribes quarreled among themselves, Sosenk, the King of the Nile country, immediately invaded Palestine. Judah could offer no resistance whatever; Sosenk entered its capital, robbing it of the treasures which Solomon had accumulated in the palace and in the sanctuary. Jeroboam, who undertook to defend himself, met with a worse fate. He was driven across the plain of Jezreel into Transjordan, and even there was given no rest. Sosenk crossed the river after him and captured Mahanaim, where Ishbaal had found safety from the Philistines, and David from Absalom. Thereafter, Israel became tributary to Egypt.[55]

No sooner had he made terms of peace with Sosenk, than Jeroboam, weakened as his army and people were, resumed the struggle for the conquest of Philistia. His efforts were in vain; he died in the midst of the war. His son, Nadab, who succeeded to the throne was equally unsuccessful; and now the restive, defeated army began to blame the home government for its failure. Baasa, the general at the front, taking advantage of the disaffection, declared a revolt, and became king in Nadab's stead (ibid. 15.27).

Realizing that war against the Philistines would be futile, the new King sought more ready, though less valuable prey, in Judah. He would have succeeded in conquering the tiny land, had not Asa, King of Judah, appealed to Ben-hadad, King of Damascus, to declare war against Israel. Ben-hadad attacked Baasa's realm from the north and compelled him to desist from further attacks on Judah.

Thwarted in this effort against the southern state, Baasa apparently returned to the Philistines. His son Elah, who continued the struggle, was killed after a reign of but two years by Zimri, a captain to whom he had entrusted half his chariots. With the army encamped against the Philistines, however, such a palace revolution was not likely to succeed. Within a week of Zimri's revolt, the army declared itself in favor of its general, Omri. Zimri, seeing no hope for success against this formidable enemy, committed suicide. Nevertheless, the opposition to the control of the army, which consisted, primarily, of the smaller landowners, continued; the courtiers declared themselves in favor of a certain Tibni, son of Ginath. The conflict between the candidates continued for a time; though Omri had the advantage of numbers, Tibni had that of prestige. Before the issue could be settled in battle, Tibni died. Omri became the undisputed master of the Kingdom (I Kings 16.9 ff.); and opened a new era in the history of Israel.

XVII. THE DOCTRINE OF PEACE AND
THE PROPHETIC MOVEMENT

That Israel entered on a new stage in its career in the reigns of Omri and his son, Ahab, was recognized both by foreign observers, who continued to call the land *mat Omri* (Omri's country) even after he died, and the native historian, who describes Ahab's reign with unique fullness and detail. Certainly the two kings were among the ablest who were called to the throne of Israel. Imitating the policy of David, Omri, the plebeian, was determined to establish a metropolitan capital as a means for the perpetuation of his dynasty, and acquired the Mount of Samaria as the site for the town (I Kings 16.24).

Military exploits, like those which David used to enrich his capital, were, of course, impossible for Omri. Since David's time, the power of Aram had become consolidated, and that of Israel had weakened. There was no possibility of Omri's acquiring the copper mines and trade routes David had possessed, or seizing the tribute he had collected. The only alternative was stimulation of trade with the Phoenicians and Arameans; in order to do this, Omri entered into treaty agreements with both of these foreign powers, possibly even accepting vassalage to them. He ceded to the Arameans valuable trading rights in Samaria, in return, doubtless, for similar privileges which they gave him elsewhere;[1] and he certainly must have entered into an exchange of goods with Tyre and Zidon.[2]

Ahab, his son and successor, was an even more clear-sighted statesman and administrator. He adopted Omri's policies and carried them to their natural culmination; but he realized that the development of a commercial metropolis was not enough to ensure the throne. He needed the loyal and devoted support of a definite class of the people in his struggle against the landed patricians; like David, he looked for this to the traders and artisans of the metropolis, the backbone of the prophetic followers of YHWH. He made one of them, Obadiah, "Servant of YHWH," his chief minister; he called his children by names which affirmed his own loyalty to YHWH — Ahaziah, "YHWH has taken hold"; Jehoram, "YHWH is all-high"; Athaliah, "YHWH is exalted." He stimulated the growth of the prophetic schools, until there were literally hundreds of prophets of YHWH in the land.

It is one of the most cruel and pathetic paradoxes in history that this worshiper of YHWH and friend of the prophets should be recorded in history as the worst of apostates. His wise plans which, carried to fruition might have made his dynasty invincible, were frustrated; and his memory, which might have become one of the most revered in Israel's annals, was execrated, through the self-contradictions in which he involved himself. Yet the rabbinic sages, with their remarkable insight into such matters, estimate him correctly; and in their legends portray him in all his facets, his strength together with his weakness, his faith together with his disloyalty.

Three factors combined to nullify Ahab's good intentions: his shameless opportunism, the character of his redoubtable Queen, and the political exigencies which he himself created.

His opportunism showed itself particularly in his relation to the prophetic party. His convictions — feeble as they were — were obviously sympathetic to prophecy. But he would not become a devotee or adherent of the party. He wanted to use it and not to be used by it. When he found that his policies, far from strengthening the plebeians, relatively weakened them, he did nothing to help them. He had intended Samaria to be a refuge for the landless *Gerim*; it actually became a center for the powerful nobility. The poor, who streamed into the capital and became its artisans and small traders, did indeed find a crust of bread; the *Grossgrundbesitzer*, who surrounded the Court and could take advantage of the opportunities opened by the alliances with Tyre and Samaria, reaped harvests of incalculably greater revenue and power.

If Omri and Ahab actually thought of David's Jerusalem in making their plans for Samaria, they sadly underestimated the difference between the wealth which they had to obtain through trade alone and that which David acquired through tribute and conquest. The treasures which flowed into Jerusalem from the copper mines in Transjordan and the payments of the provinces, remained in the national treasury and were used for public construction. The money thus went into the hands of artisans, craftsmen, and small traders. Solomon could make it his business to see that the officers of the corvée were taken from plebeian ranks. It was thus possible for him and his father to create a new patricianship of recent origin. It was quite otherwise in Samaria. Omri and Ahab had no large funds at their disposal. The trade they stimulated had to be carried on entirely by private *entrepeneurs*; and the only men who had the means to take advantage of these opportunities were the richest landowners of the kingdom. Hence it came about that the metropolitan policy which in David's day was the terror of the landowners and won their opposition, was supported by the patricians of Ahab's time!

The increase of the patricians' wealth had, however, an even more disastrous effect than the widening of the breach between them and the plebeians. It brought into the country a new form of capital — that of money — which had been practically unknown before. It is altogether probable that this same result would have followed ultimately even from the commercial revolution as David and Solomon planned it. But under Omri and Ahab it was inevitable. Their economic reforms were based entirely on the development of foreign trade, which meant the introduction of a basic form of exchange or money. This development, however, opened the way to the ruin of innumerable small landowners. In earlier times, even the most desperate circumstances were unable to divorce the peasant from his ancestral soil. A famine or a drought might involve great suffering; the farmer might see his animals perish, his wife sicken, his children die. The simple economy of the land offered him no possible remedy; but neither did it tempt him with any *ignis fatuus*, luring him and his whole family to servitude and destruction. He might borrow wheat or barley from a more fortunate neighbor. But that happened rarely, and when it did happen, he was expected to return the same amount of produce in better times. The new economy of money opened new avenues of escape — but also of destruction — for him. He could go into the city and borrow money with which to obtain his supplies. To get these funds, he had to agree to mortgage his farm, which was his capital possession, and frequently to pay high interest. Natural optimism led him to believe that he could easily redeem his property the next year. But frequently this hope was doomed to frustration. Year after year passed; in the end the mortgage on the farm was foreclosed and the peasant was indeed fortunate if he was not sold into slavery for debt.[3]

The prophets of Ahab's day realized the new danger and raised a violent outcry against what seemed to them patent injustice, although it was based on recognized forms of the law. But Ahab made no move to help them. Perhaps he thought that the patricians were too powerful to defeat; perhaps he felt that a strong metropolis would become a centralizing force in the kingdom, no matter how it was controlled; perhaps a more recondite force was at work preventing him from following his natural bent.

In his failure to deal with this difficult situation, Ahab was, however, inviting catastrophe. He was driving the small landowners, who were being threatened with loss of property, into the arms of the prophetic opposition, and he was carrying the class conflict from Samaria, where it originated, into the hinterland which had never before known it.

But perhaps a more important factor in solidifying the opposition against Ahab was the religious apostasy which he permitted the political situation and his wife to force upon him. A vassal of Phoenicia, whose assistance was essential to him in withstanding the even greater danger of absorption by Aram, he necessarily set up temples to Baal, Melkart and Astarte, the deities of his suzerain; and even permitted his wife to persecute those who opposed the innovations. No policy could have been fraught with graver peril.

Many decades might have passed before the people, generally, were aware of the results which flowed from his political and economic opportunism. They might even have forgiven him his departure from the rugged simplicity of an earlier age, his erection of his magnificent palace, and his establishment of an army containing no less than two thousand horsemen. But they could not condone the effort which he and his Queen made to establish the gods of the Zidonians, as the supreme deities of Israel. No one before him had dared commit such an obvious act of national disloyalty; and it is certain that Ahab, too, would have escaped the costly experiment had he not been under the complete control of Jezebel.

How the King who proved himself so courageous in battle, so shrewd in diplomacy, and so astute in government, became so powerless in his household relations is still an enigma. Was he another David, able to rule an empire, but not his own family? Or was his wife a Cleopatra, whose charm could break down even an Antony? Who was this strange princess, the daughter of Ethbaal, King of the Zidonians, who first displaced the Queen Mother, by law and custom the First Lady of the land, and then usurped also the prerogatives of her royal husband? Whence did her power flow — from misdirected genius, or from congenital aberration? She slaughtered hundreds of prophets because they opposed her, and even threatened the life of Elijah himself; her daughter Athaliah, who resembled her so closely, destroyed all but one member of Judah's royal family, and made herself Queen of that land for six years.

Were mother and daughter both madwomen, glorying in the sight of blood, in the infliction of pain, and in deeds of horror? Or were they normal women placed in peculiar circumstances and endowed with unusual gifts? Were their cruelty and ruthlessness a throwback to the age of Jael, that Kenite lady who could murder a fleeing general in cold blood? Or were they the heralds of a distant age, when women were to be the equals of men, in fierceness as in goodness?

Difficult as it is to answer these questions, we cannot fail to see in Jezebel certain lineaments which proclaim true greatness, whether for good or for evil. Her calmness and self-assurance, her determination and her courage, her energy and her strength demand admiration. The bravery which she displayed at that supreme moment when her son's assassin was approaching and she knew that her hour had come, touch the heart of even the hostile historian. "She painted her eyes," we are told, "and attired her head, and looked out at the window" (II Kings 9.30 ff.). Old and gray as she was, and entirely at his mercy, she fearlessly taunted him with the name of Israel's most despised traitor. "Is it peace, thou Zimri, thy master's murderer?" she cried.

In his fury, the victorious rebel ordered her thrown down from the casements, and then rushed to forget the scene in food and drink and revelry. It was futile. Even as he sat at table, the stern face with the painted eyes and well-attired hair which had looked out from the palace window continued to haunt him. "Look now after this cursed woman," he cried, "and bury her; for she is a king's daughter."

Throughout her life, when Ahab vacillated, she was firm; when he compromised, she continued to struggle; when he yielded, she cast him aside and took the reins of government into her own hands. She had little sympathy with his whimpering when, finding that the vineyard he coveted was not for sale, he came home and childishly "laid him down upon his bed, and turned away his face, and would eat no bread" (I Kings 21.4). "Dost thou now govern the Kingdom of Israel?" she cried. "Arise, and eat bread, and let thy heart be merry; I will give thee the vineyard of Naboth the Jezreelite." And she was as good as her word. She wrote letters in Ahab's name, asking the leaders of the community in which the unfortunate Naboth lived to accuse him of apostasy and treason, and to condemn him to death. This was done, and the property was confiscated to the King. Ahab uttered no word of remonstrance; but when the prophet appeared to upbraid him for the double sin of murder and robbery, he "put sackcloth upon his flesh, and fasted, and lay in sackcloth, and went softly" (21.27).

One man only, Jezebel could neither conquer nor intimidate—Elijah the Gileadite, the uncompromising exponent of the prophetic traditions of the simple life and simple worship. The sudden and unexpected appearance of this strange man, fresh from his native provincial village of Transjordan, on the stage of history has been depicted with consummate skill by the writer of the Book of Kings. The astonishment we feel when he breaks into the monotonous chronicle of kings and princes is intended to reflect, in necessarily faint measure, the amazement of the contemporary revelers of Samaria, the capital of the land, when they beheld in their midst, coming as from nowhere, the leonine figure, threatening them with destruction. Altogether naked, except for a covering of animal skin about his loins, bronzed and almost blackened by exposure to the sun and the elements, covered about his neck and chest with long strands of hair which hung down from his chest and beard, lithe, muscular, and athletic, he left a deep impression on all who saw him. For a hundred generations, from his own time until our own, he has continued to haunt man's imagination.

Within a few decades he became a legend. While those who had seen and known him were still alive, his activity came to be described in impossible hyperbole, which obscured, when it did not destroy, the historical personality. With the passing of the centuries, Jew, Christian, and Moslem vied with each other in their efforts to rebuild the gigantic character. But his real dimensions eluded them all. They could recognize in the great teacher, leader, thinker and statesman, who for a generation had single-handedly held the forces of ethical and religious disintegration in check, nothing more than a miracle worker, with magical powers over life and weather. His poetic insight and his unerring intuition, his sense of the dramatic and his overwhelming personality were all lost for them. Their Procrustean imaginations, warped by their own desires and limited by their own capacities, hewed the lines of the prophet to suit their needs, and left our rationalist generation hardly more than a mythological shadow of his real and vital being.

Yet seen in the light of the social conditions of his day, Elijah emerges as one of the supreme geniuses of western history. Not without reason did the editors of the prophetic

books couple him with Moses in their final exhortation to
the people — "Remember ye the law of Moses My servant,
which I commanded unto him in Horeb for all Israel, even
statutes and ordinances. Behold, I will send you Elijah the
prophet before the coming of the great and terrible day of
the Lord" (Mal. 3.22). How just these writers were,
appears only when we have succeeded in separating the
facts preserved in Scripture from the legendary material in
which they are embedded. From the day when he first
entered on his ministry as an ordinary village *kahin* or
priest-physician-prophet in Gilead, through the years when
he valiantly struggled against the intrusion of foreign,
heathen ideals into the life of his people, until the moment
when, feeling that his work was over, he left his colleagues
and pupils to seek peace once more in his native hills, his
powerful spirit did not once yield to the mighty forces
arrayed against him.

It is a plausible conjecture that Elijah was first brought
to Samaria by the reports which reached him in Gilead of
Ahab's apostasy. At any rate, as soon as he appeared
before the King, he announced that for three years "there
shall not be dew nor rain these years" (I Kings 17.1). The
historicity of the drought which followed is confirmed by
Phoenician traditions, which recalled it as vividly as did
those of the Hebrews.[4] In vain did Ahab search Elijah to
beg him to intercede for rain with his God. The prophet
had disappeared as remarkably as he had appeared. It was
afterwards known that he had gone to the brook Cherith
for a time, and when that brook dried up, he had made his
way to the country of the Phoenicians, wishing, doubtless,
to learn more about the forces which were drawing his
people to their foreign worship. Ultimately he returned and

called on Obadiah to arrange an interview for him with the King. When the two men met, neither was in a mood for conciliation. "Is it thou, thou troubler of Israel?" Ahab cried to Elijah. "I have not troubled Israel"; replied Elijah, "but thou, and thy father's house, in that ye have forsaken the commandments of the Lord" (I Kings 18.18). There could be peace between them only on one condition, he held; if Ahab would agree to convoke a national assembly to decide on the question of the national worship. There was nothing to be done but to yield; and Ahab agreed to the meeting on Mount Carmel.

What transpired on that memorable occasion will never be known with precision. The legend which grew up about the incident within a single generation has forever concealed its realities from us. But there can hardly be any question that the gathering did occur, and that it was the scene of Elijah's most impressive triumph. Before he had completed his argument and his appeal, the people all arose and shouted, "YHWH, He is our God; YHWH, He is our God."

But Elijah knew the character of his real adversary too well to believe the struggle was over. Having scored his magnificent victory on Mount Carmel, Elijah was now for the first time in real peril of his life. Oratory, dramatics, logic, and athletic prowess — such as he had displayed when he ran before Ahab's chariot all the way from the scene on Mount Carmel to the royal palace in Jezreel — were of no avail with the relentless Phoenician princess. Her heart was still bent on the foreign worship and on the enhancement of the royal power; and no sooner was Ahab home than he was a tool in her hands. Pondering over the futility of his efforts, the prophet withdrew to Mount Horeb for new

inspiration. There, at the foot of the Mountain of Revelation, the solution of the grievous problem came to him.
The assembly on Mount Carmel had shown — what he had
always believed — that the heart of the common people was
loyal to the God of Israel. They were kept from His service
only through two forces: the ambitions of Ahab and his
patrician courtiers, and the influence of the Phoenician
government. The remedy which suggested itself was indeed
desperate; but could anything else succeed? He determined
to initiate a movement to overthrow the house of Omri, and
to place a plebeian on the throne. But this was only the
first step. To prevent the new King from following in the
ways of Omri, Israel's allegiance must be turned from
Phoenicia to Aram, and Aram, too, must be made subject
to a government which would be amenable to prophetic
influence. "Go," he heard the voice of God saying to him
from Mount Horeb, "return on thy way to the wilderness
of Damascus; and when thou comest, thou shalt anoint
Hazael to be king over Aram; and Jehu the son of Nimshi
shalt thou anoint to be king over Israel" (I Kings 19.15 f.).
Placed under two new Kings, both chosen appointees of the
prophetic group, Aram and Israel might present a sufficiently powerful front to resist the idolatrous influences of
Phoenicia and Egypt.

Elijah was too much of a realist to believe for a moment
that this mighty program could be carried out by his few
shepherd followers. It was necessary to obtain the organized
support of the *'am ha-arez*, whom Ahab's commerical
policies were driving into the opposition; and who were
becoming even more infuriated by the reform in the tax-
collecting system, which wiped out the old tribal boundaries.
The prophet's primary concern with religious reform had

to be submerged for the moment to the peasant's demand for social change.

To obtain the full assistance of the peasant group, one of them had to be associated with the leadership of the prophetic party; Elijah decided to call on Elisha son of Shaphat, a young peasant devotee of YHWH, to join him in his task, with a view to succeeding him when the time came. "And Elisha the son of Shaphat of Abel-meholah shalt thou anoint to be prophet in thy room" (19.16).

The fundamental accuracy of the record which describes the prophet's cogitations, his decisions, and his later activities, is demonstrated by its faithful report of the changes Elijah ultimately introduced into the details of the program. He was no doctrinaire to be bound by formulated plans; his ideas adjusted themselves to the exigencies of practical life.

Acting with unsurpassed skill and craft, he decided as he made his way northward from the Wilderness of Horeb to reverse the order of proceedings. The time was not ripe for a revolution either in Israel or in Aram. Instead of going to Damascus, he appeared in Abel-meholah and called on Elisha to join him. The young man, fresh from the plough, said merely, "Let me, I pray thee, kiss my father and my mother, and then I will follow thee" (19.20); and from that day onward, he became Elijah's chosen companion.

It must have been while the prophetic party was undergoing this transformation that Ahab presented it with the slogan it needed to consolidate its forces. Adjoining the King's palace at Jezreel, a man by the name of Naboth had a vineyard. Wishing to complete his estate, the King offered to purchase Naboth's vineyard, or to replace it with another of his own. But Naboth, descended from a long line of peasants, could not bear to part with his ancestral home-stead. "The Lord forbid it me," he cried, "that I should give the inheritance of my fathers unto thee" (ibid. 21.3). It was characteristic of the Israelite form of government that the subject should dare to refuse the offer of the King, and that the King should, even for a moment, find himself helpless in the face of the refusal.

Jezebel, however, was more resourceful. She conceived the plan through which Naboth was accused of the double crime of blasphemy and treason,— of "cursing God and the king." The leaders of his community discovered false witnesses to testify against him; he was found guilty, and condemned to death, while his property was confiscated. The King had his wish; the vineyard of Naboth became Ahab's palace garden.

The affair was not one which could shock the subjects of an ordinary oriental potentate. It could hardly compare either in cruelty or perfidy with David's seduction of Bath-sheba and his murder of her husband (II Sam. 11.15); in fact, as the commentators have remarked, Jezebel did nothing that an ordinary avaricious and unscrupulous noble might not have accomplished. But this meant nothing to Elijah; the judicial murder and robbery of Naboth was characteristic of the new temper of the monarchy. In his retreat on Mount Carmel, Elijah became aware of the circumstances of the case, and without delay rushed to the winter palace of the King to utter his protest. He found Ahab walking in the newly acquired property. "Hast thou killed, and also taken possession?" he said to the King. "Thus saith the Lord: in the place where dogs licked the blood of Naboth shall dogs lick thy blood, even thine" (I Kings 21.19). Paralyzed by his consternation, deeply aware of the human significance of the prophet's warning, and perhaps stricken also by awakened remorse, the King could only reply, "Hast thou found me, O mine enemy?" "I have found thee," replied the prophet; "because thou hast given thyself over to do that which is evil in the sight of the Lord. Behold I will bring evil upon thee, and will utterly sweep thee away, and will cut off from Ahab every man-child, and him that is shut up and him that is at large in Israel. And I will make thy house like the house of Jeroboam the son of Nebat, and like the house of Baasa the son of Ahijah, for the provocation wherewith thou hast provoked Me, and hast made Israel to sin."

Ahab knew his antagonist too well to think that these were idle threats. It was obvious that a revolution was in the making, the results of which none could foresee. The arrest and death of Elijah would achieve nothing; the wily prophet had already appointed a substitute to lead the revolution should he disappear. The injustice to Naboth would rally to the prophetic standard many who were little concerned with the religious issue; it was quite likely that Ahab's proud efforts might culminate in the destruction which overtook the houses of Jeroboam and Baasa. There was nothing left to do but to submit in silent humiliation. The King rent his clothes, "put sackcloth upon his flesh, and fasted, and lay in sackcloth, and went softly" (21.27).

The prophet was not taken in by these superficial gestures. But he was no lover of violence; and if Ahab, intimidated, would submit to prophetic guidance, revolution with its horrors was unjustified. Elijah decided to take no action but to await the development of events. The prophetic party had achieved sufficient strength to be patient even with its enemies. It was impossible for either the King or Jezebel to persecute or suppress it.

But while Elijah desisted from immediate rebellion, he did not permit the incident of Naboth to be forgotten. The "blood of Naboth" became a rallying cry against oppression for generations; and when finally the dynasty fell, the name of the unforgettable peasant was on the lips of the avenging rebels!

During all these years, Elijah had concerned himself only with the internal affairs of the Kingdom; he had taken no stand on the questions of peace or war. Israel had been almost continuously at war with Aram during Ahab's reign, trying to free itself from the suzerainty of the Syrian kingdom and to regain its lost territory. But Elijah had shown no interest in the struggle. He did not support it; and, on the other hand, he apparently did not believe that the non-aggression doctrines of Samuel applied to a war which had as its purpose the liberation of the land from its conquerors.

The expansion of the prophetic party had, however, brought into it a new group, which, loyal to YHWH and opposed to Baal like the rest of the pietists, was yet nationalistic in outlook, and sought to regain for Israel all the lands which David had ruled. Perhaps they had in mind the establishment of a metropolitan commercial group such as David had dreamed of, which would constitute the backbone of the party. More likely, however, they were not so far-sighted. They were simple provincials who loved their country and wished to see it great.[5]

There was a third faction, headed apparently by a certain Micaiah son of Imlah, which opposed all war. Anticipating the principle to be announced a century later by Isaiah, they were sincere lovers of peace at all costs.

It thus came about that when Ahab, having made his peace with the prophetic party, surrounded himself with "prophets of the Lord," he had no difficulty in discovering a large number who encouraged his military measures. About to proceed with his vassal-ally, Jehoshaphat, King of Judah, against Aram, on the eve of a battle he was promised by them a speedy victory. One of them, named Zedekiah, "YHWH is righteous," even made "horns of iron," crying to the King, "With these shalt thou gore the Arameans until they be consumed" (22.11).

But this prophetic unanimity was far from satisfactory to Jehoshaphat, who insisted on seeking the advice of Micaiah son of Imlah. As was to be expected, Micaiah prophesied evil, predicting the death of the King himself. Ahab's indulgence toward the prophetic party did not include its ultra-pacifist faction, and he felt justified in throwing Micaiah into prison until he should return from battle alive and victorious. Alas, it was not to be. In spite of his show of confidence, the King took the precaution of disguising himself as a common soldier; but the trick proved futile. He was struck by a stray arrow from the opposing camp, and died as he was being taken home to Samaria.

Ahab's death momentarily increased Jezebel's prestige. As Queen Mother, custom gave her greater authority than as Queen Consort; and in addition Ahaziah was entirely under her influence. His activities might have provoked the long awaited revolution, had he reigned for any considerable time. At the end of two years, however, he fell out of a lattice in his upper chamber at Samaria, and was killed.

His brother, Jehoram, who succeeded to the throne, definitely broke with Jezebel and her party.   He realized the growing strength of the prophetic following, and tried to propitiate them by putting aside "the pillar of Baal that his father had made" (II Kings 3.2).   It was too late.   The day of the statesmanly Elijah, who could be both firm and patient, was past; the leadership of the prophetic party was in the hands of the fierce and determined peasant, Elisha.

Watching carefully for his opportunity during the thirteen years of Jehoram's rule, Elisha slowly developed a considerable following in Aram as well as in Israel.[6] At a propitious moment, when Ben-hadad, the King of Aram, lay ill, Elisha appeared in Damascus, where he was welcomed with all the reverence due to a recognized teacher and leader of an international following. Accepting the honors paid him, he persuaded Hazael, one of Ben-hadad's generals, to undertake the leadership of the peasants' cause and to overthrow the existing government. The reigning king Ben-hadad was murdered, and Hazael ascended the throne in his place.[7]

That this was no palace revolution is obvious from Elisha's rôle in it. The prophet could hardly have cared whether one prince or another ruled the distant Arameans; his trip to Damascus and the fact that his relation to the rebellion are recorded in Scripture, indicate clearly the social and prophetic nature of the effort. Returning to Samaria after the success of his venture against Ben-hadad, Elisha again bided his time for a suitable occasion to unseat also the reigning King of Israel. Before many years Hazael declared war on Israel. The Scriptures give us some ground for believing that he did so at the instigation of Elisha and the prophetic party (II Kings 8.11). But however this

may be, Elisha seized the opportunity offered by the arming
and massing of the peasantry for battle, to carry out the
long-ripening project. The King had been wounded in
battle and lay ill in his palace at Jezreel. Hearing this,
Elisha at once dispatched a messenger to the camp, at
Ramoth-gilead, to anoint Jehu, one of the generals, as Israel's
new King. Jehu, at first uncertain of the army's attitude,
hesitated to accept the call; but the secret came out, and he
was hailed as king by his fellow commanders. Proceeding at
once to Jezreel where King Joram lay sick, Jehu slew him and
Queen Jezebel, as well as King Ahaziah of Judah, who was
visiting them. Jehu immediately set out for Samaria but
paused on his way to win the support of Jehonadab the son
of Rechab, the leader of the purist-shepherd party. "And
when he departed thence he lighted on Jehonadab the son
of Rechab, coming to meet him, and said to him: 'Is thy
heart right, as my heart is with thy heart?' And Jehonadab
answered: 'It is.' 'If it be' [said Jehu] 'give me thy hand.'
And he gave him his hand; and he took him up to him
into the chariot. And he said, 'Come with me and see my
zeal for the Lord' " (II Kings 10.15).

It is clear from the story that Jehu was not of the
prophetic party himself. He represented neither the landless plebeians who were the backbone of the prophetic
following, nor the aristocratic assimilationists who had given
their support to Jezebel, but the rural peasantry who,
massed in the army, had suddenly realized their power. It
was for this reason that the prophets later found so much
to criticize in Jehu and his house. But for the moment
they preferred Jehu to Ahab.

In his efforts to win the support of the semi-nomadic
shepherds, Jehu apparently affected their characteristic

sleeveless jacket and long-fringed, girdled skirt. But it is equally characteristic of his reign that his followers, the courtiers, wore the clothes natural to men of opulence at the time. It is thus the King and princes appear on the Black Obelisk, which commemorates their appearance before Shalmaneser III, King of Assyria.[8]

Seen in the light of this analysis Jehu's rebellion and the corresponding effort of the prophetic party in Aram were of far greater importance than the simple biblical narrative would indicate. They were part of a widespread revolt of the peasant masses against the aristocratic chieftains, and were instigated by the prophetic following, who now came into power for a little time. The events corresponded altogether to the struggle which was to be enacted two centuries later in Greece when Solon introduced his reforms in Athens, and four centuries later in Italy when the plebeians demanded a redistribution of land in Rome.[9] In each of these countries, the peasants silently and quietly accepted their debased position until the new money economy, the dispossession of the old farmers from their homesteads, the growth of the cities, and the development of a concentrated proletariat, gave sudden strength to the revolutionary movements.

Both Hazael's rebellion and that of Jehu bear clear marks of a peasant revolt. As we have already noted, one of the characteristics of the ancient peasant was his lack of refinement and his brutality toward those who fell into his power. The gory tale of Jehu's needless cruelties becomes intelligible only in the light of this fact. He commands Jezebel's eunuchs to throw her out of the window to be dashed to pieces on the ground, and then leaves her body to be consumed by street curs. While this inhumanity is being carried out, he goes home to eat and drink, and only

after his refreshment reminds himself that being a Queen,
Jezebel is entitled to proper burial. His order to slaughter
the seventy sons of Ahab may be accepted as part of the
usual procedure in an oriental revolt. But his treatment of
the Baal worshipers has a refinement of cruelty quite out of
keeping with the usual Israelitish gentleness toward the
vanquished. He invites all the Baal adherents to join with
him in a special service to their god. "Ahab," he announces,
"served Baal a little; Jehu will serve him much" (II Kings
10.18). Deceived by these kind words, the unsuspecting
votaries of the foreign god assemble in great numbers at
his Temple, where Jehu offers the customary sacrifice. But
when that is done, he admits the soldiery who, standing
without, are waiting for the signal, and slaughters everyone
present.

Hazael's bloodthirstiness and brutality was of a piece
with that of Jehu. We have no record of the scenes in
Damascus when he ascended the throne, but for decades
people spoke with terror of his heartless cruelties in the
subsequent war against Israel. Elisha is said to have wept
when he offered Hazael the crown of Aram, because he
foresaw the consequences to his people. "And Hazael
said: 'Why weepeth my lord?' And he answered: 'Because
I know the evil that thou wilt do unto the children of
Israel: their strongholds wilt thou set on fire, and their
young men wilt thou slay with the sword, and wilt dash
in pieces their little ones, and rip up their women with
child' " (ibid. 8.12). That Hazael actually carried out these
horrible predictions we know from Amos (1.3).

The conflict between the assimilationist nobility and the
loyalist gentry was not limited to northern Israel. It raged

with equal fervor in Judah, which had been for some generations a vassal of the northern state. Asa, who had called on Aram to help him against Israel, had been succeeded by his son, Jehoshaphat, who accepted Ahab's suzerainty, following him in his wars and even marrying his heir-apparent, Jehoram, to Athaliah, the daughter of Ahab and Jezebel. This princess succeeded in impressing the "manner of the house of Ahab" on Judah both during the life of her husband and that of her son, Ahaziah; and when the latter died, she, a veritable Lady Macbeth, massacred all his heirs, including her own grandchildren, and seized the throne. Only one of the princes, Jehoash, an infant less than a year old, escaped, being saved by one of his aunts. For six years Athaliah reigned in her own right, holding in check both those who were loyal to the Davidic dynasty and those who were seeking a social revolution. This was the more remarkable because an enemy of her house, Jehu, was King over Israel; and large sections of her own subject population — the 'am ha-arez who ultimately deposed her, and the prophetic, plebeian group which ever after execrated her memory — opposed her. Yet she could not, of course, have held her throne single-handedly. It is obvious that her assistants were the patrician nobles who, fearing a coup of the 'am ha-arez in Judah similar to Jehu's in the North, used her as a means of maintaining their own authority. This is what is actually implied in the Scriptures, which conclude the story of the coup against her by saying: "So all the 'am ha-arez rejoiced, and the city was quiet" (II Kings 11.20). Bearing in mind that ancient records speak of the "city" when they mean the "nobility," we may rightly infer from this passage that the gentry accepted

the new King with joy, and the aristocracy accepted him
with resignation. That the aristocracy should have preferred
a woman usurper of foreign nationality to the rightful heir is
explicable only if they considered important matters of policy
at stake in her retention. What these were becomes clear
when we consider that Athaliah was the daughter of Ahab
and Jezebel. She doubtless endeavored to carry out in
Judah the policies which her family had followed in Northern
Israel. Hence we understand the zeal of the Temple priests
for the rightful heir to the throne, and the union between
ecclesiastic and militia against the princes and the nobles.
And hence, too, the vigor with which the victorious rebels
in Judah, as in Israel, turned against the foreign Baal whom
Athaliah had worshiped (II Kings 11.18). For the aristocrats, the vassalage of Judah to Israel and of Israel to
Phoenicia had been not merely a political but a cultural
relationship. Like the Hellenists of a later generation they,
as early as the ninth century B.C.E., wanted to escape
the comradeship and association of their lowly brethren —
the poor plebeians no less than the unsophisticated peasants.
But in both Judah and Israel the militia drawn from the
country revolted, and asserted their rights on the one
hand and the national will to live on the other. The double
purpose of the rebellion is clearly stated in Scripture, which
tells us: "And Jehoiada made a covenant between the
Lord and the king and the people, that they should be
the Lord's people; between the king also and the people"
(II Kings 11.17). In other words, the King and the people
undertook together to be loyal to their ancestral worship
and not to permit the intrusion of the foreign, Phoenician
Baal; while the King, on his part, granted the people
definite rights in the government. The writer of Scripture,

less interested in political and social affairs than in those of the Temple, tells us nothing of the provisions of this second covenant, which would so much interest us. But the power which the 'am ha-arez as a body exercised from this day on implies that it had replaced at least in part the *Gerousia*, or council of patrician elders, as the King's advisory board.

Nothing is mentioned in the biblical narrative of the part played in this rebellion by the plebeian shepherds, the city proletariat, or the prophetic following. Yet an incident which occurred twenty-three years later throws some light on the matter. The King, now thirty years old, was becoming impatient with the restraint exerted upon him by the priesthood, who claimed full credit for his elevation to the throne. To check their arrogance he had to seek assistance from some other powerful group. It was useless to turn to the patrician nobles, who still resented the death of Athaliah, their tool. Nor could he expect assistance from the scattered members of the 'am ha-arez, which could be assembled only in moments of crisis. In his desperation, he decided to turn to the proletariat and trading groups of Jerusalem. The manner in which he did this is described in simple words by the historian. Until Jehoash's time, the priests had been authorized to receive the voluntary offerings made by their friends for the Temple; and in return they were expected to keep the Temple structure in repair. But it turned out that the priests, taking the gifts, failed to carry out their part of the agreement, and the building suffered. Thereupon the King prohibited the priests from accepting such donations and set up a chest in which the money could be deposited for the "repair of the house of the Lord." When the chest became filled with money, the King's scribe and the High Priest together put it in bags and counted it. The money was then turned over to the proper officials of the Temple to be given "into the hands of them that did the work, that had oversight of the house of the Lord" (II Kings 12.12). It was spent for "the carpenters and the builders, that wrought upon the house of the Lord, and to the masons and the hewers of stone, and for buying timber and hewn stone to repair the breaches of the house of the Lord, and for all that was laid out for the house to repair it" (12.13). But "they reckoned not with the men, into whose hand they delivered the money to give to them that did the work, for they dealt faithfully" (12.16). To put the matter briefly, the King trusted the workers, but not the priests. Since the proletariat stood at the bottom of the social ladder and the priests at its top, the measure of this insult can readily be imagined.[10]

The King indicated further his adherence to the prophetic group when he ordered that no "cups of silver, snuffers, basins, trumpets, any vessels of gold, or vessels of silver," be made out "of the money which was brought into the house of the Lord" (12.14). As Abram Menes has shown, this rule was definitely associated with the plebeian doctrine of the simple worship. The priestly historian indicates his dissatisfaction with this quarrel by saying: "And Jehoash did that which was right in the eyes of the Lord all his days while Jehoiada the priest instructed him" (II Kings 12.3).

In spite of these important concessions to the proletariat, the real power lay in the hands of the 'am ha-arez. The reigns of Jehoash and his immediate successors were obviously periods of continued strife between this large and ambitious group of peasants and the old aristocrats, who made repeated efforts to reassert their prerogatives. This may be inferred from the fact that both Jehoash and his son, Amaziah, met violent deaths. It is highly instructive to note that when Amaziah was assassinated "the whole *'am Yehudah* took Azariah, who was sixteen years old, and made him king" (II Kings 14.21). This passage which, like some others (cf. e. g. Jer. 25.2) uses *'am Yehudah* as variant for *'am ha-arez*, shows the continued power of the gentry and their loyalty to the reigning house of David. When Azariah became ill and his son, Jotham, was appointed regent, he is said to "have judged the *'am ha-arez*" (II Kings 15.5). Here again the squireage, which means the army, appear in a special position of influence and power such as they could not have had before the coup through which they removed Athaliah.

The long and peaceful reign of Azariah brought prosperity to the country, particularly to the trading classes, stimulating the growth of Jerusalem. Describing this period, at the beginning of his ministry, Isaiah says:

"Their land also is full of silver and gold,
  Neither is there any end of their treasures;
  Their land also is full of horses,
  Neither is there any end of their chariots" (2.7 ff.).

Their enhanced prosperity enabled the trading classes of Jerusalem and the artisans who were allied with them to seek far greater power and influence than they had enjoyed even under Jehoash. Fortunately for them, they obtained as their leader a prophet — Isaiah — who, distinguished in descent, as well as by his personal gifts of spirit, mind, and eloquence, was able to translate their inchoate strivings into a vigorous program of action.

And, indeed, those were days when the Commonwealth stood in great need of wise guidance. Judah's trade had grown while Aram was having her own difficulties with Assyria. But the time had come when Aram, realizing that she could not defeat Assyria singlehandedly, sought to lure or force her smaller neighbors into a conspiracy against the Eastern Empire. Ahaz, who was king of Judah, saw that he had nothing to gain from entering into an alliance with Aram and much to lose. The success of the effort against Assyria could only leave Judah in vassalage to Aram and Northern Israel, while its failure would, of course, mean ruin. When, however, he declined to join his larger neighbors, they invaded his land, besieged his capital, and prepared to replace him with a puppet king of their own, the son of Tabeel (735 B.C.E.). Ahaz, in terror, followed the opportunistic advice of his princes and nobles and called on Assyria for succor.

This, Isaiah and his prophetic following, who had supported Ahaz's neutral policy, considered a fatal error. Isaiah (7.4) mocked the king's panic: "Keep calm and be quiet"; he said, "fear not, neither let thy heart be faint, because of these two tails of smoking fire brands, for the fierce anger of Rezin and Aram, and of the son of Remaliah." Transforming the old prophetic antipathy to war into a positive doctrine of peace, he for the first time in history laid down the principle of International Right. There was justice among nations as there was justice among individuals. Full of faith, Isaiah held that Judah should neither join in battle against Assyria nor invoke her aid.[11] God could be relied on to save His people; there was no need to turn to Tiglath-pileser. There was statesmanship as well as piety in this teaching, for Assyria would certainly of her own accord move to protect her interests, while by inviting her help Ahaz automatically accepted vassalage. The prophet did not object to nominal political subjection, or even to the payment of annual tribute to Assyria. He feared the cultural and religious submission which accompanied vassalage. The historian clearly records that when "king Ahaz went to Damascus to meet Tiglath-pileser king of Assyria, he saw the altar that was at Damascus; and king Ahaz sent to Urijah the priest the fashion of the altar and the pattern of it, ... according to all that king Ahaz had sent from Damascus; so did Urijah the priest make it against the coming of king Ahaz from Damascus" (II Kings 16.10 ff.). Isaiah had the same objection to this innovation that Elijah had to the worship of the Phoenician Baal.

For the moment, however, Isaiah and his followers were defeated. Assyria saved Judah from destruction and incidentally extended its suzerainty over both Aram and Israel.

Ahaz, the easily terrified weakling, was succeeded by his son, the strong, determined, ambitious Hezekiah. From the beginning the prophetic party recognized a friend in the new king and placed high hopes in his rule. But his sympathy was not altogether a matter of persuasion; it was largely opportunistic. In the same year in which Hezekiah had ascended the throne of Judah, Shalmaneser IV became king of Assyria. The change of world emperors was always a signal for revolt among the smaller states, and Israel, which together with Aram had been beaten so completely a few years before, now attempted to retrieve its losses. Shalmaneser invaded the land, besieged the capital, Samaria, and after a three-year siege, reduced the all but impregnable fortress. Israel lost its independence, and a large part of its population was transported to distant lands, their places being taken, according to Assyrian policy, by people from various Aramean cities. Hezekiah, whose statesmanship cannot be doubted, recognized that his time had come. What, in view of the overwhelming power of Assyria, could not be accomplished by force of arms would be gained by the peaceful penetration of traders and the deflection of Samaria's commerce to Jerusalem. If, a hundred years later, Ezekiel could speak of Jerusalem as a great international market, the foundations for that development were laid during Hezekiah's reign, when Samaria lay in ruins.

Desiring to increase the strength and prestige of his capital city, Hezekiah broke away from the rural policies which his predecessors had followed for more than a century. Perhaps, like monarchs of other ages and countries, he was glad of the opportunity to curb the growing power of the army and the squireage. To attain his purpose, Hezekiah cunningly invented a policy admirably suited to the wishes of city patrician as well as plebeian, but violently antagonistic to those of the country. He resisted all efforts to involve him in a war with Assyria, abolished the gods and the altars which Ahaz had introduced, and went so far as to suppress the village altars, the high places, which were miniature rivals of Jerusalem's Temple (II Kings 18.4).[12] The prophets had long become convinced that there was no hope of purifying Judah's religious life unless it was concentrated in one sanctuary. So long as the provincials worshiped in their local shrines, the pure theology inherited from wilderness days would inevitably become diluted with the sensual, agricultural ceremonies of the ancient

Canaanites. Many village temples had become places of religious miasma in which the strangest syncretism between Israel's religion and the cult of the agricultural deities was to be found. The recently discovered Elephantine papyri give us a vivid picture of the religion developed by a colony of these provincials in distant Egypt. The confusion of Israel's God and the local gods and goddesses is so complete that one wonders whether prophetic teaching had had any effect on these people at all.[13] Yet the forms of worship used in the villages of Judah were doubtless not essentially different from those recorded in these tablets of the Island of Yeb. The Baal ceremonies and worship were so deeply ingrained in the rural mind, they were so admirably adapted to country needs, that they were inevitably retained in large parts of the country. The farmers, ignorant of theology and incapable of casuistry, simply continued the folk ways but associated them with the national God of Israel. Just as in later days the nations of Europe, becoming Christianized, adhered to their ancient Teutonic and Celtic celebrations, merely giving them new meaning, so the ancient Hebrew peasants served God through the medium of the Canaanite forms which the prophets, loyal to the nomadic tradition, condemned. The destruction of the high places in which the syncretism flourished seemed to the prophetic following the only possible method of combating the tendency. One God and one sanctuary became the dominant thought of the party.

It has been supposed that the Jerusalem priests were the chief sponsors of this movement. This simple explanation has, however, one fatal defect — it does not accord with the known facts. Certainly the priesthood of the Temple was pleased when its sanctuary was declared God's sole temple on earth. But the Law (Deut. 18.6) gives the local village priests full right of participation in the services of the main sanctuary. It further denies to any priests the right to own land. It is inconceivable that such rules would emanate from the Jerusalem priesthood or be supported by it. It seems far more probable that the movement to eradicate the high places was initiated by the prophets who feared syncretism, and advanced by the traders of Jerusalem who sought to enhance the prestige of their metropolis.[14]

By the year 704 B.C.E., Judah had reached new heights of prosperity; the policies of Hezekiah had been successful, the land was rich and powerful, subject only to light burdens of a distant and friendly Assyrian overlord. Just at this time Sargon, King of Assyria, died, leaving the throne to the inexperienced Sennacherib. The change of rulers was again a signal for unrest among the subject peoples who had trembled before the very name of the earlier king. Chaldea, never quiescent under the rule of Assyria, declared its independence, and preparations were being made to receive back Merodach-baladan, the ancient foe of Assyria, who had been driven into the marshlands in 709. Egypt sought advantage to itself in the unsettled conditions at Nineveh; and Judah, now the foremost state in Syria, was approached by both great governments with the suggestion that it join them in a world conspiracy against the tyrant.

The temptation was great. So widespread a conspiracy, involving both Egypt and Babylonia as well as Palestine, might easily succeed against a new and untried monarch. If the allies were victorious, Judah would emerge far more powerful than it had been at any time in its history. It would control all the land governed by David and might aspire to Empire. With such stakes at hand the ambition and opportunism of Hezekiah and his aristocratic counselors asserted themselves, and he entered the conspiracy.[15]

Isaiah, whose pacifism was uncompromising, denounced the whole affair and warned Hezekiah of the grave dangers which he might incur. A strong Babylon would be not a whit less oppressive a master than a strong Assyria. Judah had ultimately nothing to gain from being yoked with such lions; its hope lay in pacific neutrality and submission.

"And Isaiah said unto Hezekiah: 'Hear the word of the Lord. Behold, the days come, that all that is in thy house, and that which thy fathers have laid up in store unto this day, shall be carried to Babylon; nothing shall be left, saith the Lord. And of thy sons that shall issue from thee, whom thou shalt beget, shall they take away; and they shall be officers in the palace of the king of Babylon.' Then said Hezekiah unto Isaiah: 'Good is the word of the Lord which thou hast spoken.' He said moreover: 'Is it not so, if peace and truth be in my days?' " (II Kings 20.16 ff.).

Read by itself, Hezekiah's reply seems unspeakably childish and selfish, even if uttered contemptuously and ironically. He is happy with peace in his own day and quite careless about the storm being prepared for his descendants. But seen in the light of the whole history the words gain in significance. Hezekiah takes Isaiah's prophecy to imply the success of the conspiracy; the prophet does not threaten destruction at the hands of Assyria but an almost eschatological defeat at the hands of Babylonia, now endeavoring in companionship with Israel to throw off Assyrian bondage. He replies, therefore, quite naturally,

"Good is the word which thou hast spoken." He could not provide for an endless future, but it was well to embark on a policy which would lead to immediate success.

Isaiah continued to preach peace and submission, appealing from the King to the people. "Woe to the rebellious children, saith the Lord, that take counsel, but not of Me, and that form projects, but not of My spirit, that they may add sin to sin; that walk to go down into Egypt, and have not asked at My mouth; to take refuge in the stronghold of Pharaoh, and to take shelter in the shadow of Egypt! Therefore shall the stronghold of Pharaoh turn to your shame, and the shelter in the shadow of Egypt to your confusion" (30.1–3).

In his effort to avoid imminent war, Isaiah rises to the most sublime picture of a pacific world which had yet come from him. He foresees a new King succeeding Hezekiah, coming forth "a shoot out of the stock of Jesse,"

> "And the spirit of the Lord shall rest on him,
> The spirit of wisdom and understanding,
> The spirit of counsel and might,
> The spirit of knowledge and fear of the Lord . . . .
> But with righteousness shall he judge the poor,
> And decide with equity for the meek of the land . . . .
> And righteousness shall be girdle of his loins,
> And faithfulness the girdle of his reins.
> And the wolf shall dwell with the lamb,
> And the leopard shall lie down with the kid;
> And the calf and the young lion and the fatling together;
> And a little child shall lead them.
> And the cow and the bear shall feed;
> Their young ones shall lie down together;

And the lion shall eat straw like the ox.
And the sucking child shall play on the hole of the asp,
And the weaned child shall put his hand on the
basilisk's den.
They shall not hurt nor destroy,
In all My holy mountain;
For the earth shall be full of knowledge of the Lord,
As the waters cover the sea" (11.1 ff.).[16]

But Isaiah's advice was not merely based on states-
manlike love of peace; it was associated with profound
religious convictions and what he and his party considered
true patriotism. The time had clearly come when Judah
had to choose between subjection to the Asiatic or the
African empire. Independence was not to be dreamed of;
it could not be had by the weak in a world based on force
and violence. Yet the empires of the Nile and the Euphrates
were so evenly balanced that Judah could, if it wished,
choose its master.

This was no novel situation for Judah or Israel. For
centuries they had been buffer states between Babylonia
and Egypt, Assyria and Egypt, Aram and Egypt. Through
all this period the prophetic party had inclined toward
Asiatic rather than African masters. When Abraham had
to choose a wife for his son, he commanded his servant to
bring him a daughter-in-law from amidst his family in
Aram, but by no means to select one from the Canaanites
of the land. Hagar took a wife for Ishmael from the land
of Egypt (Gen. 21.21), but Rebekah and Isaac, like
Abraham, sent their son Jacob to Mesopotamia for his wife.
In Deuteronomy (26.5) the Israelites are definitely declared
the descendants of a "wandering Aramean." The Law,

indeed, forbids the Judaite to despise the Egyptian (Deut. 23.8), yet it endeavors to protect the Judaite from the influences of the Nile country. The Book of Leviticus specifically mentions the "doings of the land of Egypt wherein ye dwelt," and the "doings of the land of Canaan, whither I bring you," as those to be avoided by the Israelite (Lev. 18.3). Nothing is said about the dangerous customs of Aram, Assyria or Babylonia.

This was not due to special fondness which the plebeian felt for Mesopotamia and its culture. He would have opposed Aramean, Babylonian or Assyrian assimilation with the same fervor which he used against Egypt. But while his nomadic traditions were in no danger from the kingdoms of the East in the ninth century and later; he had much to fear from the insidious influence of Egypt. The Canaanite culture was dominated by Egypt. Indeed the Hebraic traditions declared Egypt and Canaan brothers, although the two peoples were quite distinct from each other in language and in racial origin. It was their similarity in custom and manner which led Scripture to say that Mizraim (Egypt) and Canaan (the native population of Palestine) were both sons of Ham (Gen. 10.6).

Throughout the First Commonwealth the Jewish nobility preferred the standards of these Canaanite peoples, and consequently those of Egypt from which they derived. In addition to the attraction which Egypt had for the aristocrat, as the source of the Canaanite culture, it had its own especial fascination because of its size, its power, its technology, and especially its commercial associations with the *Grossgrundbesitzer*. Documents which have been preserved in the Egyptian sands leave no doubt that in all periods the wealthiest Palestinians sought a market for their products in Egypt, just as they turned to Egypt for their cultural examples and their social ambitions.

Babylonia and Assyria were too far to have much influence and Aram too small. It was natural, therefore, that the culturally nationalist plebeian should feel less fear in subjection of his country to a Mesopotamian ruler than to an Egyptian Pharaoh. The result of his antagonism was that throughout the later years of the First Commonwealth, when Egypt and Mesopotamia again became rivals for world empire, Judah was divided between a pro-Egyptian aristocracy and the pro-Babylonian plebeians. It is of the utmost interest to note how the same conflict was resurrected in the Second Commonwealth in the few decades when the Ptolemys of Egypt struggled against the Seleucids of Syria. No sooner had these successors of Alexander the Great reconstructed the ancient empires than the dichotomy in Palestine between the wealthy Egyptophiles and the poor Egyptophobes also sprang into being once again.[17]

It was thus quite impossible for Isaiah to regard with composure an alliance between Judah and Egypt. Such an alliance violated his doctrine of peace; it threatened cultural assimilation; it was certain to end in failure and destruction. But the prophet's warnings were all in vain. Hezekiah's plans were fixed and unalterable. He weighed the chances and believed that they favored him. The King thus quarreled with the plebeians on the same issue of war and peace which was destined, five centuries later, to bring about a similar rift between the Maccabean King, John Hyrkan, and the pacifist Pharisees.[18]

The event had a decisive influence not only on the life of the state but also on the character of prophecy. The prophet had entered the field of pure politics, where worship as such was not in any way involved. He denounced the King, not for sin against the ritual, or even against ethics, but against what he called divinely commanded diplomacy. The fissure in the prophetic ranks which had first become apparent in the days of Micaiah son of Imlah of Northern Israel, had at last developed into a complete cleavage. Those of the prophetic following who rejected Isaiah's doctrine of peace had to leave the party, no matter what their attitude toward his theology and ritual might be. To the two kinds of prophets which the country had known before his time, those of YHWH and those of Baal, there was added a third species — the "false" prophets, who spoke in the name of YHWH, but rejected His doctrine of peace. Carried away by war fever, these prophets, like certain poets, teachers, ecclesiastics, and philosophers of all ages, preached blind patriotism, which for them meant submission to the policy of their rulers. The struggle between the two groups of prophets of YHWH remained acute throughout the period following Isaiah.

But now events took a more unfavorable turn than even Isaiah had predicted. Sennacherib, more energetic and ruthless than his warrior father, had quickly crushed the Babylonian revolt and turned to settle matters on the Mediterranean coast. In 700 B.C.E. he appeared in Palestine at the head of his well disciplined, irresistible troops, whose very march struck terror into the hearts of the Judaites. Sweeping past the tiny kingdom of Judah, he marched the main army down the coast line against the Philistine cities who had joined the conspiracy, while a detachment was sent into the interior of Judah to ravage the countryside and the fortified towns. "And destroy to

Hezekiah the Judaite, who had not submitted to my yoke,"
Sennacherib tells us in his inscription, "forty-six of his
fenced cities and fortresses, and small towns in their vicinity without number, by breaking them down with battering
rams and the strokes of . . . . the assaults of breach-stormers
and the blows of axes and hatchets, I besieged and took,
200,150 persons;[19] small and great, male and female, horses,
mules, asses, camels, large cattle, small cattle, without
number, I brought forth from the midst of them, and
allotted as spoil. As for himself, like a caged bird in
Jerusalem, his capital city, I shut him up."[20]

In utter despair, Hezekiah turned for comfort and assistance to the prophet whose advice and warning he had
spurned.

Isaiah, leader of the pacific party, was confident.
Speaking to people who could have watched from their
ramparts the heartless destruction wrought by the Assyrian
in the lowlands about them, whose country had been
depopulated through rapine, massacre and the exile of
thousands of people, he urged stability and faith. Jerusalem,
he was certain, would not be destroyed. "Behold their
valiant ones cry without; the ambassadors of peace weep
bitterly. The highways lie waste, the wayfaring man
ceaseth; he hath broken the covenant, he hath despised
cities, he regardeth no man. The land mourneth and
languisheth; Lebanon is ashamed, it withereth; Sharon is
like a wilderness; and Bashan and Carmel are clean and
bare. Now will I arise, saith the Lord; now will I be exalted;
now will I lift Myself up. Ye conceive chaff, ye shall bring
forth stubble; your breath is a fire that shall devour you . . . .
Look upon Zion, the city of our solemn gatherings; thine

eyes shall see Jerusalem a peaceful habitation, a tent that shall not be removed; the stakes whereof shall never be plucked up, neither shall any of the cords thereof be broken" (33.7 f.). God "whose fire is in Zion, and His furnace in Jerusalem" (31.9) could not permit His household to be destroyed.

The firm faith that Jerusalem in a peculiar sense belonged to God indicates that the village altars had already been denounced by the prophet as unholy, and had consequently been suppressed by the King. If there were other sanctuaries in the land, and they had been destroyed by the Assyrian, why should Jerusalem expect special safety?

The teaching of the prophet once again coincided with highest statesmanship as well as with the need of the metropolitan citizenry. Submission to Sennacherib's new demand was impossible. He frankly declared his intention to deport the population to some other country "as goodly as yours;" indeed his treatment of the inhabitants of the other cities left no doubt of the fate of his captives, even had he been silent.

Jerusalem was awaiting with impatience news of the impending battle between Sennacherib and the Egyptians, when one of the strangest and most dramatic events in the whole of Jewish history occurred to save the city. As the Assyrian army lay encamped on the borders of the desert, a plague broke out felling 185,000 of the soldiers and forcing Sennacherib to make his way back to Nineveh with all possible speed. Two hundred years later Herodotus, wandering in the neighborhood, still heard stories of the remarkable episode. Sennacherib, in his monument, passes it over with appropriate silence, but the Scriptures gleefully report the miracle which so amazingly confirmed the prophetic prediction.

The catastrophe which had befallen Sennacherib's army, and the news that Tirhaka, the Egyptian general, was preparing to take advantage of the situation to attack him, compelled the Assyrian King to accept milder terms of peace than might have been expected. It is an error, however, to suppose that he was defeated. Holding practically all Judah in his power, he was still able to impose a victor's terms on Hezekiah. The only concession he granted the rebel king was permission to retain his throne as Assyrian vassal. Large tracts of the Judaite kingdom were transferred to the Philistines, a heavy tribute of no less than thirty talents of gold and three hundred talents of silver was paid to the conqueror, and Hezekiah's daughters — apparently he yet had no son — were taken into captivity.

While the prophet might thus look upon the issue of the war as the supreme vindication of his teachings, his opponents were hardly prepared to share in his jubilation.

Hungry, humiliated, and without hope, the Judaites lost faith in their prophet and his God. The homeless peasants were strengthened in their conviction that the destruction of the village altars had been an error. Anyone could have foreseen that no God would wish to have His sanctuaries suppressed. The prophetic teaching that Israel's God was different from all others was clearly false, witness His unwillingness or inability to bring defeat on the Assyrians when they were ravaging the country. The remarkable episode on the borders of Egypt could be rationally explained as due to the gods of that country, who were ready to defend the people. The vivid, immediate experience of famine and poverty overshadowed all the memories of the intense relief they had felt when news had come of Sennacherib's retreat; they forgot how much worse things might have been; they knew only how bad they were.

The plebeian traders of the city suffered more deeply and for a longer time than the peasants. In a few years the farmers had returned each to his land and settled down to get their food from the soil. But the trader's markets were permanently destroyed by the wholesale deportation and the loss of the national territory. The impoverishment of the farmer, who still lived within the narrowed confines of Judah, prevented his coming to the capital and engaging in the luxury of purchase; while the more numerous peasantry who had been transferred to the control of the Philistines naturally turned to other market places under their new dominions. The commercial and artisan class was thus once more reduced in position and prestige as well as in numbers and, above all, in its faith and self-confidence.

The ground was thus prepared for a counter-reformation, which would restore the cultural conditions of Ahaz's days. The gentry had been overpowered by Hezekiah and they, too, had suffered grievously in Sennacherib's devastating invasion. The time was ripe for a return of the nobles to the power which they had lost in the revolt against Athaliah. Whether this could have been accomplished in Hezekiah's day is uncertain; but the strong King died in 697 B.C.E., and was succeeded by his twelve-year-old son, Manasseh. The regents, who from the first set the tone of his rule, were, of course, of the princely aristocracy, and they proceeded to undo at once all the pro-Jerusalemite measures introduced by Hezekiah. They saw nothing blameworthy in the desire of the farmers for local altars and high places. The syncretistic worship did not disturb them, for their own was even less Judaic.

To show their loyalty to Assyria, now more powerful than ever, they brought into the Temple itself the worship of Astarte, the Queen of Heaven, and of the whole Assyrian pantheon. Such reactionary and assimilatory undertakings could not be accomplished without bloodshed, and for the first time in its history Jerusalem was the scene of religious martyrdom. The plebeian traders and artisans were satisfied with the pacific acceptance of Assyrian suzerainty; indeed little Judah could do nothing against such conquerors as Esarhaddon, who now ruled in Nineveh, and who even reduced Egypt. But they could see no purpose in the acceptance of foreign gods and worship — in the spiritual abasement before temporal power. Already impoverished by war and its aftermath, many of them were now reduced to hopeless beggary by the reëstablishment of the local sanctuaries and the consequent loss of Jerusalem's trade.

But Manasseh's counselors ruled with an iron hand. Isaiah himself, it is said, was executed for his protest against this assimilationist reaction.[21] The remnant of his party were driven into Marrano-like concealment. Its leaders were effectually silenced, so that no word of prophecy has been preserved from the whole of Manasseh's reign.

The assimilationist movement was not, however, confined to worship; it extended to the whole of life. This we know from Zephaniah, a prophet who arose immediately after the end of Manasseh's terrorism. "And it shall come to pass [in the day of the Lord's sacrifice]," he says, "that I will punish the princes, and the king's sons, and all such as are clothed with foreign apparel" (1.8).[22] Speaking at the same time, Jeremiah, incensed at the change of worship, condemns it primarily as betrayal of inherited custom:

"Hath a nation changed its gods,
Which yet are no gods?
But My people hath changed its glory,
For that which doth not profit . . . .
For My people have committed two evils:
They have forsaken Me, the fountain of living waters,
And hewed them out cisterns, broken cisterns,
Which can hold no water" (2.11 ff.).

But while the prophetic party could be driven into a spore-like trance, it could not be utterly destroyed. Rooted in the economic life of the people, its teachings needed but the refreshing influence of more favorable conditions to be restored to full vitality. There are indications that the pietists, unable to bring their sacrifices either to the Temple which had been defiled, or outside of it because of their belief that it alone was God's chosen sanctuary, were driven to the establishment of private prayer meetings as a new mode of worship. Hitherto prayer had been frequently resorted to, but only as supplementing sacrifice. The much harassed pietists who remained loyal to their partisan teachings were now fast becoming convinced that the animal offering was unnecessary and that real communion with God could be had only through prayer. A member of the school, living somewhat later, but writing in the spirit of teachings inaugurated during this period, attributed to Solomon a prayer at the dedication of the Temple which would make of the sanctuary not a place for hecatombs and holocausts but of a "house of prayer for all nations." "And hearken Thou," he asks of God, "to the supplication of Thy servant and of Thy people Israel when they shall pray toward this place; yea, hear Thou in heaven Thy dwelling place; and when Thou hearest, forgive" (I Kings 8.30). And then he continues, "Moreover concerning the stranger that is not of thy people Israel when he shall come out of a far country for Thy name's sake — for they shall hear of Thy great name, and of Thy mighty hand, and of Thine outstretched arm — when he shall come and pray toward this house; hear Thou in heaven Thy dwelling-place, and do according to all that the stranger calleth to Thee for; that all the peoples of the earth may know Thy name, to fear Thee, as doth Thy people Israel, and that they may know that Thy name is called upon this house which I have built" (ibid. 41–3). Throughout the thirty-nine verses composing this remarkable prayer, there is not a single mention of the altar or bloody sacrifices. The unsuspecting reader might suppose that the structure to which it refers was a great synagogue instead of a place intended for the regular Temple ritual.[23]

Entirely under the control of the Assyrians and contemptuous of the plebeians, Manasseh could hardly have been aware of the deepened religious spirit which was permeating the submerged opposition. Still less could he have understood the forces which, released during the long respite of his peaceful reign, were destined to produce a new and invigorated prophetic party before the end of the century. As in the early days of Hezekiah, before he had joined the conspiracy against Assyria, so now Jerusalem was the unrivaled trade center for the whole of Palestine.[24] The country had long since recovered from the destruction wrought by Sennacherib. Fields were again being ploughed and planted; the shops and roads were once more busy; the land had returned to normalcy. The Chronicler (II, 33.11) does indeed speak of a rebellion of Manasseh against Assyria, but the record is unsupported by the Book of Kings, which would certainly have made mention of such momentous facts as Manasseh's being led in captivity to Assyria, his repentance, and his return to power. The Assyrian annals tell of Assur-bani-pal's invasion of the coast country, but are silent about any trouble in Judah. We are thus left to assume that the story in Chronicles was merely intended to emphasize the importance and value of repentance.

With the ordinary commerce of the country flourishing, the artisan and trading classes of Jerusalem, who had lost their influence in the tragic years at the end of Hezekiah's reign, were regaining prestige and power. We have already seen to what an extent their personal interests coincided with the teachings of prophecy. They could easily be convinced of the wickedness of the agricultural rites so much favored in rural sections; and they were ready to move for the concentration of worship at the capital. Their superior sophistication enabled them to understand the conception of One Invisible God; while their being massed in a large city made it possible for them to create new urban customs, replacing the older rural ceremonies in which they had no interest. Nothing in their experience called for gods and goddesses of fertility; the sex customs associated with Canaanite worship were revolting to them. The idolatrous priests seemed mere profligates; the prophets defending them downright deceivers. The plebeians might be forced by hostile rulers to submit to the current religion; but no sooner was the hand of the oppressor removed than they would of necessity return to their natural tendency to side with the prophets. Persecution was inevitably helpless against a faith that drew its strength neither from logic nor sentimentality, but from the economic and social life of its adherents. Setting themselves against such natural forces, Manasseh and his courtiers were like Thor trying to empty the horn which the crafty giants had connected with the eternal ocean itself. The more he drank, the more water appeared, for even a god is no match for the endless, aboriginal sea.

Manasseh died in his sin and was succeeded by his equally worthless son, Amon, whose only virtue, from the prophetic point of view, consisted in the brevity of his reign. In 639 B.C.E. he was assassinated, and there came to the throne his eight-year-old child, Josiah, who, remaining under the tutelage of regents and guardians for a time, ultimately restored the policies of Hezekiah and reversed completely the trend of the preceding fifty-seven years.

Times were propitious for such a change. The Assyrian Empire, whose favor Manasseh had continuously sought, was now rapidly declining. The great Scythian invasion, which began about the year 640, had apparently initiated the fatal attack on the Empire; and when Assur-bani-pal died in 626 B.C.E., it must have been clear to some observers that the end of his Empire could not be long delayed. His many bitter conflicts, his fierce ravaging of subject countries, his ruthless revenge had only staved off the evil day. His weaker successors could not hold the reins of power in their hands. In the year 625 B.C.E., Nabopolassar, a Chaldean, was appointed Babylonian viceroy, and the foundations for revolt were thus laid. Before two decades had passed, the mighty city of Nineveh yielded to the joint armies of Medes and Chaldeans and reaped the bitter harvest of hatred which her kings had for two centuries sown throughout the known world. Fire and sword mercilessly destroyed everything: man, woman and beast; house, temple and fortress. Buried under dust and débris, the city's very name was wiped from the face of the earth, so that later historians could not identify its place. Only the modern archaeologist, with his map and his spade, has at last restored its remains to view.

Not many years passed before the victorious Babylonians, risen to new power, sought to impose their rule on the whole of the Empire. But pending their rise, the nations of Western Asia breathed freely. As early as 645 B.C.E. the Assyrians had withdrawn from Egypt, and not long afterward their hold on Palestine began to slacken. Thus from the beginning of his reign, Josiah had the opportunity, which had come to his great-grandfather before him, of making Judah coterminous with Israel. But again, as in Hezekiah's day, the conquest of the northern lands was not to be made by soldiers and the sword, but by the infiltration of merchants, craftsmen and artisans.

The year 626 B.C.E., when Josiah attained his majority and when Assur-bani-pal, the last of the great Assyrian kings, died, marked the beginning of Jeremiah's prophecy. This can hardly be a coincidence. It is obvious that the new king had already decided to befriend those whom his father had persecuted, and that he felt free to do so without interference from his Assyrian suzerain.

Jeremiah's early prophecies are filled with demands for reformation of the village sanctuaries. In 621 B.C.E. the king finally undertook the purification of the Temple from the last remnants of the foreign worship which his grand-

father had introduced. This was, in effect, a formal declaration of independence from Assyria, whose gods had stood
in the Temple for almost fifty years.

In the course of the cleaning and rebuilding process,
Hilkiah, the priest, came upon the ancient code, which had
lain hidden in the sacred precincts since the days of
Hezekiah, prohibiting the provincial sanctuaries and con-
centrating all religious authority as well as worship in the
capital. Josiah lost no time in putting the ordinances into
effect and, imitating the ruthlessness which the Judaite
kings had learned from their Assyrian masters, he proceeded
to destroy every last vestige of village worship in the land.

The reformation could not be carried out without harshness, cruelty, and widespread suffering. The prophetic
following, embittered by the persecution which Manasseh
had visited on them, turned on their opponents, breaking
down and defiling their altars and houses of worship, dispossessing their priests and destroying all memory of
idolatry and provincial sanctuaries. Deuteronomic law had
provided that the village priests should have equal rights
with those of Jerusalem in the central sanctuary, but the
leaders of the Reformation could not bring themselves to
admit into the sacred portals those who had so recently
been their foremost antagonists. "Nevertheless," the record
tells us, "the priests of the high places came not up to the
altar of the Lord in Jerusalem, but they did eat unleavened
bread among their brethren" (II Kings 23.9). In other
words, they were given some of the minor priestly dues,
but not the major rights in the meat sacrifices of the
Temple.

It was inevitable that political power should remain in
the hands of the nobility. Mankind had not yet progressed

to the stage where workers and traders could actually control a government. But the plebeians, who recalled the persecutions of Manasseh and the violent revulsion against them under his reign, were loath to trust the sincerity of the reformation. They recalled similar changes under Hezekiah and knew how little they affected the people's hearts or their daily lives. When a delegation representing King Josiah came to Huldah, the prophetess, to ask her opinion about the newly discovered Book of the Law, she said to them, "Thus saith the Lord, the God of Israel: 'Tell ye the man that sent you unto me: Thus saith the Lord: Behold, I will bring evil upon this place, and upon the inhabitants thereof, even all the words of the book which the king of Judah hath read; because they have forsaken Me, and have offered unto other gods, that they might provoke Me with all the work of their hands; therefore My wrath shall be kindled against this place, and it shall not be quenched.' " Nevertheless, she was willing to give Josiah the comforting assurance that if he carried out the will of God he would be gathered to his grave in peace, "neither shall thine eyes see the evil which I will bring upon this place" (II Kings 22.15 ff.).

Jeremiah, too, admiring Josiah for his courage and his virtue, yet realized that the reformation depended on too uncertain factors. Isaiah had believed that Jerusalem would never be taken by the foreign conqueror; but that had been in the golden age of Hezekiah, when Messianic possibilities seemed near, when the royal power seemed adequate to meet the difficult problems of the state and the faith, when the prophets had not yet taken the full measure of the opposition to their policies. Since that day Manasseh and his counselors had disillusioned the most sanguine. Jeremiah and his group realized that the nobility and the gentry might be pushed into the background for a moment, but their restoration was as inevitable as the return of the tides. Only exile and deportation could bring about a reconstruction of the Commonwealth. The awful predictions of Deuteronomy would have to be fulfilled before the patricians and the gentry would be sufficiently chastened to accept prophetic guidance.

The fears of the prophets were justified all too grimly. In the year 608 B.C.E. Pharaoh Necho of Egypt, realizing the waning power of Assyria and hoping to annex Western Asia to his African dominion, undertook an expedition against Nineveh. Josiah went to meet him at Megiddo, in northern Palestine, to discuss the status of his kingdom in the event of Pharaoh's victory. Apparently dissatisfied with Josiah's attitude toward himself, Pharaoh slew him. His body was brought back to Jerusalem for burial and immediately the 'am ha-arez, who had been in the background so long, reasserted their right to appoint the king. Passing over Eliakim, the eldest son of Josiah, they chose Jehoahaz, the second son, who presumably agreed with their anti-Egyptian, militaristic policy. But the reasons which made Jehoahaz acceptable to the 'am ha-arez made him unacceptable to Pharaoh, who sent for him from his camp at Riblah, and as soon as he arrived, threw him in chains, to be taken to Egypt. Reversing the selection of the 'am ha-arez, Pharaoh appointed Eliakim king, changing his name to Jehoiakim.

Soon afterward Necho was defeated at Carchemish by the young Nebuchadnezzar, King of Babylonia, who showed himself heir to the ability and ambition as well as the ruthlessness of the Assyrians. The effort to extend the dominion of Pharaoh into Asia was frustrated; Babylonia, not Egypt, was to succeed Assyria. Again as in Hezekiah's day, Judah had to choose its master and now, as then, the aristocrat favored Egypt, the plebeian Mesopotamia.

Jehoiakim, placed on the throne by Pharaoh and representing the nobility, was definitely pro-Egyptian; yet he realized that the country needed, above all, to be welded together again into a single unit. He desisted from all persecution, permitted the rural high places to be rebuilt and their priests to return to them, and at the same time gave full recognition and protection to the central sanctuary in Jerusalem.

The extent to which Judah became subject to Babylonia after the battle of Carchemish is uncertain. Probably Nebuchadnezzar's rule was not at first more severe than that of Assyria had been during the last years of its decline. The Babylonians, having defeated Egypt, were apparently satisfied at first with obtaining expressions of fealty and friendship from the Judaite buffer state, separating them from their great enemy in Africa. But as Nebuchadnezzar's power increased, he began to dream of a great Babylonian Empire similar to that of Assyria, which had just been overthrown. It must have been exorbitant demands which at length, in the year 598, drove Jehoiakim, the careful and cautious ruler, into revolt. Nebuchadnezzar lost no time in invading the land; he laid siege to the capital and finally took it. Jehoiakim had died during the war and was succeeded by his eighteen-year-old son, Jehoiachin, whom Nebuchadnezzar carried off to Babylonia, together with "all men of might, even seven thousand, and the craftsmen and the smiths a thousand, all of them strong and apt for war."[25]

Nebuchadnezzar then appointed Josiah's third son king, changing his name to Zedekiah.

The ruler of the dwindling state was at heart a member of the prophetic, pacifist party, as his brother, Jehoahaz, and their father, Josiah, had been. But he was weak and fickle, altogether unable to withstand the pressure of the nobles. Again and again he made overtures to Jeremiah but found it impossible to follow the counsel of the prophet. False prophets, representing the views of the gentry, were continually urging him to rebellion; Egypt was sending its agents and promising assistance; the army officers who were in Babylonia demanded action for their deliverance.

In the first years of his reign Zedekiah sent agents to Babylon to offer homage to the king; but apparently this was unsatisfactory to Nebuchadnezzar, for in the fourth year Zedekiah himself undertook the long journey.[26] Jeremiah took advantage of each of these occasions to send letters to the exiles in Babylonia. That he was able to do this indicates that the ambassadors sent in the first instance, and some of the members of the entourage which accompanied Zedekiah in the second, were of the prophetic following.

Finally, in 588, Zedekiah, no longer able to restrain the princes, entered upon his fatal rebellion against Babylonia. Within a few months the great army of Nebuchadnezzar appeared in Judah and encamped against the walls of Jerusalem. Hundreds of the prophetic party deserted the defenders and threw themselves on the mercy of the Chaldeans. Zedekiah's courage, never strong, altogether failed him and he turned to Jeremiah for advice. But the prophet's warning to yield could not be carried out by the vacillating king, so powerless was he in the hands of his courtiers.

In July, 586 B.C.E., the Chaldeans made a breach in the wall and entered the city. The King fled but was pursued and captured near Jericho. Brought to Riblah before Nebuchadnezzar, he was adjudged guilty of treason, blinded and taken in fetters to Babylonia. Some seventy others of the nobility, including the chief priest, and his second, were condemned to death by the King. The walls of Jerusalem were torn down, the Temple and all the important houses burned, and the city left in ruins. Archaeological excavations show that similar devastation overtook all the other important centers of Judaite life.[27] A large portion of the population was sentenced to deportation but "the poorest of the land" were left behind to look after the fields and vineyards (II Kings 25.12).

The Babylonian general Nebuzaradan dealt kindly with Jeremiah, in whom he recognized the leader of the pacifists (Jer. 39.11 ff.). Even more significantly he appointed as governor of the land a member of the prophetic party, Gedaliah, whose father, Ahikam, the son of Shaphan, had on several important occasions figured as a friend of the plebeians. In fact, thirty-five years earlier, he had been a member of the delegation sent by King Josiah to the prophetess, Huldah, for advice regarding the newly discovered Book of the Law (II Kings 22.12), and during the reign of Jehoiakim he had once saved Jeremiah from the death which threatened him (Jer. 26.24).[28]

But Gedaliah's rule was brief. Within two months he was murdered by one of the princes who had escaped the soldiers of Nebuchadnezzar. With him the last vestige of Jewish self-government disappeared. A Babylonian governor succeeded him and Judah became simply a district within the Empire.